AI-POWERED SAP®
FINANCE

AI-POWERED SAP® FINANCE

How to Transform your Enterprise Systems With Generative AI

The Definitive Guide to Generative AI in SAP Finance
Future-Proof Your SAP Career Today

MOHAMMED HAFEEZ BAIG

DEDICATION

This book is dedicated to **my parents**, whose unwavering encouragement and values continue to guide me; to **my son, Haroon Baig**, whose presence inspires me to build with intention and hope; and to **my mentors**, whose wisdom and belief in my potential have shaped this journey in countless ways.

Their support has not only fueled this work but also reminded me why knowledge should be shared and made useful.

And to you, the reader — thank you for allowing this effort to find its purpose through your hands and mind.

DISCLAIMER

This book, *AI-Powered SAP® Finance*, is an independently authored work created by **Mohammed Hafeez Baig**, based on the author's personal experience, industry research, and professional expertise in SAP Finance and emerging AI technologies.

SAP®, SAP S/4HANA®, SAP Fiori®, SAP Business Technology Platform® (SAP BTP), SAP Analytics Cloud® (SAC), and other SAP product names and services referenced in this book are registered trademarks or trademarks of SAP SE in Germany and other countries. All other product and service names mentioned are the trademarks of their respective companies.

This publication is **not affiliated with, sponsored by, endorsed by, or officially connected to SAP SE** or any of its subsidiaries or affiliates. Any references to SAP products or platforms are for educational and informational purposes only.

The views, frameworks, and recommendations expressed in this book are solely those of the author and contributors, and do not represent the official policies, perspectives, or roadmap of SAP SE or any specific organization.

Every effort has been made to ensure that the information in this book is accurate and up-to-date at the time of publication. However, the author makes no representations or warranties regarding the completeness, suitability, or accuracy of the content. Readers are advised to consult official SAP documentation and professional advisors when implementing SAP or AI solutions in enterprise environments.

The case studies, examples, and scenarios included in this book are either based on public information, anonymized client experiences, or fictionalized composites used to illustrate key concepts.

By reading this book, you agree that the author and publisher shall not be held liable for any loss, damage, or consequences arising from the use of information presented herein.

CONTENTS

UNIT 4: APPLYING THE SOLUTION

UNIT 5: ROADMAP – FROM SAP ASPIRANT TO AI LEADER

INTERVIEWS

INTRODUCTION

Bridging the Gap: AI in SAP Finance

Why This Book?

The purpose of this book is to address a critical gap in how the SAP ERP system functions today and how it will evolve with the advancements in Artificial Intelligence (AI). Businesses currently rely on ERP systems like SAP to manage their financial and operational processes efficiently. While these systems are highly structured and optimized for current business needs, the integration of AI into SAP remains largely unexplored—leaving organizations without clear guidance on how to harness AI's full potential.

In this book, I will focus specifically on SAP Finance, providing real-world examples and step-by-step guidance on how AI can be effectively integrated into SAP with a focus on FICO. By using SAP Finance as a primary example, I will demonstrate practical AI applications, enabling SAP professionals, consultants, and businesses to adopt AI-driven solutions with confidence and clarity.

Artificial Intelligence is revolutionizing industries at an unprecedented pace, and businesses that embrace AI will gain a significant competitive edge. AI has the power to transform enterprise operations, making them more intelligent, automated, and efficient. However, despite the growing awareness of AI's potential, there is no clear roadmap for integrating AI into SAP and ERP processes—this is the void this book aims to fill. The lack of AI adoption in SAP Finance is not due to a lack of interest or awareness—rather, it stems from the absence of practical implementation strategies. Many businesses and professionals recognize the benefits of AI, but they face major challenges, such as:

- *Understanding how AI fits into SAP and its various functions.*
- *Identifying the right AI tools to enhance ERP processes.*

- *Overcoming resistance to change in traditional SAP workflows.*
- *Making a strong business case for AI-driven transformation to justify investments.*

This book is designed to bridge this gap. We will explore in detail how SAP Finance operates today, the challenges it faces, and how AI-driven transformation can enhance its capabilities. **Unlike many discussions on AI that remain theoretical, this book provides step-by-step insights, practical tools, and actionable strategies** to help SAP professionals, business leaders, and enterprises successfully integrate AI into their ERP systems.

This book is more than just an introduction to AI—it is a structured roadmap to help organizations future-proof their SAP Finance operations. By adopting AI, businesses can unlock new levels of efficiency, automation, and innovation.

If you're a company leveraging SAP, an SAP consultant, or an SAP end-user, you cannot afford to ignore this shift. AI is not just a technological trend—it is the future of business. Organizations that fail to integrate AI into their SAP enterprises will struggle to remain competitive, while those that embrace AI-driven transformation will achieve unparalleled efficiency, cost savings, and growth. This book will provide you with the knowledge, tools, and strategies you need to successfully adopt AI in SAP Finance—before it becomes an industry necessity.

Who Should Read This Book?

This book is designed for a diverse audience, including:

1. **SAP Consultants** – Professionals working in SAP who want to stay ahead in AI-driven ERP innovations.

2. **FinTech Professionals** – Individuals in the financial technology sector looking to understand AI's role in ERP systems.

3. **Business Stakeholders** – Decision-makers who want to leverage AI to optimize their SAP-based financial operations.

4. **SAP Decision Makers** – CIOs, CFOs, and IT leaders exploring AI adoption within SAP environments.

5. **Recent Graduates** – Those aspiring to enter the SAP industry and gain a competitive edge with AI knowledge.

6. **AI Professionals & Enthusiasts** – Individuals interested in AI applications within enterprise systems.

7. **Anyone Interested in SAP Finance & AI** – Professionals looking to enhance their understanding of SAP Finance and AI-driven ERP transformations.

What You'll Learn

- Insights into **current SAP Finance operations**
- A **structured roadmap** for AI adoption
- Key **AI tools and technologies** for SAP
- **Step-by-step guidance** on AI integration
- **Real-world examples** of AI in **SAP Finance production support**

This book provides actionable insights that will help SAP professionals, consultants, and enterprises understand how AI can transform SAP Finance and streamline ERP processes for long-term success.

Why This Book is a Game Changer

There is no book on the market today that specifically focuses on AI adoption in SAP Finance. While AI is widely discussed in the tech world, most SAP professionals lack concrete, practical knowledge on how to integrate AI into their business processes.

This book is not just informational—it's transformational. It provides a hands-on approach, equipping businesses and consultants with the tools and frameworks necessary to integrate AI before it becomes a necessity.

Additionally, this book does not just introduce AI concepts—it also provides a comprehensive deep dive into the current SAP Finance process. A dedicated chapter explores SAP Finance in detail, ensuring that readers gain a strong foundational understanding of SAP business processes before implementing AI. This knowledge is typically acquired only through years of experience or by reading multiple books. By combining this essential SAP Finance foundation with AI-driven strategies, this book serves as a one-stop guide for both seasoned professionals and newcomers looking to master AI in SAP Finance.

This book is your starting point—a guide to ensuring your SAP Finance processes remain future-proof in an AI-driven world. With this book, I aim to empower SAP professionals—from beginners to seasoned experts—to embrace AI.

Now is the time to start integrating AI into SAP Finance—before it becomes an absolute necessity. If you're serious about SAP Finance, AI, and the future of ERP, this book is for you.

You may find some aspects redefined and re-mentioned throughout the book, especially in Units 2 and 3, which are designed to build your foundational knowledge and reinforce your learning.

Let's embark on this journey together and take the first step toward transforming SAP with AI.

UNIT 1

Understanding the Problem

Introduction

In today's fast-paced digital world, businesses are striving to integrate AI into their financial systems to enhance efficiency, automation, and decision-making. However, despite the potential, SAP Finance faces significant roadblocks in AI adoption—challenges that organizations must first understand before they can overcome.

This unit serves as a crucial foundation for our journey. Across Chapters 1 to 5, we will take a deep dive into the existing problems, uncover the root causes, and analyze the barriers preventing seamless AI integration into SAP Finance. Why is AI adoption in finance not as smooth as expected? What technical, operational, or strategic challenges stand in the way? How do these issues impact businesses?

Before jumping into solutions, we must first fully grasp the problem. By the end of this unit, you will have a clear and thorough understanding of these challenges, setting the stage for the solutions and strategies that we will explore in the following units. Get ready to challenge conventional thinking, break down complex issues, and gain the insights needed to drive innovation in SAP Finance with AI!

CHAPTER 1

The Knowledge Gap in AI Integration with SAP

The Role of AI in SAP: Understanding the Knowledge Gap and Path to Implementation.

AI is set to play a transformative role in our lives, rapidly becoming the new paradigm through which businesses and individuals operate. With significant advancements already taking place across industries, SAP Finance is no exception to this shift. There is a growing realization that AI will eventually take over many financial processes, making them more efficient and intelligent. However, despite this awareness, many SAP consultants, users, and businesses struggle with a fundamental challenge—they don't know how to get started. The lack of clarity on where to begin, how to implement AI, and how to effectively leverage it for optimizing SAP Finance processes creates a significant knowledge gap, leaving organizations uncertain about the next steps in integrating AI into their workflows.

Imagine a finance team that once spent weeks closing the books, manually reconciling transactions, and ensuring compliance with strict regulatory standards. Now, with AI-powered automation, those same tasks are completed in a fraction of the time, with greater accuracy and efficiency. This is not a distant future, it's happening now.

To truly grasp AI's impact on SAP Finance, let's take the case of Siemens, a global leader in industrial manufacturing. Siemens faced challenges with its financial closing processes—manual reconciliations, data inconsistencies, and compliance risks led to delays and inefficiencies. By integrating SAP S/4HANA with AI-driven automation, Siemens was able to reduce its financial close cycle by 60% while ensuring higher accuracy in reporting. Similarly, Deloitte, a leading consulting firm, implemented AI-powered fraud detection in SAP Finance for one of its multinational clients. The AI algorithms analyzed historical transaction patterns, flagging irregularities in real time, which resulted in a 40% reduction in financial fraud incidents. These are not hypothetical scenarios—companies across industries are already leveraging AI within SAP Finance to optimize processes, minimize risks, and improve decision-making. By examining such real-time case studies, SAP professionals can better understand AI's tangible benefits and how to implement them effectively.

Many SAP Finance professionals, consultants, and business leaders find themselves at a crossroads: they recognize AI's growing influence but struggle to understand how to integrate it into their workflows effectively. The challenge is not just about learning a new technology—it's about overcoming a significant knowledge gap. Despite AI's increasing presence in SAP's ecosystem, many professionals lack the structured education, technical exposure, and strategic guidance needed to implement AI solutions effectively. Questions like, "Where do I start?" "Which AI tools are relevant to SAP Finance?" and "How will this impact my role?" remain largely unanswered.

This chapter explores why this knowledge gap exists, the risks of ignoring it, and what professionals and businesses must do to bridge it. AI isn't just another IT trend—it's the next frontier in digital transformation. And those who fail to adapt risk being left behind.

Today, as we speak, there's a growing realization that AI will eventually take over many processes, making them more efficient. However, despite this awareness, many SAP consultants, SAP users, and businesses using SAP struggle with a fundamental challenge—they don't know how to get started. The lack of clarity on where to begin, how to implement AI, and how to effectively leverage it for optimizing SAP Finance processes creates a significant knowledge gap.

This knowledge gap exists for several reasons, such as:

Lack of AI Education – While many people sense that AI will play a crucial role in the future, their understanding of what AI truly is remains limited. This is not just speculation, but a fact supported by numerous examples and technological advancements. The first challenge is a lack of foundational knowledge about artificial intelligence.

Limited Depth of Knowledge – Even those who are aware of AI often have only a surface-level understanding. This highlights the urgent need for upskilling. Similar to how the internet was a novel concept 20–25 years ago, AI is now at a stage where professionals need to upgrade their skills to stay relevant. The good news is that SAP professionals already have a strong foundation, so integrating AI into their workflow will not be as difficult as it may seem.

Absence of a Structured Learning Approach – Even if someone is eager to learn, they often lack clear guidance. While there are numerous AI courses, certifications, and college programs available, what's missing is a structured approach tailored specifically for SAP Finance professionals. AI is a vast field, covering areas such as generative AI, machine learning, and data engineering. As SAP consultants and users, we don't necessarily need to become AI developers—we are the facilitators and end-users of SAP systems. However, we do need a precise, structured framework to understand how AI can be applied within SAP Finance processes.

Even among those who possess AI knowledge, hesitation and resistance persist. This reluctance stems largely from the inherent complexity of ERP systems and the deeply ingrained belief that each enterprise operates with a unique set of data and processes. Unlike generic solutions, SAP Finance is not a "one-size-fits-all" framework, leading many professionals to question whether AI can truly adapt to the intricacies of their specific business environment.

Why is the AI Knowledge Gap an Issue in SAP Finance?

The AI knowledge gap in SAP Finance is not just a minor inconvenience, it has serious implications for businesses, professionals, and the overall efficiency of financial systems. AI is rapidly becoming a core component of digital transformation, and SAP Finance, being at the heart of enterprise resource planning (ERP), cannot afford to lag behind. Here's why this gap is a critical issue:

Missed Opportunities for Efficiency and Automation

SAP Finance involves complex processes such as financial planning, forecasting, compliance, and risk management. AI has the potential to automate and optimize these functions, reducing manual effort, improving accuracy, and enhancing decision-making. However, due to the lack of AI knowledge, many finance professionals continue to rely on traditional, labor-intensive workflows, leading to inefficiencies and slower business processes.

Increased Risk of Job Displacement

As AI adoption grows, organizations will favor employees who can work alongside AI-driven tools rather than those who resist them. SAP Finance professionals who fail to understand AI's role in financial reporting, fraud detection, and predictive analytics risk becoming obsolete. The gap isn't just about missing out on opportunities—it's about job security in a rapidly evolving market.

Difficulty in Implementing AI-Driven SAP Solutions

SAP has been integrating AI into its suite, including SAP S/4HANA, SAP Analytics Cloud (SAC), and intelligent automation tools. However, most finance teams lack the technical expertise to implement and make full use of these AI-powered features. This results in underutilization of existing tools, leading companies to invest in AI but fail to see a return on that investment due to a skills gap.

Challenges in Compliance and Risk Management

Finance professionals deal with strict regulatory requirements, tax laws, and auditing standards. AI can enhance compliance by identifying anomalies and automating compliance checks. However, without the proper understanding of how AI functions, there is a risk of misinterpretation, incorrect implementations, or resistance from compliance teams who see AI as a black-box system rather than a tool for risk mitigation.

Data Silos and Lack of AI-Driven Insights

SAP Finance relies on vast amounts of structured and unstructured data. AI can help in deriving insights, detecting patterns, and improving financial decision-making. However, the knowledge gap prevents organizations from using AI effectively for data-driven insights, leaving them with fragmented data silos and reliance on outdated reporting methods.

Additional Issues in SAP, Especially SAP Finance

Beyond the AI knowledge gap, SAP Finance faces several other pressing challenges:

Complexity of SAP S/4HANA Migrations

With SAP pushing for S/4HANA adoption, many companies struggle with the migration process. The complexity of data transformation, system integration, and business process reengineering creates major hurdles, especially for those unfamiliar with AI-powered automation tools that can simplify the transition.

Integration Challenges with Emerging Technologies

SAP Finance is increasingly expected to integrate with blockchain, IoT, and AI-driven predictive analytics. However, these technologies require a level of expertise that many SAP professionals lack, leading to disconnected systems and inefficient workflows.

Shortage of SAP Finance Talent

There is a growing demand for SAP Finance professionals who understand AI, automation, and cloud-based ERP solutions. However, the supply of such talent remains limited, making it difficult for companies to find the right skill sets for their digital transformation initiatives.

Rising Costs of SAP Implementation and Maintenance

SAP implementations are expensive, and without proper AI knowledge, businesses often overspend on customization and manual workarounds instead of leveraging AI to optimize workflows and reduce costs.

Resistance to Change in Finance Departments

Finance teams tend to be risk-averse and hesitant to adopt AI-driven changes due to concerns about accuracy, compliance, and reliability. This resistance slows down digital transformation and creates friction between finance and IT teams.

The Consequences of Ignoring AI Integration in SAP Finance

If these issues persist and organizations fail to act, the consequences will extend beyond mere inefficiencies. The long-term risks could significantly impact businesses, SAP professionals, and the overall competitiveness of enterprises. Let's explore each issue in detail and the potential fallout of inaction.

To summarize this chapter, I broadly classified the issues into 5 categories in addition to the knowledge gaps.

Knowledge and Skill Gaps

These issues stem from a lack of education, expertise, and structured learning pathways for AI in SAP Finance.

- Lack of AI Education – Many professionals have limited exposure to AI fundamentals.
- Limited Depth of Knowledge – Even those familiar with AI often have only a superficial understanding.
- Absence of a Structured Learning Approach – No tailored roadmap exists for SAP Finance professionals to upskill in AI.
- Skill Gap Between IT and Finance Teams – AI requires cross-functional expertise, which is currently lacking.

Psychological and Organizational Resistance

These challenges are related to hesitation, fear of change, and skepticism about AI's role in financial processes.

- Resistance to Change in ERP Enterprises – Professionals believe each company has unique data and processes that AI cannot standardize.
- Fear of Losing Control Over Decision-Making – Finance teams worry that AI automation could override human oversight.
- Trust and Reliability Concerns – AI is seen as a "black box," making it difficult to trust its outputs.
- Organizational Inertia and Legacy System Dependence – Businesses are slow to change due to deeply embedded processes.

Technical and Implementation Challenges

These issues arise from the complexities of integrating AI within existing SAP Finance frameworks.

- Difficulty in Implementing AI-Driven SAP Solutions – Lack of technical expertise leads to underutilization of AI features.
- Data Silos and Lack of AI-Driven Insights – Fragmented data prevents AI from delivering meaningful insights.
- Integration Challenges with Emerging Technologies – AI must work alongside blockchain, IoT, and predictive analytics.
- Complexity of SAP S/4HANA Migrations – AI adoption is hindered by ongoing migration challenges.

Regulatory and Compliance Concerns

These challenges stem from strict financial regulations and the uncertainty surrounding AI governance.

- Challenges in Compliance and Risk Management – AI must align with SOX, IFRS, and other financial regulations.
- Uncertainty Around AI Regulations and Compliance – Lack of clear legal frameworks increases hesitation.

Financial and Business Constraints

These barriers are related to cost, ROI concerns, and the difficulty in justifying AI investments.

- Lack of Clear Business Cases for AI in SAP Finance – Organizations struggle to define AI's tangible benefits.
- Rising Costs of SAP Implementation and Maintenance – AI adoption requires additional resources and investments.
- Cost and Resource Constraints – Many companies lack the budget to experiment with AI-driven tools.

Summary of Classification

Knowledge & Skill Gaps – Lack of AI education, structured learning, and cross-functional expertise.

Psychological & Organizational Resistance – Fear of change, trust issues, and legacy system dependence.

Technical & Implementation Challenges – Integration difficulties, data silos, and migration issues.

Regulatory & Compliance Concerns – AI's alignment with financial regulations remains unclear.

Financial & Business Constraints – Uncertainty about AI's ROI and high implementation costs.

Why This Needs to Be Addressed Urgently

SAP Finance is at a crossroads. Companies that embrace AI and automation will gain a competitive edge, while those that fail to upskill their workforce will fall behind. The AI knowledge gap is not just about missing out on innovation—it's about whether SAP Finance professionals can remain relevant in an era where AI-driven decision-making is becoming the norm.

Many of the challenges highlighted above are genuine concerns that require thorough evaluation and open discussion among professionals in the SAP Finance space, alongside AI experts. There is an urgent need for SAP Finance professionals to upskill in AI-driven SAP technologies so that we can collectively determine the best path forward. AI adoption is inevitable, and the sooner we start this conversation, the better prepared we will be for the transformation ahead. I do not claim to have all the answers, but I am sharing my insights based on years of experience working with SAP Finance across various industries and domains, as well as my recent expertise in SAP Generative AI. Let this serve as a starting point—a catalyst for discussion and exploration—as we navigate this journey together.

Now that we have looked at the knowledge gaps, in the next chapter, let's discuss why AI in SAP Finance is an under-discussed topic.

The integration of AI with SAP Finance presents immense opportunities, yet many organizations struggle to bridge the knowledge gap. A lack of understanding about AI's capabilities, implementation strategies, and real-world applications often leads to hesitation in adopting AI-driven financial solutions. Without proper awareness and education, businesses risk falling behind in an increasingly data-driven world.

This lack of knowledge is a key reason why AI in SAP Finance remains an under-discussed topic. Many finance professionals and decision-makers either underestimate its potential or overlook its relevance due to uncertainty and misconceptions. In the next chapter, we will explore why AI's role in SAP Finance has not received the attention it deserves and how this oversight is shaping the future of financial transformation.

CHAPTER 2

Why AI in SAP Finance is Currently Overlooked

Artificial Intelligence (AI) has revolutionized industries across the globe, from healthcare to logistics and customer service. However, one segment where AI's full potential remains largely untapped is SAP Finance. Despite SAP's continued push towards intelligent enterprise solutions with S/4HANA, Business Technology Platform (BTP), and SAP Analytics Cloud (SAC), AI's role in SAP Finance is still not widely discussed or leveraged.

This chapter explores why AI in SAP Finance remains an under-discussed topic, the challenges preventing its widespread adoption, and why mastering AI in SAP Finance represents a massive opportunity for finance professionals and enterprises alike.

The Traditional Mindset in Finance: Resistance to AI

Finance has always been a sector driven by accuracy, compliance, and risk mitigation. Financial professionals, especially in large enterprises using SAP Finance, are conditioned to trust structured processes that are rule-based and well-documented. The idea of integrating AI, which is inherently probabilistic and continuously learning, often raises concerns about:

Regulatory Compliance: Finance professionals must adhere to strict laws such as IFRS, GAAP, SOX (Sarbanes-Oxley), and GDPR. AI models introduce black-box decision-making, making it difficult to ensure auditability and compliance.

Risk Aversion: Unlike other departments that can afford to experiment, finance teams are highly risk-averse. Even a minor financial miscalculation can lead to regulatory fines or loss of investor trust.

Historical Preference for Rule-Based Systems: Finance has always been about deterministic processes (i.e., fixed rules and configurations in SAP FICO). AI introduces a layer of probabilistic decision-making, which goes against traditional financial principles.

Real-World Example: Why Banks Were Slow to Adopt AI

Even in the banking industry, which has massive financial resources for technological adoption, AI-driven automation faced significant resistance initially. Banks only started adopting AI aggressively in fraud detection and risk assessment after rigorous validation processes. Similarly, finance teams in SAP environments remain hesitant to embrace AI until they see proven reliability.

Lack of Awareness Among SAP FICO Professionals

SAP Finance professionals are experts in configuration, customization, and compliance, but many lack exposure to AI/ML. The skill gap between traditional SAP consultants and AI-driven SAP innovations is significant because:

SAP Finance training rarely covers AI: Standard SAP Finance courses focus on GL, AP, AR, asset accounting, tax configurations, and reporting, but they do not emphasize machine learning (ML) applications in financial forecasting, fraud detection, or automation.

Few SAP FICO consultants have AI expertise: Most SAP Finance professionals have deep domain knowledge in finance and accounting, but lack technical exposure to AI technologies such as TensorFlow, Python, or AI models in SAP BTP.

SAP certifications are still catching up: SAP offers certifications in Finance, S/4HANA, and SAC, but AI-specific training for SAP Finance professionals is still limited.

Impact on Enterprises

Because most SAP Finance teams do not have AI expertise, companies struggle to implement AI-driven automation. This results in slower adoption of AI in financial processes, leading to missed opportunities in efficiency, cost savings, and predictive analytics.

Limited Real-World Implementations and Case Studies

Unlike AI in sales, supply chain, or customer service, where successful AI applications are widely discussed and documented, AI in SAP Finance lacks high-profile success stories. This creates a perception gap—many CFOs and finance teams believe AI in SAP Finance is still experimental, even though AI-driven invoice processing, financial reconciliation, and anomaly detection already exist.

Why Finance Lags Behind Other SAP Modules

SAP Supply Chain & Logistics (SAP EWM, TM): AI is widely used in demand forecasting, warehouse automation, and transportation route optimization.

SAP Sales & Customer Service (SAP CRM, C4C): AI is actively used in chatbots, lead scoring, and customer sentiment analysis.

SAP Finance (SAP FICO, S/4HANA Finance): AI is still underutilized for predictive analytics, anomaly detection, and financial automation.

This lack of high-visibility case studies discourages adoption, as finance professionals often rely on industry benchmarks before implementing new technology.

Complexity of AI Integration in SAP Finance

Integrating AI into SAP Finance is not as straightforward as implementing AI in CRM or supply chain management. AI in SAP Finance requires:

Deep Integration with SAP S/4HANA & BTP

AI-driven finance solutions must be embedded into SAP's core ERP system, requiring expertise in SAP BTP, SAC, and ML models.

Data Quality & Volume Issues

AI requires large amounts of structured data. However, many companies still have legacy financial systems with inconsistent or incomplete data.

High Initial Costs

Implementing AI in SAP Finance requires investment in data engineering, AI expertise, and SAP consultants with AI knowledge.

Skills Gap in SAP AI Tools

SAP professionals who understand both AI/ML and SAP Finance are rare, making it hard for enterprises to implement AI-driven financial solutions.

Regulatory and Compliance Concerns

One of the biggest reasons why AI in SAP Finance remains under-discussed is regulatory complexity. Financial data is highly sensitive, and any AI-driven automation must adhere to strict compliance laws:

- Sarbanes-Oxley Act (SOX): Requires strict financial controls; AI models must be auditable.
- General Data Protection Regulation (GDPR): Restricts how financial data is processed using AI.
- International Financial Reporting Standards (IFRS): AI-driven financial forecasts must comply with IFRS principles.

Many CFOs and finance leaders are concerned about AI-driven decisions violating compliance laws, making them hesitant to implement AI in SAP Finance.

Lack of Clear AI Use Cases in SAP Finance

Unlike AI in supply chain, HR, or customer service, where use cases like chatbots and demand forecasting are well-documented, AI in SAP Finance lacks widespread awareness of high-impact use cases.

Key AI Opportunities in SAP Finance

AI-Powered Financial Anomaly Detection

- o Detect fraudulent transactions or unusual financial patterns before audits.

AI-Driven Predictive Cash Flow Forecasting

o   AI can predict future cash flow based on historical data, reducing liquidity risk.

Automated Journal Entry & Financial Reconciliation

o   AI can auto-classify financial transactions, reducing manual accounting work.

Intelligent Invoice Processing

o   AI can automatically extract invoice details, reducing processing time and errors.

Conversational AI for Finance Teams

o   AI-powered chatbots can answer financial queries in real-time for CFOs and controllers.

Why These Use Cases Are Underutilized

–   CFOs are unaware of AI's capabilities in SAP Finance.

–   Finance professionals are not trained in AI integration.

–   AI vendors rarely target SAP Finance as a priority market.

This presents a huge opportunity for SAP professionals who bridge AI and SAP Finance.

Key Takeaway:

AI in SAP Finance remains under-discussed due to risk aversion, lack of awareness, and regulatory concerns. However, this also presents a once-in-a-generation opportunity for SAP professionals who integrate AI with finance.

If you're a SAP Finance consultant, now is the time to learn AI and become a leader in AI-driven financial transformation.

Why AI in SAP Finance is a Massive Opportunity

Because AI in SAP Finance is under-discussed and underutilized, there is a huge gap for professionals who can:

Upskill in AI & SAP BTP: Learning SAP AI Core, SAP Data Intelligence, and machine learning can open high-value career opportunities.

Develop AI-Driven SAP Finance Solutions: AI-powered financial analytics tools and automation bots can revolutionize finance teams.

Help Enterprises Navigate Compliance & AI Adoption: Professionals who understand both finance regulations and AI implementation will be in high demand.

AI in SAP Finance is often overlooked in strategic discussions, not because of its lack of potential, but due to a combination of skepticism, uncertainty, and resistance to change. While AI is revolutionizing various industries, its role in enterprise finance remains under-discussed, leaving many organizations hesitant to explore its full capabilities.

One key reason for this hesitation is the abundance of myths and misconceptions surrounding AI in finance. Concerns about job displacement, data security, and implementation complexity often cloud the conversation, preventing businesses from fully embracing AI-driven transformation. In the next chapter, we will debunk these myths, separating fact from fiction to provide a clearer perspective on AI's true impact in enterprise finance.

CHAPTER 3

The Myths and Misconceptions About AI in Enterprise Finance

Introduction

Artificial Intelligence (AI) has been heralded as a game-changer in enterprise finance, promising increased efficiency, accuracy, and better decision-making. However, despite its growing adoption, numerous myths and misconceptions still surround its implementation. A common belief is that AI adoption is not easy because every enterprise is unique, leading to challenges in standardization. Another widespread notion is that AI's effectiveness is solely dependent on the quality of data it processes. While both statements have elements of truth, they often serve as barriers rather than stepping stones for enterprises looking to leverage AI in financial operations.

This chapter aims to debunk these myths and offer a nuanced understanding of AI's role in enterprise finance. We will discuss why AI is more adaptable than many believe, explore the crucial role of data in AI performance, and highlight practical strategies for overcoming perceived challenges.

Myth 1: "AI Adoption is Not Feasible Because Every Enterprise is Unique."

One of the most common misconceptions about AI in enterprise finance is that because every company operates differently—with unique workflows, legacy systems, and financial strategies—AI solutions cannot be easily implemented. While it is true that no two enterprises are identical, AI systems today are designed with flexibility in mind.

AI is More Adaptable Than You Think

AI models are not static, one-size-fits-all systems; they are highly adaptable tools that can be trained and fine-tuned to cater to specific business needs. Many leading AI solutions come with configurable features that allow them to integrate seamlessly with diverse financial systems.

For instance, AI-powered financial forecasting tools can be customized to recognize industry-specific trends, whether for retail, manufacturing, or healthcare. Through machine learning (ML), these tools continuously learn from an enterprise's historical data, making them increasingly effective over time.

Additionally, AI can integrate with enterprise resource planning (ERP) systems like SAP S/4HANA, Oracle ERP Cloud, or Microsoft Dynamics, making it easier for businesses to apply AI-driven automation without overhauling existing infrastructure. Companies that invest in AI adoption discover that, rather than being a rigid framework, AI is a flexible ally that molds itself around business-specific needs.

Case Study: AI in Financial Planning & Analysis (FP&A)

Consider a global corporation with subsidiaries across multiple countries. Each subsidiary operates under different regulatory frameworks, tax structures, and market conditions. Traditional FP&A teams often struggle with consolidating and analyzing such complex financial data.

However, AI-powered tools like SAP Analytics Cloud (SAC) enable enterprises to unify disparate financial data sources, normalize data, and provide real-time, predictive insights. AI's adaptability allows each subsidiary to tailor its analytics models without disrupting the overarching financial strategy of the enterprise.

Myth 2: "Your AI is Only as Good as Your Data."

A common adage in AI discussions is: "Your AI is only as good as your data." While this statement holds some truth, it is often misunderstood. Businesses frequently assume that unless they have perfect, clean, and abundant data, AI will be ineffective. This leads to unnecessary hesitation in AI adoption.

AI Can Work With Imperfect Data

Real-world data is rarely perfect. It is often messy, incomplete, and inconsistent. However, AI systems today are designed to handle imperfect data through advanced data cleansing techniques, anomaly detection, and intelligent inference.

For example, AI-powered finance systems can use data imputation techniques to fill in missing values, making historical data more usable for predictive modeling. Additionally, machine learning models can detect and correct errors in financial transactions, reducing the risks of manual data entry mistakes.

Data Governance and AI Performance

While AI can work with imperfect data, enterprises still need strong data governance policies to maximize AI's potential. Investing in data management frameworks ensures that AI models receive structured and relevant data, improving their predictive capabilities. Implementing data lakes, metadata management, and real-time data integration enhances AI's ability to generate meaningful insights.

Companies leading the AI revolution in finance, such as JP Morgan and Goldman Sachs, focus not only on acquiring vast amounts of data but also on refining their data pipelines to ensure quality and relevance. The lesson here is not that AI fails without perfect data, but that data management is a continuous process that enhances AI's accuracy over time.

AI's Ability to Learn and Adapt

A key feature of modern AI is continuous learning. Unlike traditional rule-based financial systems, AI models improve with every data point they process. Even if an enterprise starts with imperfect data, AI refines its predictions and insights as more data flows in. The key is to start, iterate, and refine, rather than waiting for a utopian dataset.

Myth 3: "AI Will Replace Human Financial Experts."

Another widespread myth is that AI will completely replace financial analysts, accountants, and CFOs. In reality, AI is designed to augment human expertise, not replace it.

AI as a Co-Pilot, Not a Replacement

AI excels at automating repetitive tasks, detecting anomalies, and processing large volumes of data at unprecedented speeds. However, it lacks the human intuition required for complex decision-making, strategic planning, and ethical considerations.

For example, while AI can generate financial forecasts, human financial analysts are needed to interpret those predictions, contextualize them within market dynamics, and make strategic decisions. AI assists in identifying trends, but financial experts provide the critical thinking necessary to act on those insights.

The Future of AI and Human Collaboration

Rather than eliminating jobs, AI is reshaping finance roles. Financial professionals who embrace AI-driven tools enhance their productivity and decision-making capabilities. For instance:

- AI-powered reconciliation tools help accountants process transactions faster, allowing them to focus on financial analysis rather than manual data entry.
- AI-driven risk management models provide deeper insights into financial risks, enabling CFOs to make proactive strategic decisions.
- AI-based chatbots assist with customer queries in financial services, freeing up human advisors for more complex interactions.

Companies that adopt AI see improved efficiency without sacrificing human expertise. The future of enterprise finance is not about AI vs. humans but AI working alongside humans.

Myth 4: "AI is Too Expensive and Only for Large Enterprises."

Many smaller enterprises hesitate to adopt AI, assuming that it requires significant investments in infrastructure, data science teams, and machine learning expertise. While AI implementation does require investment, it is increasingly accessible to businesses of all sizes.

Cloud-Based AI Solutions Lower the Barrier

Cloud computing has democratized AI adoption. AI-driven financial tools are now available as cloud-based solutions, offering cost-effective options without requiring heavy upfront investments in hardware or specialized personnel.

For example, AI-powered financial automation tools like QuickBooks AI, Xero, and SAP AI Core allow businesses to leverage machine learning for financial processes without maintaining in-house AI teams. Subscription-based models also make AI implementation scalable, allowing enterprises to start small and expand as needed.

Return on Investment (ROI) Justifies AI Adoption

Enterprises that invest in AI often see significant returns, including:

- Reduced financial fraud through AI-driven anomaly detection.
- Faster financial close processes with automated reconciliations.
- Improved cash flow forecasting, leading to better financial planning.

These benefits lead to long-term cost savings, making AI adoption not just a competitive advantage but a necessity in today's financial landscape.

Takeaway: AI is Not a Myth, But a Reality

AI adoption in enterprise finance is often misunderstood due to myths surrounding its feasibility, data dependence, job implications, and cost. While challenges exist, they are not impossible to overcome or too difficult to deal with successfully. AI is flexible, capable of handling imperfect data, designed to augment rather than replace human expertise, and more accessible than ever.

For enterprises willing to invest in data quality, governance, and AI-driven tools, the rewards far outweigh the challenges. The key is to start small, experiment, and refine AI applications over time. The future of enterprise finance is not about whether AI will be adopted but about how well enterprises will leverage it to drive innovation and efficiency.

In the end, AI in finance is as good as the data, the strategy, and the people guiding its adoption. With the right approach, AI is not a distant dream—it is a present-day reality transforming finance as we know it.

CHAPTER 4

The Current Limitations of SAP Finance Without AI

Introduction

SAP Finance is a robust and powerful system that has helped enterprises manage their financial operations efficiently for decades. However, despite its capabilities, the platform has yet to fully embrace artificial intelligence (AI) at the level necessary to unlock its true potential. While SAP has made significant strides in AI through Business Technology Platform (BTP) and other intelligent solutions, the overall adoption of AI within SAP Finance remains slow.

This lack of AI-driven transformation has left financial processes underutilized, missing out on opportunities for automation, predictive insights, fraud detection, and process optimization. In an era where financial technology is rapidly evolving, this sluggish adoption presents challenges for businesses looking to scale, streamline operations, and make data-driven decisions in real-time.

This chapter will explore the current limitations of SAP Finance due to the lack of AI integration, highlighting the gaps in automation, predictive analytics, compliance, and user experience. It will also discuss why AI adoption in SAP Finance is moving at a slow pace and how enterprises can accelerate this transformation.

The Current State of SAP Finance: Efficiency Without Intelligence

SAP Finance, particularly with S/4HANA, offers a robust foundation for financial processes. From General Ledger Accounting to Financial Closing and Treasury Management, SAP provides a structured and integrated environment to manage financial data. However, without AI, the system remains largely **reactive rather than**

proactive, relying on human intervention for decision-making, error detection, and complex reconciliations.

Some of the primary limitations of SAP Finance in its current form include:

Limited Automation in Transaction Processing

Despite advancements in automation within SAP Finance, the majority of financial processes still require significant **manual intervention**. Areas like **invoice processing, bank reconciliation, tax compliance, and intercompany transactions** demand human effort, increasing the risk of errors and inefficiencies.

- **Accounts Payable & Receivable:** While SAP has features like automatic payment runs and workflow approvals, **invoice matching and fraud detection remain largely manual.** AI-powered Optical Character Recognition (OCR) and machine learning could enhance invoice processing by automating validation and reconciliation.
- **Bank Reconciliation:** Traditional SAP Finance systems still require **manual matching of bank transactions**, whereas AI could instantly classify transactions, detect anomalies, and flag fraudulent activities.

Lack of Predictive Analytics for Financial Forecasting

Financial forecasting in SAP is primarily based on **historical data and static models.** This makes it difficult for businesses to proactively prepare for future financial challenges.

- **Revenue & Cash Flow Predictions:** Without AI, financial teams rely on static forecasting tools, which lack real-time adaptability. AI could enable predictive cash flow analysis by detecting **patterns in customer payments, market trends, and external economic indicators.**
- **Budgeting & Variance Analysis:** SAP's standard budgeting modules require manual data entry and adjustments, whereas AI-powered predictive analytics could automatically highlight risks and recommend budget adjustments.

Inefficient Month-End and Year-End Closing

The **financial close process** is one of the most time-consuming aspects of SAP Finance. Traditional financial closing involves multiple layers of **data reconciliation, error handling, compliance checks, and approvals.**

- **High Dependency on Manual Review:** Without AI, finance teams must manually identify discrepancies and validate reports, leading to **delays in financial closure.**
- **Data Inconsistencies:** Organizations using multiple ERP systems struggle with **data harmonization**, something AI could assist with by identifying mismatches and reconciling financial records across different systems.

Weak Fraud Detection and Compliance Monitoring

SAP Finance has built-in controls for fraud prevention, but without AI-driven **pattern recognition and anomaly detection**, businesses remain vulnerable to financial fraud and compliance risks.

- **Procurement & Expense Fraud:** AI could flag **duplicate invoices, fake vendors, and irregular transactions** in real-time, reducing the risk of financial fraud.
- **Regulatory Compliance:** SAP Finance relies on predefined rules for compliance, but AI could dynamically monitor regulatory changes and recommend necessary adjustments in tax laws, IFRS compliance, and SOX regulations.

Lack of Personalized Financial Insights for Decision-Makers

Financial decision-makers using SAP often rely on **static reports and dashboards** that require manual interpretation. AI-driven financial insights could offer **real-time scenario analysis**, allowing CFOs to simulate different financial strategies and instantly see their impact.

- **Decision Automation:** AI could recommend **cost-saving strategies, investment opportunities, and liquidity management solutions** based on real-time financial data.
- **Sentiment Analysis:** AI could analyze **market sentiment, economic conditions, and competitor activities** to provide **contextual insights** into financial risks and opportunities.

Why AI Adoption in SAP Finance is Lagging

Despite these evident limitations, the adoption of AI in SAP Finance remains slow. Several factors contribute to this hesitancy, including:

Lack of AI Awareness & Expertise Among Finance Teams

Many finance professionals **lack AI expertise**, making it difficult for organizations to fully leverage AI-powered SAP solutions. Finance leaders are **hesitant to adopt AI-driven automation**, fearing job redundancies or errors in critical financial processes.

High Implementation Costs and Complexity

Integrating AI into SAP Finance requires investment in **AI models, data processing capabilities, and change management.** Many companies hesitate to adopt AI due to **high upfront costs and the complexity of migrating to AI-powered modules**.

Security and Data Privacy Concerns

Financial data is **highly sensitive**, and organizations fear that AI-driven financial automation could **increase exposure to cybersecurity threats and data breaches.** Compliance with **GDPR, CCPA, and SOX regulations** further complicates AI adoption in finance.

Slow Adoption of SAP BTP & AI-Powered Solutions

SAP is actively working on AI-powered capabilities through **SAP Business Technology Platform (BTP)**, but the adoption rate is slow. Many enterprises still rely on **legacy SAP ECC or outdated S/4HANA versions**, delaying AI-driven transformation.

How AI Can Unlock the Full Potential of SAP Finance

To overcome these limitations, businesses must embrace AI-powered solutions in SAP Finance. AI can **revolutionize financial operations** by:

Enabling Intelligent Automation

AI can automate end-to-end financial processes, reducing manual effort and increasing efficiency.

- **AI-powered invoice processing** can match invoices with purchase orders in real-time.
- **Chatbots and voice assistants** can provide financial insights on demand.

- **Smart workflow automation** can accelerate financial approvals and document processing.

Predictive Analytics for Financial Planning

AI-driven predictive models can forecast cash flow, revenue, and risks with higher accuracy.

- **Dynamic forecasting** adjusts financial models based on real-time market conditions.
- **Automated variance analysis** detects budget deviations and suggests corrective actions.

Strengthening Compliance and Fraud Prevention

AI can monitor transactions and detect suspicious activities with high accuracy.

- **Machine learning models** can flag unusual spending patterns.
- **AI-powered tax compliance** can dynamically adjust tax calculations based on regulatory changes.

Enhancing User Experience with AI Assistants

SAP Finance users can leverage AI-powered assistants for a seamless experience.

- **Conversational AI** can provide instant financial insights via chatbots.
- **AI-driven dashboards** can highlight critical financial KPIs without manual reporting.

Takeaway: The Need for Rapid AI Adoption in SAP Finance

SAP Finance has long been a cornerstone of enterprise financial management, but without AI, it remains **underutilized and overly dependent on human intervention**. Despite SAP's efforts to integrate AI through **SAP BTP and intelligent financial automation**, adoption is not happening at the pace it should.

Businesses must actively **embrace AI-driven automation, predictive analytics, and compliance monitoring** to unlock the full potential of SAP Finance. The longer AI adoption is delayed, the more enterprises risk inefficiencies, financial losses, and missed opportunities for growth.

SAP Finance without AI is **like a high-performance car without a GPS**—it can function, but it lacks the intelligence to navigate efficiently. The time to accelerate AI adoption is now.

Despite its robust capabilities, traditional SAP Finance systems still struggle with inefficiencies such as manual data reconciliation, delayed financial reporting, and limited forecasting accuracy. These challenges create operational bottlenecks, increase compliance risks, and hinder strategic decision-making.

To overcome these limitations, businesses need a transformative approach—one that enhances efficiency, accuracy, and agility. This is where AI steps in. By leveraging AI-driven automation, predictive analytics, and intelligent workflows, organizations can unlock the full potential of SAP Finance. The next chapter explores why AI is not just an option but a strategic necessity in modern financial transformation.

CHAPTER 5

The Business Case for AI in SAP Finance

Introduction

Artificial Intelligence (AI) is transforming the financial landscape, and SAP Finance is no exception. As a seasoned SAP Finance consultant, I have seen businesses struggle with process inefficiencies, data silos, and compliance challenges. AI presents an opportunity to not only automate tasks but to also add predictive insights, streamline operations, and enable better decision-making.

In this chapter, I will explore the undeniable business case for AI in SAP Finance, breaking down its impact into automation, predictive analytics, compliance, fraud detection, and financial planning. The objective is to convince finance and IT professionals that AI is not just a futuristic technology—it is an immediate necessity for businesses looking to remain competitive.

AI-Driven Automation in SAP Finance

One of the most significant advantages of AI in SAP Finance is the automation of repetitive tasks. Traditionally, finance teams spend countless hours on processes like invoice matching, reconciliations, and journal entries. AI-driven automation reduces manual intervention, leading to higher efficiency and lower operational costs.

Key Benefits:

- **Accounts Payable and Receivable Automation**: AI-powered bots can process invoices, match them with purchase orders, and flag discrepancies without human intervention.
- **Expense Management**: AI can categorize expenses, validate them against policies, and streamline approval workflows.

- **Bank Reconciliations**: Instead of manually matching bank statements with ledger entries, AI algorithms can perform reconciliations in real-time, reducing errors and delays.

From an SAP perspective, AI can be integrated with SAP Finance modules such as **SAP S/4HANA Finance**, **SAP Concur**, and **SAP Invoice Management (VIM)** to create a seamless, automated financial ecosystem.

Real-World Example

A leading global retail chain implemented AI-driven invoice processing within SAP S/4HANA. Before AI adoption, their accounts payable team manually handled over 100,000 invoices annually, leading to delayed payments and reconciliation errors. By deploying an AI-based system integrated with SAP Finance, they achieved a **60% reduction in processing time**, significantly reducing overhead costs and improving vendor satisfaction.

Predictive Analytics for Smarter Decision-Making

AI is not just about automation; it's also about intelligence. Predictive analytics is a game-changer in SAP Finance, enabling CFOs and financial analysts to make data-driven decisions proactively.

How AI Enhances Predictive Analytics:

- **Cash Flow Forecasting**: AI models analyze historical data and external factors (e.g., economic indicators) to predict future cash flows with greater accuracy.
- **Revenue Forecasting**: Businesses can anticipate revenue trends by leveraging machine learning models that detect patterns in sales, customer behavior, and market dynamics.
- **Cost Optimization**: AI can analyze spending patterns, suggest cost-saving opportunities, and forecast budget variances before they occur.

SAP's AI-driven **SAP Analytics Cloud (SAC)** is an excellent example of how businesses can leverage predictive analytics within their SAP Finance landscape. With AI, financial forecasts become more reliable, reducing uncertainty and enabling better strategic planning.

Case Study

A manufacturing company facing volatile raw material costs leveraged SAP Analytics Cloud with AI-based predictive models. By incorporating real-time market price fluctuations and supply chain disruptions into their forecasting models, they improved procurement strategies and saved **$10 million annually** through optimized cost planning.

Strengthening Compliance and Risk Management

Compliance and risk management are major concerns for finance teams, especially in industries that face stringent regulatory requirements. AI provides a proactive approach to compliance by detecting anomalies, ensuring adherence to financial policies, and automating audits.

AI's Role in Compliance and Risk Mitigation:

- *Regulatory Compliance*: AI-powered compliance monitoring tools continuously check transactions against regulatory frameworks like IFRS, GAAP, and SOX.
- *Audit Automation*: AI can analyze financial records in real-time, flagging suspicious transactions and ensuring adherence to accounting policies.
- *Risk Assessment*: Machine learning models assess financial risk by analyzing credit scores, historical data, and market conditions.

SAP solutions such as **SAP GRC (Governance, Risk, and Compliance)** can be augmented with AI to provide real-time compliance insights and risk assessments.

Example from the Banking Sector

A global bank integrated AI into SAP GRC for real-time compliance tracking. Previously, compliance audits took **three months** to complete. With AI, real-time alerts reduced compliance review cycles to just **one week**, enabling faster corrective actions and mitigating regulatory fines.

Fraud Detection and Prevention

Fraudulent activities in finance can cause massive financial and reputational damage. AI's ability to detect patterns and anomalies makes it a powerful tool for fraud prevention.

How AI Prevents Fraud:

- *Real-Time Anomaly Detection*: AI algorithms analyze transactional data to identify unusual patterns and flag potential fraud.
- *Identity Verification*: AI-powered systems authenticate users by analyzing behavioral patterns, preventing unauthorized access.
- *Supplier and Vendor Fraud Detection*: AI can cross-check vendor details with transaction histories to identify suspicious activities.

By integrating AI into **SAP Fraud Management**, businesses can proactively mitigate fraud risks, ensuring financial integrity.

Notable Case

A multinational corporation using SAP S/4HANA detected an **85% reduction in fraudulent transactions** after implementing AI-driven fraud monitoring. The system flagged suspicious transactions in real-time, allowing auditors to act before payments were made.

AI in Financial Planning and Analysis (FP&A)

Financial planning and analysis (FP&A) is a crucial function where AI can provide unmatched value. AI-powered tools enhance the accuracy and efficiency of financial planning by processing vast amounts of data in real time.

Key Benefits:

- *Dynamic Budgeting*: AI-driven models adjust budgets based on real-time financial data, making financial planning more adaptive.
- *Scenario Analysis*: AI simulates multiple financial scenarios, allowing businesses to prepare for best and worst-case situations.
- *Data-Driven Decision-Making*: AI-powered dashboards and visualization tools provide CFOs with real-time financial insights.

SAP's **Integrated Business Planning (IBP) and SAP Analytics Cloud (SAC)** leverage AI to enhance FP&A processes, ensuring agility in financial decision-making.

Corporate Example

A Fortune 500 company adopted AI-powered SAP IBP for financial planning. The AI model detected hidden inefficiencies and suggested cost optimizations, leading to a **15% improvement in net profit margins** within a year.

Challenges and Considerations

While the business case for AI in SAP Finance is strong, there are challenges that businesses must consider before adoption.

Common Challenges:

- *Data Quality and Integration*: AI requires clean, structured data, which may require significant effort in data governance and preparation.
- *Change Management*: Employees may resist AI-driven automation, requiring proper training and change management strategies.
- *Cost and ROI Considerations*: Implementing AI requires investment in technology and expertise. Organizations need to assess the return on investment (ROI) before committing to AI adoption.
- *Security Concerns*: AI systems must comply with data protection laws to ensure financial data remains secure and confidential.

Despite these challenges, businesses that successfully integrate AI with SAP Finance gain a competitive edge through efficiency, intelligence, and risk mitigation.

Takeaway: AI is No Longer Optional in SAP Finance

The business case for AI in SAP Finance is no longer about "if" but "when and how" businesses will implement it. AI-driven automation, predictive analytics, compliance monitoring, fraud detection, and FP&A enhancements all contribute to making SAP Finance more intelligent and efficient. Organizations that embrace AI in SAP Finance today will lead the financial transformation of tomorrow. AI will redefine finance functions in ways we never imagined before. The time to act is now.

As we move forward, it's crucial to ground ourselves in the fundamentals. Mastering the basics of SAP Finance—its architecture, core modules, and key processes—is the foundation for integrating advanced technologies like AI. In the next unit, we'll break down SAP Finance from the ground up, making complex concepts simple and giving you the clarity needed to build toward innovation with confidence. Let's get into it.

WHAT'S NEXT

In the upcoming unit, we will pause to understand the entire SAP FICO process holistically—from both a **technical SAP module perspective** and a **real-world business process perspective**. This section is carefully designed to ensure that you not only know **what** to automate with AI but also **why** it matters in the broader context of enterprise operations.

The next unit is a culmination of my years of hands-on experience, project learnings, and process insights. The information covered is so comprehensive that going through it will feel like reading several SAP Finance and Business Process books—all distilled into one cohesive narrative.

Whether you are a beginner or a seasoned consultant, this next step will provide the clarity and confidence you need to build intelligent, future-ready SAP Finance systems. Let's begin.

UNIT 2

Mastering the Basics

Mastering SAP Finance: From Fundamentals to Advanced Insights

Introduction to SAP Finance

This unit provides a comprehensive exploration of SAP Finance, serving as both an introduction for newcomers and a structured refresher for experienced consultants. The objective is to establish a solid foundational understanding that will support advanced topics in subsequent chapters.

We begin by addressing fundamental concepts, such as the role of **Enterprise Resource Planning (ERP) systems** and their significance in modern enterprises. From there, we will navigate through SAP's core modules before narrowing our focus to SAP Finance. Each submodule will be examined in detail, covering key functionalities, essential concepts, and critical system integrations within the **SAP FICO framework**.

Following the previous chapter's discussion on AI-driven finance, this section emphasizes why mastering core SAP Finance principles remains essential. While innovation continues to transform financial management, a deep understanding of SAP Finance fundamentals is the key to navigating and leveraging these advancements effectively.

This unit, along with its chapters, is designed to be the **only resource an SAP Finance consultant truly needs** to gain a complete and practical understanding of this domain. Whether you are starting your journey in SAP Finance or looking to refine your expertise, this book equips you with the knowledge required to **become an effective team member and a valuable contributor to any SAP Finance project**. Every topic covered has been carefully selected and structured based on years of professional experience, ensuring that **if you focus on this unit, you will develop a comprehensive and holistic understanding of SAP Finance**.

Unlike most resources available today, which either focus on isolated aspects or require reading multiple books, this book consolidates everything in one place. To achieve this level of expertise, one would typically need to study numerous books, sift through documentation, or gain years of hands-on experience. **This book eliminates that gap** by presenting a structured, all-encompassing guide to SAP Finance, allowing professionals to gain clarity, confidence, and the skills necessary to excel in the field.

By the end of this unit, you will have a well-rounded and structured understanding of SAP Finance, setting the stage for the more advanced concepts and industry trends that lie ahead. So, let's dive in—because from here on, we embark on a deep and insightful journey into SAP Finance that will transform the way you approach this space!

CHAPTER 1

Understanding ERP and SAP

What is ERP?

Enterprise Resource Planning (ERP) is an integrated system used by organizations to manage business processes efficiently. ERP software enables the seamless flow of information across departments, ensuring all facets of an enterprise operate cohesively. By centralizing data management, ERP systems eliminate redundancy, enhance productivity, and improve decision-making.

ERP acts as the backbone of an enterprise, offering a unified database that integrates core business functions such as finance, supply chain, human resources, customer relationship management, and manufacturing. It streamlines business processes by automating routine tasks, reducing errors, and improving operational efficiency.

The Evolution of SAP ERP: From R/3 to S/4HANA to Rise with SAP

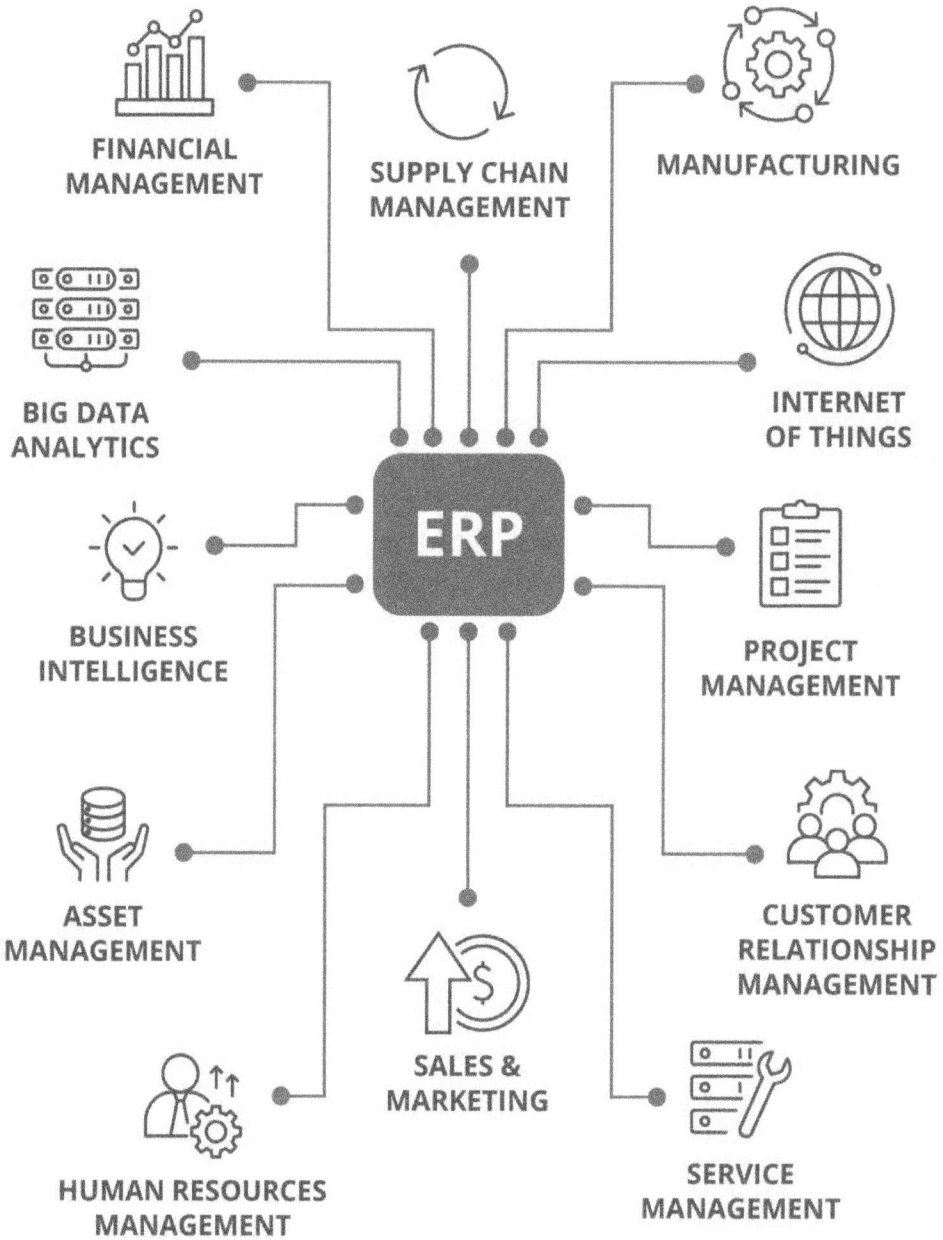

FINANCIAL MANAGEMENT

SUPPLY CHAIN MANAGEMENT

MANUFACTURING

BIG DATA ANALYTICS

INTERNET OF THINGS

BUSINESS INTELLIGENCE

ERP

PROJECT MANAGEMENT

ASSET MANAGEMENT

SALES & MARKETING

CUSTOMER RELATIONSHIP MANAGEMENT

HUMAN RESOURCES MANAGEMENT

SERVICE MANAGEMENT

Functions of ERP

ERP systems serve multiple functions across an organization. Some key functions include:

Financial Management – Tracks financial transactions, manages accounts payable/receivable, and ensures compliance with accounting standards like IFRS and GAAP.

Supply Chain Management – Streamlines procurement, inventory management, and logistics, ensuring optimal resource utilization.

Human Resource Management (HRM) – Handles employee payroll, performance management, recruitment, and benefits administration.

Customer Relationship Management (CRM) – Enhances customer service by managing client data, sales, and marketing.

Manufacturing and Production – Manages production planning, scheduling, and quality control.

Reporting and Analytics – Provides real-time insights into business performance through data visualization and reporting tools.

Compliance and Risk Management – Ensures regulatory compliance and minimizes financial and operational risks.

Uses of ERP

ERP systems are implemented in various industries to optimize business operations. Their primary uses include:

Improving Efficiency – Automates routine processes, reducing human errors and increasing productivity.

Enhancing Decision-Making – Offers real-time data for informed strategic planning.

Facilitating Collaboration – Ensures different departments can share data seamlessly.

Reducing Costs – Streamlines operations and eliminates unnecessary expenses.

Enhancing Customer Service – Improves response times and customer interactions.

Types of ERP Systems

ERP systems are categorized based on their deployment models:

On-Premise ERP – Installed on company servers, offering full control over data and security.

Cloud-Based ERP – Hosted on external servers, providing remote access, scalability, and lower maintenance costs.

Hybrid ERP – A combination of on-premise and cloud-based models, balancing control and flexibility.

While several ERP vendors exist, **SAP dominates the ERP market**, making it the industry leader.

SAP ERP and Its Market Leadership

SAP (Systems, Applications, and Products in Data Processing) is the world's leading ERP software provider. With an extensive range of solutions, SAP helps businesses optimize their processes and drive innovation. The dominance of SAP is due to several factors:

Comprehensive and Scalable Solutions – SAP ERP caters to businesses of all sizes and industries.

Global Adoption – Over 400,000 customers across 180+ countries use SAP.

Industry-Specific Customization – SAP offers tailored solutions for manufacturing, retail, finance, healthcare, and more.

Continuous Innovation – SAP continuously enhances its products, incorporating AI, IoT, and analytics.

Strong Integration Capabilities – SAP seamlessly integrates with third-party applications and other SAP products.

History of SAP and Its Evolution

Founded in 1972 by five former IBM engineers in Germany, SAP has grown into a global technology giant. Its evolution can be divided into key phases:

SAP R/1 (1972) – The first real-time financial accounting system.

SAP R/2 (1979) – Expanded to cover materials management and production planning.

SAP R/3 (1992) – Introduced a client-server architecture, enhancing scalability and multi-module integration.

SAP ECC (2004) – The most widely used version before S/4HANA, integrating finance, logistics, HR, and more.

SAP S/4HANA (2015) – A modernized, cloud-compatible ERP with an in-memory database for real-time processing.

The Evolution of SAP ERP: From R/3 to S/4HANA to Rise with SAP

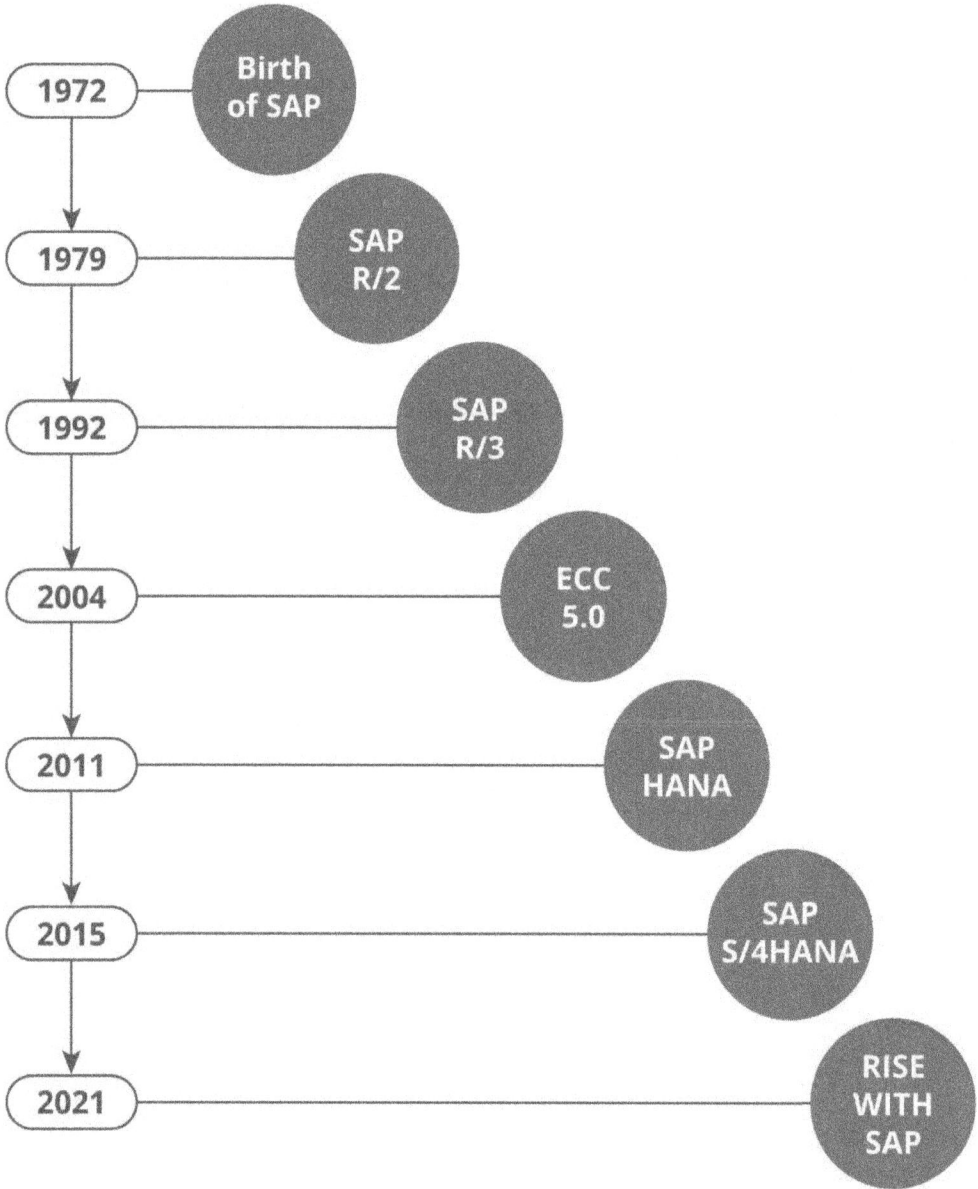

1972 — Birth of SAP

1979 — SAP R/2

1992 — SAP R/3

2004 — ECC 5.0

2011 — SAP HANA

2015 — SAP S/4HANA

2021 — RISE WITH SAP

SAP ECC vs. SAP S/4HANA

SAP ECC (ERP Central Component) was the dominant ERP system until the launch of SAP S/4HANA. The transition from ECC to S/4HANA marks a significant technological leap, focusing on speed, efficiency, and digital transformation.

Key Differences Between SAP ECC and SAP S/4HANA

1. Database Technology –
   - SAP ECC operates on traditional relational databases like Oracle, IBM DB2, and Microsoft SQL Server.
   - SAP S/4HANA runs exclusively on SAP HANA, an in-memory database that processes transactions and analytics in real time, enabling faster decision-making.
2. User Experience –
   - SAP ECC uses the traditional SAP GUI, which is functionally rich but outdated in design.
   - SAP S/4HANA employs SAP Fiori, a modern, web-based, and mobile-responsive user interface, offering an intuitive experience and enhanced productivity.
3. Data Model Simplification –
   - SAP ECC contains multiple tables storing redundant data, leading to complexity and inefficiency.
   - SAP S/4HANA eliminates redundant tables and aggregates, reducing database size and improving system performance.
4. Cloud and AI Integration –
   - SAP ECC is primarily an on-premise solution, requiring extensive customization for cloud adoption.
   - SAP S/4HANA is cloud-compatible, supporting SaaS models and AI-driven analytics for smarter business processes.
5. Financial and Controlling Integration –
   - SAP ECC separates FI (Financial Accounting) and CO (Controlling) modules, requiring reconciliation.
   - SAP S/4HANA merges FI and CO into a single data model, eliminating reconciliation efforts and providing real-time financial insights.

SAP ECC VS SAP S/4HANA

AREAS OF DIFFERENCE	SAP ECC	SAP S/4HANA
DATA PROCESSING	Traditional batch processes	Uses real time analytics
DATABASE	DB2, Oracle, SQL, Server, and SAP MaxDB	HANA database
DEPLOYMENT	On-premises	On-premises, cloud, as well as hybrid
FUNCTIONALITIES	Comes with built-in analytics and reporting tools, embedded with SAP GUI	Business Partner Approach with CVI, embedded with SAP Fiori 3.0, flexible workflows, etc
GENERAL LEADER (GL)	Classic GL or new GL	New GL; prerequisite for new asset accounting
FILES & ARCHITECTURE	Separate customer and vendor files. Traditional R/3	Combined business partner files. In-memory architecture

SAP Modules

SAP ERP consists of multiple modules, each catering to different business functions. These modules integrate seamlessly, ensuring smooth data flow and operational efficiency.

Major SAP Modules

1. Financial Accounting (FI) –
   o Manages general ledger, accounts payable/receivable, and financial reporting.
   o Ensures compliance with IFRS, GAAP, and local regulations.
2. Controlling (CO) –
   o Focuses on internal cost accounting, budgeting, and profitability analysis.
   o Provides insights into cost drivers and revenue streams.
3. Materials Management (MM) –
   o Oversees procurement, vendor management, and inventory control.
   o Automates purchase orders, invoice verification, and stock transfers.
4. Sales and Distribution (SD) –
   o Manages customer orders, billing, and pricing.
   o Ensures smooth order-to-cash processing.
5. Production Planning (PP) –
   o Facilitates manufacturing processes, scheduling, and resource planning.
   o Aligns supply chain with demand forecasts.
6. Human Capital Management (HCM) –
   o Handles employee records, payroll, recruitment, and talent management.
   o Ensures compliance with labor laws and workforce planning.
7. Extended Warehouse Management (EWM) –
   o Optimizes warehouse logistics, storage, and distribution.
   o Enhances real-time inventory tracking and movement control.

These modules interact with each other to form a robust ERP ecosystem, streamlining business operations efficiently.

SAP Modules
Types of SAP Module

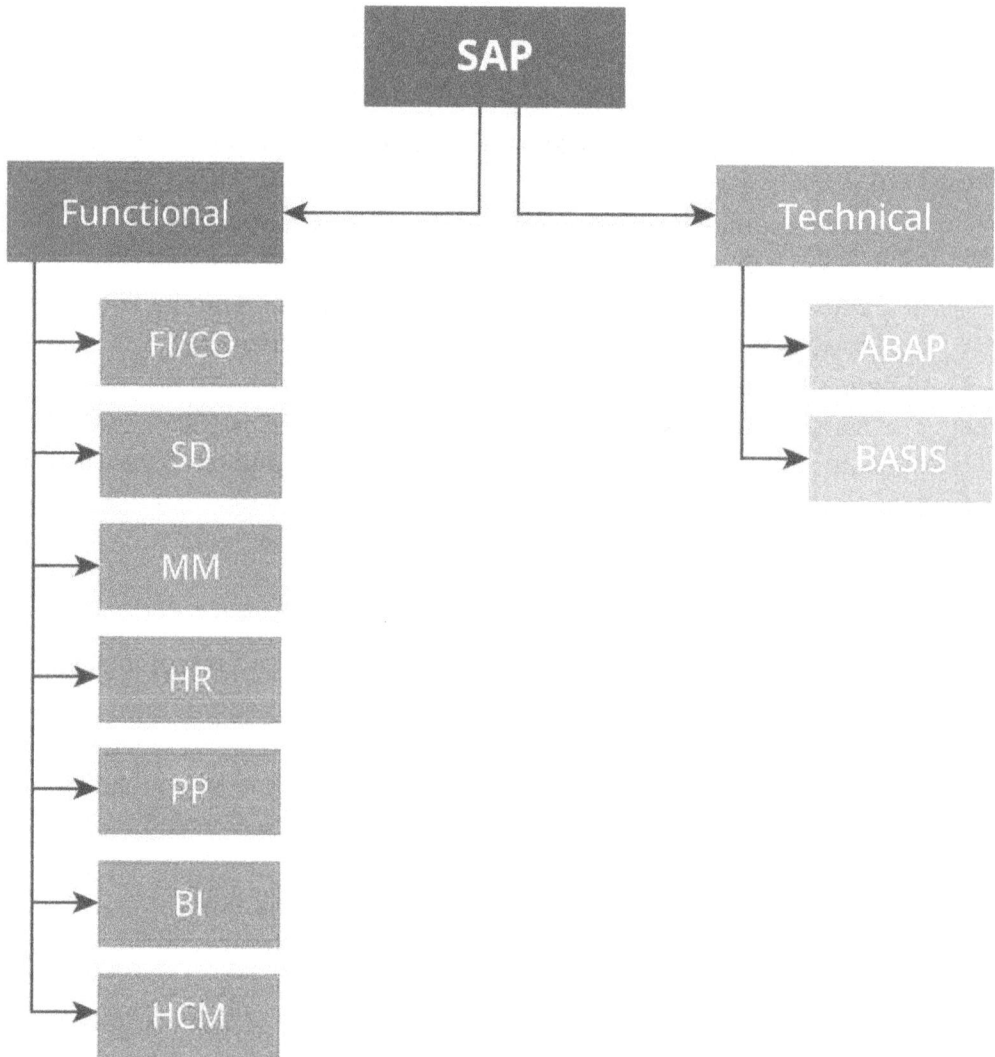

SAP Overview - Most important Modules

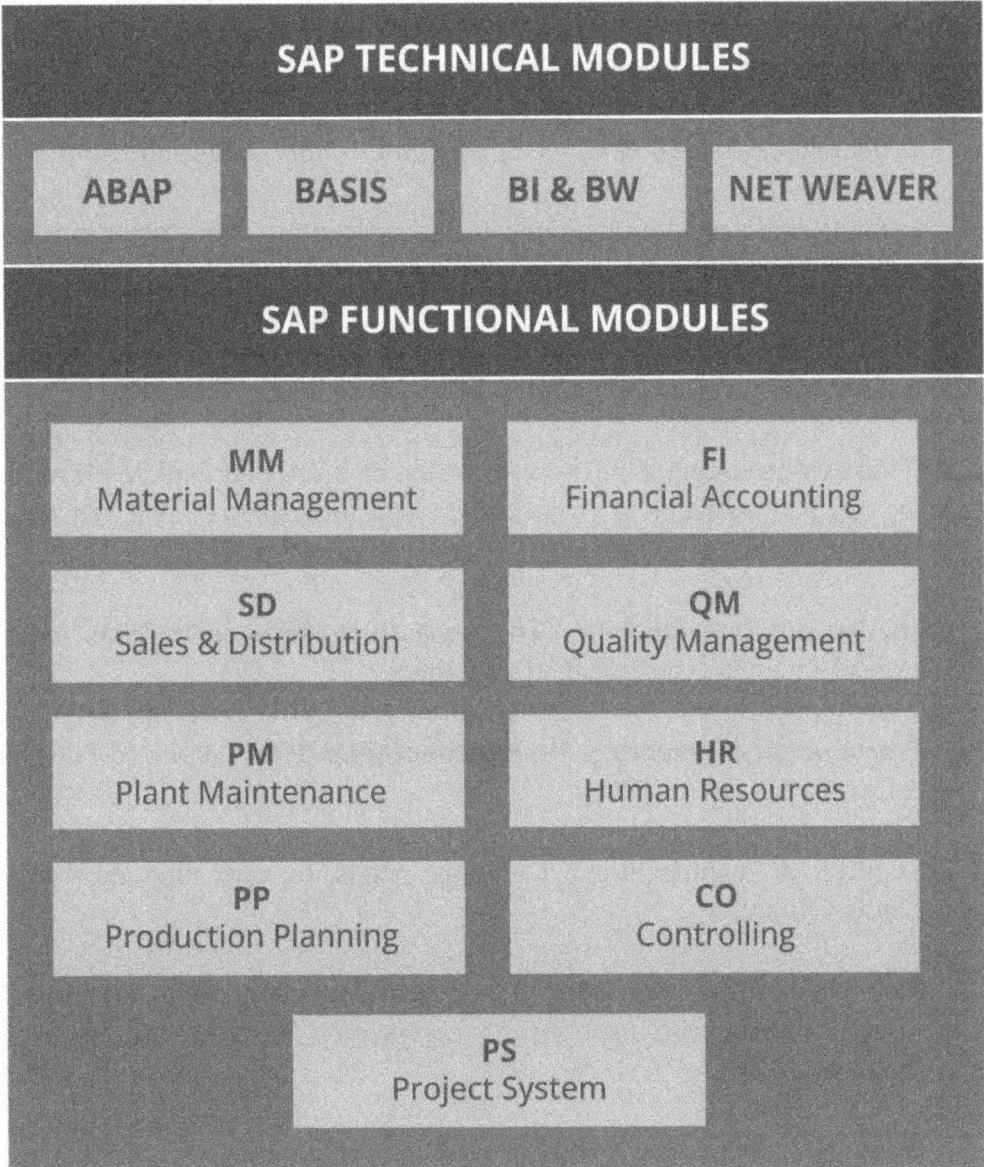

SAP TECHNICAL MODULES

| ABAP | BASIS | BI & BW | NET WEAVER |

SAP FUNCTIONAL MODULES

MM Material Management	**FI** Financial Accounting
SD Sales & Distribution	**QM** Quality Management
PM Plant Maintenance	**HR** Human Resources
PP Production Planning	**CO** Controlling

PS Project System

Interaction Between SAP Modules: A Deeper Dive

SAP's core strength lies in its seamless integration of different business functions, ensuring smooth data flow across departments. This eliminates isolated data silos and allows organizations to operate efficiently. Let's break down the key interactions between modules with relatable examples:

1. **Order Processing (SD & FI)** – From Customer Order to Revenue Recognition

   Example: Imagine you run an online electronics store. A customer purchases a laptop from your website.

   Sales & Distribution (SD): The SD module processes the customer order, generates an invoice, and updates delivery schedules.

   Financial Accounting (FI): The moment the order is confirmed, the FI module records the transaction as accounts receivable (money owed by the customer). Once payment is received, it updates the company's revenue.

   Key Benefit: This integration ensures accurate revenue tracking, reduces manual data entry, and avoids billing errors.

2. **Procurement & Inventory Management (MM & FI)** – Tracking Purchases & Expenses

   Example: A manufacturing company needs to buy raw materials to produce furniture.

   Materials Management (MM): The purchasing team places an order for wood and metal with a supplier. Once delivered, the MM module updates inventory records.

   Financial Accounting (FI): The FI module automatically records this as an expense (accounts payable) and ensures the supplier is paid on time.

   Key Benefit: This integration helps businesses keep track of procurement costs, avoid duplicate purchases, and ensure suppliers are paid efficiently.

3. ***Manufacturing & Costing (PP & CO)*** – Planning Production & Analyzing Costs

   Example: A car manufacturing plant schedules the production of 500 vehicles.

   Production Planning (PP): The PP module determines how many cars should be produced, schedules production, and allocates required resources.

   Controlling (CO): The CO module calculates production costs, including raw materials, labor, and overhead expenses, ensuring profitability.

   Key Benefit: Businesses can optimize production efficiency, reduce waste, and maintain cost control, making operations more profitable.

4. ***Warehouse & Logistics (EWM & MM)*** – Managing Storage & Movement of Goods

   Example: An e-commerce company stores thousands of products in multiple warehouses.

   Extended Warehouse Management (EWM): When a new shipment arrives, EWM assigns an optimal storage location. When a customer places an order, EWM ensures the item is picked, packed, and shipped efficiently.

   Materials Management (MM): MM updates the stock levels in real time, ensuring accurate inventory tracking and preventing stockouts.

   Key Benefit: This integration optimizes storage space, reduces delivery delays, and prevents inventory discrepancies.

   These interactions eliminate data silos, ensuring a unified business view.

SAP Modules

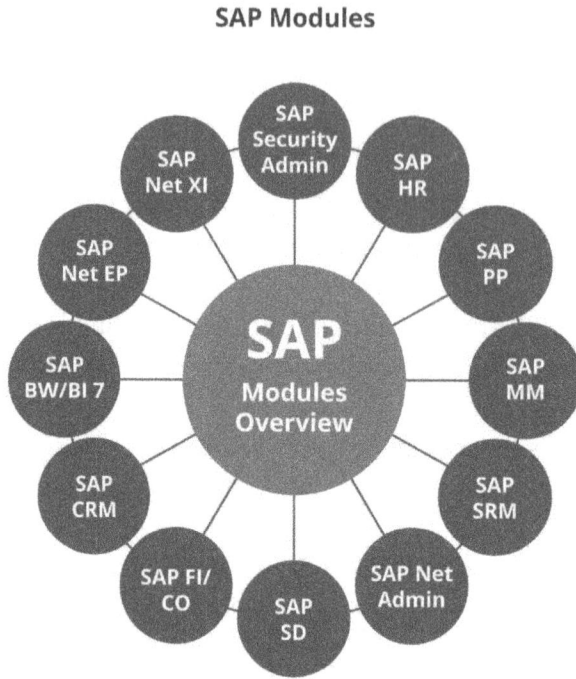

How SAP Modules Work Together in a Business: A Comprehensive Example

Let's take the example of a custom furniture company to understand how different SAP modules interact seamlessly from customer order to final delivery and payment.

Step 1: Customer Places an Order (Sales & Distribution - SD & Financial Accounting - FI)

💡 **Scenario:** A customer orders a **custom-built oakwood dining table** from your furniture company's website.

🪁 **SAP Process Flow:**

- The **Sales & Distribution (SD)** module captures the order details (customer information, product type, price, quantity, and delivery date).
- The system automatically checks if the item is in stock or needs to be produced.
- The **Financial Accounting (FI)** module records this order as **accounts receivable** (an amount owed to the company).

☑ **Benefit:** The business gets real-time visibility into incoming revenue and can track customer payments efficiently.

Step 2: Production Planning & Scheduling (PP & Controlling - CO)

💡 **Scenario:** Since the table is a custom order, it needs to be manufactured.

📌 **SAP Process Flow:**

- The **Production Planning (PP)** module checks production capacity and schedules manufacturing.
- A **Bill of Materials (BOM)** is generated, listing the required raw materials (oakwood, screws, varnish, etc.).
- The **Controlling (CO)** module calculates the cost of production (raw materials, labor, machine usage, overhead expenses).

☑ **Benefit:** This ensures the company **optimizes production costs** and **sets profitable pricing**.

Step 3: Raw Materials Procurement (Materials Management - MM & FI)

💡 **Scenario:** The company realizes they don't have enough oakwood in stock.

📌 **SAP Process Flow:**

- The **Materials Management (MM)** module automatically triggers a **purchase requisition** to buy more oakwood.
- The purchasing team selects a supplier and issues a **purchase order (PO)** via MM.
- Once the supplier delivers the wood, MM updates inventory records.
- The **Financial Accounting (FI)** module records the transaction as an **accounts payable** entry (company owes money to the supplier).

☑ **Benefit:** Ensures a **smooth supply chain**, prevents production delays, and keeps track of expenses.

Step 4: Manufacturing the Dining Table (PP & EWM - Extended Warehouse Management)

💡 **Scenario:** The production team starts building the table.

➹ **SAP Process Flow:**

- The **PP module** assigns work to the production floor, ensuring machines and workers are ready.
- Once the table is completed, the **EWM (Extended Warehouse Management) module** directs it to the warehouse for storage.
- Inventory levels are **automatically updated** to reflect the new finished product.

☑ **Benefit:** Reduces **manual tracking errors** and **optimizes warehouse space**.

Step 5: Order Fulfillment & Delivery (EWM & SD)

💡 **Scenario:** The customer is expecting delivery within 10 days.

➹ **SAP Process Flow:**

- The **EWM module** assigns the **best warehouse location** for easy access.
- The **SD module** generates a **delivery note and shipping label**, ensuring proper logistics.
- The table is shipped via a third-party carrier, and **tracking details are shared with the customer**.

☑ **Benefit:** Faster **order fulfillment, accurate tracking, and improved customer satisfaction**.

Step 6: Customer Payment & Financial Reconciliation (FI & CO)

💡 **Scenario:** The customer receives the table and makes an online payment.

➹ **SAP Process Flow:**

- The **FI module** records the payment, marking the invoice as **paid** and closing the accounts receivable entry.

- The **CO module** updates profitability reports to show how much profit was made from the sale.

☑ **Benefit:** Ensures accurate **financial tracking and profitability analysis**.

Final Outcome: SAP in Action

- ◆ *Customer Satisfaction: The customer receives their order on time and makes payment.*
- ◆ *Operational Efficiency: The company tracks every stage in real-time, reducing manual errors.*
- ◆ *Financial Visibility: The company can analyze sales revenue, production costs, and profits with accurate reports.*
- ◆ *Seamless Data Flow: No duplication of work, ensuring a smooth business process.*

Types of Data in SAP

In SAP, data is the foundation for all business processes. Understanding the various **types of data** is crucial for configuration, customization, and effective process execution. SAP data can be broadly categorized into six major types:

1. Master Data

Master Data is the core data that remains consistent over time and is used repeatedly across transactions and processes. It represents key business entities and is critical for business operations.

- ◆ Examples of Master Data:

  - **Customer Master (SD / FI):** Includes general data (name, address), company code data (reconciliation account), and sales area data (pricing, shipping).
  - **Vendor Master (MM / FI):** Similar to customer master, with general, accounting, and purchasing data.
  - **Material Master (MM / PP):** Contains details such as basic data, purchasing, sales, accounting, and storage information.
  - **G/L Accounts (FI):** Used for recording accounting transactions.
  - **Employee Master (HCM):** Includes personnel information, payroll data, etc.

- ***Asset Master (FI-AA):*** Used for fixed asset tracking.

☑ Key Characteristics:

- Stored centrally and used across multiple modules.
- Relatively static, but can be maintained periodically.
- Crucial for reporting and transaction consistency.

2. Transaction Data

Transaction Data refers to the data generated from day-to-day business transactions. It changes frequently and is dynamic in nature.

- ◆ Examples of Transaction Data:

  - Sales Orders (SD)
  - Purchase Orders (MM)
  - Accounting Documents (FI)
  - Goods Movement (MM)
  - Production Orders (PP)
  - Time Sheet Entries (HCM)

☑ Key Characteristics:

- Time-dependent and used to record specific business events.
- Typically linked to master data.
- Often stored in transactional tables (like BKPF/BSEG for accounting).

3. Configuration (Customizing) Data

Configuration Data or **Customizing Data** defines how the system behaves. This is set up during implementation using the SAP Implementation Guide (IMG) and stored in the system client.

- ◆ Examples of Configuration Data:

  - Company Codes, Plants, Sales Organizations
  - Account Groups and Number Ranges
  - Tax Codes and Chart of Accounts
  - Tolerance Groups and Posting Periods

☑ Key Characteristics:

- Created and modified by consultants.
- Stored client-specifically.
- Transported across systems (e.g., from development to quality to production).

4. Organizational Data

Organizational Data represents the legal and organizational structure of a company in SAP. It forms the framework on which transactions are processed and master data is maintained.

- Examples of Organizational Data:

  - Company Code (FI)
  - Plant (MM, PP)
  - Sales Organization (SD)
  - Controlling Area (CO)
  - Personnel Area (HCM)

☑ Key Characteristics:

- Defines how business units are structured.
- Used as a basis for data access and reporting.
- Configured during initial implementation.

5. Reporting Data (Analytical Data)

Used in SAP BW/4HANA, SAP Analytics Cloud, and other reporting solutions, this data is used to analyze and visualize trends, patterns, and KPIs.

- Examples of Reporting Data:

  - Key Figures and Characteristics in BW
  - Planning Data in SAC
  - Aggregated Financial Statements
  - Dashboard Metrics

☑ Key Characteristics:

- Derived from transactional and master data.
- Often stored in data warehouses or analytical systems.
- Used for decision-making and performance analysis.

6. Technical Data

Behind the scenes, SAP stores metadata and technical configuration to support functional operations.

- Examples:

  - Table Definitions
  - Program Code and Function Modules
  - User Authorizations
  - Transport Logs

Summary Table:

Type of Data	Description	Examples
Master Data	Core business entities used across processes	Customer, Vendor, Material
Transaction Data	Data generated during business transactions	Sales Order, Invoice, Goods Receipt
Configuration Data	System setup and customization	Chart of Accounts, Posting Keys
Organizational Data	Structure of company and business units	Company Code, Plant, Sales Org
Reporting Data	Aggregated or analytical data for reporting	KPI Dashboards, SAC Models
Technical Data	Metadata and system-level info	Tables, ABAP Programs, Authorizations

Why SAP is Essential for Modern Businesses

By integrating all departments, SAP allows businesses to:

- ☑ **Reduce manual work** and improve efficiency
- ☑ **Track financial performance** in real-time
- ☑ **Optimize production and inventory management**
- ☑ **Deliver products on time** and enhance customer experience
- ☑ **Make data-driven decisions** for long-term growth

SAP acts as the **central nervous system** of a company, ensuring **seamless collaboration between departments** and driving **profitability**.

Why SAP is the Undisputed Leader in ERP

By seamlessly connecting departments, SAP eliminates inefficiencies and enables businesses to:

- ✔ **Improve decision-making** with real-time data
- ✔ **Reduce manual work** and errors
- ✔ **Enhance customer satisfaction** with faster order fulfillment
- ✔ **Optimize costs and profitability**

SAP's **end-to-end process integration** ensures that businesses run smoothly and remain competitive in the digital era.

Wrapping Up & Looking Ahead

Enterprise Resource Planning (ERP) systems, especially SAP, have transformed the way businesses operate by seamlessly integrating core functions and driving efficiency. The shift from SAP ECC to SAP S/4HANA is a testament to how technology keeps evolving, enabling organizations to become more agile, data-driven, and future-ready.

Well done on completing this introductory chapter! You've taken your first important steps into the world of ERP systems, understanding what they are, why they matter, and how SAP stands out as a global leader in this space. We explored the overall architecture of SAP, the purpose of its key modules, and how they work together to streamline business processes across an enterprise.

Now that you have a solid foundation, it's time to zoom in on one of the most critical areas of any organization: Finance.

In the next chapter, we'll dive deep into the book's niche, SAP Finance (FI) module—unpacking its structure, core functionalities, real-world use cases, and how it plays a central role in ensuring accurate, timely, and compliant financial operations. Whether you're new to finance or looking to strengthen your technical grasp, this is where theory meets real business impact.

Let's get started—the heart of SAP is calling.

CHAPTER 2

Mastering SAP Finance

This chapter isn't just another section in the book—it's the most important one when it comes to understanding the SAP Finance (FI) module. If you're serious about mastering SAP Finance, pay close attention to every aspect covered here. A solid grasp of these concepts will not only give you a strong foundation in financial processes but also set you up for success in understanding Enterprise Resource Planning (ERP) as a whole.

For newcomers or those looking to build a career in SAP Finance, I cannot stress this enough: absorb every detail in this chapter. If needed, read it again and again until the concepts are crystal clear. Mastering this material will give you a significant head start and make the rest of your SAP journey much smoother.

What You'll Learn in This Chapter

The SAP FI module consists of several key submodules, each playing a vital role in an organization's financial operations. In this chapter, we'll explore these in depth, including:

General Ledger (G/L): The backbone of financial accounting, tracking all financial transactions.

Accounts Payable (AP): Managing an organization's obligations to vendors and suppliers.

Accounts Receivable (AR): Handling incoming payments and customer balances.

Asset Accounting (AA): Recording and managing fixed assets like buildings, machinery, and vehicles.

Banking: Managing cash transactions and bank-related processes.

We'll not only cover the purpose and key concepts of each submodule but also:

- *How each submodule functions within SAP.*
- *The business processes they support.*
- *How they interact with other SAP modules.*
- *Essential transaction codes (T-codes) you'll use daily.*
- *Important SAP tables that store financial data—critical for consultants and users.*

By the end of this chapter, you'll have a clear and structured understanding of SAP Finance, making it easier to navigate real-world financial processes within an organization.

Let's Dive In! Without further ado, let's get started. If you're **new to SAP Finance**, make this chapter your top priority—it's your **launchpad to success**!

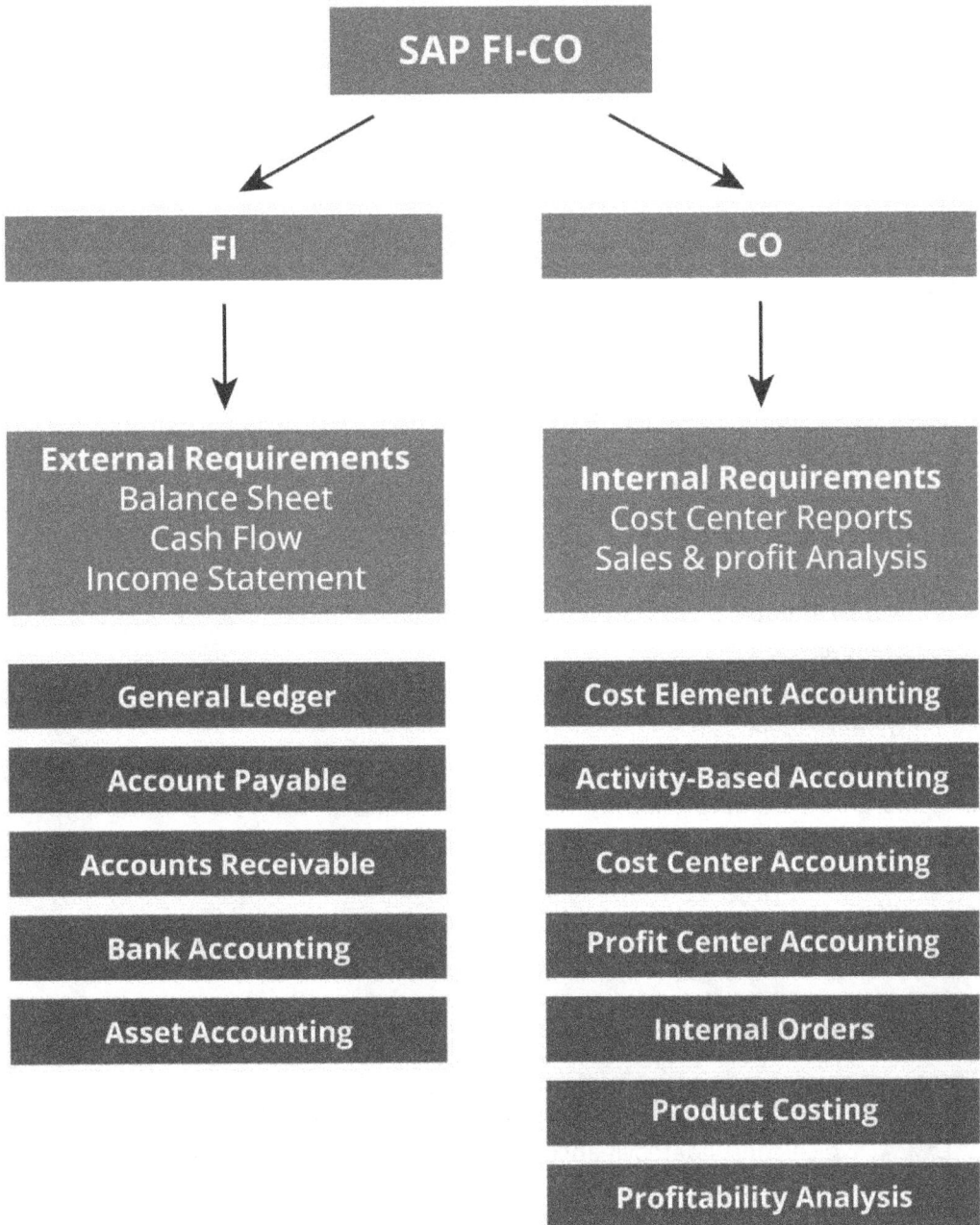

SAP FI-CO

FI

CO

External Requirements
Balance Sheet
Cash Flow
Income Statement

Internal Requirements
Cost Center Reports
Sales & profit Analysis

General Ledger

Account Payable

Accounts Receivable

Bank Accounting

Asset Accounting

Cost Element Accounting

Activity-Based Accounting

Cost Center Accounting

Profit Center Accounting

Internal Orders

Product Costing

Profitability Analysis

SAP Finance - General Ledger (GL)

Introduction to General Ledger (GL)

The General Ledger (GL) in SAP Finance (FI) serves as the central repository for recording and managing all financial transactions within an organization. It plays a critical role in ensuring that financial data is accurate, up-to-date, and compliant with financial reporting standards such as IFRS, GAAP, and local statutory requirements.

SAP GL provides a structured approach to financial accounting, integrating seamlessly with other SAP modules like Accounts Payable (AP), Accounts Receivable (AR), Asset Accounting (AA), Controlling (CO), and Material Ledger (ML). It enables organizations to track their financial activities, generate financial statements, and support decision-making processes by maintaining real-time and historical financial data.

Key Features of SAP General Ledger:

- *Real-time financial data processing:* Ensures immediate updates and financial transparency.
- *Multiple currency handling:* Supports transactions in various currencies to meet global business needs.
- *Multi-GAAP and multi-ledger support:* Allows companies to maintain different accounting principles in parallel.
- *Automatic account determination:* Reduces manual errors by automatically determining GL accounts for financial postings.
- *Flexible reporting:* Enables businesses to generate financial statements, trial balances, and detailed financial reports.

Evolution of SAP General Ledger:

With the release of SAP S/4HANA Finance, SAP introduced the Universal Journal (ACDOCA), which consolidates financial transactions from FI (General Ledger, AP, AR), CO, AA, and ML into a single table. This advancement eliminates redundancy, improves reporting capabilities, and enhances performance in financial data processing.

The General Ledger (GL) in SAP Finance (FI) serves as the central accounting system, maintaining all financial transactions in real-time. It provides an accurate and comprehensive view of an organization's financial position, ensuring compliance with financial reporting standards like IFRS, GAAP, and local statutory requirements.

SAP S/4HANA Finance introduced Universal Journal (ACDOCA), which combines FI (General Ledger Accounting, Accounts Payable, Accounts Receivable), Controlling (CO), Asset Accounting (AA), and Material Ledger (ML) in a single table.

Functions of General Ledger

The GL module in SAP FI performs several critical financial functions, including:

- **Recording Transactions:** Capturing all financial transactions in real time.
- **Financial Reporting:** Generating balance sheets, profit & loss statements, and trial balances.
- **Reconciliation:** Integrating with sub-ledgers like **Accounts Payable (AP), Accounts Receivable (AR), and Asset Accounting (AA)**.
- **Multi-currency Handling:** Supporting multiple currencies for global financial reporting.
- **Audit and Compliance:** Ensuring regulatory compliance and audit readiness.
- **Period Closing Activities:** Assisting in monthly, quarterly, and yearly financial closings.

Main Components of General Ledger

The SAP GL comprises several key components:

1. **Chart of Accounts (COA):** A structured list of **GL accounts** categorized by assets, liabilities, revenue, and expenses.
2. **Company Code:** Represents an independent legal accounting entity within SAP.
3. **Fiscal Year Variant:** Defines the financial year structure (e.g., calendar year, April to March, etc.).
4. **Posting Periods:** Controls which periods are open for posting transactions.
5. **Field Status Variant:** Determines mandatory, optional, and suppressed fields in transactions.
6. **Document Types & Number Ranges:** Classifies transactions and assigns number ranges for control.
7. Ledger Concept:
   - **Leading Ledger:** Used for statutory reporting.
   - **Non-Leading Ledger:** Used for additional reporting needs (e.g., local GAAP, tax reporting).
8. **Number Ranges:** Defines the numerical sequencing for financial documents.

9. **Posting Keys:** Determines whether a posting is debit or credit and specifies the account type.
10. **Financial Statement Version (FSV):** Defines the structure of financial reports like balance sheets and income statements.

Flow of General Ledger (GL)

The typical flow of transactions in SAP GL follows:

1. **Business Transactions:** Initiated from different modules (e.g., Sales, Procurement, Payroll, etc.).
2. **Document Posting:** Transactions are posted to the GL via journal entries.
3. **Automatic Account Determination:** System automatically determines GL accounts for postings.
4. **Integration with Sub-Ledgers:** Updates AP, AR, and Asset Accounting (AA).
5. **Period-End Processing:** Includes **reconciliations, accruals, adjustments**, and **financial reporting**.
6. **Financial Statements Generation:** Balance sheet and profit & loss (P&L) statements are generated.

Data flow from Transactional Postings to Balance Sheet

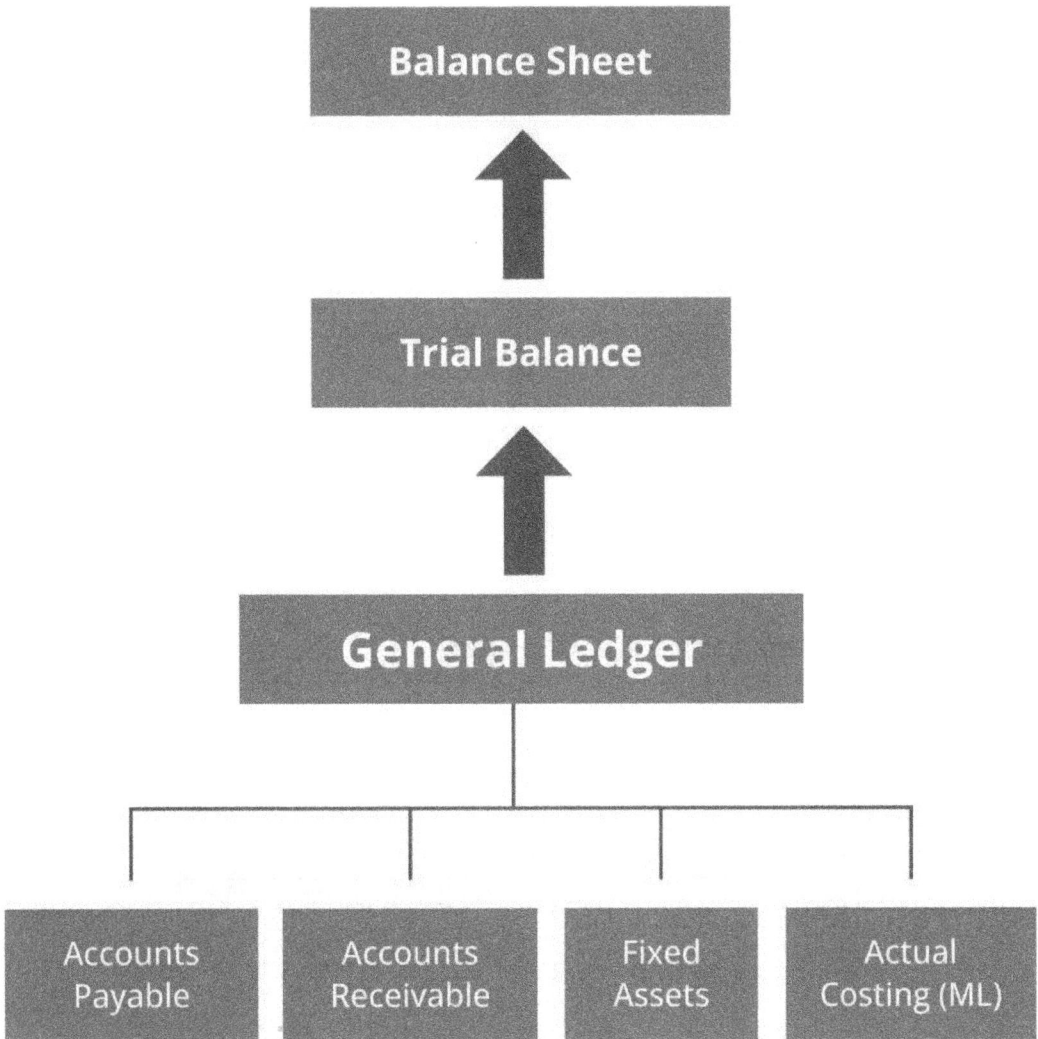

Balance Sheet

↑

Trial Balance

↑

General Ledger

| Accounts Payable | Accounts Receivable | Fixed Assets | Actual Costing (ML) |

Process of General Ledger (GL)

The General Ledger process involves:

1. **GL Master Data Creation**
   - Define Chart of Accounts
   - Maintain GL Account Groups
   - Create GL Accounts (FS00)

2. **Transaction Posting**
   - Enter Financial Documents (FB50, F-02, etc.)
   - Automatic Posting from Sub-Ledgers (AP, AR, AA, etc.)

3. **Period-End Processing**
   - Open & Close Posting Periods (OB52)
   - Perform Reconciliations (F.13, F.19)
   - Accruals and Deferrals (FBS1, FBV1)

4. **Reporting & Analysis**
   - Financial Statements (S_ALR_87012284, S_ALR_87012301)
   - Trial Balance (S_ALR_87012277)

Important T-Codes for General Ledger

T-Code	Description
FS00	Maintain GL Account Master Data
OB52	Open/Close Posting Periods
F-02	Post Document
FB50	Enter GL Account Document
FB60	Enter Vendor Invoice
FB70	Enter Customer Invoice
FBL3N	Display GL Account Line Items
FAGLB03	Display GL Balances
F.01	Financial Statements
F.10	Balance Sheet Adjustment
F.08	GL Account Balances (New GL)

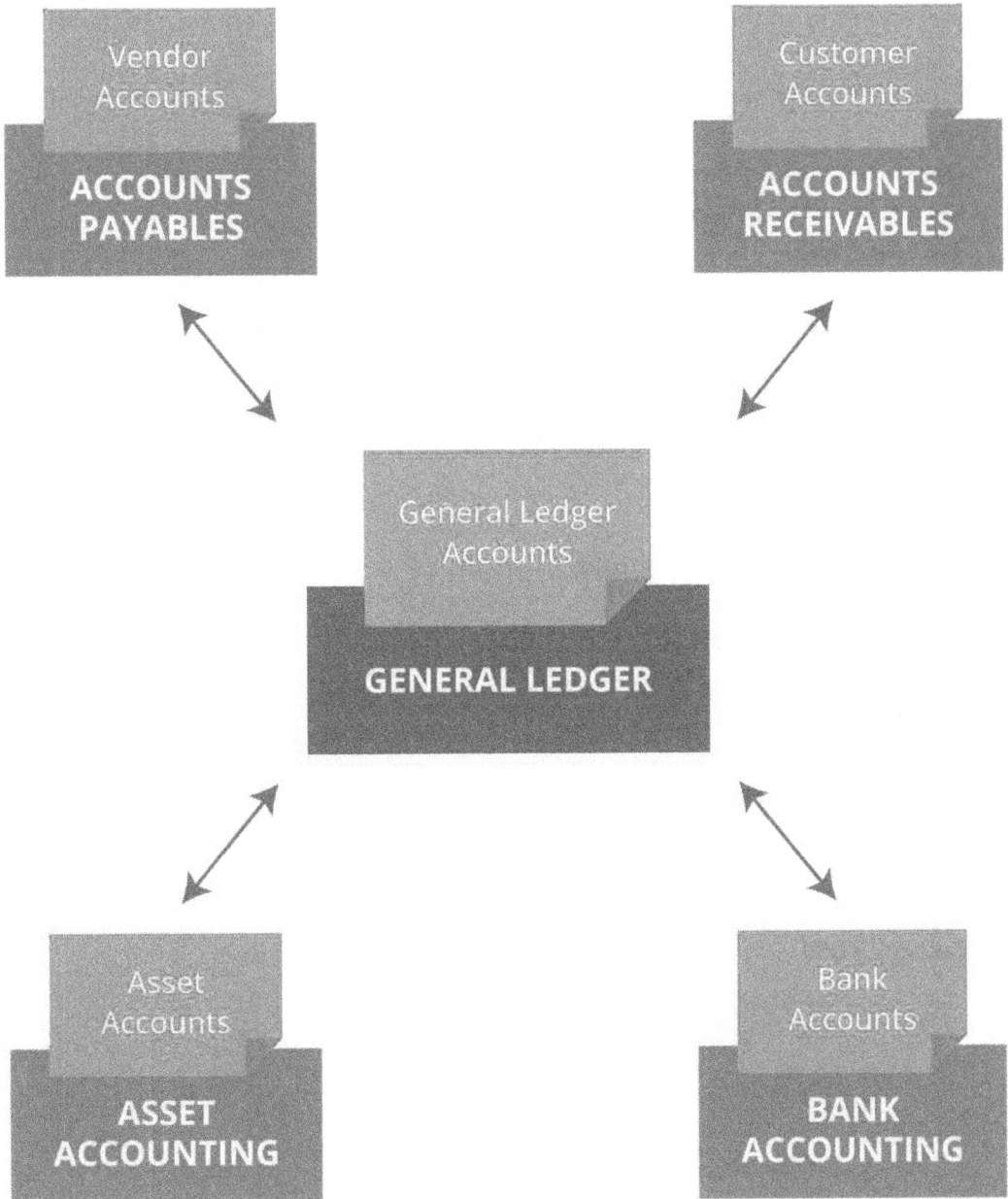

Vendor Accounts

ACCOUNTS PAYABLES

Customer Accounts

ACCOUNTS RECEIVABLES

General Ledger Accounts

GENERAL LEDGER

Asset Accounts

ASSET ACCOUNTING

Bank Accounts

BANK ACCOUNTING

Journal Entries in General Ledger

Journal entries form the foundation of financial postings. Each entry consists of:

Example 1: Vendor Invoice Posting (Accounts Payable)

Debit: Expense Account (600000) $1,000
Credit: Vendor Account (300001) $1,000
T-Code: *FB60*

Example 2: Customer Invoice Posting (Accounts Receivable)

Debit: Customer Account (200001) $2,500
Credit: Revenue Account (400000) $2,500
T-Code: *FB70*

Example 3: Bank Payment Posting

Debit: Vendor Account (300001) $1,000
Credit: Bank Account (100000) $1,000
T-Code: *F-53*

Example 4: Accrual Posting

Debit: Expense Account (600100) $500
Credit: Accrued Liabilities (250100) $500
T-Code: *FBS1*

Important Tables in General Ledger

SAP uses several key tables to store GL-related data:

Table Name	Description
SKA1	Chart of Accounts Master Data
SKB1	GL Account Master Data (Company Code Level)
BKPF	Accounting Document Header
BSEG	Accounting Document Line Items
FAGLFLEXA	New GL Line Items Table
ACDOCA	Universal Journal Entry Table (S/4HANA)
BSIS	GL Account Transactions (Dr Side)
BSAS	GL Account Transactions (Cr Side)
BSIK	Open Vendor Items
BSID	Open Customer Items

Advanced Topics in General Ledger

1. *New General Ledger (New GL)*

   - Introduced in SAP ECC 6.0 and enhanced in S/4HANA.
   - Includes functionalities like *document splitting, parallel ledgers, and segment reporting*.

2. *Parallel Accounting*

   - Allows multiple ledgers to be maintained for different accounting principles (e.g., IFRS, GAAP, Tax Ledger).
   - Implemented using *Non-Leading Ledgers or Ledger Groups*.

3. *Intercompany Transactions*

   - Handles financial transactions between different legal entities within the same group.
   - Key T-Codes: *FBU1 (Post Intercompany Document), FBICR3 (Reconciliation)*.

4. ***Cross-Company Transactions***

- Transactions between company codes in the same client but different legal entities.
- Key T-Codes: ***FB50 (Enter GL Account Document), F.01 (Financial Statements for Multiple Company Codes)***.

Conclusion

The **SAP General Ledger** is the backbone of financial accounting, integrating with all sub-modules like **Accounts Payable, Accounts Receivable, Asset Accounting, and Controlling**. With **S/4HANA Finance**, the **Universal Journal (ACDOCA)** streamlines financial transactions, ensuring real-time reporting and compliance. A solid understanding of GL processes, T-codes, journal entries, and tables is essential for **SAP FI consultants, accountants, and finance professionals** managing enterprise financial operations efficiently.

SAP Finance - Accounts Payable (AP)

Introduction to Accounts Payable (AP)

Accounts Payable (AP) in SAP Finance (FI) is responsible for managing an organization's short-term obligations to suppliers and vendors. It ensures timely payments, proper tracking of outstanding liabilities, and compliance with financial policies.

SAP AP automates the procure-to-pay (P2P) process, integrating with Materials Management (MM) for invoice verification and General Ledger (GL) for financial reporting. It supports multi-currency transactions, automatic payments, tax calculations, and reconciliation with vendor accounts.

Key Features of SAP Accounts Payable:

- **Vendor Management:** Maintains detailed records of vendor transactions.
- **Invoice Processing:** Supports manual and automated invoice entry.
- **Payment Processing:** Facilitates check, bank transfer, and electronic payment methods.
- **Reconciliation and Reporting:** Ensures accurate financial statements.
- **Integration with Other Modules:** Works closely with **MM, GL, and Asset Accounting (AA)**.

Evolution of AP in SAP:

With SAP S/4HANA Finance, AP functionalities are streamlined within the Universal Journal (ACDOCA), reducing redundancy, improving reconciliation, and enabling real-time financial analytics.

MPP Process Flow Diagram
Accounts Payable

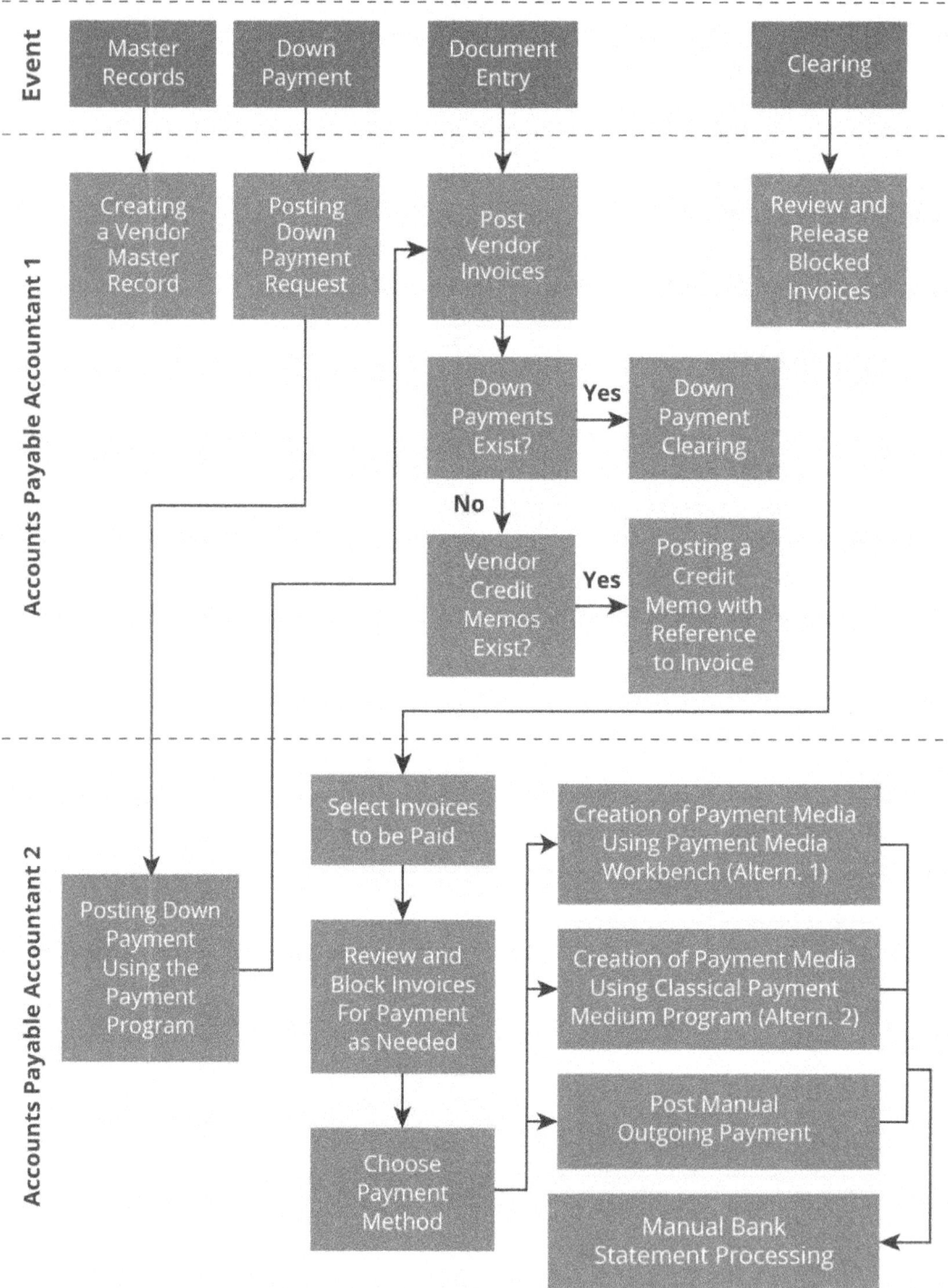

Event

Master Records → Creating a Vendor Master Record

Down Payment → Posting Down Payment Request

Document Entry → Post Vendor Invoices

Clearing → Review and Release Blocked Invoices

Accounts Payable Accountant 1

Post Vendor Invoices → Down Payments Exist?

Down Payments Exist? — **Yes** → Down Payment Clearing

Down Payments Exist? — **No** → Vendor Credit Memos Exist?

Vendor Credit Memos Exist? — **Yes** → Posting a Credit Memo with Reference to Invoice

Accounts Payable Accountant 2

Posting Down Payment Using the Payment Program

Select Invoices to be Paid → Review and Block Invoices For Payment as Needed → Choose Payment Method

Creation of Payment Media Using Payment Media Workbench (Altern. 1)

Creation of Payment Media Using Classical Payment Medium Program (Altern. 2)

Post Manual Outgoing Payment

Manual Bank Statement Processing

Functions of Accounts Payable

The AP module in SAP FI serves several core functions:

- *Vendor Invoice Management:* Tracks invoices from receipt to payment.
- *Invoice Verification:* Ensures proper matching with Purchase Orders (PO) and Goods Receipts (GR).
- *Payment Processing:* Manages payment runs for timely vendor settlements.
- *Credit Management:* Helps maintain vendor credit limits and conditions.
- *Tax Calculations:* Computes applicable taxes (e.g., VAT, GST, withholding tax).
- *Automatic Clearing and Reconciliation:* Matches vendor open items with payments.

Main Components of Accounts Payable

SAP AP consists of several key components:

1. *Vendor Master Data:* Stores vendor-specific details like name, payment terms, and bank details.
2. *Invoice Posting:* Records incoming invoices from vendors.
3. *Payment Program (F110):* Automates bulk payments.
4. *Withholding Tax Management:* Deducts and reports applicable taxes.
5. *Down Payments and Advances:* Manages partial payments before final invoice settlement.
6. *Automatic Clearing of Open Items:* Matches invoices with payments for reconciliation.
7. *Integration with Materials Management (MM):* Ensures that payments align with purchase orders and goods receipts.
8. *Open and Close Posting Periods:* Defines which financial periods are open for posting transactions.
9. *Document Types and Number Ranges:* Controls invoice and payment postings.
10. *Payment Terms and Conditions:* Defines discount policies and due dates.

Flow of Accounts Payable (AP)

1. *Purchase Order (PO) Creation* (via MM module)
2. *Goods Receipt (GR) Posting* (integration with MM)
3. *Invoice Verification & Entry* (MIRO, FB60)
4. *Approval Workflow* (if required)

5. **Payment Processing** (F110 for automatic payments, F-53 for manual payments)
6. **Clearing Open Items** (F.13 for automatic clearing)
7. **Financial Reporting** (Vendor Balances, Trial Balance, P&L Statement)

Process of Accounts Payable (AP)

1. **Vendor Master Data Setup**
   - Maintain vendor details (FK01, FK02, XK01, XK02)
   - Assign company code, payment terms, and tax codes

2. **Invoice Entry & Verification**
   - Manual Invoice Posting (FB60)
   - Invoice Verification (MIRO for PO-based invoices)
   - Reversing Incorrect Invoices (FB08)

3. **Payment Processing**
   - Automatic Payment Run (F110)
   - Manual Payments (F-53 for outgoing payments, F-58 for checks)
   - Down Payment Processing (F-48)

4. **Period-End Activities**
   - Open and Close Posting Periods (OB52)
   - Vendor Reconciliation (F.13, FBL1N)
   - AP Reporting (S_ALR_87012082, S_ALR_87012085)

Important T-Codes for Accounts Payable

T-Code	Description
FK01 / FK02	Create/Change Vendor Master Record
XK01 / XK02	Create/Change Vendor Centrally
FB60	Enter Vendor Invoice
MIRO	Invoice Verification for PO-based invoices
F110	Automatic Payment Run
F-53	Manual Vendor Payment
F-44	Clear Vendor Account
FBL1N	Vendor Line Item Display
F.13	Automatic Clearing
S_ALR_87012082	Vendor Balances Report

Journal Entries in Accounts Payable

Example 1: Vendor Invoice Posting

Debit: Expense Account (600000) $5,000
Credit: Vendor Account (300001) $5,000
T-Code: *FB60*

Example 2: Payment to Vendor

Debit: Vendor Account (300001) $5,000
Credit: Bank Account (100000) $5,000
T-Code: *F-53*

Example 3: Down Payment to Vendor

Debit: Vendor Advance (180000) $2,000
Credit: Bank Account (100000) $2,000
T-Code: *F-48*

Important Tables in Accounts Payable

Table Name	Description
LFA1	Vendor Master (General Section)
LFB1	Vendor Master (Company Code Section)
BSIK	Open Vendor Items
BSAS	Cleared Vendor Items
BKPF	Accounting Document Header
BSEG	Accounting Document Line Items
BSAK	Cleared Vendor Transactions
BSIK	Open Items for Vendors

Advanced Topics in Accounts Payable

1. **Vendor Payment Blocks**
   - Prevents payment processing for specific invoices.
   - Used for invoice verification and approval workflows.

2. **Automatic Invoice Processing via IDocs & OCR**
   - Automates invoice receipt and posting using Electronic Data Interchange (EDI) and Optical Character Recognition (OCR).

3. **Withholding Tax Configuration**
   - Applies local tax regulations to vendor payments.
   - Key tables: **WITH_ITEM, T059Z**.

4. **Foreign Currency Transactions & Exchange Rate Handling**
   - Manages vendor payments in multiple currencies.
   - Exchange rate determination via **OB08**.

5. **GR/IR Clearing Account**
   - Used to track goods received but not yet invoiced.
   - Key T-Code: **F.19** for automatic clearing.

Closing Statement and Conclusion

The **Accounts Payable (AP) module in SAP FI** plays a crucial role in managing vendor liabilities, ensuring timely payments, and maintaining accurate financial records. Its seamless integration with **MM, GL, and Treasury** enables efficient financial operations. With SAP S/4HANA Finance, real-time analytics and automation further streamline AP processes, reducing manual effort and improving compliance. Understanding **AP workflows, T-codes, journal entries, and advanced topics** is essential for **finance professionals, SAP consultants, and accounting teams** managing enterprise-wide accounts payable operations efficiently.

SAP Finance - Accounts Receivable (AR)

Introduction to Accounts Receivable (AR)

Accounts Receivable (AR) in SAP Finance (FI) is a critical module that manages the money owed to an organization by its customers. It ensures that all transactions related to customer payments, invoices, credit memos, and outstanding balances are accurately recorded and managed efficiently.

AR plays a key role in the financial health of a business, as it directly affects cash flow and working capital. The AR process starts from the point of issuing an invoice to a customer and extends to payment collection, adjustments, and reconciliation. With SAP's robust capabilities, businesses can streamline AR operations, reducing manual efforts and improving financial visibility.

SAP AR integrates with other SAP modules, such as Sales and Distribution (SD), Controlling (CO), and Treasury (TR), to provide comprehensive financial management.

Functions of Accounts Receivable

The SAP Accounts Receivable module provides various functions to manage and track customer-related financial transactions, including:

- **Customer Master Data Management**: Storing customer details, including credit limits, payment terms, and contact information.
- **Invoice Processing**: Generating and managing customer invoices based on sales transactions.
- **Incoming Payments**: Processing payments received from customers via various channels (e.g., bank transfer, check, electronic payment methods).
- **Credit Management**: Monitoring customer credit limits to minimize financial risk.
- **Dunning Process**: Automating reminders for overdue invoices and escalating collection efforts.
- **Reconciliation and Reporting**: Ensuring that customer balances match the general ledger and providing insights into receivables.
- **Integration with Other Modules**: Collaborating with SD for order processing, CO for profitability analysis, and TR for cash management.

Accounts Receivable Process Flow in SAP

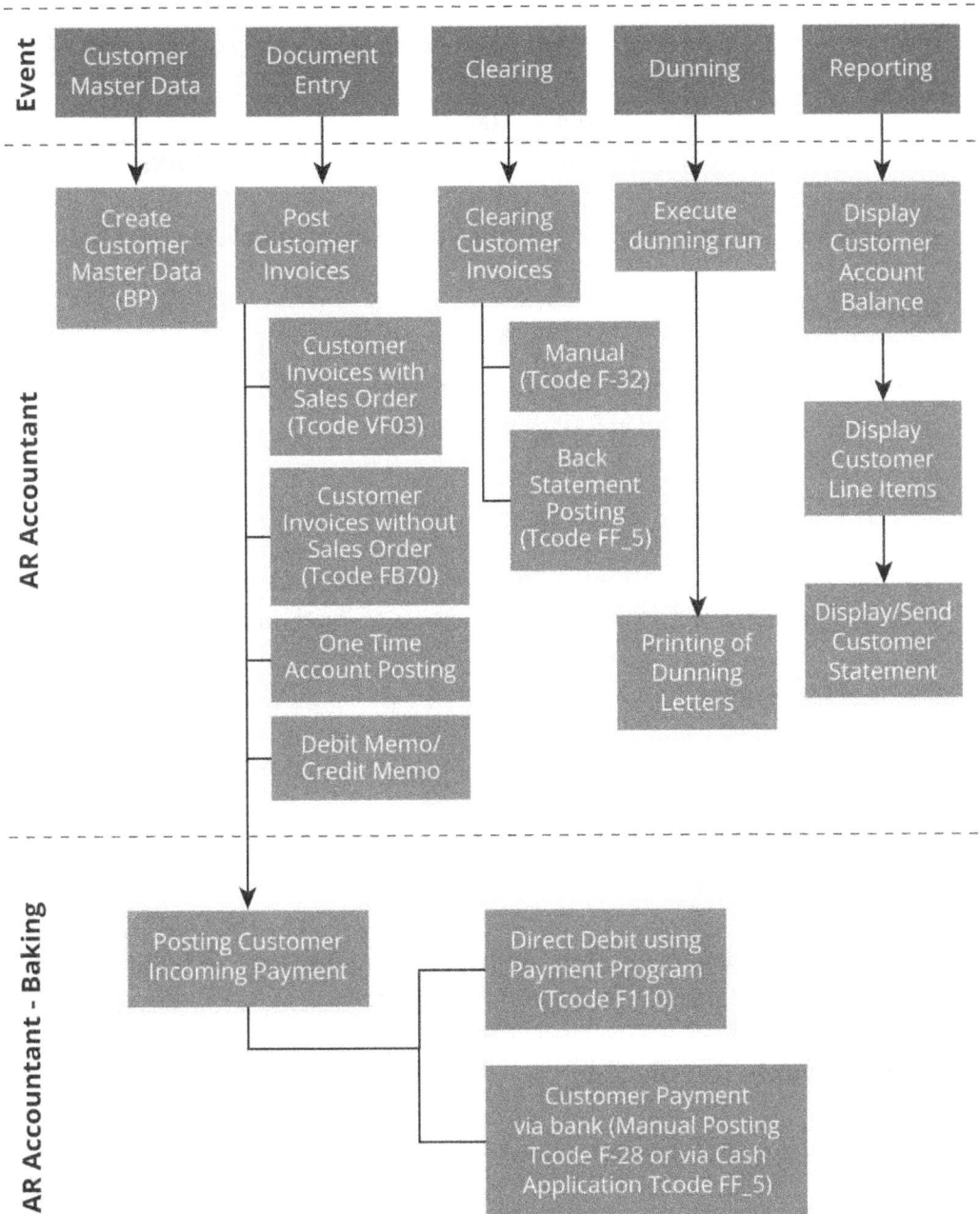

Event

| Customer Master Data | Document Entry | Clearing | Dunning | Reporting |

AR Accountant

- Create Customer Master Data (BP)
- Post Customer Invoices
  - Customer Invoices with Sales Order (Tcode VF03)
  - Customer Invoices without Sales Order (Tcode FB70)
  - One Time Account Posting
  - Debit Memo/ Credit Memo
- Clearing Customer Invoices
  - Manual (Tcode F-32)
  - Back Statement Posting (Tcode FF_5)
- Execute dunning run
  - Printing of Dunning Letters
- Display Customer Account Balance
  - Display Customer Line Items
  - Display/Send Customer Statement

AR Accountant - Baking

- Posting Customer Incoming Payment
  - Direct Debit using Payment Program (Tcode F110)
  - Customer Payment via bank (Manual Posting Tcode F-28 or via Cash Application Tcode FF_5)

Main Components of Accounts Receivable

a) Customer Master Data

Customer master data contains all relevant details about a customer, including:

- General Data: Name, address, contact details
- Company Code Data: Payment terms, dunning procedures, reconciliation accounts
- Sales Area Data: Credit limits, pricing conditions, and delivery information

b) Document Posting

Each financial transaction related to customers, such as invoices, payments, or credit memos, is recorded in SAP as a document.

c) Dunning Process

The dunning process is used to remind customers of overdue payments. It includes multiple levels, from simple reminders to legal notices.

d) Credit Management

SAP's Credit Management functionality assesses a customer's creditworthiness and helps prevent excessive risk exposure.

e) Payment Processing

SAP facilitates payment receipts from customers through different methods, including checks, wire transfers, and direct debits.

Flow of Accounts Receivable

The AR process typically follows this flow:

1. **Sales Order Processing (SD Module)** – A customer places an order.
2. **Delivery & Goods Issue** – The ordered goods/services are delivered.
3. **Billing Document Generation** – An invoice is created in SAP FI.
4. **Invoice Posting in AR** – The customer's account is debited.
5. **Payment Receipt** – The customer pays through available payment channels.

6. **Clearing the Open Items** – Once payment is received, the outstanding balance is cleared.
7. **Dunning Process** (if required) – Reminders are sent for overdue payments.

Process of Accounts Receivable

Step 1: Customer Master Data Creation

T-Code: **XD01** (Create Customer)

Step 2: Invoice Posting

T-Code: **FB70** (Enter Customer Invoice)

- The system generates an accounting entry:
  Customer A/c (Dr.) XXX
  Revenue A/c (Cr.) XXX

Step 3: Incoming Payment Processing

T-Code: **F-28** (Incoming Payment Processing)

- Accounting entry:
  Bank A/c (Dr.) XXX
  Customer A/c (Cr.) XXX

Step 4: Dunning Process (Overdue Payment Reminders)

T-Code: **F150** (Dunning Run)

Step 5: Reconciliation and Reporting

T-Code: **FBL5N** (Customer Line Item Display)

Important T-Codes in Accounts Receivable

T– Code	Description
XD01	Create Customer
XD02	Change Customer
XD02	Display Customer
FB70	Customer Invoice Posting
F–28	Incoming Payment
F–32	Clearing of Customer Open Items
FBL5N	Customer Line Item Display
F150	Dunning Process Execution
FD33	Customer Credit Management Display
S_ALR_870121	AR Aging Report

Journal Entries in Accounts Receivable

Invoice Posting

Customer A/c (Dr.) XXX
Revenue A/c (Cr.) XXX

Payment Receipt

Bank A/c (Dr.) XXX
Customer A/c (Cr.) XXX

Discount Allowed (if applicable)

Cash A/c (Dr.) XXX
Discount Allowed A/c (Dr.) XXX
Customer A/c (Cr.) XXX

Bad Debt Write-off

Bad Debt Expense A/c (Dr.) XXX
Customer A/c (Cr.) XXX

Important SAP Tables in Accounts Receivable

Table	Description
KNA1	General Customer Master
KNB1	Customer Master (Company Code)
BSID	Accounting: Secondary Index for Customers
BSEG	Document Line Items
FAGLFLEXA	New General Ledger Accounting
F150D	Dunning History Table

Advanced Topics in Accounts Receivable

a) *Integration with SAP Treasury and Risk Management*

- Cash flow forecasts and liquidity planning.

b) *Automatic Incoming Payments Processing*

- SAP can automatically clear payments using EBS (Electronic Bank Statement) or Lockbox functionality.

c) *Accounts Receivable Aging Analysis*

- SAP generates aging reports to analyze outstanding balances based on due dates.

d) *Dispute and Collections Management*

- SAP provides tools for tracking disputed invoices and customer collections.

e) *Credit Risk Management*

- Businesses use SAP Credit Management (FSCM) to assess customer credit risk and define credit limits.

Closing Statement and Conclusion

Accounts Receivable in SAP Finance plays a crucial role in maintaining the financial health of an organization. **It provides real-time visibility into outstanding customer balances, automates the invoicing and collection process, and minimizes credit risks.**

With the integration of various SAP modules, **AR helps businesses optimize their working capital and ensure accurate financial reporting**. Mastering SAP AR functionalities, such as customer master data, invoice processing, credit management, and reconciliation, is essential for finance professionals to streamline receivables and improve cash flow management.

SAP Finance - Asset Accounting (AA)

Introduction to Asset Accounting (AA)

Asset Accounting (FI-AA) is a sub-module of SAP Finance (FI) that focuses on managing and tracking fixed assets. It integrates with other SAP modules such as General Ledger (FI-GL), Controlling (CO), Plant Maintenance (PM), and Materials Management (MM).

Asset Accounting plays a crucial role in financial reporting as it enables organizations to track asset values, depreciation, revaluation, asset transfers, retirements, and scrapping. The sub-module ensures compliance with multiple accounting standards, such as IFRS, US GAAP, and local tax regulations.

Key features of FI-AA include:

- Recording asset acquisitions
- Calculating depreciation automatically
- Supporting multiple valuation methods
- Managing asset retirements and transfers
- Handling revaluations and impairments
- Generating financial reports related to assets

Functions of Asset Accounting

The core functions of SAP FI-AA include:

- **Asset Acquisition**: Recording the purchase of assets through integration with FI-AP or directly via manual entry.
- **Asset Depreciation**: Automatic calculation of depreciation based on assigned methods.
- **Asset Transfers**: Moving assets between company codes, cost centers, or locations.
- **Asset Retirement**: Managing asset disposals, whether through sales or scrapping.
- **Asset Revaluation**: Adjusting asset values due to market fluctuations or impairment.
- **Asset Reporting**: Generating reports for financial statements, tax calculations, and internal management.

Assets Flow in SAP from Asset Master Creation until Asset Write off.

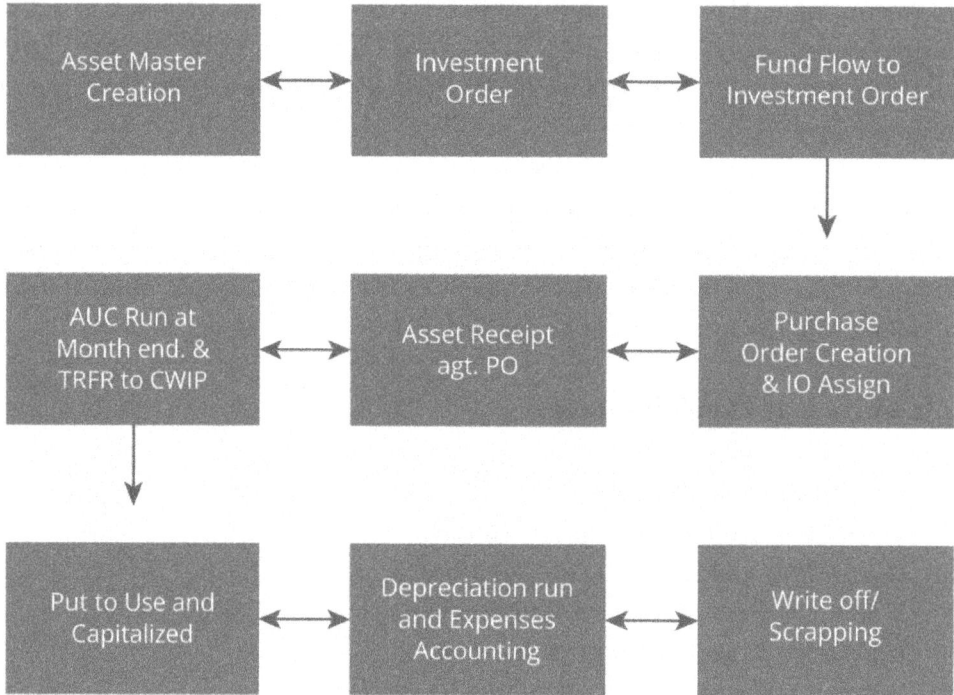

Asset Master Creation	⟷ Investment Order	⟷ Fund Flow to Investment Order
AUC Run at Month end. & TRFR to CWIP	⟷ Asset Receipt agt. PO	⟷ Purchase Order Creation & IO Assign
Put to Use and Capitalized	⟷ Depreciation run and Expenses Accounting	⟷ Write off/ Scrapping

Main Components of Asset Accounting

a) Chart of Depreciation

Defines the depreciation methods, rules, and calculations for asset valuation. Each company code is assigned to a chart of depreciation.

b) Asset Classes

Asset classes categorize assets, such as buildings, machinery, furniture, and vehicles. Each asset class determines:

- Depreciation area
- Account determination
- Number range for asset master records

c) Depreciation Areas

Depreciation areas allow an organization to maintain different depreciation calculations for statutory, tax, or internal reporting.

d) Asset Master Records

Each asset is created as a master record that includes:

- Asset class
- Cost center
- Useful life
- Depreciation key

e) Integration with Other SAP Modules

- **FI-GL**: Posts asset transactions directly into the general ledger.
- **CO**: Assigns assets to cost centers, internal orders, or WBS elements.
- **MM**: Facilitates asset acquisition through purchase orders and goods receipts.
- **PM**: Links assets to maintenance records for tracking usage and repairs.

Flow of Asset Accounting

1. Asset Master Data Creation (AS01/AS02/AS03)
2. Asset Acquisition (F-90, ABZON, or integration with MM-FI)
3. Asset Capitalization
4. Depreciation Run (AFAB)
5. Asset Transfers (ABUMN, ABT1N)
6. Asset Retirement/Sale (ABAON, ABAVN)
7. Period-End Closing and Reporting

Process of Asset Accounting

Step 1: Asset Master Data Creation

Each fixed asset must have a master record, which includes its details and accounting attributes.

Step 2: Asset Acquisition

Assets can be acquired through purchase (invoice verification), internal development, or direct capitalization.

Step 3: Asset Depreciation

Depreciation methods include:

- Straight-line depreciation
- Declining balance depreciation
- Units of production depreciation

Step 4: Asset Transfer

Assets can be transferred within or between company codes.

Step 5: Asset Retirement

Retirement occurs when an asset is sold, scrapped, or written off.

Step 6: Year-End Closing

At the end of the fiscal year, depreciation is finalized, reports are generated, and balances are carried forward.

T-Codes for Asset Accounting

T-Code	Description
AS01	Create Asset Master Record
AS02	Change Asset Master Record
AS03	Display Asset Master Record
F-90	Asset Acquisition with Vendor
ABZON	Asset Acquisition without Vendor
AFAB	Execute Depreciation Run
ABAVN	Asset Retirement without Revenue
ABAON	Asset Retirement with Revenue
ABUMN	Transfer Asset within Company Code
ABT1N	Transfer Asset to Another Company Code
AW01N	Asset Explorer
AR02	Asset Balances Report

Journal Entries

Transaction	Debit	Credit
Asset Purchase	Asset A/C	Vendor A/C
Depreciation	Depreciation Expense	Accumulated Depreciation
Asset Sale	Customer A/C	Asset A/C
Asset Scrap	Loss on Disposal	Asset A/C
Asset Transfer	Receiving Asset A/C	Transferring Asset A/C

Key Tables in Asset Accounting

Table	Description
ANKA	Asset Classes
ANLA	Asset Master Data
ANLC	Asset Value Fields
ANEP	Asset Line Items
ANEK	Asset Document Header
T093	Asset Accounting Customizing
TABA	Asset Transactions

Advanced Topics in Asset Accounting

a) Parallel Valuation in Asset Accounting

Allows multiple valuation approaches, such as book depreciation for internal reporting and tax depreciation for compliance.

b) Asset Under Construction (AUC)

Manages assets in progress that have not yet been capitalized.

c) Lease Accounting (IFRS 16)

Manages leased assets under IFRS 16 guidelines, treating leases as assets with amortization schedules.

d) Asset Impairment

A process where asset values are adjusted due to significant reductions in recoverable value.

Conclusion

SAP FI-AA is a critical module for tracking and managing an organization's fixed assets. It integrates seamlessly with other SAP modules to ensure proper financial control, reporting, and compliance.

By leveraging Asset Accounting, businesses can effectively manage asset life cycles, maintain regulatory compliance, and optimize financial performance. Understanding the core processes, T-codes, and journal entries is essential for mastering this module and ensuring accurate financial reporting in SAP systems.

SAP Finance - Bank Accounting (BA)

Introduction to Bank Accounting (BA)

SAP Bank Accounting (BA) is an essential component of SAP Financial Accounting (FI) that enables businesses to efficiently manage their bank transactions, including processing payments, bank statements, and reconciliations. The module integrates seamlessly with other SAP FI modules like Accounts Payable (AP), Accounts Receivable (AR), and General Ledger (GL), ensuring a smooth financial workflow.

With globalization and digital banking advancements, organizations require a robust bank accounting system to track cash flows, monitor bank balances, and automate financial processes. SAP Bank Accounting offers real-time integration, automated bank reconciliation, and compliance with financial regulations, making it a crucial tool for businesses.

Functions of Bank Accounting

The primary functions of SAP Bank Accounting include:

- *Management of Bank Master Data:* Storing details about bank accounts, account types, bank keys, and bank groups.
- *Processing Incoming and Outgoing Payments:* Managing payments via various methods like electronic transfers, checks, direct debits, and wire transfers.
- *Bank Statement Processing:* Automatic or manual uploading and processing of bank statements.
- *Reconciliation of Bank Accounts:* Ensuring bank transactions recorded in SAP match the actual transactions in the bank.
- *Cash Positioning and Liquidity Management:* Tracking available cash and future cash flows.
- *Automated Clearing of Bank Transactions:* Identifying and matching open items with bank statement records.

SAP FI-Bank Accounting Diagram

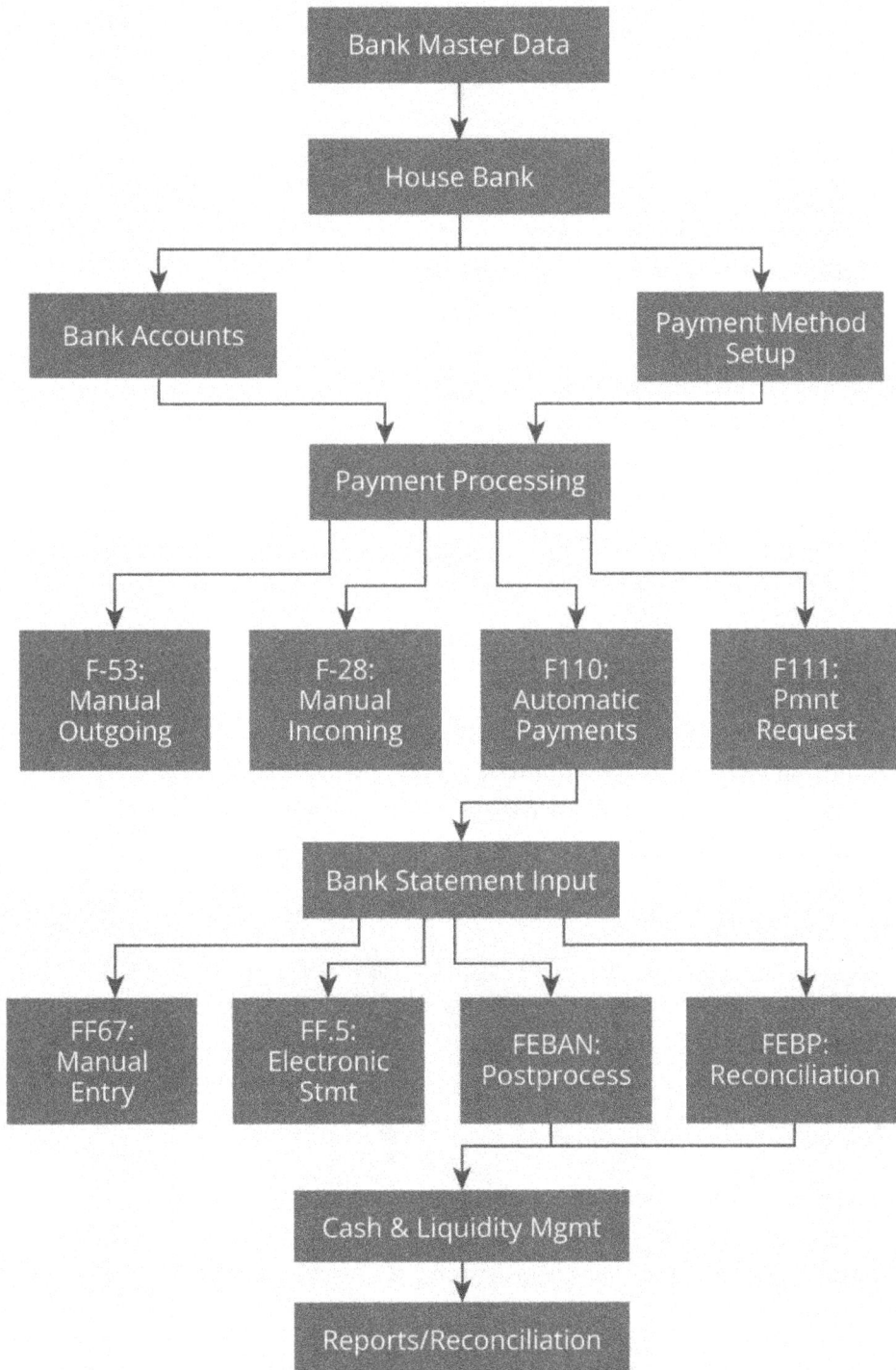

Bank Master Data

House Bank

Bank Accounts

Payment Method Setup

Payment Processing

F-53: Manual Outgoing

F-28: Manual Incoming

F110: Automatic Payments

F111: Pmnt Request

Bank Statement Input

FF67: Manual Entry

FF.5: Electronic Stmt

FEBAN: Postprocess

FEBP: Reconciliation

Cash & Liquidity Mgmt

Reports/Reconciliation

Main Components of Bank Accounting

SAP Bank Accounting consists of the following key components:

a) Bank Master Data (FI12, FI13)

This includes:

- Bank Key: Unique identifier for a bank.
- Bank Account: Company's account details.
- Bank Country: Country where the bank operates.

b) Bank Reconciliation Process

This involves:

- Uploading bank statements.
- Matching transactions with SAP records.
- Clearing open items.

c) Electronic Bank Statement (EBS)

- Automates bank statement processing.
- Uses MT940, BAI, CAMT formats.
- Requires configuration in SAP for proper execution.

d) Payment Program (F110)

This component processes automatic payments for vendors and customers based on predefined rules.

e) Check Management

- Manual and automatic check processing.
- Check encashment and voiding of checks.
- Integration with payment transactions.

Flow of Bank Accounting

The typical flow of Bank Accounting in SAP follows these steps:

1. **Creation of Bank Master Data:** Define bank key and bank accounts.
2. **Transaction Recording:** Payments and receipts are recorded in SAP.
3. **Bank Statement Upload:** Electronic bank statements are imported.
4. **Reconciliation Process:** Matching system transactions with bank transactions.
5. **Clearing Process:** Resolving unmatched transactions.
6. **Reporting:** Generating financial statements and cash flow reports.

Process of Bank Accounting

The standard process of SAP Bank Accounting includes:

1. **Defining House Banks (FI12):** Configuring banks in SAP and linking them to company codes.
2. **Setting Up Payment Methods (FBZP):** Defining payment methods like wire transfer, checks, and electronic funds transfer.
3. **Executing Payment Runs (F110):** Automating vendor and customer payments.
4. **Uploading Bank Statements (FF_5, FEBAN):** Importing electronic bank statements.
5. **Reconciliation and Clearing (FEBA, F.13):** Matching and clearing bank transactions.
6. **Generating Reports:** Extracting cash flow and bank transaction reports.

Important T-Codes

Here are some crucial SAP T-codes for Bank Accounting:

T-Code	Description
FI12	Maintain House Banks
FI13	Display Bank Details
F110	Automatic Payment Program
FF_5	Upload Electronic Bank Statements
FEBAN	Bank Statement Processing
F.13	Automatic Clearing
FEBA	Post Process Bank Statement
FBZP	Payment Program Configuration

Journal Entries in Bank Accounting

Below are some common journal entries related to bank transactions:

Bank Incoming Payment (Customer Receipts)

Bank Account Dr. xxxx
Customer Account Cr. xxxx

Bank Outgoing Payment (Vendor Payment)

Vendor Account Dr. xxxx
Bank Account Cr. xxxx

Bank Charges Entry

Bank Charges Expense Dr. xxxx
Bank Account Cr. xxxx

Bank Interest Earned

Bank Account Dr. xxxx
Interest Income Cr. xxxx

Important Tables in Bank Accounting

Table	Description
BNKA	Bank Master Data
PAYR	Payment Data (Checks, Transfers)
REGUH	Settlement Data from F110
REGUP	Line Items in Payment Program
FEBKO	Bank Statement Header Data
FEBEP	Bank Statement Line Items

Advanced Topics in Bank Accounting

a) Lockbox Processing

Lockbox is a banking service for bulk check deposits. SAP allows automation of check collection and processing by linking customer payments to outstanding invoices.

b) Multi-Bank Connectivity (MBC)

SAP provides MBC, which enables real-time bank connectivity, reducing manual intervention in payment processing and reconciliation.

c) Bank Communication Management (BCM)

BCM ensures secure and efficient payment processing by enabling approval workflows for outgoing payments.

d) In-House Cash Management

Large organizations with multiple subsidiaries use SAP In-House Cash to manage intercompany payments and centralize cash flow monitoring.

e) Machine Learning for Bank Reconciliation

SAP leverages AI and ML to automate transaction matching and reconciliation, reducing errors and manual efforts.

Conclusion

SAP Bank Accounting is an indispensable module for managing an organization's financial transactions with banks. **By automating bank statement processing, reconciliation, and payment execution, businesses can achieve better financial control and reduce operational risks.** With advanced features like electronic bank statements, multi-bank connectivity, and machine learning for reconciliation, SAP continues to evolve, ensuring efficient cash management and banking operations.

Mastering SAP Bank Accounting is crucial for financial professionals, as **it directly impacts cash flow visibility, compliance, and financial reporting.** As businesses continue to embrace digital transformation, understanding and leveraging SAP BA can drive efficiency and accuracy in financial processes.

Congratulations on reaching the end of this comprehensive chapter! You've just taken a deep dive into the foundational pillars of SAP Finance—General Ledger (GL), Accounts Payable (AP), Accounts Receivable (AR), Asset Accounting (AA), and Bank Accounting (BA). Throughout this chapter, we've covered critical aspects such as process flows, key transactions (T-codes), underlying tables, and the main components that make up each functional area.

By now, you should have a strong grasp of how these elements come together to support core financial operations within SAP.

But Finance doesn't function in a silo.

Up next, we move into the exciting world of FI Integration—where Finance intersects with other key modules like Materials Management (MM), Sales and Distribution (SD), and Controlling (CO). You'll learn how transactions in logistics trigger financial postings, how integration points are configured, and why cross-functional understanding is essential in real-world implementations.

Stay with me—things are about to get even more connected, practical, and powerful.

CHAPTER 3

SAP Finance Integration – The Nerve Center of Enterprise Operations

Why Integration is the Heart of SAP Finance

In the fast-paced world of enterprise operations, no department works in a vacuum. Every decision, transaction, and process ripples across the organization — whether it's a sales team sealing a deal, procurement ordering raw materials, HR processing payroll, or production planning for the next manufacturing run.

Picture this: A sales rep closes a high-value order. Instantly, inventory levels need to be updated. Procurement has to replenish stock. Finance must record the receivable. None of this can wait. Everything must happen seamlessly, accurately, and in real time.

This is where SAP Finance (FI) integration steps in — not as an isolated accounting tool, but as the central nervous system of your ERP landscape. SAP, by design, is built as a fully integrated ERP system, where actions in one module automatically trigger corresponding processes in others. That means a transaction initiated in Sales and Distribution (SD), Materials Management (MM), or Human Capital Management (HCM) can instantly create a financial entry in FI — no double entry, no lag, no mess.

Think of it as a chain reaction: One action sparks many, all synchronized to keep your operations and your books aligned. This automatic integration does more than just reduce effort — it fuels:

- Accuracy, by eliminating manual posting errors.
- Speed, through real-time data flow across departments.
- Compliance, with full audit trails of who did what, when, and why.
- Clarity, allowing business users to make smart decisions based on live data.
- Efficiency, reducing delays between operational activity and financial visibility.

Let's not forget the big picture: when departments don't integrate well, it leads to fragmented data, manual workarounds, duplicated efforts, and compliance nightmares. With SAP Finance integration, however, the right data flows to the right place, at the right time — automatically.

In this chapter, we'll dive deep into how SAP FI integrates with the major business modules:

- Materials Management (MM) – so that every goods receipt and invoice receipt is captured financially.

- Sales and Distribution (SD) – to ensure billing and incoming payments reflect as revenues and receivables.

- Controlling (CO) – where internal costs and allocations are tracked for transparency and planning.

- Production Planning (PP) – capturing costs as goods are manufactured and inventories change.

- Project System (PS) – recording expenditures, revenues, and settlements related to large-scale projects.

We'll walk through each integration point, explain what triggers the financial postings, highlight relevant configuration steps, and most importantly — show why these connections matter in real-life business scenarios.

So, whether you're a consultant, a finance professional, or a curious learner, strap in — we're about to explore how SAP Finance becomes the ultimate translator between business operations and financial truth.

FI-MM Integration (Procure-to-Pay)

Turning Procurement into Financial Events

Overview

The integration between Financial Accounting (FI) and Materials Management (MM) represents one of the most frequently used and crucial intersections in SAP. In nearly every business, procurement activities — buying goods or services — have financial consequences.

Without this integration, companies would have to manually create journal entries every time goods were received or invoices were posted. That would be error-prone, inefficient, and vulnerable to fraud or compliance violations.

SAP solves this with tight real-time coupling between MM and FI. Every logistical movement (like goods receipt or invoice receipt) triggers an automatic accounting entry in FI — thereby ensuring that the financial books reflect reality immediately and accurately.

Business Scenarios

- *A manufacturing company receives raw materials from a vendor — SAP automatically books inventory and creates a corresponding liability.*
- *A retail chain posts a vendor invoice — SAP updates accounts payable and records the tax liability.*
- *During payment runs, SAP clears outstanding vendor balances based on invoice and payment matching.*

FI-MM integration

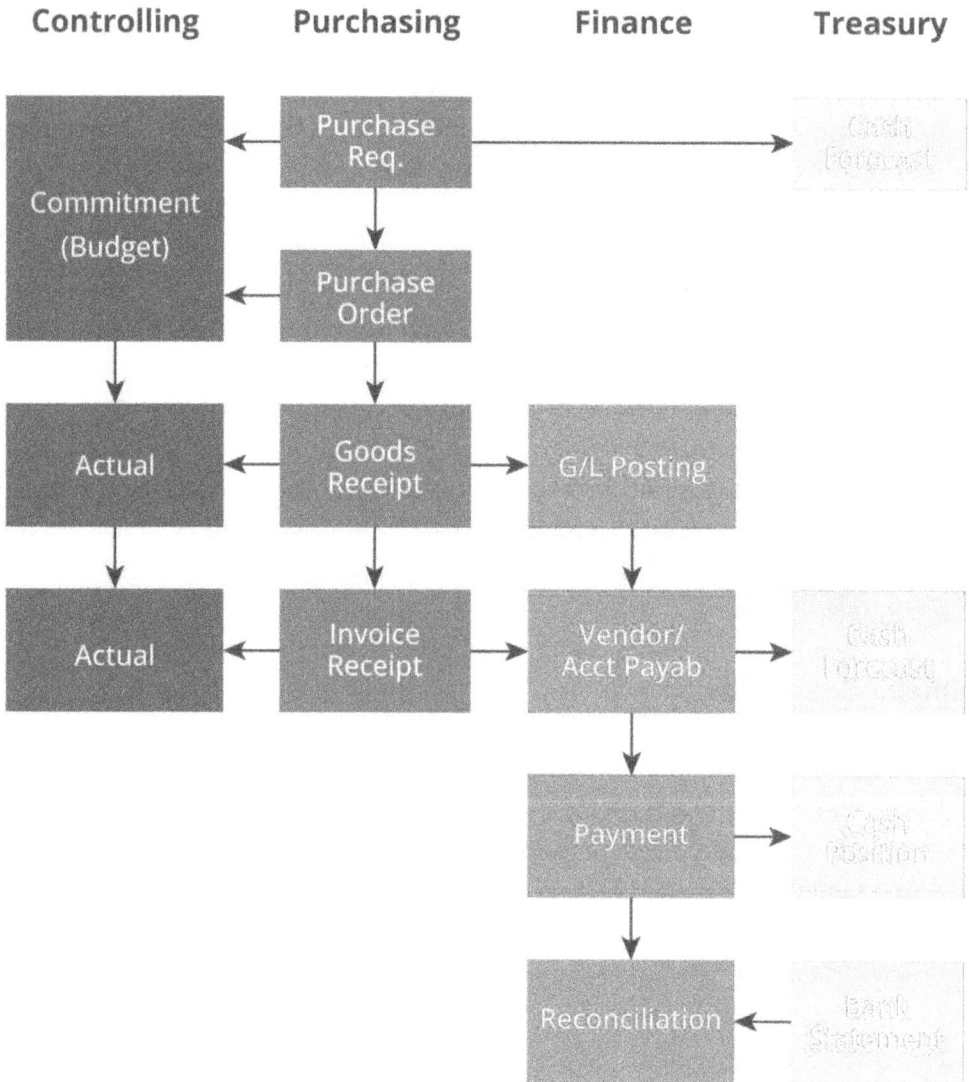

Controlling	Purchasing	Finance	Treasury

Commitment (Budget)

Purchase Req.

Cash Forecast

Purchase Order

Actual

Goods Receipt

G/L Posting

Actual

Invoice Receipt

Vendor/ Acct Payab

Cash Forecast

Payment

Cash Position

Reconciliation

Bank Statement

Key Integration Points

MM Process Step	FI Impact	Explanation
Purchase Order (PO) Creation	No direct FI entry	A PO is a commitment to purchase but does not trigger accounting until goods or invoices are received. However, it updates commitment values in CO if commitment management is active.
Goods Receipt (MIGO)	Dr. Inventory / Cr. GR/IR	Inventory value is capitalized (valuated stock). The GR/IR account is a clearing account used until the invoice is received. Valuation is based on standard, moving average, or MAP price.
Invoice Receipt (MIRO)	Dr. GR/IR / Cr. Vendor	The liability is recognized. This clears the GR/IR and establishes a payable to the vendor. Differences between invoice and GR (e.g., quantity or price) are handled via tolerances.
Vendor Payment (F110 / F-53)	Dr. Vendor / Cr. Bank	The outstanding liability is cleared, and the bank account is credited. Depending on configuration, cash discounts are calculated and posted to separate accounts.

Key Configuration:

- **OBYC** – Automatic Account Determination (used to link MM movement types with GL accounts)
- **Transaction Codes**:
  - ME21N – Create Purchase Order
  - MIGO – Goods Receipt
  - MIRO – Invoice Posting
  - F110 – Automatic Payment Run

Configuration Linkage:

- **Transaction OBYC** *maps movement types (e.g., 101 – goods receipt) to GL accounts based on valuation class, valuation area, and transaction key.*
- **Transaction OMWD** *is used to determine valuation class per material type and plant.*

FI-SD Integration (Order-to-Cash): From Sale to Revenue Recognition

Overview

The integration of SAP Sales and Distribution (SD) with SAP Finance (FI) is critical to track how sales translate into revenue and receivables. Sales processes — such as fulfilling customer orders, generating invoices, and collecting payments — all have financial consequences.

Thanks to this integration, when a billing document is created in SD, it automatically posts an accounting document in FI. This process recognizes revenue, applies applicable taxes, and updates customer receivables in real time. This ensures that:

- Finance gets timely, accurate revenue data.
- Receivables are managed effectively.
- Sales-related financial information is available for performance tracking.

Business Scenarios

- *A distribution company ships products to a client and creates a billing document. SAP posts revenue, sales tax, and a customer receivable automatically.*

- *A financial controller can run a real-time aging report to understand how much is owed by customers — without waiting for batch processes or manual updates.*

- *Sales revenue is posted to the correct GL and profit center based on the product or region, supporting profitability analysis.*

SD-FI Integration

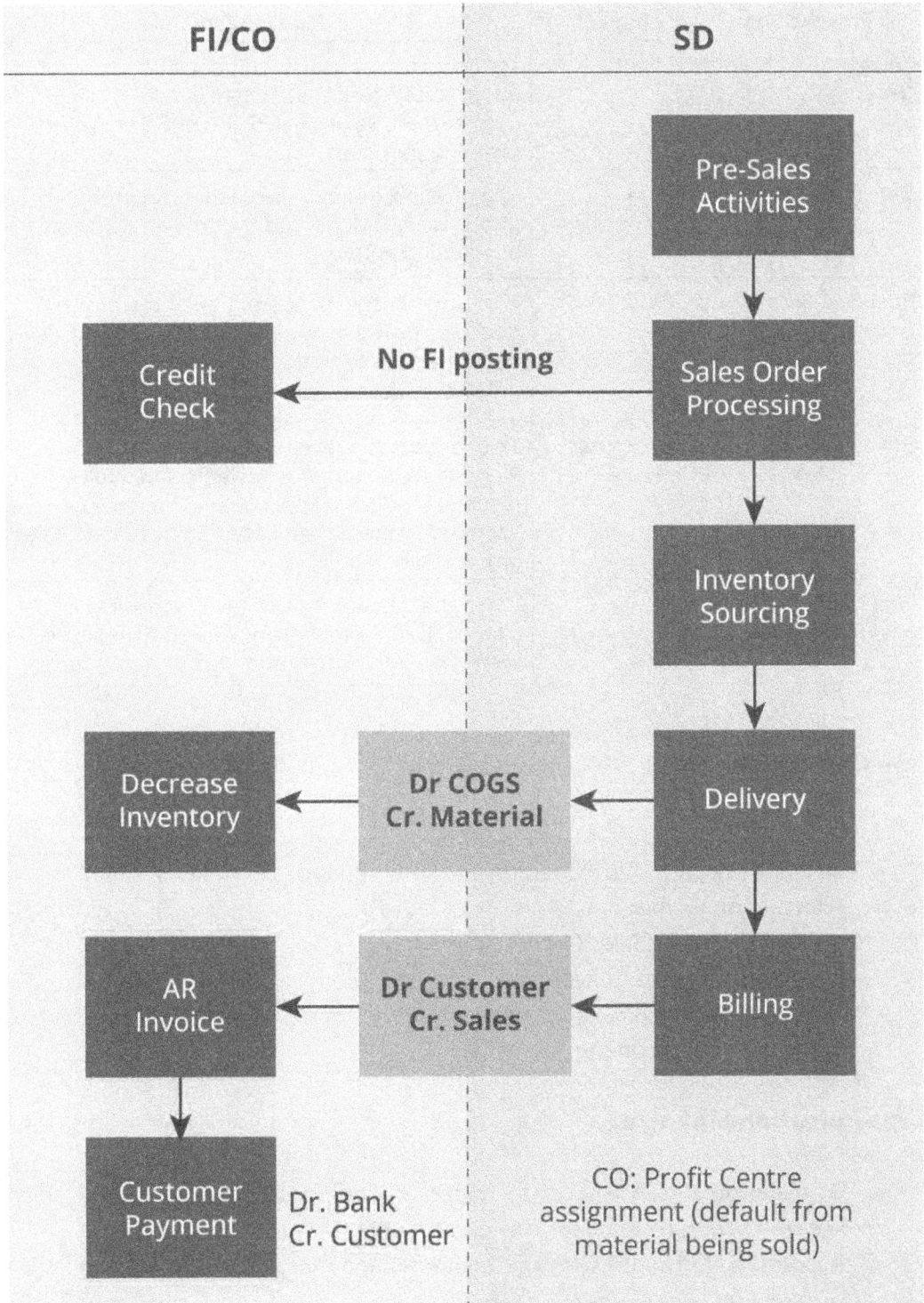

FI/CO	SD

Pre-Sales Activities

↓

No FI posting

Credit Check ← Sales Order Processing

↓

Inventory Sourcing

↓

Decrease Inventory ← **Dr COGS Cr. Material** ← Delivery

↓

AR Invoice ← **Dr Customer Cr. Sales** ← Billing

↓

Customer Payment   Dr. Bank Cr. Customer

CO: Profit Centre assignment (default from material being sold)

Key Integration Points

SD Process Step	FI Impact	Explanation
Sales Order (VA01)	No FI entry	This is a commercial document indicating intent to sell. However, it can update commitment values in CO-PA or SD tables for planning purposes.
Delivery (VL01N)	No FI entry (normally)	The physical goods movement is recorded. If goods issue is done, this triggers a valuation and accounting entry.
Post Goods Issue (PGI)	Dr. COGS / Cr. Inventory	This is the financial recognition of the cost of goods sold. The inventory account is credited, and the corresponding COGS account is debited. PGI also reduces stock in MM.
Billing (VF01)	Dr. Customer / Cr. Revenue & Tax	This triggers the revenue recognition in FI. It creates a customer receivable and books revenue (and tax if applicable). The revenue account is determined based on customer, sales org, and product type.
Incoming Payment (F-28)	Dr. Bank / Cr. Customer	When the customer pays, their receivable is cleared. Cash discounts or short payments can be posted based on predefined payment terms.

Key Configuration:

- **VKOA** – Account determination for SD
- Revenue Account Determination via condition types (e.g., KOFI, KOFK)
- **Transaction Codes:**
  - VA01 – Create Sales Order
  - VL01N – Create Delivery
  - VF01 – Create Billing Document
  - F-28 – Post Incoming Payment

Configuration Linkage:

- **Transaction VKOA** is used to map SD condition types (like PR00 – price, MWST – tax) to revenue and tax GL accounts.
- **Account Assignment Group** in customer and material master influences the GL selection.

FI-CO Integration (Controlling and Internal Financial Transparency)

Overview (Cost and Profit Tracking)

The integration of SAP Finance (FI) with Controlling (CO) is a foundational element of the SAP ecosystem. While FI tracks external financial reporting, CO is responsible for internal management accounting. The two must work hand-in-hand to ensure that every financial transaction is not just posted to the GL but is also internally allocated, analyzed, and reported based on business needs.

FI and CO integration is fundamental to internal and external reporting. Every FI document must be reconciled with corresponding cost elements in CO to facilitate performance analysis.

Whenever a cost-related transaction is posted in FI (such as salaries, rents, or utility bills), the system simultaneously asks: Where should this cost be tracked in CO? This is where cost objects like cost centers, internal orders, or WBS elements come into play.

The dual posting ensures that every dollar (or euro, rupee, or yen) spent is aligned with both legal accounting requirements and managerial performance tracking.

Business Scenarios

- *When payroll expenses are posted to FI, they're also assigned to respective cost centers in CO — enabling department-level budgeting.*
- *Marketing expenses can be tracked via internal orders and compared against allocated budgets.*
- *Controlling data supports profitability analysis (CO-PA) by linking revenues and costs to products, customers, or market segments.*

Integration Elements

- Primary Cost Elements: Represent GL accounts in CO (e.g., salary, rent).
- Secondary Cost Elements: Internal costs (e.g., assessments, settlements).
- Cost Centers / Profit Centers: Help allocate and report expenses and revenues.

FI-CO Sync Mechanism:

- When a financial transaction (e.g., expense booking) is posted in FI, the system checks if a cost object is mandatory.
- This links cost centers, internal orders, or projects for internal tracking.

Transaction Codes:

- OKB9 – Default Account Assignments
- KS01 – Create Cost Center
- KSB1 – Cost Center Reports

Key Integration Points

FI Process Step	CO Impact	Explanation
Expense Posting (FB60, FB01)	Cost is assigned to a CO object	When an expense is booked, SAP prompts for a cost object — Cost Center, Internal Order, WBS, etc. This creates a parallel CO document for internal reporting.
Payroll Posting	Costs flow to CO objects	Salaries and wages can be distributed to multiple cost centers (e.g., HR, IT, Admin). Overheads and employer contributions are also tracked.
Asset Depreciation	Depreciation costs assigned to CO	Asset Accounting integrates with CO to push planned and actual depreciation values to cost centers or internal orders.
Assessment & Distribution (KSU5/ KSV5)	Allocates costs from one cost center to others	These are periodic processes that distribute indirect costs (like admin expenses) to operational centers based on statistical keys.

Configuration Linkage:

- **OKB9** defines default cost elements and cost centers for automatic assignments.
- **KA01, KSB1, KS03** help manage and report cost centers and actuals.

FI-PP Integration (Production Planning): Capturing the Cost of Goods Manufactured

Overview

The integration of SAP Production Planning (PP) with SAP Finance (FI) and Controlling (CO) ensures that production costs are accurately captured and reflected in both inventory valuation and profitability analysis.

This integration becomes especially important in manufacturing environments where goods are produced rather than purchased. As raw materials are consumed and finished goods are produced, the system must keep track of material movements, labor costs, and overhead allocations. These all tie back to financial accounting through direct and indirect postings.

SAP allows costs to be collected on production orders, settled to inventory or CO objects, and ultimately reflected in the balance sheet and income statement.

Business Scenarios

- A company issues raw materials for a production order — SAP reduces raw material inventory and posts a work-in-progress (WIP) cost.
- Finished goods are received into inventory — the system calculates the standard or actual cost and updates the balance sheet.
- At period-end, variances (e.g., scrap, inefficiencies) are settled to cost centers or profit centers.

Processes Involved

- Planned Orders → Production Orders
- Goods Issue (GI) to production: Dr. Production Order / Cr. Raw Materials Inventory
- Goods Receipt (GR) from production: Dr. FG Inventory / Cr. Production Order
- Order Settlement: Dr./Cr. Variance → Cost Center or Profitability Segment

Key Configuration:

- Account determination via OBYC
- Valuation classes tied to material master

Transaction Codes:

- CO01 – Create Production Order
- MB1A – Goods Issue
- MB31 – Goods Receipt
- KO88 – Order Settlement

Key Integration Points

PP Process Step	FI/CO Impact	Explanation
Production Order Creation (CO01)	No FI entry	The order acts as a cost collector but does not trigger accounting. It holds planned costs for comparison.
Goods Issue (MB1A/MIGO)	Dr. Production Order / Cr. Raw Material Inventory	When raw materials are consumed, inventory is reduced, and production order costs are increased. It reflects material consumption cost.
Activity Confirmation (CO11N)	Dr. Production Order / Cr. Cost Center	Labor and machine costs are posted as internal activity allocations. This moves costs from cost centers to the order.
Goods Receipt (MB31)	Dr. FG Inventory / Cr. Production Order	Finished goods are added to inventory. Costs from the order are reversed out and transferred to the finished goods account.
Order Settlement (KO88)	Transfers variance to cost center or inventory	If there's a difference between planned and actual costs, it is settled to price difference accounts, cost centers, or CO–PA segments.

Configuration Linkage:

- **OBYC** settings for transaction keys like BSX (inventory), GBB (offsetting entries), and FRL (production differences).
- Order types are defined to determine how production orders behave financially.

FI-PS Integration (Project System): Financial Control Over Projects

Overview

In businesses that manage complex, long-term projects — such as construction, IT implementations, or R&D initiatives — **SAP Project System (PS)** integrates tightly with FI and CO to ensure that **costs and revenues are monitored and accounted for at every phase**.

Projects in SAP are broken down into **WBS (Work Breakdown Structure)** elements, which act like cost objects. All expenses, whether material, labor, or service-related, are posted against WBS elements. These are rolled up into budgets, reported upon, and ultimately settled to relevant receivers (assets under construction, cost centers, etc.).

This integration helps companies **avoid project overruns, ensure cost transparency**, and comply with financial regulations for capital and operating projects.

Business Scenarios

- A capital investment project (e.g., building a new plant) records costs like construction, equipment, and consulting fees. At completion, the WBS element is settled to an Asset Under Construction (AuC).
- A customer project (e.g., software implementation) has billing milestones. Revenues and costs are tracked at the project level for margin analysis.
- Budget overruns are flagged in real-time, allowing project managers to take corrective actions.

Common Objects:

- **WBS Elements**: Work Breakdown Structures for planning and monitoring
- **Network Activities**: Define tasks and dependencies
- Financial postings are tracked per WBS or network

Key Transaction Codes:

- CJ01 – Create Project
- CJ20N – Project Builder
- CJ88 – Project Settlement

Key Integration Points

PS Process Step	FI/CO Impact	Explanation
Project/WBS Creation (CJ01)	No FI entry	The project acts as a planning and controlling structure. Budgets and structures are defined, but no accounting entries are posted.
Expense Posting to WBS (FB60/F-90)	Dr. Expense GL / Cr. Vendor, CO object=WBS	External costs like consulting or materials are booked to WBS elements, aiding cost tracking.
Internal Activity Posting	Dr. WBS / Cr. Cost Center	Time booked by internal employees or machine usage gets posted from sender to receiver.
Revenue Recognition (Milestone Billing)	Dr. Customer / Cr. Revenue	If a customer project is billed via PS, revenue is posted, and WBS elements are credited.
Settlement (CJ88)	Costs moved to asset or cost center	At project completion or periodically, WBS costs are settled to receiving objects like Assets under Construction (AuC) or cost centers.

Configuration Linkage:

- **Settlement Rules** in WBS define how and where the costs are settled.
- **CJ88 and KO88** are key transactions to perform period-end activities.

Integration Best Practices

1. **Automatic Postings:** Use OBYC (MM), VKOA (SD), and OKB9 (CO) to define automatic GL account determination.
2. **Consistent Master Data:** Ensure material, vendor, customer, cost center, and GL data is consistently maintained.
3. **Real-time Reconciliation:** Use tools like **GR/IR Clearing (F.13)** and **Customer-Vendor Reconciliation (F.19)** to keep books clean.
4. **Monitor Interfaces:** For third-party integration or external systems, monitor IDoc and BAPI transactions.

Takeaway

Understanding how SAP Finance integrates with other modules transforms your financial system from a data recording tool to a real-time business insight engine. These integrations automate data flow, improve compliance, reduce redundancy, and enable agile decision-making.

In your SAP journey, mastering these integrations is crucial. You must think beyond transactional entries and embrace how financial data is interconnected with every other process — from a purchase in MM to revenue recognition in SD or cost allocations in CO.

In the next chapter, we'll shift our focus from module-level integrations to end-to-end business processes that drive enterprise operations. We'll explore how SAP enables seamless execution of key processes such as Order-to-Cash (O2C), Procure-to-Pay (P2P), Record-to-Report (R2R), Hire-to-Retire (H2R), and more. By breaking down these core cycles, we'll see how multiple SAP modules collaborate behind the scenes — and how Finance plays a vital role at every step of the journey.

CHAPTER 4

From Modules to End-to-End Business Processes – SAP's Integrated Execution Engine

In the previous chapters, we explored how SAP Finance integrates with individual modules like Sales and Distribution (SD), Materials Management (MM), and Human Capital Management (HCM). While those module-level connections are crucial, they only tell part of the story. Now, it's time to zoom out and view the bigger picture—how SAP orchestrates end-to-end business processes that power the modern enterprise.

SAP is far more than a set of standalone functional components; it's a unified business process platform that enables companies to operate cohesively across departments, geographies, and industries. Whether it's fulfilling customer orders, managing procurement, consolidating financials, or supporting the employee lifecycle, SAP's architecture is designed to ensure that information flows seamlessly—not just within modules, but across them.

At the heart of this capability lie the core enterprise processes:

- Order-to-Cash (O2C) – how organizations sell, fulfill, and collect revenue for their goods and services.
- Procure-to-Pay (P2P) – how they source, purchase, and pay for materials and services.
- Record-to-Report (R2R) – how financial data is captured, consolidated, and analyzed to inform strategy.
- Hire-to-Retire (H2R) – how human capital is recruited, developed, and retained over the employee lifecycle.

These processes aren't just operational workflows—they are strategic pillars that directly impact profitability, agility, and customer satisfaction. Each one involves multiple SAP modules working in tandem, with Finance acting as the central nervous system of the enterprise.

Finance isn't just a passive recipient of data—it's an active enabler of these processes. From recording revenue and expenses to enforcing controls and generating real-time insights, Finance ensures that operations are not only efficient but also compliant, auditable, and optimized for performance. With innovations like SAP S/4HANA and SAP Analytics Cloud, Finance can now deliver predictive insights and scenario modeling, further elevating its strategic role.

In the sections that follow, we'll break down each of these end-to-end processes. You'll see how SAP modules interlink, where Finance steps in, and why a process-driven view is essential for designing efficient, scalable, and future-ready SAP landscapes.

This chapter is not just about integration—it's about transformation. It's about understanding how to move from functional excellence to process excellence, where Finance is not just a back-office function but a strategic partner driving enterprise value.

Let's dive into each process and uncover how SAP truly runs the business.

Order-to-Cash (O2C)

Overview:

Order-to-Cash covers the entire journey from receiving a customer order to collecting payment. It is the revenue-generating engine of a business.

Key Steps:

1. Customer Inquiry / Quotation (SD)
2. Sales Order Creation (SD)
3. Availability Check & Delivery (SD + MM)
4. Shipping & Transportation (SD)
5. Billing (SD + FI)
6. Payment Receipt (FI-AR)

SAP Order to Cash O2C Process

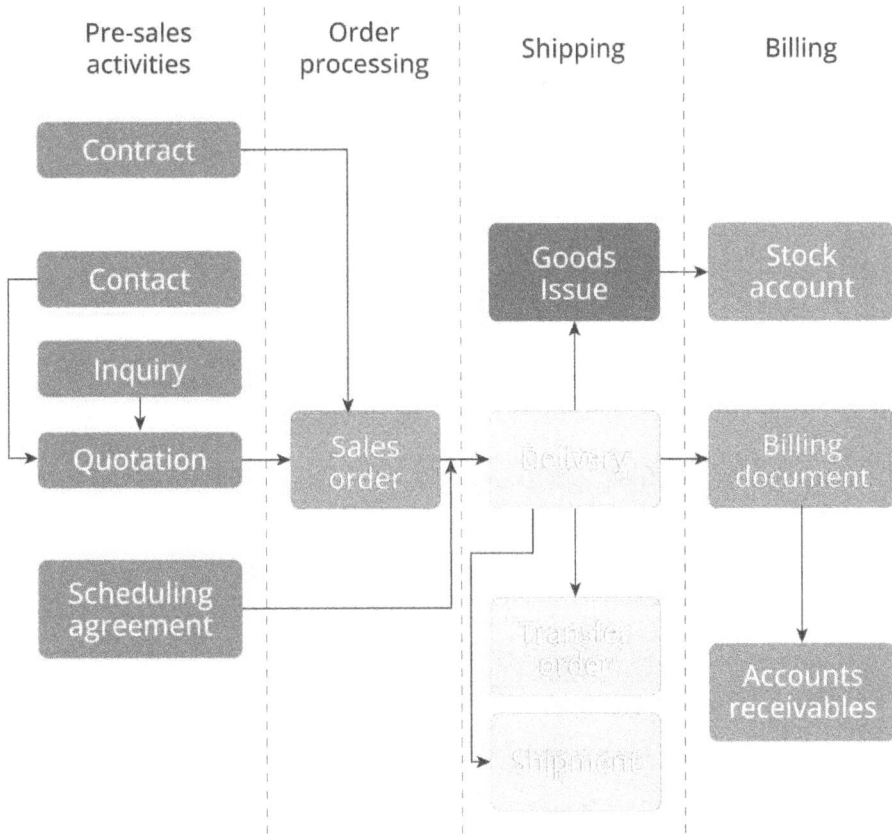

Pre-sales activities	Order processing	Shipping	Billing

Contract → Sales order

Contact

Inquiry

Quotation → Sales order

Scheduling agreement

Goods Issue → Stock account

Delivery → Billing document

Transfer order

Shipment

Billing document → Accounts receivables

Modules Involved:

- SD (Sales and Distribution)
- MM (Materials Management)
- FI (Financial Accounting)
- CO (Controlling)
- **GTS (Global Trade Services)** – for exports/imports
- LE (Logistics Execution)

Finance Touchpoints:

- Customer credit management (FI-AR / FSCM)
- Revenue posting (FI)
- Tax calculation (FI-TX)

- Dunning and collection (FSCM-Collections)
- Reconciliation and reporting (FI-GL)

SAP ensures that when a delivery is made, the inventory value is adjusted, revenue is recognized when billing occurs, and customer balances are updated—all in real time. With embedded analytics and tools like SAP Analytics Cloud (SAC), the entire process can be monitored for bottlenecks or aging receivables.

Order to Cash Process Flow in SAP

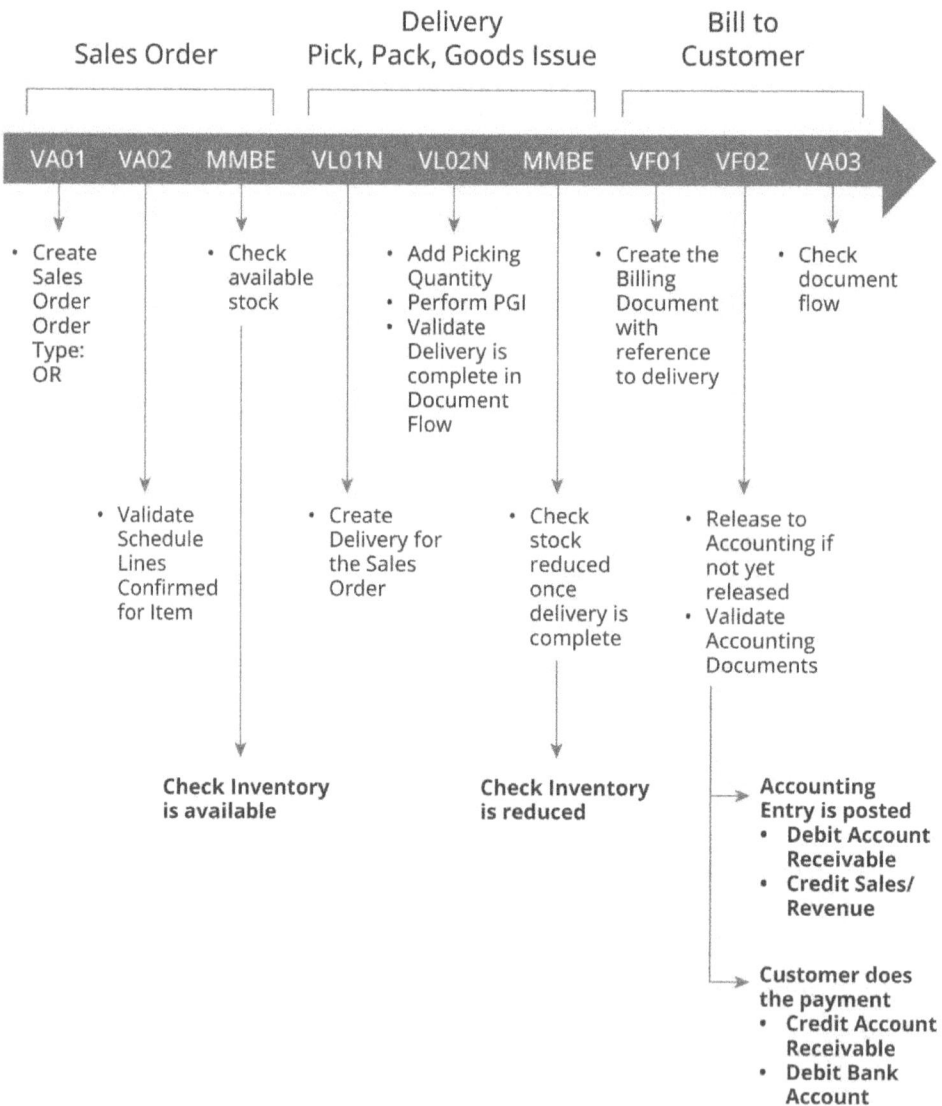

Sales Order — VA01, VA02, MMBE

Delivery Pick, Pack, Goods Issue — VL01N, VL02N, MMBE

Bill to Customer — VF01, VF02, VA03

- Create Sales Order Order Type: OR
- Check available stock
- Add Picking Quantity
- Perform PGI
- Validate Delivery is complete in Document Flow
- Create the Billing Document with reference to delivery
- Check document flow

- Validate Schedule Lines Confirmed for Item
- Create Delivery for the Sales Order
- Check stock reduced once delivery is complete
- Release to Accounting if not yet released
- Validate Accounting Documents

Check Inventory is available

Check Inventory is reduced

Accounting Entry is posted
- **Debit Account Receivable**
- **Credit Sales/ Revenue**

Customer does the payment
- **Credit Account Receivable**
- **Debit Bank Account**

Procure-to-Pay (P2P)

Overview:

Procure-to-Pay spans the lifecycle from identifying a purchasing need to paying the vendor. It ensures companies have the materials and services needed to operate efficiently.

Key Steps:

1. Purchase Requisition (MM)
2. Purchase Order Creation (MM)
3. Goods Receipt (MM + WM/EWM)
4. Invoice Receipt (FI + MM)
5. Vendor Payment (FI-AP)

Modules Involved:

- MM (Materials Management)
- FI (Financial Accounting)
- CO (Controlling)
- EWM (Extended Warehouse Management)
- VIM (Vendor Invoice Management)

Finance Touchpoints:

- Purchase order commitments (FI-FM / CO)
- GR/IR clearing (FI-MM integration)
- Vendor liabilities and invoice verification (FI-AP)
- Payment processing (FI)
- Cash forecasting and treasury (FSCM-CM)

P2P Process Flowchart
Procure to Pay

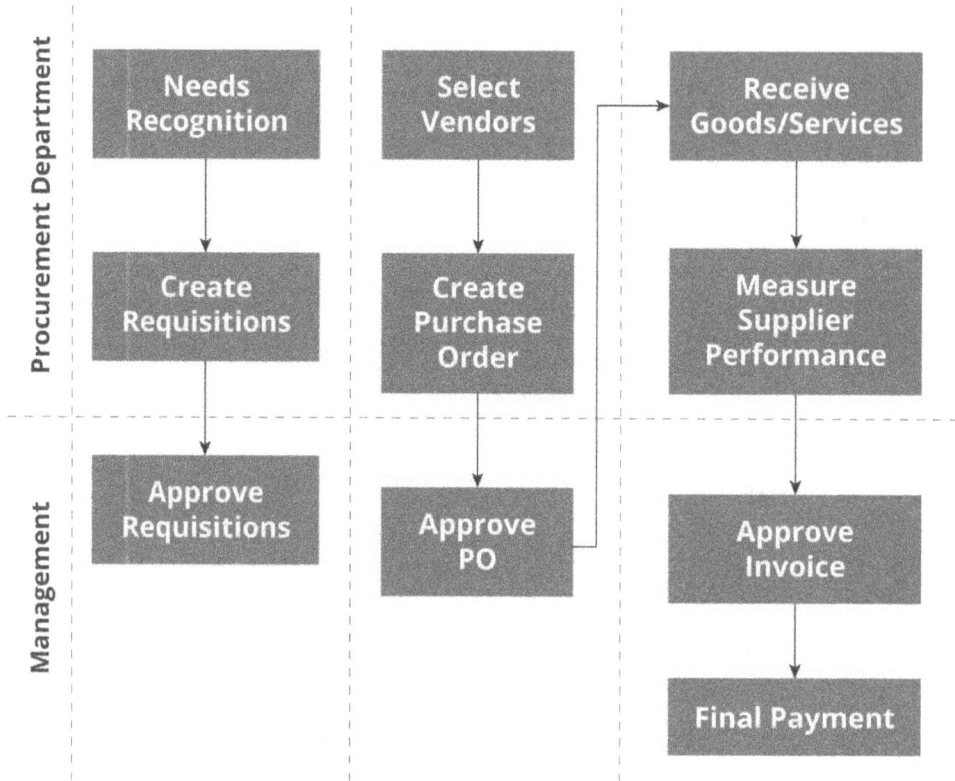

SAP handles procurement with automation and compliance in mind. When a purchase is approved and a goods receipt is posted, the system triggers accounting entries for inventory valuation. Upon invoice receipt, liabilities are recorded, and payments are scheduled—ensuring Finance is involved every step of the way.

Record-to-Report (R2R)

Overview:

Record-to-Report is the backbone of corporate financial management. It includes all the steps to record transactions, consolidate accounts, and report financial performance.

Traditional record to report process diagram

Following slide outlines record to report diagram which are used by many organization for preparing financial report. The record to report process begins with recording transactions, preparing, analysing and reporting.

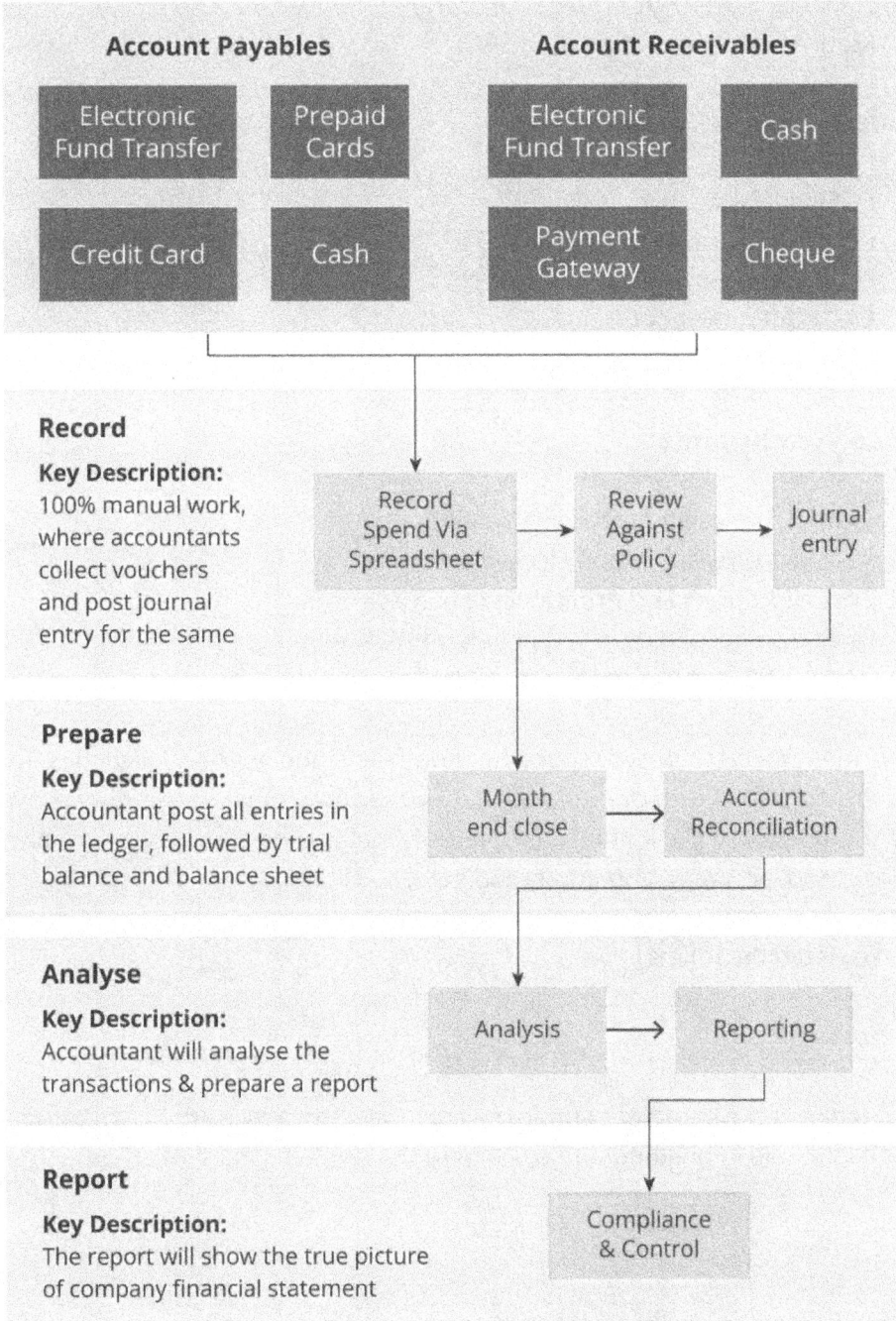

Key Steps:

1. Transaction Recording (FI, CO, MM, SD, etc.)
2. Period-End Close (FI, CO, FM, etc.)
3. Consolidation (FI-LC or Group Reporting)
4. Financial Statement Preparation (FI)
5. Management Reporting (CO, SAC)

Modules Involved:

- FI (Financial Accounting)
- CO (Controlling)
- FM (Funds Management)
- SAC (SAP Analytics Cloud)
- BPC or Group Reporting

Finance Touchpoints:

- Journal entries and recurring postings
- Accruals, provisions, and closing activities
- Cost allocations and profitability analysis
- Financial consolidation (e.g., intercompany eliminations)
- GAAP/IFRS compliance and audit trails

SAP provides powerful tools to speed up month-end and year-end activities. Through real-time integration with operational systems, transactional data is always available for reporting. Closing Cockpits, Automated Accrual Engines, and Central Finance help improve speed, accuracy, and audit readiness.

Hire-to-Retire (H2R)

Overview:

Hire-to-Retire is the complete employee lifecycle—from recruitment to offboarding. It plays a vital role in building and sustaining the human capital of an organization.

Key Steps:

1. Recruitment (SAP SuccessFactors / HCM)
2. Onboarding (SuccessFactors / HCM)
3. Employee Master Data Maintenance (PA/OM)
4. Payroll & Time Management (PY/PT)
5. Performance Management and Development (SF PM/GM)
6. Retirement / Exit Process (HCM)

Recruit to Retire

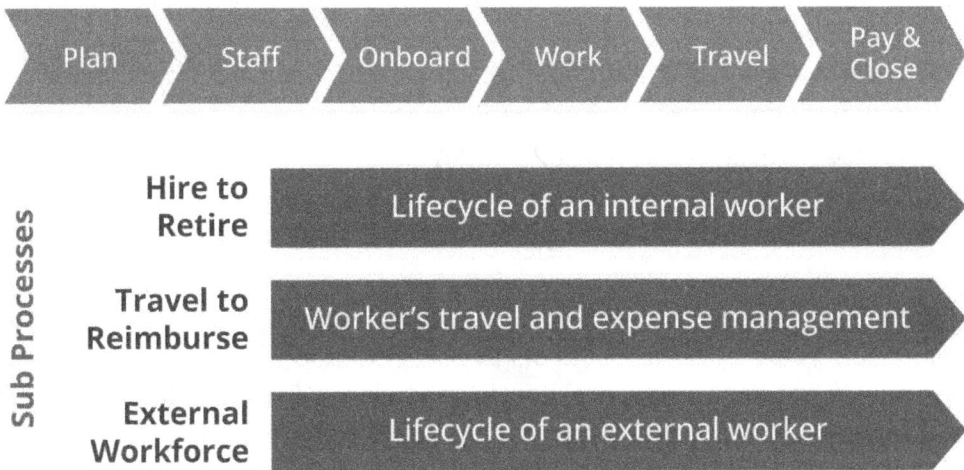

Modules Involved:

- SAP HCM / SAP SuccessFactors
- FI (Financial Accounting)
- CO (Controlling)
- Payroll
- Time Management
- Benefits / Compensation

Finance Touchpoints:

- Payroll posting to FI/CO
- Cost center assignments
- Travel & expense management

- Budgeting for headcount and salary planning (CO-OM)
- Accruals for bonuses and leave liabilities

SAP ensures that HR events reflect immediately in the Finance system. When an employee is hired, their cost center and payroll data flow into Controlling for internal reporting and to Financial Accounting for actual cost posting. Integration with Travel Management and Benefits ensures accurate reimbursement and forecasting.

Beyond the Big Four: Other End-to-End Cycles

- **Design-to-Operate (D2O):** Covers product lifecycle management, from design through manufacturing to delivery. Involves PLM, PP, QM, MM, and EWM.
- **Lead-to-Cash (L2C):** A broader version of O2C that starts from marketing and lead nurturing (CRM), including CPQ (Configure Price Quote), and ends with revenue recognition and customer payment.

The Finance Thread: Weaving Through All Processes

No matter which process you examine, Finance is at the core. Whether it's customer billing in O2C, vendor payments in P2P, payroll entries in H2R, or closing journals in R2R—Finance ensures compliance, control, and clarity. Financial data is not just an output of these processes but a real-time, integral component.

In SAP, this is enabled by:

- **Universal Journal (ACDOCA)** – a single source of truth for financial and controlling data
- **Integration Frameworks** – preconfigured and extensible scenarios for tight process flows
- **Fiori Apps** – role-based dashboards for real-time insight and action
- **Embedded Analytics & Machine Learning** – to detect anomalies, predict cash flow, or optimize working capital

Takeaway:

End-to-end business processes are where SAP's true power comes alive. They break down functional barriers and create a unified enterprise experience—where information flows seamlessly and actions are tightly coordinated. Finance, with its cross-functional visibility and compliance responsibilities, is the thread that connects all modules and ensures the business runs smoothly and profitably.

Next Chapter Preview: SAP Closing Process – Bringing it All Together

While the daily flow of transactions powers business operations, the closing process is where everything converges. It's the final checkpoint—a moment to validate, reconcile, and crystallize business performance into financial results. In the next chapter, we'll explore the SAP Closing Process in detail: its phases, key activities, tools, best practices, and how Finance collaborates with other teams to deliver accurate and timely financial closings.

CHAPTER 5

SAP Finance Closing Process – Month-End & Year-End

Introduction

Closing the books in SAP Finance is one of the most critical tasks in the financial lifecycle of any organization. Whether it's month-end or year-end, these closings are pivotal moments where finance, controlling, and operations intersect to reflect the company's performance, ensure data accuracy, comply with accounting standards, and prepare for internal and external reporting.

Inaccurate or incomplete closings can lead to compliance issues, poor decision-making, and loss of credibility with stakeholders. Therefore, having a streamlined, consistent, and automated closing process in SAP is not just beneficial—it's essential.

SAP's integrated ERP framework enables companies to handle complex closing activities efficiently by combining data across various modules such as FI, CO, MM, SD, and Asset Accounting. Through standardized processes and automation tools like the Financial Closing Cockpit (FCC) and SAP S/4HANA Universal Journal, SAP empowers finance teams to close faster and more accurately.

This chapter will walk you through the essential aspects of SAP Finance closing, covering both month-end and year-end closings, key steps, best practices, transaction codes, and key considerations that every SAP professional must know.

Month-End Closing Process in SAP Finance

Purpose

- Finalize financial data for the month
- Accurately reflect monthly financial performance
- Prepare for management reporting and external disclosures
- Ensure all sub-modules (AA, AP, AR, CO, MM, SD) are reconciled and closed

Key Steps and T-Codes

Step	Description	Transaction Code
1	Close MM Module (Material Ledger/ Inventory Valuation)	MMRV, CKMLCP
2	Close SD Module (Revenue recognition, Billing)	VF04, VF44
3	Post Recurring Entries	F.14, FBD1
4	Post Accruals & Provisions	FBS1, F.81
5	Depreciation Run (Asset Accounting)	AFAB
6	Open Next Period (FI/CO)	OB52, OKP1
7	Execute Foreign Currency Valuation	F.05, FAGL_FC_VAL
8	Reconcile Intercompany Transactions	FBICR3, FBICRC0
9	Run Balance Sheet and P&L Reports	F.01, S_ALR_87012284
10	Transfer Data to CO (Cost Centers, Internal Orders)	KSV5, KSU5, KSII
11	Run Financial Statements (for approval & review)	S_ALR_87012284, F.01
12	Close Period in FI	OB52
13	Use Financial Closing Cockpit (Optional)	FCLOCO

Key Considerations for Month-End

- Ensure all invoices and expenses are posted.
- Unposted documents must be reviewed and corrected.
- Run GR/IR clearing (*F.13*) to clean up open items.
- Validate asset capitalization and transfers.
- Perform reconciliation of sub ledgers with the general ledger.
- Ensure open items in AR and AP are reviewed.

Year-End Closing Process in SAP FI

Purpose

- Complete financial year with accurate books
- Carry forward balances to the new fiscal year
- Perform legal and tax-related closings
- Prepare for external audits and statutory reporting

Key Steps and T-Codes

Step	Description	Transaction Code
1	Perform all Month-End Activities for December	Same as above
2	Close Asset Fiscal Year	AJAB
3	Carry Forward Asset Balances	AJRW
4	Close CO Periods	OKP1, KSV5, KSU5
5	Carry Forward Customer/Vendor Balances	F.07
6	Carry Forward GL Balances	F.16
7	Close Fiscal Year in FI	OB52, year-end period closure
8	Final Run of Reports for External Use	F.01, S_PL0_86000028
9	Archive Financial Documents (optional)	SARA
10	Create New Fiscal Year	OB29, if not already done

Key Considerations for Year-End

- Perform a dry run of year-end activities in a test environment.
- Coordinate with external auditors on adjustments.
- Review all manual journal entries.
- Verify that the fiscal year variant settings are correct.
- Lock periods after closure to prevent postings.
- Run **SAP S/4HANA reconciliation ledger** if applicable.

Automation & Tools

SAP Financial Closing Cockpit (FCC)

FCC enables structured, automated, and monitored financial closing processes. It includes:

- Task templates and dependencies
- Status tracking
- Automated job scheduling
- Email notifications

Use: Transaction Code FCLOCO

SAP S/4HANA Universal Journal (ACDOCA)

- Centralized table for all financial components (FI, CO, AA, ML)
- Simplifies reconciliation and closing steps
- Real-time reporting and consistency

Reporting and Analytics Post-Closure

Report	Description	T-Code
Trial Balance	Summarized balances	S_ALR_87012277
P&L Statement	Profitability view	F.01, S_PL0_86000028
Balance Sheet	Snapshot of financial position	F.01
Open Items Analysis	Review outstanding AR/AP	FBL1N, FBL5N, FBL3N
Aging Report	Customer/vendor aging	S_ALR_87012178

Common Challenges & Best Practices

Challenges

- Delays due to manual entries or coordination issues
- Errors in intercompany postings or FX valuation
- Incomplete asset depreciation or transfer
- Unreconciled subledger-G/L balances

Best Practices

- Create a month-end/year-end checklist and timeline
- Automate routine tasks with FCC or batch jobs
- Perform regular data quality audits
- Leverage workflow for approvals
- Conduct training for involved users

Additional Critical Considerations in SAP Finance Closing

Manual Adjustments and Journal Entries

- Late adjustments like audit corrections, misposted entries, or accruals often need manual posting.
- Use **FB50**, **FB01**, or **F-02** for manual entries.
- Create **posting templates** for recurring manual adjustments.
- Validate and approve entries using workflows.

Accrual Engine and Provisions

Use the **Accrual Engine** for recurring accruals:

- Configure Accrual Object types (e.g., rent, bonus, warranties)
- T-codes: **ACE** transactions (e.g., **ACEPOST**, **ACE_PROCI**)
- It supports IFRS and US GAAP-based accrual logic.

Tax Reporting and Compliance

- Perform tax calculations and reporting (e.g., VAT, GST, Withholding Tax)
- Run **tax reconciliation** and **reporting** via T-codes like:
  - **S_ALR_87012357** (Tax reconciliation)

    ○   **RFUMSV00** (VAT reports)
- Submit digital filings (e.g., SAF-T, e-Invoicing where required)

Bank Reconciliation and Cash Management

- Ensure that all **bank statements** (electronic or manual) are posted and reconciled.
- T-codes:
  - **FF67** – Manual Bank Statement Entry
  - **FEBAN** – Bank Statement Post-processing
  - **FF.5** – Upload Electronic Bank Statements
- Review **Cash Position and Liquidity Forecasts**

Document Parking, Blocking, and Release Workflow

- Clear all **parked documents**: T-code **FBV0**, **FBV2**
- Review **blocked invoices/payments**: T-code **MRBR**, **F110**
- Use **workflow reports** to ensure no stuck approvals (e.g., payment blocks or invoice approvals)

Audit Trails and SOX Compliance

- Enable **Change Logs** and **Document Change History**
- Review **authorization logs** (e.g., changes made to OB52)
- Maintain **Segregation of Duties (SoD)** compliance
- Use GRC tools if applicable

KPIs for Financial Closing Performance

Consider setting up and monitoring KPIs to measure and improve the closing process:

- Days to close books (DCO)
- Number of manual journal entries
- Unreconciled balances
- Aging of open items
- Variance from forecast

Multi-Currency and Group Consolidation

- Foreign Currency Revaluation (**F.05**) should be thoroughly tested
- Group consolidation using **SAP S/4HANA Group Reporting** or **EC-CS**
- Intercompany reconciliation and elimination entries for group-level reporting

Closing Calendar

Implement and publish a **Closing Calendar**:

- Assign owners to each closing task
- Set deadlines and dependencies
- Automate with **SAP Financial Closing Cockpit** or external tools (e.g., Black-Line, Redwood)

Post-Closing Adjustments and Audit Period

- Allow for **"soft closure"** where financials are reviewed but not yet locked
- Make use of **special periods (13–16)** for audit adjustments
- Ensure proper **documentation** and **audit trails** for all post-closing entries

Key Takeaways

- **Discipline & Standardization** are key to successful financial closings in SAP.
- Understand the **integration between modules** (FI, CO, MM, SD, AA) to ensure clean financials.
- Use **automated tools** like Financial Closing Cockpit to minimize manual intervention and errors.
- Master critical **T-codes** like **F.01**, **F.16**, **AJAB**, **F.05**, and **F.07** for efficient execution.
- Develop a strong communication and coordination plan across departments for timely closure.
- Perform **early testing** of year-end processes and ensure alignment with **audit requirements**.
- Periodic **training and documentation** can reduce dependency on key users and improve consistency.

In this chapter, we explored the end-to-end SAP Finance closing process, covering both month-end and year-end activities in detail. From key steps and T-codes to module integration, compliance considerations, and automation tools like the

Financial Closing Cockpit, we highlighted the importance of a disciplined, structured approach to closing the books. By aligning processes across Finance, Controlling, Asset Management, MM, and SD, organizations can ensure accurate financials, reduce closing cycle time, and stay audit-ready. Whether it's recurring entries, depreciation runs, foreign currency valuations, or balance carryforwards, each task plays a vital role in achieving a clean and compliant close.

As the books are closed and the financial data is finalized, the next critical phase begins—transforming that data into actionable insights. Financial reporting is not just about compliance; it's about telling the story of the business through numbers. Whether it's internal management reports, statutory statements, or executive dashboards, accurate and timely financial reporting forms the foundation for informed decision-making. In the next chapter, we'll explore the power and purpose of financial reporting in SAP, the tools available, and how organizations can leverage them to drive strategy, transparency, and trust.

CHAPTER 6

SAP Finance Reporting – Driving Business Insights Through Data

In the dynamic world of enterprise finance, accurate and timely reporting isn't just a compliance necessity - it's a strategic tool that drives informed decisions, identifies opportunities, and flags risks in real-time. SAP Finance Reporting empowers finance professionals to access real-time financial data, generate precise reports, and analyze trends that align with business goals. Whether it's monitoring profitability, tracking cash flows, or preparing for audits, SAP's robust reporting capabilities serve as the backbone for intelligent financial management.

SAP Finance Reporting goes far beyond traditional financial statements. It integrates seamlessly with various modules (FI, CO, SD, MM, etc.), allowing enterprises to generate internal and external reports, manage compliance, support tax filings, and enable management to make strategic decisions. From classic reports in SAP GUI to modern visual dashboards in SAP Fiori and SAP Analytics Cloud (SAC), SAP's reporting landscape is vast, flexible, and powerful.

In this chapter, we'll explore the key aspects of SAP Finance Reporting—process steps, important transaction codes, reporting tools, and best practices. This foundation sets the stage for understanding how data flows across SAP and how it can be extended to third-party integrations, which we'll cover in the next chapter.

Types of SAP Finance Reports

SAP Financial Accounting (FI) provides a variety of reports to support both internal and external reporting needs:

- ***General Ledger Reports*** – For balance sheets, profit & loss statements.
- ***Accounts Payable (AP) Reports*** – Vendor aging, open items, due dates.

- **Accounts Receivable (AR) Reports** – Customer balances, overdue receivables.
- **Asset Accounting Reports** – Asset balances, depreciation, acquisitions/disposals.
- **Controlling Reports** – Cost center reports, internal orders, profit center reports.
- **Special Purpose Ledger (SPL) Reports** – Custom reporting for specific structures.

Key SAP Reporting Tools

SAP offers various tools and platforms to generate financial reports, each with its unique capabilities:

a. Classic SAP GUI Reports

- Accessible via transaction codes.
- Real-time and customizable with selection criteria.
- Suitable for operational and reconciliation purposes.

b. Report Painter / Report Writer

- Used primarily for CO reporting (e.g., cost center reporting).
- Offers layout customization for end users.
- T-code: **GRR1, GR55, GRR2**

c. Drilldown Reporting

- Provides summarized reports with options to drill down into details.
- Used in profitability analysis and account balance views.
- T-codes: **KE30, FAGLL03, S_ALR_87012284**

d. SAP Query (SQ01/SQVI)

- Allows users to create custom reports without needing ABAP.
- Joins multiple tables and creates user-friendly output.

e. SAP Fiori Analytical Apps

- Role-based dashboards with real-time KPIs and charts.
- Enhances user experience with drill down navigation and graphical views.

f. SAP Analytics Cloud (SAC)

- Cloud-based reporting and planning tool.
- Combines financial data with visual dashboards, predictive analysis, and collaborative features.

Commonly Used Transaction Codes (T-Codes)

Report Area	Transaction Code	Description
General Ledger Reporting	FAGLB03, FBL3N	G/L line item reports and balances
Trial Balance	S_ALR_87012277	Trial balance by chart of accounts
Profit & Loss Statement	S_ALR_87012284	P&L by cost element/cost center
Balance Sheet	S_ALR_87012279	Balance sheet structure
Accounts Receivable Reports	FBL5N, FD10N	Customer line items and balances
Accounts Payable Reports	FBL1N, FK10N	Vendor line items and balances
Asset Accounting	AW01N, AR01	Asset Explorer, Asset history sheet
Cost Center Reports	S_ALR_87013611	Cost centers: Actual vs. Plan/Variance
Internal Orders	KO88, KOB1	Settlement reports and actual line items

Reporting Process Flow in SAP

While the specifics vary depending on the report type, the typical reporting process in SAP Finance includes:

Step 1: Data Entry & Posting

- Financial transactions are entered (invoices, payments, journal entries).
- Real-time postings update ledgers.

Step 2: Data Enrichment

- Assignments to cost centers, internal orders, and profit centers enhance reporting dimensions.

Step 3: Period-End Closing Activities

- Accruals, depreciation runs, foreign currency revaluation, etc., are completed.
- Ensures accuracy and completeness of data.

Step 4: Report Execution

- Users run standard or customized reports.
- Apply filters such as company code, fiscal year, cost center, GL account.

Step 5: Analysis & Export

- Drill down into transaction details for reconciliation.
- Export to Excel or integrate with SAC/Fiori for visualization.

Reporting Considerations and Best Practices

- **Reconciliation**: Always reconcile sub-ledger and general ledger balances before reporting.
- **Period Consistency**: Ensure proper period selection (posting date vs. document date).
- **Authorizations**: Sensitive data should be protected via proper user roles.
- **Data Aging**: Ensure data is archived or cleaned periodically to enhance performance.
- **Real-time Reporting**: Use Fiori or SAC for faster insight and interactive analysis.
- **Customization**: Use SAP Query or SAC stories for business-specific reports.

Common Challenges in SAP Finance Reporting

- **Data Overload**: Too much data without filters can lead to slow reports.
- **Inconsistent Master Data**: Inaccurate cost centers, GL accounts, or document types affect report quality.
- **Performance Issues**: Poor system performance during peak closing times.
- **User Training**: End users may struggle without proper training on report usage or interpretation.

SAP Finance Reporting stands as a powerful pillar in enterprise performance management. When executed effectively, it provides visibility, compliance, and a pathway to strategic insights. From classic SAP GUI screens to real-time analytics in Fiori and SAC, organizations can adapt the right tools for their size, industry, and business needs.

Yet, reporting doesn't end within SAP alone. The future lies in connected ecosystems. Businesses often need to pull or push financial data to and from third-party platforms, whether it's tax engines, banking platforms, BI tools, or external ERPs. Understanding these integrations is crucial to unlocking seamless operations and enhanced decision-making.

Key Takeaways

- SAP offers robust financial reporting tools, including classic reports, Report Painter, SAP Query, Fiori apps, and SAP Analytics Cloud.
- Common transaction codes cover G/L, AP, AR, Asset, and CO reporting areas.
- Accurate reporting begins with clean postings, correct master data, and proper period closing.
- Consider user roles, data performance, and reconciliation as part of reporting hygiene.
- SAP Finance Reporting is the backbone of compliance, internal control, and strategic decision-making.

In the next chapter, we'll explore SAP Third-Party Integrations—how SAP Finance connects with external systems to streamline bank reconciliations, automate tax compliance, enhance reporting capabilities, and enable real-time data exchange across platforms. We'll dive into integration technologies like IDocs, APIs, BAPIs, and middlewares that make SAP a truly connected enterprise solution.

CHAPTER 7

SAP Third-Party Integrations

Introduction: Bridging Ecosystems for Seamless Business

Think of your SAP system as the heart of your enterprise, pumping financial, operational, and logistical data throughout every department. But even the heart needs external specialists—banks, tax authorities, logistics providers, payroll systems—to function fully. These external parties are like external organs delivering oxygen, nutrients, and medicine. The integration between SAP and third-party systems forms the lifeline of a well-functioning, digitally connected enterprise.

Third-party integrations in SAP aren't just a technical exercise, they are a strategic necessity. Whether it's syncing bank statements, validating tax invoices, or integrating with cloud-based HR systems, these connections streamline operations, improve accuracy, and enable real-time decision-making. In this chapter, we explore types of third-party integrations, integration methods, process steps, key considerations, and real-life use cases to help you make informed decisions.

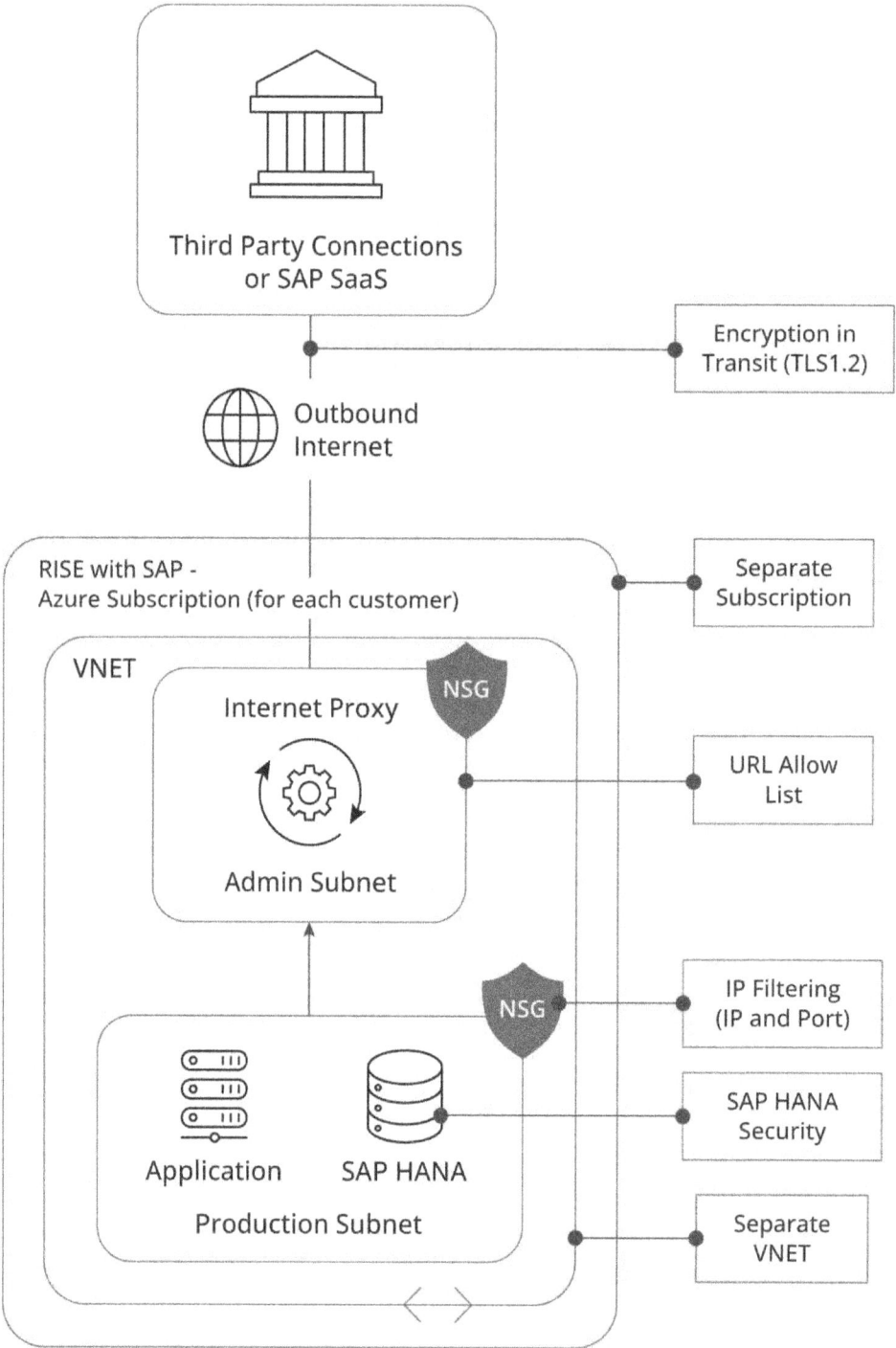

Types of SAP Third-Party Integrations

1. Financial Institutions (Bank Integrations)

- **Purpose:** Automate payment processing and bank statement reconciliation
- **Interfaces:** SWIFT, MT940, BAI2, CAMT.053, EBICS
- **SAP Tools:** Bank Communication Management (BCM), Payment Medium Workbench (PMW), Electronic Bank Statement (EBS)

2. E-Invoicing and Tax Engines

- **Purpose:** Real-time invoice validation and tax compliance
- **Popular Tools:** Vertex, Sovos, Avalara, SAP Document Compliance
- **Integration:** SAP PI/PO, SAP CPI, XML/JSON APIs

3. Payroll and HR Systems

- **Purpose:** Synchronize HR and payroll data
- **Platforms:** Workday, ADP, SuccessFactors
- **Integration:** IDocs, BAPIs, web services

4. Logistics and Warehouse Providers

- **Purpose:** Integrate with third-party logistics (3PL) and transportation systems
- **Examples:** FedEx, DHL, UPS
- **Data Exchanged:** Shipping, delivery, tracking

5. E-commerce and CRM Systems

- **Purpose:** Connect SAP with customer-facing platforms
- **Platforms:** Salesforce, Shopify, Magento
- **Integration:** SAP CPI, Middleware, APIs

6. Analytical and BI Tools

- **Purpose:** Share data for reporting and analytics
- **Examples:** Power BI, Tableau, Qlik
- **Method:** OData, CDS Views, extractors

Integration Approaches and Tools

1. IDocs (Intermediate Documents)

- **Use Case:** Batch data exchange
- **T-Codes:** WE02, WE20, WE19

2. BAPIs (Business Application Programming Interfaces)

- **Use Case:** Real-time, synchronous communication
- **T-Code:** BAPI (Explorer)

3. ALE (Application Link Enabling)

- **Use Case:** Distributed communication using IDocs

4. SAP PI/PO (Process Integration/Orchestration)

- **Use Case:** Middleware for message transformation and routing

5. SAP CPI (Cloud Platform Integration)

- **Use Case:** Cloud-to-cloud and cloud-to-on-premise integration

6. REST/SOAP APIs

- **Use Case:** API-based direct communication
- **Tool:** SAP API Hub

Typical Integration Process

1. Requirement Gathering

- Define business need and scope
- Identify systems and data to be exchanged

2. Interface Design

- Choose integration technology (IDoc, API, etc.)
- Map fields and define data formats

3. Configuration and Development

- Maintain partner profiles, RFC destinations
- Configure middleware, develop custom logic if needed

4. Testing

- Conduct unit, integration, and performance testing

5. Deployment and Monitoring

- Go live and monitor via logs and alerts
- Tools: SM37, WE02, SLG1

Important SAP T-Codes for Integration

T-Code	Description
WE02	Display IDoc
WE20	Partner Profiles
WE19	Test IDoc
SM59	RFC Destination Configuration
SXMB_MONI	PI/PO Message Monitoring
SLG1	Application Log
SM37	Background Job Monitoring
FBZP	Bank Configuration
OBPM1	Payment Format Configuration

Integration Readiness Checklist

- Clear business use case defined
- Data mapping document prepared
- Integration method chosen
- Error handling strategy in place
- Compliance requirements reviewed
- User training conducted

Real-Life Case Study: Global Manufacturing Company

Challenge: Automate tax invoice validation and logistics tracking across multiple countries.

Solution: Implemented SAP Document Compliance and SAP PI to connect with tax authorities in India, Mexico, and Brazil. Set up API-based tracking with DHL and FedEx.

Result: Reduced manual work by 80%, ensured compliance, and improved customer satisfaction through real-time tracking.

Integration with External Tax Calculation Engines

SAP S/4HANA

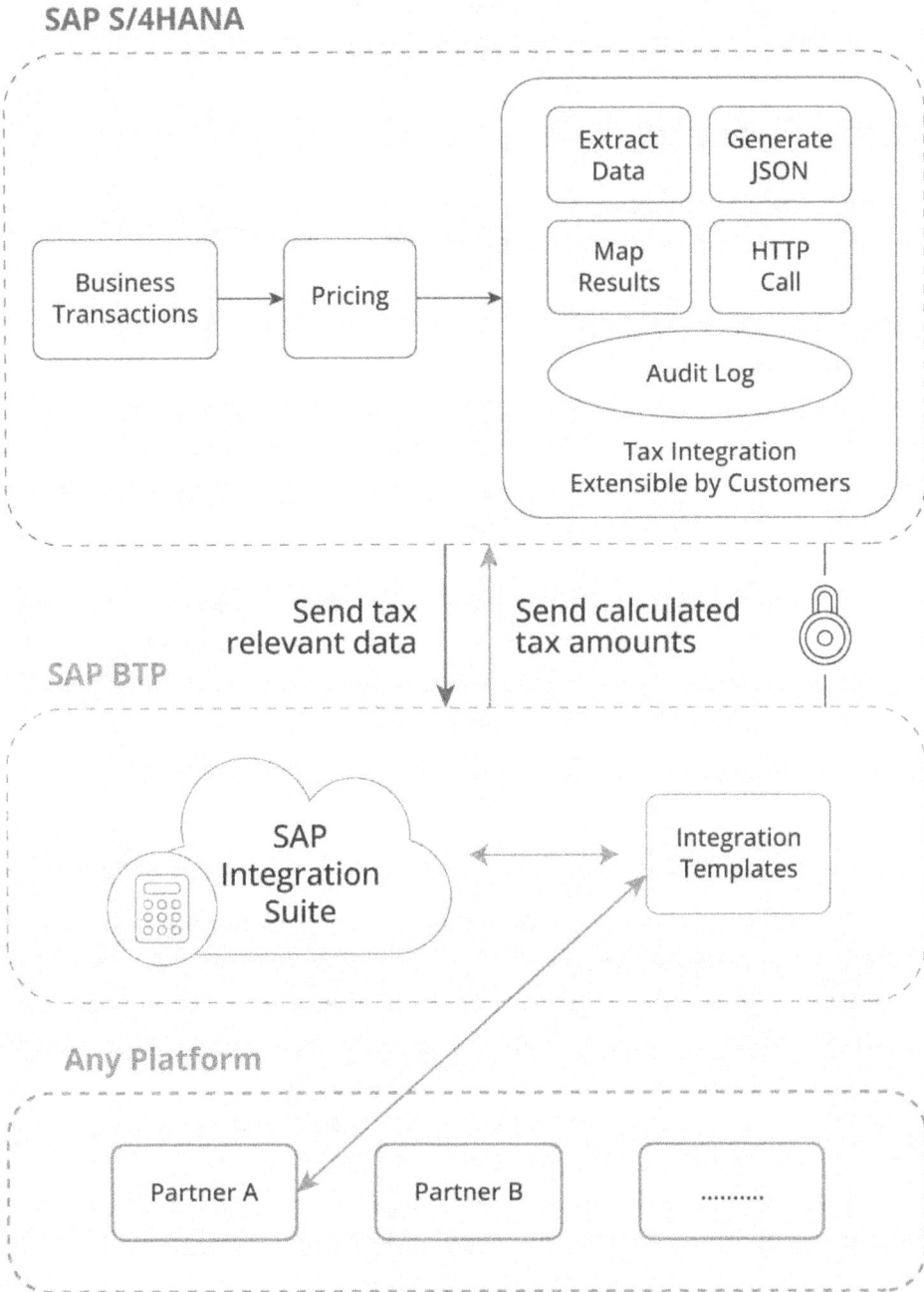

Business Transactions → Pricing →

Extract Data | Generate JSON
Map Results | HTTP Call
Audit Log

Tax Integration
Extensible by Customers

Send tax relevant data →
Send calculated tax amounts

SAP BTP

SAP Integration Suite ↔ Integration Templates

Any Platform

Partner A | Partner B | ....

Common Pitfalls to Avoid

- Hardcoding endpoints or values in logic
- Lack of automated error handling
- Ignoring country-specific compliance needs
- Not scaling the integration for high volumes

Suggested Integration Tools

- SAP Integration Suite
- SAP Application Interface Framework (AIF)
- Seeburger BIS for EDI
- EPI-USE Labs API Toolkit
- Ariba Network for supplier collaboration

Pause and reflect—how many third-party systems does your SAP environment currently talk to? Are they fully automated or still semi-manual? What would breaking those silos mean for your business efficiency?

SAP third-party integrations act as digital bridges that connect your ERP with the world around it. From bank automation to e-commerce connectivity, they fuel operational excellence and real-time business intelligence. By mastering integration design, tools, and monitoring practices, organizations can unlock massive productivity gains and enhance agility.

Key Takeaways

- SAP supports diverse third-party integrations including banks, tax engines, logistics, and HR systems
- Integration methods range from IDocs and BAPIs to APIs and middleware
- Success depends on clear scoping, secure communication, robust testing, and monitoring
- Real-world examples prove that automation can lead to drastic efficiency gains

While third-party integrations extend SAP's capabilities outward, the next layer of mastery lies in optimizing internal processes. SAP's Cross-Application Components and Enabling Elements provide foundational functions that enhance consistency, control, and automation across the system.

These elements include vital functions like Indirect Tax Configuration, Account Determination, Exchange Rate Management, Cost Center Allocations, Internal Orders, Number Range Management, and more. They serve as the rule engines and configuration backbones for Finance, Logistics, and Controlling modules. From managing dunning and payments to handling business partners and document splitting, these tools ensure seamless financial and operational orchestration.

In the next chapter, we'll explore each of these powerful tools—understanding how they enable process automation, ensure compliance, and act as the silent drivers of end-to-end integration within SAP.

CHAPTER 8

SAP Cross-Application Components and Enabling Elements

In the vast and interconnected ecosystem of SAP, success hinges not only on core modules like Finance (FI), Controlling (CO), Materials Management (MM), and Sales and Distribution (SD), but also on the seamless collaboration enabled by cross-application components and configuration elements, often referred to as "enabling elements." These foundational tools form the backbone of integrated business processing—they ensure consistency, automate transactions, facilitate compliance, and provide the agility required for businesses to operate efficiently across departments and geographies.

SAP is renowned not just for its powerful functional modules, but for the underlying Cross-Application Components and Enabling Elements that bind these modules into a unified, intelligent enterprise. These elements are the glue that transforms SAP from a collection of siloed applications into a harmonized, enterprise-wide solution. They drive secure, consistent, and efficient data and process flows across all business functions. Without these elements, an organization's SAP system would be fragmented, with modules operating in isolation—leading to inconsistencies, duplication of efforts, and manual reconciliations.

Whether it's automating payment processes, managing multi-currency operations, or ensuring timely reconciliation of accounts, these enabling elements play a critical role. They directly influence data flow between modules, connect operational processes with financial accounting, and empower enterprises to standardize, optimize, and scale with confidence. From workflow automation and classification systems to product lifecycle management, data archiving, and inter-system communications, these components ensure finance stays aligned with business operations at all times.

In this chapter, we delve deep into the top 15 most widely used SAP **enabling elements,** exploring their core functions, relevance, and their profound impact on SAP Finance and the broader SAP enterprise system. By the end of this chapter, you'll not only understand what these components are, but also why they are essential to designing a scalable, integrated, and future-ready SAP landscape.

1. **Account Determination** A cornerstone in SAP's integration architecture, account determination automatically maps business transactions in MM, SD, and other modules to the correct General Ledger (G/L) accounts in FI. This ensures seamless financial postings without manual intervention and supports compliance with financial reporting requirements.

2. **Indirect Taxes (VAT, GST, Sales Tax)** Tax configurations, such as VAT or GST, ensure organizations comply with country-specific tax regulations. Integrated directly with financial transactions, these configurations ensure correct tax calculations, postings, and reporting – crucial for legal compliance and audit readiness.

3. **Exchange Rate Management** In a globalized economy, organizations transact in multiple currencies. SAP's exchange rate configuration supports daily operations by maintaining consistent and up-to-date currency rates for conversions, impacting AR, AP, asset valuation, and financial consolidation.

4. **Automatic Payment Program (APP)** APP is a powerful automation tool used in Accounts Payable to process vendor payments efficiently. It consolidates open invoices, generates payment proposals, and executes payments via various formats (check, ACH, etc.), minimizing errors and improving vendor relationships.

5. **Dunning Procedure** An essential element in Accounts Receivable, the dunning program helps manage overdue customer payments. SAP allows organizations to define dunning levels and customize correspondence, improving cash flow and enforcing payment discipline.

6. **Reconciliation Accounts** These G/L accounts serve as connectors between sub-ledgers (customers, vendors, assets) and the general ledger. All postings in sub-ledgers automatically flow into reconciliation accounts, ensuring data integrity and consistency in financial statements.

7. **Document Splitting** Critical for segment and profit center reporting, document splitting enables businesses to produce accurate financial statements under multiple accounting principles (e.g., IFRS and GAAP). It breaks down accounting entries by dimension, supporting legal and managerial reporting needs.

8. **Tax Procedure & Configuration** Beyond just indirect taxes, SAP's tax procedure settings accommodate complex scenarios such as withholding tax, input/output tax offsets, and jurisdiction-based tax rules. These configurations ensure correct tax liability calculations and posting.

9. **Internal Orders** Internal Orders enable tracking of specific activities or cost objects, often used for short-term projects, events, or maintenance work. They facilitate budget tracking, cost control, and internal reporting, often serving as a bridge between operational and financial planning.

10. **Business Partner Configuration** With S/4HANA, Business Partner (BP) has become the central master data object, replacing traditional customer and vendor master data. BP unifies and simplifies data management, enhancing consistency across procurement, sales, and finance.

11. **Cost Center Allocation & Distribution** These processes distribute or allocate costs across various cost centers based on defined rules or usage, ensuring accurate internal cost tracking and reporting. These tools are vital for cost transparency and performance management.

12. **Electronic Bank Statement (EBS) Configuration** EBS automates the import and reconciliation of bank transactions with accounting records, significantly reducing manual work in bank reconciliations. Treasury and finance teams rely heavily on this for real-time cash visibility.

13. **Asset Accounting (FI-AA)** Asset Accounting manages the entire lifecycle of fixed assets, from acquisition to retirement. It integrates closely with purchasing and finance processes, providing key functions like depreciation, revaluation, and asset transfers.

14. **Intercompany Processes** Large enterprises with multiple legal entities use intercompany configuration to facilitate seamless transactions between them. It ensures proper accounting entries, tax handling, and reporting for consolidated financial statements.

15. **Workflow Management** Workflows automate approval processes across procurement, finance, and HR. With clearly defined process paths and role-based approvals, workflows reduce delays, improve compliance, and enhance transparency.

Impact on SAP Finance and Enterprise Operations

These enabling elements are not siloed features; they are embedded in nearly every SAP transaction. From initiating a purchase requisition to recording revenue from sales, these components ensure that the right data flows to the right place in real time. They strengthen the integrity of financial postings, support compliance with global accounting standards, and provide actionable insights for decision-making. Most importantly, they transform SAP from a transactional system to a strategic enterprise platform.

Key Takeaways

- SAP Enabling Elements are critical building blocks for cross-functional business processes.
- They ensure automated, consistent, and compliant financial postings across modules.
- Components like Account Determination, Exchange Rate Management, and Business Partner Configuration play a pivotal role in Finance.
- These elements enhance efficiency, governance, and reporting across the enterprise.

Without these cross-application components, an organization's SAP system would be fragmented—each module operating independently, leading to inconsistencies, duplication of efforts, and manual reconciliations. Whether it's workflow automation, classification, product lifecycle management, or document and data archiving, these components play a pivotal role in creating a harmonized environment. Their impact on SAP Finance is especially profound, as finance is interwoven with every other function in the enterprise.

What Are Cross-Application Components?

Cross-Application Components (CACs) are functionalities in SAP that span multiple modules and application areas, providing shared services or foundational capabilities across the system. These are not standalone modules, but reusable and integrative elements that enhance data consistency, process automation, and user experience.

Key characteristics include:

- Used across multiple modules (e.g., FI, SD, MM, PP, etc.)
- Enhance process consistency and standardization
- Support enterprise-wide compliance and automation
- Enable cross-functional reporting and integration

Key SAP Cross-Application Components and Enabling Elements

SAP Business Workflow

SAP Business Workflow automates business processes that require human interaction, approvals, and decision-making. It ensures tasks like invoice approvals, purchase requisitions, and journal entry validations follow a consistent and traceable path.

Use in SAP Finance:

- Invoice approvals (MM-FI)
- Payment release workflows
- Journal entry approval processes (via Fiori apps)
- Purchase requisition to PO flow with financial validations

Key Transactions:

- SWDD – Workflow Builder
- SWIA – Workflow administration
- SWNCONFIG – Notification settings

Document Management System (DMS)

SAP DMS allows organizations to manage documents (like PDFs, CAD files, invoices) within the SAP system. It ensures compliance, secure storage, version control, and easy retrieval.

Impact on Finance:

- Storing supporting documentation for vendor invoices
- Archiving financial records for audits
- Documenting internal approvals for accounting entries

Classification System

This component allows for grouping and categorizing objects using characteristics and classes (e.g., materials, vendors, assets). It is widely used in logistics but supports Finance in controlling assets and cost objects.

Use in Finance:

- Classify assets by type or use case for better depreciation tracking
- Categorize cost centers or internal orders for detailed reporting

Engineering Change Management (ECM)

ECM helps manage revisions and updates to master data—essential for industries like manufacturing or utilities. While it is heavily used in materials and BOMs, its impact is also seen in controlling costs and asset valuation.

Archiving and Data Retention

SAP offers tools to archive old data in compliance with legal requirements. This is critical for Finance, where historical data must be retained for auditing but shouldn't overload the live system.

Financial Impact:

- Archiving posted documents (FI)
- Managing retention of audit-relevant financial data
- Enhancing system performance by reducing data volume

Key Transactions:

- **SARA** – Archive Administration

Batch Management and Serial Numbering

Used mainly in logistics, but essential in Finance for **inventory valuation**, **asset tracking**, and **audit trail accuracy**. Every serial number has financial implications in stock accounts.

SAP ALE/IDocs (Application Link Enabling)

Facilitates communication between SAP systems (or SAP and non-SAP systems) using **Intermediate Documents (IDocs)**. In Finance, it enables:

- Transfer of financial documents between systems
- Synchronization of master data (vendors, customers, GL accounts)

Key Transactions:

- **WE02** – IDoc display
- **BD87** – Reprocess IDocs

SAP Business Partner (BP) Approach

Business Partner is a unified master data concept used across SAP S/4HANA for customers, vendors, and employees. It ensures consistency across modules and is especially significant in Finance, where accurate master data is crucial.

Change Documents and Logging

Change documents record when key data points are altered (e.g., bank account change for a vendor). For Finance, this is essential for internal controls, audits, and fraud prevention.

Key Transaction:

- **SCDO** – Display/change document objects

SAP Event Management (EM)

Enables real-time visibility into business process events across the supply chain. From a financial standpoint, it helps with:

- Tracking goods in transit (impacting GR/IR clearing)
- Monitoring delays that could lead to financial penalties or accruals

SAP Variant Configuration (VC)

VC helps build customizable products with multiple options. From a Finance perspective, it supports cost estimation, pricing, and profitability analysis for complex sales scenarios.

How Cross-Application Components Impact SAP Finance

These components impact Finance in several key ways:

- **Automation and Efficiency**: Workflows and master data synchronization reduce manual processes.
- **Data Integrity**: Centralized data management (via Business Partner or DMS) ensures consistent financial reporting.
- **Audit and Compliance**: Archiving, change logs, and document management provide traceability.
- **Cost and Profitability Control**: Classification and variant configuration offer granular insights into financial data.
- **Process Integration**: ALE/IDoc ensures data exchange for intercompany transactions and global financial consolidation.

Cross-Application Integration Across the SAP Landscape

Component	Functional Modules Impacted	Finance Involvement
Workflow	FI, MM, SD, HR	Approvals, audit trail
DMS	FI, QM, PP, SD	Document retention, compliance
ALE/IDoc	FI, MM, SD, HR	Data replication, system integration
Archiving	FI, MM, SD	Data retention policies
Classification	FI, CO, MM	Reporting, cost tracking
Business Partner	FI, SD, MM, HR	Master data harmonization

Cross-Application Components and Enabling Elements are the invisible framework that turns SAP from a collection of functional modules into a seamless, intelligent digital core. They underpin the agility, reliability, and consistency of business processes, ensuring that Finance operates not as a silo, but as a fully integrated function within the enterprise. Understanding and leveraging these components is critical for SAP Finance professionals who wish to drive automation, reduce risks, and deliver value to their organizations.

Key Takeaways

- Cross-Application Components provide essential services like workflow, document handling, classification, and system integration across all SAP modules.
- These elements ensure **data consistency**, **auditability**, and **automation**, which are vital for SAP Finance operations.
- Tools like **SAP Workflow**, **ALE/IDoc**, and **Business Partner Master Data** directly impact financial accuracy and compliance.
- SAP Finance benefits significantly from system-wide features like archiving, change documents, and classification, aiding in performance, governance, and strategic planning.
- A strong grasp of these components prepares SAP professionals for designing and managing complex enterprise systems.

As we've explored the foundational elements that enable integration across the SAP landscape, it's time to shift our focus from the system infrastructure to **how businesses model and improve their processes**. In the next chapter, we delve into **SAP Signavio**, SAP's powerful business process management suite. You'll learn how to visualize, optimize, and transform processes across Finance and other domains using Signavio's collaborative and data-driven tools. Let's explore how intelligent process design can drive continuous improvement and innovation.

CHAPTER 9

Business Process Design with SAP Signavio

In the ever-evolving digital enterprise landscape, agility and efficiency have become non-negotiable. Businesses must rapidly adapt to new market conditions, compliance requirements, and customer expectations. At the heart of this transformation lies Business Process Design — a discipline that aligns strategy with execution, enabling organizations to visualize, model, and optimize their end-to-end operations. Enter SAP Signavio, a powerful suite of cloud-based tools designed to transform how companies understand, manage, and continuously improve their business processes.

SAP Signavio is not just another process modeling tool. It is a comprehensive Business Process Transformation Suite that integrates deeply with SAP's Intelligent Enterprise ecosystem. From capturing current workflows to simulating future-state scenarios, Signavio empowers business and IT stakeholders to collaborate in real-time, co-create better processes, and drive value across the enterprise. Whether you're migrating to SAP S/4HANA or reimagining your operating model, SAP Signavio helps ensure that your digital transformation is grounded in process excellence.

Key Components and Modules of SAP Signavio

SAP Signavio offers a modular and scalable architecture. Each module caters to different business needs, but together they provide a unified view of process management:

SAP Signavio Process Manager

- **Purpose**: Design, model, and document business processes.
- **Functions**: BPMN 2.0 modeling, process documentation, and hierarchical process landscapes.

- **Use Case**: Create as-is and to-be process models, align them with business strategy, and use them as a blueprint for ERP implementation or redesign.

SAP Signavio Process Intelligence

- **Purpose**: Analyze real-time process data using process mining.
- **Functions**: Discover inefficiencies, identify bottlenecks, and suggest automation opportunities.
- **Use Case**: Improve P2P, O2C, and R2R processes by analyzing how they actually perform in your ERP systems.

SAP Signavio Collaboration Hub

- **Purpose**: Provide a centralized platform for business users to collaborate on processes.
- **Functions**: Feedback management, commenting, and shared views.
- **Use Case**: Enable cross-functional teams to co-author, review, and approve process designs, fostering greater alignment.

SAP Signavio Journey Modeler

- **Purpose**: Map customer journeys and link them to internal business processes.
- **Functions**: Customer touchpoint analysis, pain point tracking, experience KPIs.
- **Use Case**: Integrate customer experience data with operational data to drive customer-centric improvements.

SAP Signavio Process Governance

- **Purpose**: Ensure process compliance and lifecycle management.
- **Functions**: Approval workflows, policy management, and audit trails.
- **Use Case**: Create robust governance for critical processes and ensure regulatory compliance.

Use Cases and Applications

SAP Signavio supports a wide range of use cases across industries:

- **Digital Transformation**: Standardize and streamline processes before migrating to SAP S/4HANA.

- *Compliance & Risk Management*: Monitor process deviations, ensure adherence to policies, and support audits.
- *Operational Excellence*: Reduce costs and cycle times by optimizing business workflows.
- *Customer Experience*: Align internal operations with external expectations using journey modeling.
- *Sustainability*: Design energy-efficient and compliant business operations.

Key Functions and Capabilities

- *Model-Driven Process Management*: Enables businesses to use visual modeling languages to communicate complex workflows simply and clearly.
- *Live Insights*: With process mining, gain real-time insights into how processes function in practice.
- *Collaboration*: Foster enterprise-wide engagement with shared access, workflows, and version control.
- *Integration with SAP Ecosystem*: Seamless interaction with SAP S/4HANA, SAP Analytics Cloud, and SAP Business Technology Platform (BTP).
- *KPI and Benchmarking*: Evaluate processes against industry standards to identify areas of improvement.

Future of Business Process Design with SAP Signavio

As enterprises increasingly embrace **automation**, **AI**, and **hyper-personalization**, business process design will evolve from a static, one-time effort to a **continuous, data-driven discipline**. SAP Signavio is already adapting with features like:

- AI-Powered Process Suggestions
- Automated Process Discovery
- Predictive Analytics for Process Performance

With the rise of Composable ERP and modular business capabilities, SAP Signavio will play a central role in designing adaptable, resilient, and intelligent processes that can flex as the business evolves.

Business process design is no longer a back-office function; it is a strategic imperative. SAP Signavio empowers organizations to place processes at the center of their digital journey, bringing clarity, collaboration, and control to every transformation effort. As we transition into a future where agility and compliance are paramount, tools like SAP Signavio provide the transparency and structure needed to thrive.

Key Takeaways

- SAP Signavio is a holistic suite for business process transformation, integrating process modeling, mining, governance, and customer journey mapping.
- It supports core ERP transformation initiatives, especially SAP S/4HANA migrations.
- Collaboration, transparency, and continuous improvement are key pillars of its design.
- It empowers enterprises to visualize current performance, redesign for efficiency, and prepare for the future of intelligent operations.

With strong process foundations established using SAP Signavio, the next critical focus is ensuring regulatory compliance and financial integrity within those processes. In the upcoming chapter, we will explore how Compliance & SAP Finance work hand-in-hand to uphold trust, meet legal standards, and manage risk in a digitized business world.

CHAPTER 10

Compliance & SAP Finance

The Unseen Backbone of Financial Integrity

In an increasingly complex and globally interconnected business world, the pressure on organizations to comply with a growing list of financial regulations has never been higher. Missteps in compliance can result in penalties, loss of reputation, and erosion of investor and customer trust. On the flip side, companies that embed compliance into their core business processes not only avoid risk—they gain a competitive edge, improve operational discipline, and foster long-term sustainability.

SAP Finance sits at the epicenter of this compliance-driven transformation. Far more than a transactional system, SAP provides the architecture, tools, and intelligent workflows needed to automate, monitor, and enforce compliance across every financial process. Whether a company is operating solely in the United States or across dozens of countries, SAP ensures that its financial practices adhere to local laws, international standards, and internal policies—all within a unified and transparent system.

In this chapter, we will explore key compliance frameworks and how SAP supports them. From the stringent internal control requirements of the **Sarbanes-Oxley Act (SOX)** to the standardized accounting rules of **GAAP** and the global comparability of **IFRS**, compliance is no longer optional—it is foundational. We will also cover industry-specific regulations like **GxP** in life sciences and the built-in governance provided by **SAP Best Practices** and the **SAP Activate methodology**.

Finance departments must now do more than close the books—they must build controls into their systems, validate transactions in real-time, and deliver audit-ready data on demand. SAP not only enables this paradigm—it empowers it.

Sarbanes-Oxley (SOX) Compliance in SAP

Overview:

Enacted in 2002 in the wake of corporate scandals involving Enron, WorldCom, and others, the **Sarbanes-Oxley Act (SOX)** was designed to protect investors by increasing the transparency and accuracy of corporate disclosures. It requires public companies to establish robust internal controls over financial reporting (ICFR) and mandates that both management and external auditors attest to the effectiveness of these controls.

Key SOX Requirements in SAP:

Because most financial data and reporting flow through ERP systems like SAP, the ERP environment is heavily scrutinized during SOX audits. SAP must demonstrate that:

- Financial data cannot be tampered with
- Only authorized users have access to sensitive transactions
- Changes to master data and configuration are tracked
- There are clear audit trails and signoffs for financial postings

SAP Capabilities for SOX:

SAP provides built-in and extended capabilities through the SAP GRC suite (Governance, Risk, and Compliance):

- *Access Controls*: Segregation of duties (SoD) ensures no single user has conflicting roles (e.g., initiating and approving a payment).
- *Audit Trails*: SAP automatically logs user actions, system changes, and configuration edits.
- *Change Management*: SAP Solution Manager and GRC tools help track all changes in configurations and master data with version control and approvals.
- *Workflow Controls*: Posting journal entries or vendor invoices may require multi-level approvals to ensure integrity.

With SAP GRC, companies can proactively monitor compliance risks and automate checks that were once manual and error-prone.

GAAP (Generally Accepted Accounting Principles)

GAAP serves as the standard framework for financial accounting used by most U.S.-based companies. It encompasses a set of rules and procedures for financial reporting, including recognition, measurement, presentation, and disclosure. Adhering to GAAP ensures that financial statements are consistent, comparable, and transparent—allowing investors and regulators to make informed decisions.

Implementation in SAP:

SAP Finance offers a powerful structure that aligns naturally with GAAP principles:

- **Multi-ledger Accounting**: SAP allows companies to configure a **leading ledger** for primary reporting (e.g., GAAP) and **non-leading ledgers** for other standards or internal views.
- **Revenue Recognition**: SAP RAR (Revenue Accounting and Reporting) complies with ASC 606 under GAAP, allowing rules-based revenue recognition with clear audit trails.
- **Depreciation & Asset Accounting**: SAP FI-AA manages lifecycle accounting for fixed assets. You can configure different depreciation areas based on GAAP rules.
- **Consolidation and Elimination**: SAP supports intercompany eliminations and consolidated financial reporting as required under GAAP.

Example:

*A U.S.-based multinational may use GAAP as its leading ledger for consolidated financials, while simultaneously maintaining IFRS or local GAAP ledgers for its subsidiaries—using the **parallel ledger** framework within SAP.*

IFRS (International Financial Reporting Standards)

IFRS is the most widely adopted accounting standard globally, required or permitted in over 140 countries. Developed by the International Accounting Standards Board (IASB), IFRS promotes comparability and transparency across borders. Multinational corporations need to prepare financial statements in accordance with both local standards (e.g., GAAP) and IFRS for global stakeholders.

IFRS Requirements Supported in SAP

SAP provides several critical functionalities to comply with IFRS:

- Parallel Ledger Accounting: Companies can maintain IFRS and GAAP books simultaneously without duplicating data entry.
- IFRS 15 (Revenue Recognition): SAP RAR handles performance obligations, contract liabilities, and revenue allocations.
- IFRS 16 (Lease Accounting): SAP Contract & Lease Management enables companies to capitalize leases and manage right-of-use assets and lease liabilities.
- IFRS 9 (Financial Instruments): SAP Treasury and Risk Management supports classification, measurement, and impairment of financial assets.

Use Case:

A European pharmaceutical company might prepare its statutory financials under IFRS, but its U.S. subsidiary still needs GAAP compliance. SAP makes it seamless through ledger configurations and reporting structures, ensuring compliance with both sets of standards.

GxP Compliance in SAP (Life Sciences and Regulated Industries)

What is GxP?

GxP stands for "Good x Practice" where "x" can be Manufacturing (GMP), Laboratory (GLP), or Clinical (GCP). These are quality guidelines to ensure products are safe, pure, and effective. Regulatory agencies like the FDA (U.S.), EMA (Europe), and others require strict adherence to these practices.

SAP Support for GxP:

- **System Validation**: SAP must be validated for its intended use (IQ/OQ/PQ protocols). This ensures the system performs as designed.
- **Audit Trails**: SAP logs must show who performed what action and when. This includes changes to configurations, data entries, and workflows.
- **Electronic Signatures and Authorizations**: Compliance with 21 CFR Part 11 mandates secure, role-based access and auditable approvals.

- **Change Management**: SAP Solution Manager or Change Request Management (ChaRM) ensures any changes to the system go through a controlled and documented process.
- **Training Logs and SOPs**: Integration with Document Management Systems (DMS) helps manage Standard Operating Procedures (SOPs), critical for GxP audits.

Real-world Example:

A biotech firm using SAP S/4HANA in a GxP environment must validate every module used in the production or release of drugs—from materials management to batch release, asset tracking, and financial reporting—ensuring traceability and regulatory alignment.

SAP Best Practices for Compliance

SAP has developed a vast library of **Best Practices** to help organizations implement compliant, efficient, and industry-specific processes quickly and securely. These best practices are embedded into the **SAP Activate Methodology**, which provides a guided implementation framework with a strong focus on governance, risk, and documentation.

Key Compliance-Oriented Best Practices:

- *Standardized Business Processes*: These come with standard validations, approval flows, and master data setups aligned with industry norms and regulatory frameworks.
- *Workflow Templates*: Ready-to-use workflows ensure segregation of duties and prevent policy violations.
- *Documentation and Traceability*: Every activity in Activate is logged, including sign-offs, process modeling, testing evidence, and training.

Role of SAP Activate Methodology:

- Ensures risk management, documentation, and compliance tasks are embedded from the design phase.
- Faster deployment of compliant processes.
- Less risk of customization errors or process gaps.
- Audit-ready documentation from project inception.

Compliance in SAP Finance is not a reactive approach to avoid penalties—it is a proactive strategy to build business integrity, stakeholder trust, and operational excellence. By integrating SAP's powerful financial modules with governance and compliance tools, companies can create a robust ecosystem that ensures adherence to local and global regulations. With built-in best practices, real-time monitoring, and automation, SAP makes compliance an ongoing, manageable, and strategic aspect of enterprise finance.

Compliance is not a one-time task—it's a continuous commitment. SAP Finance, when properly configured and governed, becomes the guardian of financial integrity and regulatory adherence. From GxP in life sciences to dual ledger reporting for GAAP and IFRS, to automated SOX controls and SAP Best Practices, the ecosystem provides a powerful toolkit for CFOs, auditors, and finance professionals.

Key Takeaways:

SOX compliance in SAP is achieved through automated controls, audit trails, and segregation of duties.

GAAP and IFRS are supported via parallel ledgers, revenue recognition modules, and multi-currency management.

GxP compliance in SAP ensures validation, electronic record integrity, and traceability.

SAP Best Practices provide a compliant, standardized blueprint for financial processes.

Governance tools like **SAP GRC** help enforce access control, risk management, and policy adherence.

SOPs, Work Instructions, and Spec Docs are essential artifacts for compliance and audits.

With compliance as a solid cornerstone, organizations are well-positioned to embark on their SAP implementation journey with clarity and confidence. In Chapter 11: SAP Implementation Projects, we'll navigate the full project lifecycle—from initial planning and blueprinting to execution and go-live. We'll explore the key types of implementations, including Greenfield (starting from scratch), Brownfield (system migration), and Hybrid models that combine both.

You'll also gain insights into essential project documentation such as Functional Specifications, Technical Specifications, Standard Operating Procedures (SOPs), and Work Instructions—and understand how these documents align to drive a successful, controlled, and value-driven SAP rollout.

Now, let's move forward—from a compliance-driven financial foundation to mastering the art and science of SAP implementation.

CHAPTER 11

SAP Implementation Projects

SAP implementation projects represent one of the most critical undertakings for organizations aiming to digitally transform their operations. These projects are multifaceted, often requiring months or even years of careful planning, cross-functional collaboration, and rigorous execution. At their core, SAP implementation projects aim to deliver a powerful enterprise system that streamlines processes, enhances data visibility, and supports strategic decision-making across various business functions.

Successful implementation isn't just about installing software; it's about embedding new ways of working, aligning people, processes, and technology, and enabling continuous improvement. Given the scale, cost, and complexity involved, understanding every phase, stakeholder, and deliverable is key. This chapter explores the lifecycle of SAP implementation projects, their methodologies, types, and what happens once the initial go-live is achieved.

Phases of an SAP Implementation Project

SAP projects typically follow structured methodologies such as **SAP Activate**, **ASAP (Accelerated SAP)**, or custom hybrid models. Each methodology consists of clearly defined phases:

Project Preparation:

- Define project scope, objectives, timelines, and team structure.
- Assign roles and responsibilities (project manager, functional/technical consultants, business stakeholders).
- Establish governance and change management strategy.

Business Blueprint (Explore Phase in Activate):

- Conduct workshops to gather requirements.
- Document business processes using Business Process Model and Notation (BPMN) or process maps.
- Identify gaps between standard SAP functionality and business needs.

Realization:

- Configure the SAP system based on the business blueprint.
- Perform unit testing and integration testing.
- Develop custom objects (WRICEF: Workflows, Reports, Interfaces, Conversions, Enhancements, Forms).

Final Preparation:

- Conduct user acceptance testing (UAT).
- Finalize cutover plans and data migration.
- Train end-users and establish support structures.

Go-Live and Support:

- Transition from project mode to live system.
- Execute cutover activities and monitor system stability.
- Begin hypercare support and resolve initial issues.

Types of SAP Implementation

1. Greenfield Implementation:

   - A fresh start. Implementing SAP from scratch without legacy system constraints.
   - Ideal for organizations without an existing ERP or those undergoing major digital transformation.

2. Brownfield Implementation:

   - A system conversion. Migrating an existing legacy ERP (like SAP ECC) to S/4HANA.
   - Retains existing configurations and customizations where possible.

3. Bluefield Implementation:

   - A hybrid approach. Selectively transfers data and processes from the legacy system.
   - Combines the advantages of both greenfield and brownfield.
   - Often used during S/4HANA transformation projects.

Key Stakeholders in SAP Implementation

- **Project Sponsor / Executive Steering Committee:** Provides strategic direction and budget approvals.
- **Project Manager:** Oversees planning, execution, and delivery.
- **SAP Consultants (Functional & Technical):** Responsible for solution design, configuration, and development.
- **Business Process Owners:** Provide business input, validate functionality, and lead UAT.
- **Change Management & Training Leads:** Ensure user adoption and readiness.
- **Basis & Security Teams:** Manage infrastructure, system access, and compliance.

Critical Documentation in SAP Projects

- **Project Charter**: High-level overview of objectives, scope, timelines, and governance.
- **Business Blueprint Document (BPD)**: Process flows and requirements.
- **Functional Specification Document (FSD)**: For custom developments.
- **Technical Specification Document (TSD)**: Technical design of custom objects.
- **Test Scripts & Test Logs**: For all types of testing.
- **Cutover Plan**: Step-by-step guide for transitioning to the live system.
- **End-User Manuals and Training Materials**
- **Change Requests and Risk Logs**

Go-Live and Beyond: Types of SAP Projects Post-Implementation

After the initial go-live, the nature of SAP-related work evolves into other types of projects:

1. Production Support (AMS – Application Management Services):

    o   Day-to-day support for end-users.
    o   Issue resolution, incident management, monitoring, and minor changes.

2. Enhancement Projects:

    o   Adding new functionalities, reports, workflows, or automation post go-live.
    o   Often initiated based on evolving business needs.

3. Rollout Projects:

    o   Deploying the existing SAP solution to new geographies or business units.
    o   Includes localization, translation, and legal compliance setup.

4. Upgrade or Migration Projects:

    o   System upgrades (e.g., ECC to S/4HANA).
    o   Cloud migration (on-premise to cloud).

5. Archival and Decommissioning Projects:

    o   Managing legacy data.
    o   System retirement, especially during mergers, acquisitions, or divestitures.

SAP implementation projects are the foundation of enterprise transformation. They demand not just technical know-how but deep process understanding, excellent stakeholder communication, and meticulous documentation. Each phase builds upon the last, and success relies heavily on planning, governance, and user engagement.

Understanding what lies beyond go-live is equally crucial. Whether it's support, enhancements, or system upgrades, the SAP journey is continuous.

Key Takeaways

- *SAP implementation is a multi-phase, high-stakes project involving strategic planning and cross-functional collaboration.*
- *Choose the right implementation strategy (greenfield, brownfield, or bluefield) based on your organization's needs.*
- *Stakeholder roles and documentation are critical to project governance and success.*
- *Post-implementation activities like support, enhancements, and migrations are vital for long-term value.*

With the implementation complete and the system live, the focus shifts to ensuring its stability and usability for business users. In the next chapter, we will explore SAP Production Support, diving into ticket management, SLAs, root cause analysis, minor enhancements, and how support teams ensure smooth operations post go-live.

CHAPTER 12

SAP Production Support - 100+ Common Issues

This chapter takes us deep into one of the most critical and foundational areas of SAP: **Production Support**. Arguably one of the most important chapters in this book, it goes beyond being a mere catalog of issues and resolutions. It lays the groundwork for everything that follows—especially the **AI-based solutions** we'll explore in the next unit. As we examine over 100 real-world SAP Finance production support issues, it becomes clear that these are not just system glitches or user errors, but patterns and pain points that lend themselves perfectly to **automation, prediction, and intelligent resolution**. This chapter is your essential starting point—a practical and strategic lens through which we begin to reimagine SAP Finance operations with the power of **AI and machine learning**.

The Engine Room of SAP Operations

Production support in SAP is where strategy meets execution. It is the critical post-go-live phase where the system is actively used by business users and the focus shifts from implementation to **system stability, issue resolution, user support, and continuous improvement**.

In Finance, even minor disruptions—like a blocked invoice or an unposted journal entry—can cascade into larger operational setbacks. That's why production support is not only about fixing issues but about ensuring **compliance, performance, and trust** in financial data.

This chapter provides a categorized exploration of **100+ common SAP issues**, their implications, and practical troubleshooting tips. We'll also cover SLA management, user roles, documentation, and real-world support strategies. Whether you're an SAP

FICO consultant, a business analyst, or an AI enthusiast looking to identify automation opportunities, this chapter is your roadmap.

What is SAP Production Support?

SAP Production Support refers to the **ongoing monitoring, maintenance, and enhancement** of the SAP system post-implementation. Once a system goes live, users start entering real-time business data, and the system becomes mission-critical. The support team ensures:

- Smooth day-to-day operations
- Quick resolution of user-raised tickets
- Continuous compliance with financial and business regulations
- System improvements, enhancements, or fixes based on user feedback

SAP Production Support System

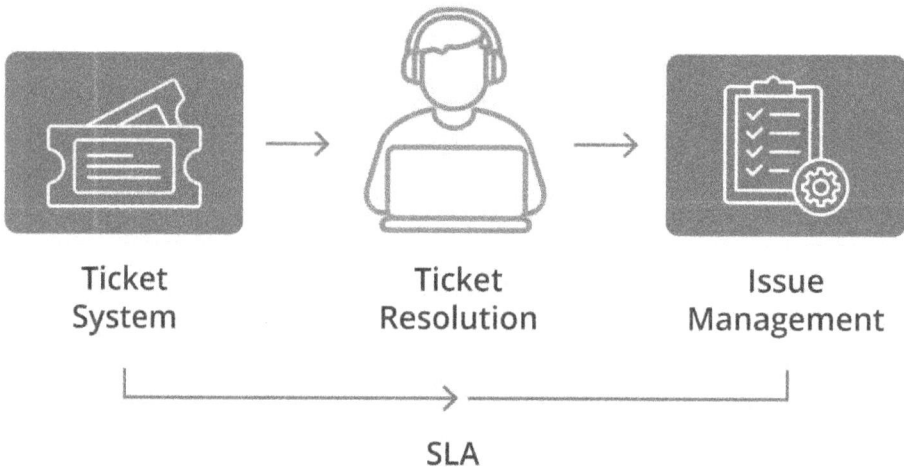

Ticket System → Ticket Resolution → Issue Management

SLA

Categories of SAP Production Support Issues (Finance-Focused)

1. Master Data Issues

- Incorrect or missing GL accounts
- Vendor/customer master data not maintained or duplicated
- Cost center assignment errors
- Tax code not defined for a country

2. General Ledger (FI-GL)

- Error in balance carryforward
- Document not posted due to missing assignment field
- Document splitting issues
- Exchange rate difference not correctly updated

3. Accounts Payable (FI-AP)

- Vendor invoice blocked for payment
- Payment proposal not picking up vendors
- Withholding tax not calculated
- Parked document errors
- Duplicate invoice detection failures

4. Accounts Receivable (FI-AR)

- Dunning program not picking up customers
- Lockbox failure to post incoming payments
- Customer credit limit errors
- Discrepancies in incoming payment clearing

5. Asset Accounting (FI-AA)

- Asset not capitalized properly
- Depreciation not posted
- Useful life incorrectly maintained
- Intercompany asset transfers failed

6. Bank Accounting

- Electronic bank statement not processed
- Payment run did not generate file
- Bank key not maintained
- MT940 interpretation errors

7. Controlling (CO)

- Cost center planning not reflecting
- Internal order settlement failed
- Profit center derivation errors
- Actual vs plan variance issues

8. Tax & Compliance

- GST/VAT calculation errors
- Reverse charge mechanism failures
- Missing country-specific tax configurations

SAP Production Support Lifecycle

1. Issue Reported (via ticketing system like ServiceNow, Remedy, Jira)
2. Impact Analysis
3. Root Cause Analysis
4. Resolution or Workaround
5. Testing in QA environment
6. Transport to Production
7. Closure with User Confirmation
8. Documentation and Knowledge Base update

SLAs (Service Level Agreements)

Each issue is assigned a priority:

- **P1 (Critical):** System down, financial closing blocked – Response in 15 mins, resolution in 4 hours
- **P2 (High):** Payment runs or business operations affected – Resolution within 8 hours

- **P3 (Medium):** Business user requests or data inconsistencies – Resolution in 2–3 business days
- **P4 (Low):** Cosmetic issues or enhancement requests – Resolution time varies

SLA tracking ensures timely issue resolution and improved user confidence.

Users & Stakeholders Involved

- **End Users:** Accountants, AP/AR clerks, treasury, auditors
- **Key Users/Super Users:** Department leads and SMEs
- **SAP Functional Consultants:** First-line support
- **Basis & ABAP Teams:** For technical/system-related fixes
- **Support Managers:** Escalation, reporting, and SLA adherence

Tools & Documentation in Production Support

- **Ticketing Systems:** ServiceNow, Jira, BMC Remedy
- Knowledge Base Articles (KBA)
- SAP Notes and OSS Messages
- Transport Requests (TRs)
- Issue Logs and Change Management Register
- Runbooks and SOPs (Standard Operating Procedures)

Common SAP FICO Production Support Issues

100+ Common SAP Finance Issues

FI-GL (General Ledger)

S.No	Issue
1	Document not posted due to missing assignment field
2	Exchange rate not updated
3	Incorrect fiscal year variant
4	Document splitting error
5	Balance carryforward not executed
6	Parked document cannot be posted
7	GL account blocked for posting
8	Incorrect profit center assignment
9	Tax code not defined for company code
10	Ledger not updated correctly

FI-AP (Accounts Payable)

S.No	Issue
1	Vendor invoice blocked for payment
2	Duplicate invoice detected
3	Withholding tax not calculated
4	Payment proposal missing vendors
5	Vendor master data missing
6	Blocked invoice not released
7	Payment run terminated
8	Bank details not maintained
9	Error in vendor reconciliation
10	Parked AP invoice cannot be posted

FI-AR (Accounts Receivable)

S.No	Issue
1	Customer dunning not triggered
2	Lockbox posting failed
3	Customer credit limit exceeded
4	Payment advice not processed
5	Unapplied cash on account
6	Invoice incorrectly cleared
7	Customer master data incomplete
8	Error in incoming payment processing
9	AR aging report not updated
10	Dispute case not closed

FI-AA (Asset Accounting)

S.No	Issue
1	Depreciation not calculated
2	Asset master data incomplete
3	Intercompany asset transfer failed
4	Asset not capitalized
5	Useful life not updated
6	Asset retired but not posted
7	Asset not linked to cost center
8	Error in revaluation
9	Asset under construction issues
10	Duplicate asset numbers

CO (Controlling)

S.No	Issue
1	Cost center not assigned
2	Internal order settlement failed
3	Profit center derivation missing
4	Variance calculation incorrect
5	Actual vs plan discrepancy
6	Primary cost element not created
7	Statistical key figure not maintained
8	Error in cost allocation cycle
9	CO document not generated
10	Plan data not updated

Bank Accounting

S.No	Issue
1	Electronic bank statement upload failed
2	House bank not maintained
3	Payment file not generated
4	Bank key missing
5	Check printing error
6	MT940 file not interpreted
7	Bank reconciliation failed
8	Incorrect bank GL posting
9	Payment medium format not found
10	Signatory not assigned to bank

Tax & Compliance

S.No	Issue
1	VAT not calculated
2	Reverse charge mechanism error
3	GST code not maintained
4	Country-specific tax configuration missing
5	Tax report discrepancies
6	Tax jurisdiction not found
7	Error in input tax adjustment
8	Withholding tax type not assigned
9	Incorrect tax base amount
10	Tax invoice not generated

FI-MM Integration

S.No	Issue
1	Error in GR/IR clearing due to quantity mismatch
2	PO invoice not posting due to missing GR
3	Incorrect movement type affecting FI posting
4	GR reversal not updating accounting document
5	Account assignment category not configured
6	Error in MIRO due to vendor account group
7	Posting period not open for PO invoice
8	Duplicate GR postings causing reconciliation issues
9	Incorrect tax code flow from PO to MIRO
10	Error during automatic account determination

FI-SD Integration

S.No	Issue
1	Accounting document not generated for billing
2	Incorrect GL account assignment during invoice posting
3	Revenue account determination not working
4	Error in credit memo accounting entry
5	Posting date not matching billing date
6	Rebate settlement not posted in accounting
7	Delivery-related billing not creating FI document
8	Intercompany billing not triggering accounting entry
9	Manual condition types not reflected in revenue
10	Tax jurisdiction code missing in SD invoice

Access Related (Authorization)

S.No	Issue
1	Error FINS_ACDOC_AUTH004 when accessing ACDOCA
2	User not authorized to create customer master
3	Access denied to execute depreciation run (AFAB)
4	Missing authorization for open item clearing
5	Inability to release parked documents due to authorization
6	No access to T-code OB52 for period opening
7	Authorization error for maintaining OBYC settings
8	Role missing for viewing asset explorer (AW01N)
9	Error in cost center report access
10	Access not provided for GL master creation

Bank Accounting (Extended)

S.No	Issue
1	Bank reconciliation report not showing latest entries
2	Duplicate entries in bank statement upload
3	Mapping error in manual bank statement
4	Bank payment not triggered due to signatory issue
5	Error in check lot number range assignment
6	Manual reconciliation posting not allowed
7	Bank file format not matching bank requirement
8	Incorrect assignment of external transaction types
9	Bank statement not clearing open items
10	Issue with house bank account assignment to company code

General Access/Technical Issues

S.No	Issue
1	Background job stuck in SM37
2	Authorization error when changing payment terms
3	SAP GUI freezing during FB60 posting
4	RFC connection error during IDOC posting
5	Incorrect role mapping after transport
6	SAP standard report missing for user
7	Authorization object for vendor display not assigned
8	Error in screen variant during transaction run
9	SM13 update error after posting
10	Job logs not available for failed jobs

Best Practices in Production Support

- Maintain clear documentation and root cause analysis (RCA)
- Regular training and enablement for business users
- Version control for transports and notes
- Weekly status updates and trend reports
- Track recurring issues for automation or process reengineering

By exploring over 100 common issues across key SAP Finance submodules, you now have a solid grasp of the real-world challenges organizations face and how to resolve them. You've also seen how critical elements like **SLAs**, **documentation**, and **collaboration** contribute to the success of support operations.

SAP Production Support is the unseen engine that keeps financial systems running smoothly day in and day out. While implementation brings systems to life, it's the **production support phase** that determines their real value and sustainability. This chapter has shown that being effective in support requires more than just technical know-how—it calls for business acumen, problem-solving agility, and proactive communication with users and stakeholders.

SAP Production Support is where theory meets reality. Every ticket tells a story—a process flaw, a data miss, or a training gap. It's also where innovation begins. As the number of tickets increases, patterns emerge. These patterns are fertile ground for AI applications such as predictive maintenance, smart ticket routing, and automated financial reconciliations.

Key Takeaways

- *Production support is mission-critical and dynamic in nature, demanding strong analytical, functional, and communication skills.*
- *Categorizing issues based on modules helps in streamlined troubleshooting.*
- *SLAs ensure timely delivery and business continuity.*
- *A solid documentation culture is the backbone of successful SAP support.*
- *AI can be used to **predict common issues**, **automate solutions**, and **reduce manual intervention** in financial processes*

Throughout this chapter, we've explored over 100 of the most common issues that SAP Finance users and consultants come across in real-world production environments. From document posting errors and GR/IR mismatches to blocked payments and access denials, these problems can disrupt daily operations if not resolved quickly and correctly. We grouped them by sub-modules like FI-GL, FI-AP, FI-AR, Asset Accounting, Controlling, FI-MM, FI-SD, Bank Accounting, and more—giving you a full picture of where things typically go wrong and what to watch out for. Consider this your survival kit for the unpredictable world of SAP production support.

Now, when you're staring at an error message or a user is panicking about a payment run failure, you might wonder, "Where do I even begin?" That's where a solid approach helps. First, figure out what kind of issue it is—data, config, access, or system-related. Use SAP's built-in tools like ST22, SM13, SLG1, and SM37 to investigate. But also remember—experience is your best teacher. As you work through more tickets and solve more problems, you'll naturally build your own internal playbook. And don't worry—nobody knows everything. Sometimes, a quick Google search can save hours of trial and error. Plus, there's an incredible community of SAP professionals out there. Platforms like the SAP Community Network (SDN) at www.sdn.sap.com are filled with real questions, real solutions, and real users, just like you, sharing what worked (and what didn't).

Now that we've thoroughly explored the common challenges in SAP Finance production support, it's time to shift our focus toward solutions and strategic applications. In Unit 4, we take a significant step forward into the evolving landscape of AI-driven SAP Finance. This next section will demonstrate how many of the issues identified in this chapter can be transformed into use cases for automation, predictive analytics, and intelligent resolution. Rather than reacting to problems after they occur, the goal is to anticipate and prevent disruptions before they impact operations. This is where traditional SAP support begins to evolve into a more proactive, data-informed, and intelligent support model—powered by the capabilities of artificial intelligence.

Before we dive into AI-powered solutions in Unit 3, the final chapter of this unit takes a brief yet important detour—one that focuses on career growth and specialization. In the next chapter, we'll explore the various advanced paths SAP Finance consultants can pursue beyond day-to-day support. From Central Finance, Group Reporting, and SAP S/4HANA Embedded Analytics to Treasury, FSCM, Controlling, and the emerging integration of AI and Data Science in Finance, you'll gain a clear understanding of the specialization areas that are shaping the future of SAP. This chapter will help you identify where your interests and skills align, and how you can position yourself for long-term success in the SAP ecosystem.

UNIT 2 SUMMARY

SAP Finance – From Fundamentals to Future-Proofing Your Career

Unit 2 provided a comprehensive dive into the foundational and advanced concepts of SAP Finance (SAP FI), offering both technical and functional insights into how the financial module supports core business operations within the SAP ecosystem. We explored the major sub-modules like FI-GL (General Ledger), FI-AP (Accounts Payable), FI-AR (Accounts Receivable), Asset Accounting (FI-AA), Bank Accounting, and Controlling (CO). Additionally, we discussed essential integration points with other SAP modules such as MM, SD, HCM, and PP, laying the groundwork for understanding SAP Finance in real-world scenarios.

Through detailed walkthroughs and real-time examples, Unit 2 emphasized the **critical role of financial transparency, compliance, and efficiency** within an integrated enterprise system. Learners gained practical insights into how SAP Finance enables organizations to meet statutory requirements, manage financial performance, and align accounting processes with strategic business goals. The interplay between financial postings and logistics data was showcased to highlight the interconnected nature of enterprise operations.

In addition to mastering the technical configurations and process flows, the unit encouraged learners to **think beyond the transaction layer**, focusing on business impact, reporting accuracy, and operational excellence. Whether it's ensuring timely vendor payments, precise revenue recognition, or reliable asset tracking, SAP Finance serves as the backbone of enterprise decision-making. With these skills as a foundation, learners are now well-positioned to specialize in advanced areas and contribute meaningfully to digital transformation initiatives in finance.

Key Takeaways from Unit 2: SAP Finance

1. ***Comprehensive Understanding of Financial Accounting Configuration***
   Gained in-depth knowledge of configuring core SAP FI components, ensuring alignment with real-world business requirements and statutory compliance.

2. ***Integrated Financial Data Across Modules***
   Explored seamless real-time integration of SAP FI with other modules such as MM, SD, and HCM, emphasizing the accuracy and consistency of financial transactions across enterprise processes.

3. ***Advanced Ledger and Document Management Techniques***
   Developed expertise in handling complex financial structures, including document splitting, parallel ledger configuration, tax processing, and multi-ledger accounting.

4. ***Management Reporting through SAP Controlling (CO)***
   Introduced to key CO functionalities supporting internal reporting and cost analysis, including cost center, profit center, and internal order management.

5. ***Structured Financial Period-End Close Activities***
   Covered standardized approaches to month-end and year-end closing processes, including reconciliations, accruals, and system validations to ensure timely and accurate financial reporting.

6. ***Effective SAP Production Support and Incident Resolution***
   Learned industry best practices for supporting live SAP Finance environments, including incident management, ticket lifecycle handling, root cause analysis, and stakeholder communication.

By understanding these topics, consultants are now better equipped to handle implementation, configuration, and support-related responsibilities across varied SAP Finance landscapes.

Recommendations: Specializations for SAP FICO Consultants to Consider

As the SAP ecosystem evolves, FICO consultants have immense opportunities to expand their skill sets and remain competitive. Below are recommended specialization paths for those looking to grow beyond core FI/CO knowledge:

1. SAP FSCM (Financial Supply Chain Management)

- *Why*: Enhances the ability to manage working capital, collections, credit, and disputes.
- *Focus Areas*: Credit Management, Dispute Management, Collections Management, Electronic Bill Presentment and Payment (EBPP).
- *Value*: High demand in large enterprises optimizing cash flows and reducing DSO.

2. SAP COPA (Profitability Analysis)

- *Why*: Key for enabling profitability tracking by customer, region, product, etc.
- *Focus Areas*: Costing-Based and Account-Based COPA, integration with SD, Realignment.
- *Value*: Strong demand in FP&A, sales analysis, and financial forecasting roles.

3. SAP BTP (Business Technology Platform)

- *Why*: Central to SAP's future – supports extensibility, analytics, and AI/ML use cases.
- *Focus Areas*: Data integration, CAP (Cloud Application Programming), Fiori/UI5, Workflows.
- *Value*: Helps FICO consultants become solution architects and technical enablers.

4. SAP Signavio (Process Intelligence & Optimization)

- *Why*: Drives business process excellence using modeling and real-time process mining.
- *Focus Areas*: Financial process modeling, simulation, and optimization.
- *Value*: Enhances your ability to consult on process transformation projects.

5. SAP Analytics Cloud (SAC)

- *Why*: FICO consultants can transition into financial planning and reporting roles.
- *Focus Areas*: Planning models, stories (dashboards), integration with S/4HANA.
- *Value*: Adds strategic reporting and FP&A capability to your toolkit.

6. SAP S/4HANA Central Finance (cFIN)

- **Why**: Centralizes finance data from multiple systems into one source of truth.
- **Focus Areas**: Replication of FI/CO data, AIF monitoring, mapping of source systems.
- **Value**: Ideal for consultants working with large, global enterprise clients.

7. SAP GRC (Governance, Risk, and Compliance)

- **Why**: Supports compliance and internal control in financial systems.
- **Focus Areas**: Access Control, Risk Management, Process Control.
- **Value**: High relevance in regulated industries like banking, pharma, and utilities.

8. SAP and Generative AI (SAP Joule & AI CoPilot)

- **Why**: SAP is embedding GenAI into core products like S/4HANA and SAC.
- **Focus Areas**: Use of SAP's Joule AI assistant, scenario-based AI modeling, BTP AI services.
- **Value**: Future-proof skill with rising demand for AI-powered finance automation and insights.

SAP Finance is no longer limited to transactional accounting. With the move toward **S/4HANA**, **Cloud**, **AI**, and **Integrated Analytics**, today's FICO consultants must evolve into digital finance strategists. By pursuing one or more of the above specialization areas, you will not only broaden your technical capabilities but also position yourself as a trusted advisor in the rapidly transforming world of intelligent finance.

Now, finally, without any further delay, let's move on to the next milestone in **Unit 3**. After building a strong foundation in SAP Finance fundamentals, it's time to shift our focus to practical solutions—and in today's world, that solution is **AI**. Artificial Intelligence is transforming finance by enabling automation, real-time insights, and smarter decision-making. **In Unit 3, we will be exploring *The Solution: Leveraging Generative AI in SAP*** to understand how FICO consultants can adapt and grow with these cutting-edge tools.

UNIT 3

The Solution – Leveraging
Generative AI in SAP

In the first two units of this book, we laid a strong foundation.

In Unit 1, we explored the business challenges enterprises face today — from manual finance processes and disconnected systems to the growing need for intelligent automation, real-time insights, and agile decision-making. We discussed the urgency to adapt, innovate, and move beyond traditional ERP landscapes.

Unit 2 provided a deep dive into SAP Finance, examining how core modules, integration touchpoints, and business processes like Order-to-Cash (O2C), Procure-to-Pay (P2P), and Record-to-Report (R2R) form the digital backbone of modern enterprises. We explored the current state of SAP implementations, production support, financial closing, and the day-to-day realities of finance operations in a connected ecosystem.

Now, in **Unit 3,** we move into the heart of transformation — **the solution.**

This unit marks the beginning of a forward-looking journey into how Generative AI is set to redefine the SAP landscape. The rise of Large Language Models (LLMs) and the integration of Generative AI capabilities across SAP's toolsets are no longer just futuristic concepts — they are real, scalable, and ready to be implemented today.

We'll begin with the fundamentals — introducing Generative AI and its place in the broader AI ecosystem, followed by a walkthrough of the technologies that power it, including LLMs. Then, we'll delve into SAP's own offerings — SAP Business AI, SAP Generative AI Hub, and SAP AI Core — understanding their architecture, capabilities, and potential use cases.

This unit is practical, hands-on, and solution-driven. It's about tools, techniques, and real-world application. It's about helping you answer the question: How can I apply Generative AI within SAP to drive value in finance and beyond?

Whether you're a consultant, business user, data analyst, or tech strategist, this unit equips you with the clarity, context, and confidence to begin your journey with Generative AI in the SAP ecosystem.

Let's unlock the future — one intelligent solution at a time.

CHAPTER 1

Introduction to Generative AI and the Generative AI Landscape

Before We Begin

In this chapter, we're not diving too deep into the technical intricacies of Generative AI. Instead, we're laying the foundation—touching the surface to get a high-level understanding of key concepts, technologies, and the evolving landscape.

Think of this as your orientation session into the world of Gen AI. The following chapters in this unit will gradually become more technical and detailed, expanding on the ideas introduced here—diving into architectures, tools, SAP-supported platforms, and enterprise-grade applications.

This unit is inspired by the Generative AI learning path SAP recommends for developers and consultants. It is designed not only for individual professionals looking to upskill—but also for SAP consultants, business teams, architects, and innovation leaders working to integrate Generative AI into existing landscapes or build new AI-driven solutions from the ground up.

Whether you're a SAP professional, functional or technical consultant, developer, architect, project manager, or simply a tech enthusiast—this chapter is your first step into a transformative space where AI meets enterprise innovation, and where business processes are no longer just automated—but intelligently augmented and co-created with AI.

As the name of this unit suggests, it aims to equip you with a structured understanding and practical path for exploring Generative AI-powered enterprise solutions—grounded in the SAP ecosystem. From tools like SAP AI Core and SAP AI Launchpad to techniques like prompt engineering, orchestration, and RAG, you'll see how modern SAP landscapes can be extended and enhanced with the power of Gen AI.

This unit will guide you to not only understand Gen AI but to begin thinking about how to design, implement, and govern Gen AI-powered use cases that are reliable, scalable, and business-aligned.

Let's begin the journey.

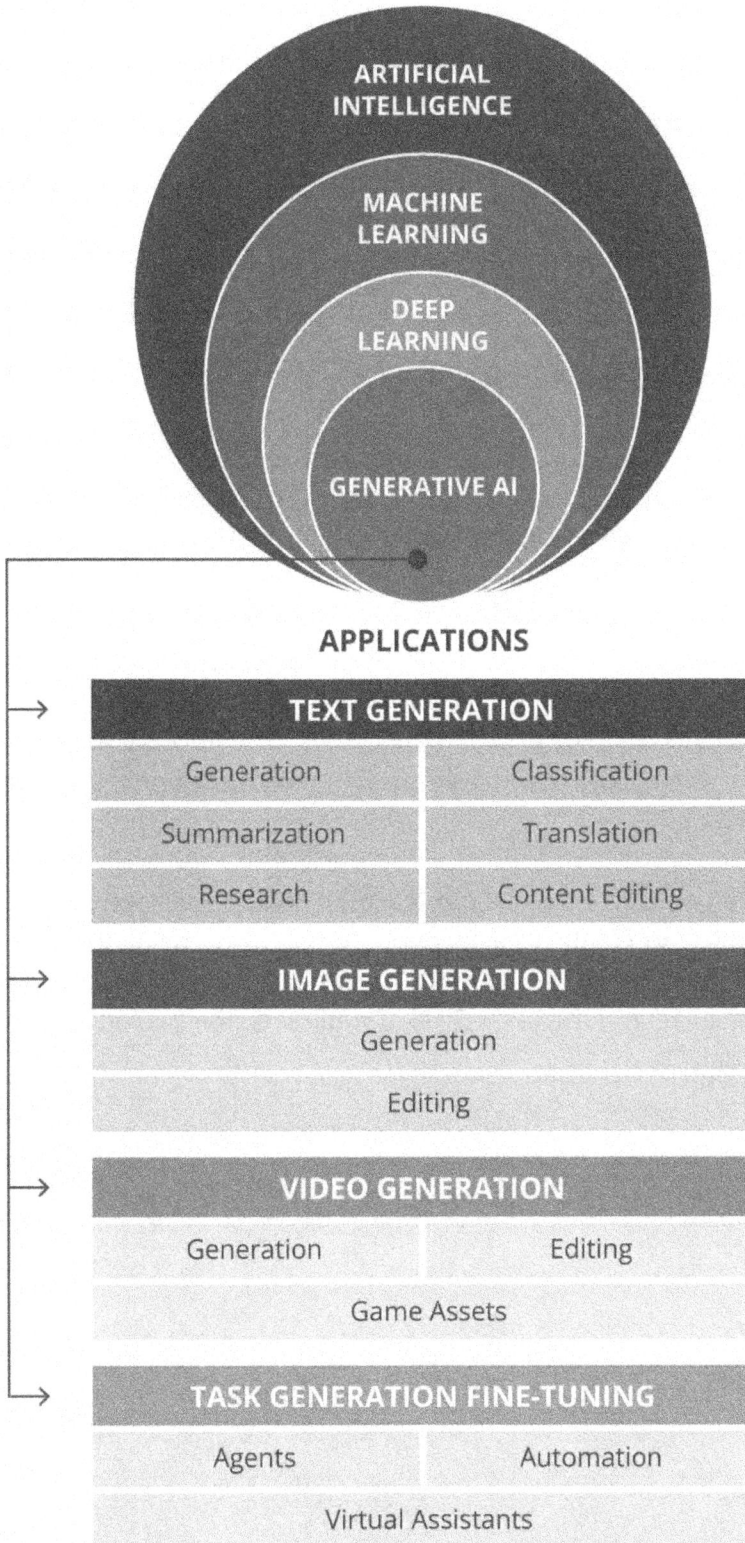

ARTIFICIAL
INTELLIGENCE

MACHINE
LEARNING

DEEP
LEARNING

GENERATIVE AI

APPLICATIONS

TEXT GENERATION

Generation	Classification
Summarization	Translation
Research	Content Editing

IMAGE GENERATION

Generation

Editing

VIDEO GENERATION

Generation	Editing

Game Assets

TASK GENERATION FINE-TUNING

Agents	Automation

Virtual Assistants

In 2022, a piece of digital art titled Théâtre D'opéra Spatial won first place in a fine art competition. The twist? It wasn't painted by a human. It was generated by an AI model known as Midjourney.

This incident stirred a global conversation. Could machines now be artists? Could they write poems, craft business strategies, develop apps, and analyze financial statements? The answer lies in a revolutionary field within Artificial Intelligence—**Generative AI.**

What is Generative AI?

Generative AI (Gen AI) is a groundbreaking subset of Artificial Intelligence that empowers machines to **create**—not just analyze or automate. It generates **text, images, audio, video, and even code** by learning from massive datasets and identifying patterns and relationships within them.

Unlike traditional AI systems that follow rule-based logic, generative AI systems **learn from existing data and create something new**. They simulate human creativity and language understanding, allowing machines to compose emails, generate legal documents, draw artwork, write stories, summarize reports, and even mimic human conversations.

At its core, Generative AI leverages **deep learning**—specifically **neural networks**—to power this ability to create. The technology behind it includes **transformers**, **autoencoders**, **latent diffusion models**, and most popularly, **Large Language Models (LLMs)** such as OpenAI's GPT, Google's Gemini, Meta's LLaMA, and Anthropic's Claude.

GenAI Framework

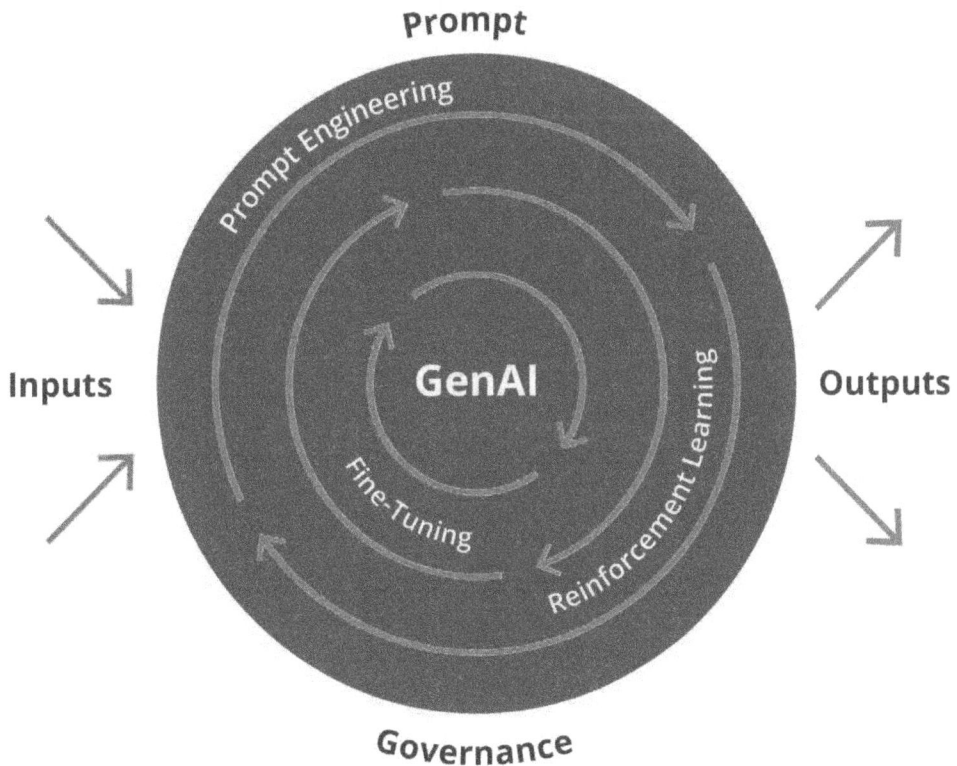

Key Concepts Behind Generative AI

To understand Gen AI, let's first break down the key elements that make it possible:

- **Artificial Intelligence (AI):** The broader discipline of making machines exhibit human-like intelligence.
- **Machine Learning (ML):** A subset of AI where machines learn from data without being explicitly programmed.
  - **Supervised Learning:** The model is trained on labeled data.
  - **Unsupervised Learning:** The model finds patterns in unlabeled data.
- **Deep Learning:** A specialized area of ML using layered neural networks to simulate the human brain.

- **Artificial Neural Networks (ANNs):** Multi-layered networks that process information and identify complex relationships.
- **Generative Models:** These models are trained to generate new outputs (text, images, etc.) based on patterns in the training data.
- **Stochastic Models:** The outputs are probabilistic, meaning the same input may yield different outputs each time.

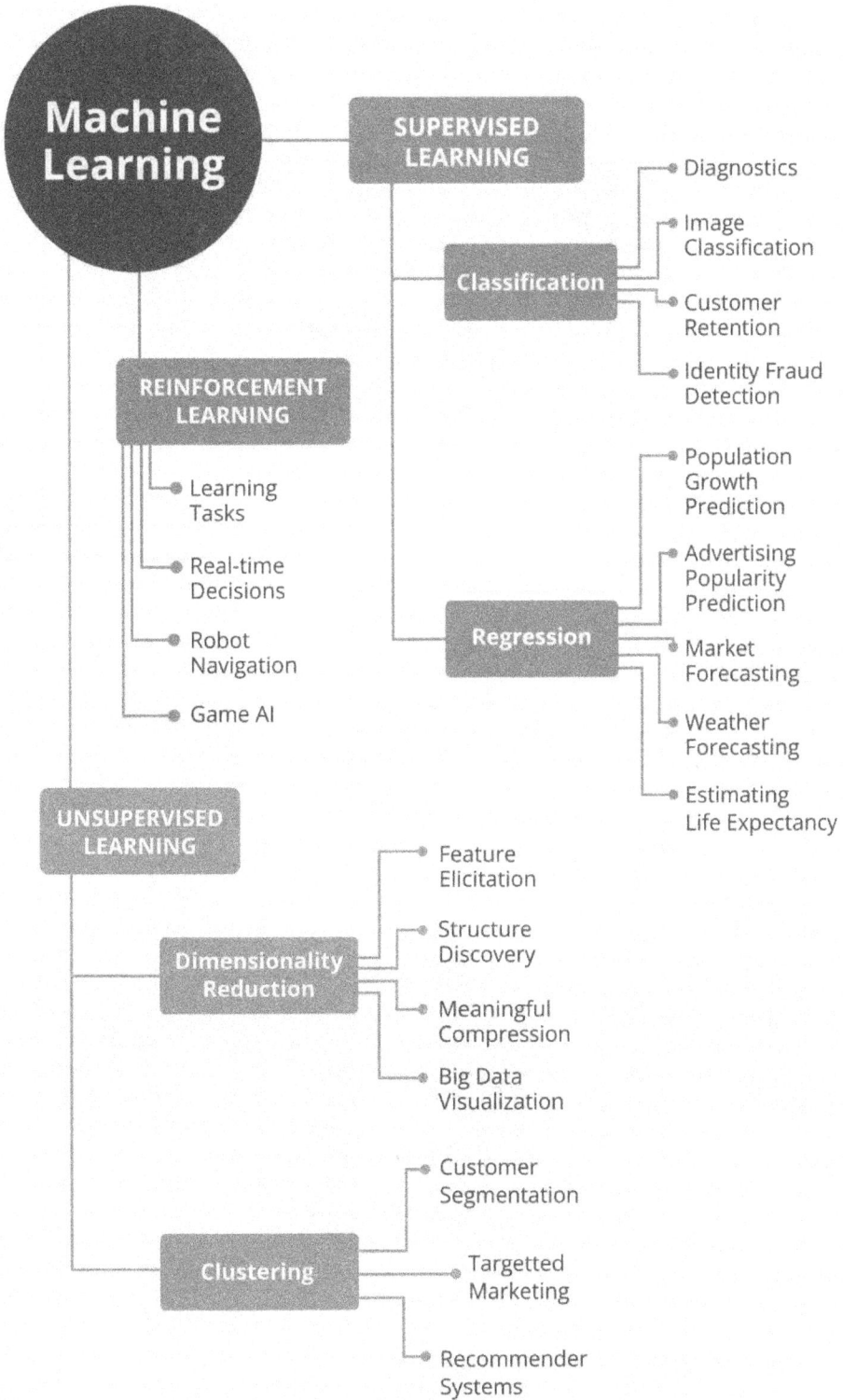

Machine Learning

SUPERVISED LEARNING

Classification
- Diagnostics
- Image Classification
- Customer Retention
- Identity Fraud Detection

Regression
- Population Growth Prediction
- Advertising Popularity Prediction
- Market Forecasting
- Weather Forecasting
- Estimating Life Expectancy

REINFORCEMENT LEARNING
- Learning Tasks
- Real-time Decisions
- Robot Navigation
- Game AI

UNSUPERVISED LEARNING

Dimensionality Reduction
- Feature Elicitation
- Structure Discovery
- Meaningful Compression
- Big Data Visualization

Clustering
- Customer Segmentation
- Targetted Marketing
- Recommender Systems

7 steps of machine learning

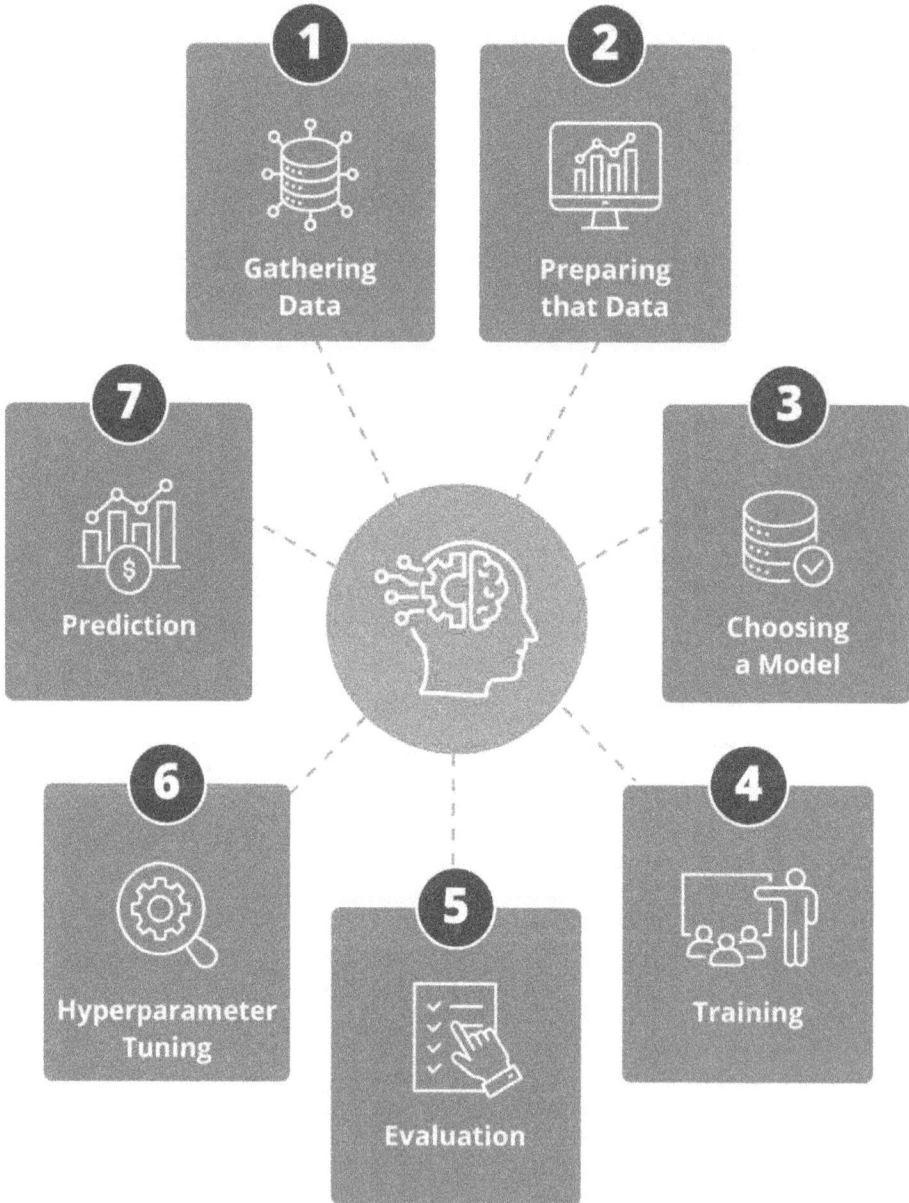

1. Gathering Data
2. Preparing that Data
3. Choosing a Model
4. Training
5. Evaluation
6. Hyperparameter Tuning
7. Prediction

How Does Generative AI Work?

1. **Training Phase:** The model learns patterns from a vast dataset. For LLMs, this could be hundreds of gigabytes or even terabytes of text.

2. **Prompt Phase:** A user gives an input or *prompt* (e.g., "Write a business plan").

3. **Inference Phase:** The model generates new content based on its training.

4. **Fine-tuning/Adaptation:** The model can be further specialized using custom data to perform better at specific tasks.

3 STEPS HOW
Generative AI Works

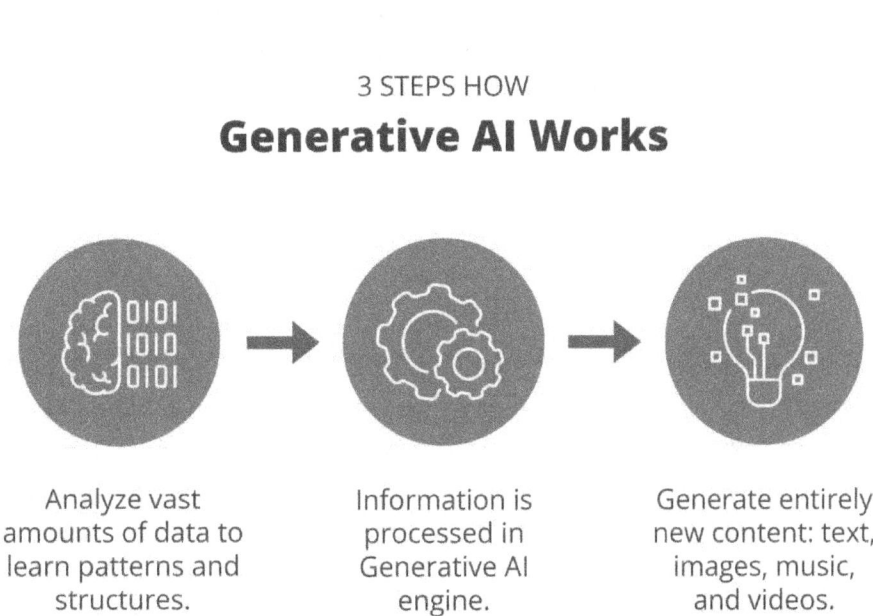

| Analyze vast amounts of data to learn patterns and structures. | Information is processed in Generative AI engine. | Generate entirely new content: text, images, music, and videos. |

The Generative AI Landscape

Generative AI is no longer a futuristic concept or a niche tool used only in research labs. It has rapidly evolved into a foundational technology that's reshaping how businesses think about automation, creativity, and problem-solving.

Across industries — from healthcare and finance to retail, manufacturing, and software — generative AI is driving a new wave of innovation. Companies are using it to generate content, summarize data, draft reports, enhance customer experiences, write code, and even simulate business scenarios. What used to take hours of manual effort can now be achieved in minutes, with AI assisting or even taking the lead.

This shift isn't just about speed or convenience — it's about unlocking new capabilities. Teams can now explore ideas, test strategies, and build solutions that weren't practical or even possible before. And with tools becoming more accessible through APIs, low-code platforms, and built-in assistants, generative AI is no longer reserved for technical experts. Business users, analysts, and consultants are increasingly finding ways to tap into its potential.

At the same time, the landscape is still evolving. New models are emerging, standards are being shaped, and questions around trust, bias, privacy, and governance are becoming central to the conversation. Navigating this space requires not only enthusiasm for what AI can do, but also a thoughtful approach to how it should be used — especially in enterprise environments.

This chapter aims to unpack where generative AI is now, where it's headed, and how organizations like SAP are shaping its future by embedding it into real-world tools and workflows.

As this landscape grows, the most exciting part isn't just the technology itself — it's what people choose to do with it. Whether you're a developer building new features, a business user exploring automation, or a strategist rethinking entire workflows, generative AI is now part of your toolbox. The opportunity is wide open: to experiment, to challenge old assumptions, and to bring fresh ideas to life in ways that were never possible before. The question isn't if you'll engage with AI — it's how creatively and responsibly you'll use it.

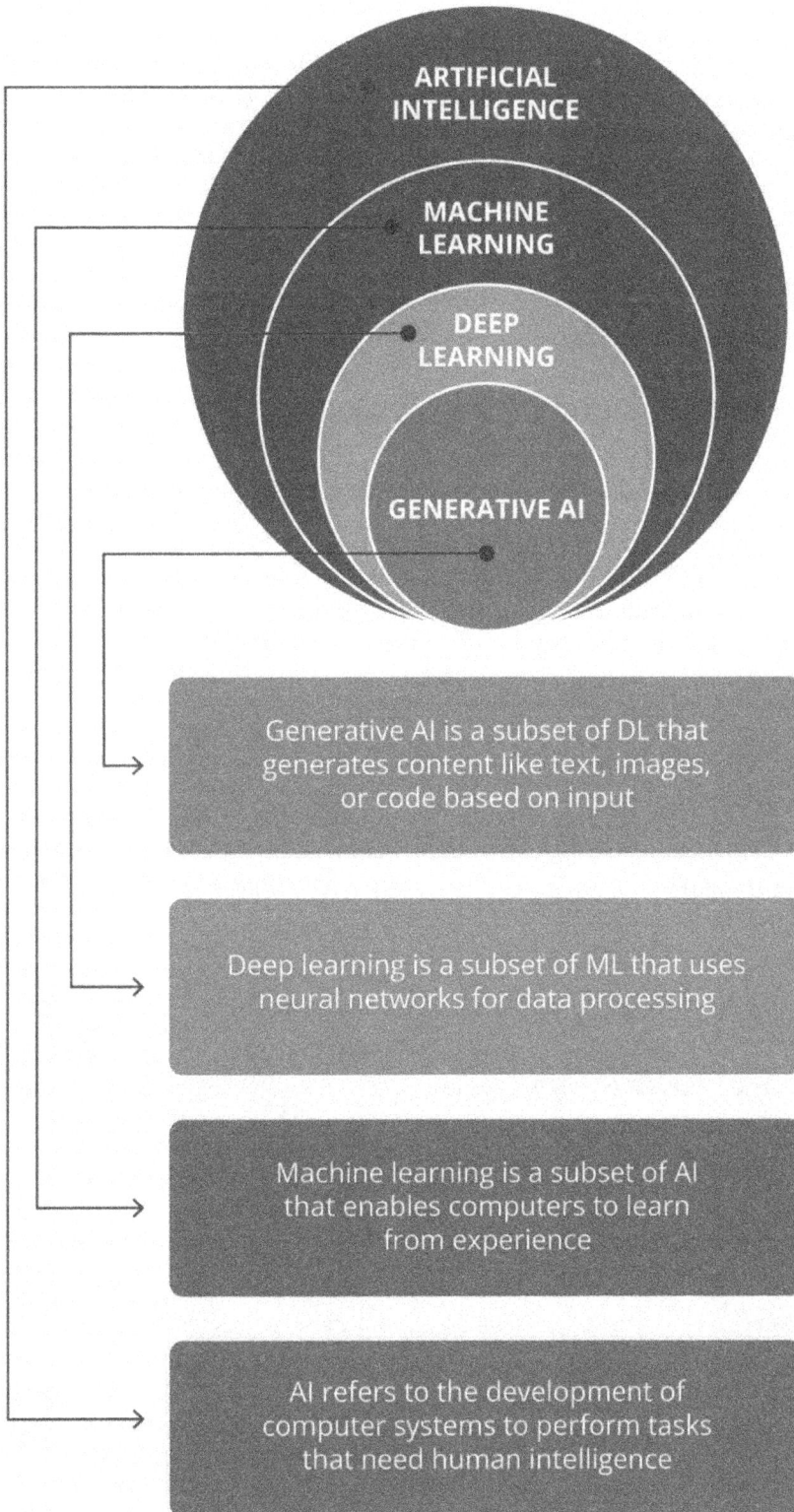

ARTIFICIAL
INTELLIGENCE

MACHINE
LEARNING

DEEP
LEARNING

GENERATIVE AI

Generative AI is a subset of DL that
generates content like text, images,
or code based on input

Deep learning is a subset of ML that uses
neural networks for data processing

Machine learning is a subset of AI
that enables computers to learn
from experience

AI refers to the development of
computer systems to perform tasks
that need human intelligence

1. Core Technologies

- Large Language Models (LLMs): These are transformer-based models trained on huge corpora of text and code (e.g., GPT-4, Claude, LLaMA).
- Multimodal Models: Capable of handling multiple types of inputs such as text + image (e.g., Gemini, GPT-4V).
- Latent Diffusion Models: Used for image generation (e.g., Stable Diffusion, DALL·E).
- Autoencoders: Used in compressing and reconstructing data in generation tasks.

2. Open vs. Closed Source Ecosystem

- Open Source Models: Like BLOOM, Mistral, LLaMA (Meta), Falcon – often funded by public or community organizations, transparent, and free to use.
- Closed Source Models: Like GPT (OpenAI), Claude (Anthropic) – developed by private companies with proprietary code, often paid services.

3. Infrastructure & Tools

- LLM Orchestration Frameworks: Agent-based systems that use tools/APIs to complete complex tasks.
- Vector Databases (e.g., Pinecone, FAISS): Store and retrieve semantically encoded knowledge for fast, context-aware searches.
- Prompt Engineering: Crafting precise prompts to influence model output.
- Retrieval Augmented Generation (RAG): Embedding domain-specific knowledge and combining it with generative power.
- Fine-tuning & Customization: Adapting foundational models to enterprise needs or industry-specific tasks.

4. Use Cases Across Industries

- Banking & Finance: Fraud detection, report generation, risk analysis.
- Healthcare: Medical imaging, drug discovery, patient communication.
- Retail & E-Commerce: Virtual shopping assistants, personalized recommendations, product design.
- Manufacturing: Predictive maintenance, quality control, design simulation.
- Education: AI tutors, content creation, adaptive testing.

5. Governance, Ethics & Safety

- **Human-in-the-loop (HITL):** Ensures human oversight for decision-making.
- **Output Validation & Red Teaming:** Cross-checking for accuracy, bias, hallucinations.
- **AI Ethics & Compliance:** Fairness, explainability, transparency.
- **Continuous Monitoring:** Regular feedback loops to improve performance and safety.

The Mindset Shift: AI-First Strategy

Generative AI isn't just a tool—it's a new mindset. Companies are now adopting **AI-first strategies**, where AI becomes the foundation of digital transformation. This shift requires:

- Building data pipelines.
- Redesigning business processes.
- Embedding AI in every layer of technology and operations.
- Training teams and developing governance frameworks.

This transition is similar to how businesses once moved from on-premise software to cloud-based platforms. Except now, the scale and speed are unprecedented.

SAP and Generative AI

SAP is actively integrating Generative AI into its suite of offerings. Here are key innovations:

- SAP Joule: An AI-powered assistant embedded in SAP products.
- SAP AI Core & AI Launchpad: Platforms to build, manage, and deploy AI models.
- SAP Build with Gen AI: Low-code tools enhanced by AI for app creation.
- SAP BTP + Gen AI: Leveraging AI capabilities within SAP's Business Technology Platform.
- Partnerships: Collaborations with Microsoft (Copilot for SAP), Google Cloud, and others to extend AI functionality.

A complete set of services for AI developers on SAP BTP

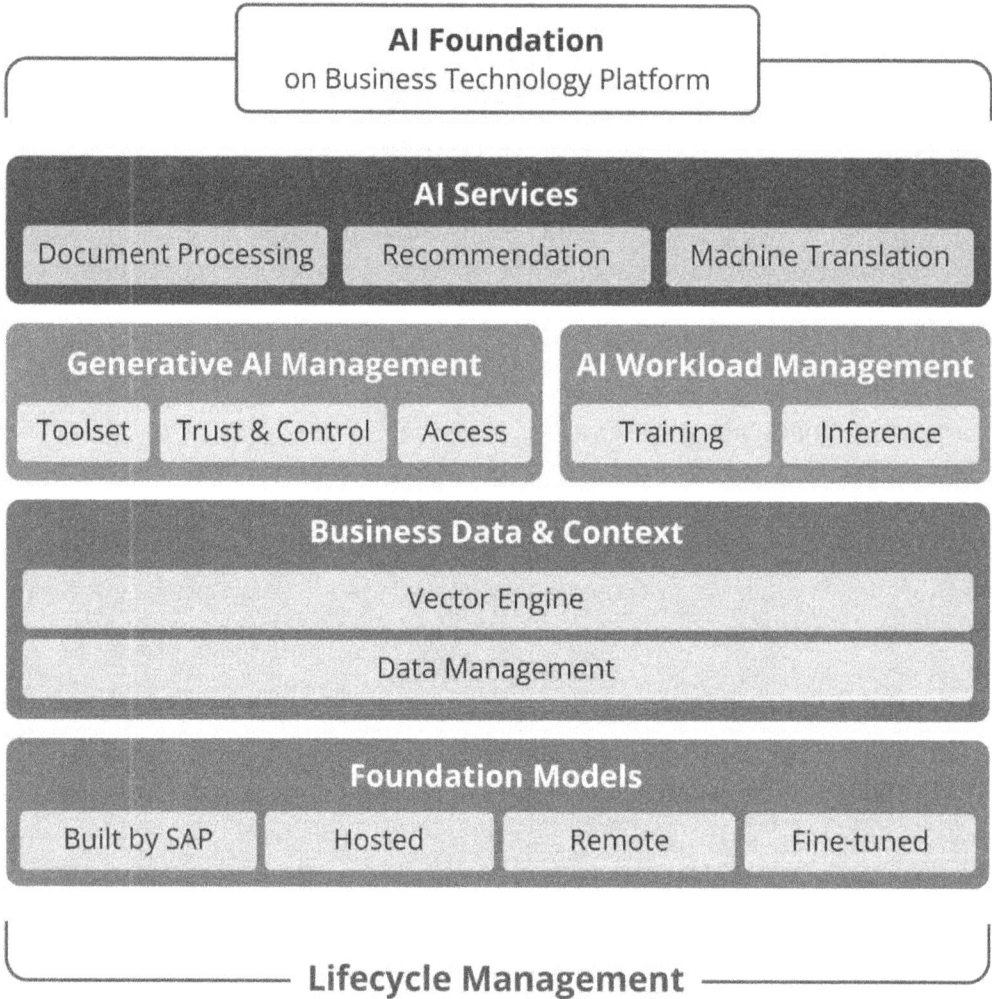

AI Foundation
on Business Technology Platform

AI Services

Document Processing | Recommendation | Machine Translation

Generative AI Management

Toolset | Trust & Control | Access

AI Workload Management

Training | Inference

Business Data & Context

Vector Engine

Data Management

Foundation Models

Built by SAP | Hosted | Remote | Fine-tuned

Lifecycle Management

Limitations and Challenges of Generative AI

While powerful, Gen AI comes with limitations:

- Hallucinations: Models can produce incorrect or fabricated content.
- Bias: AI inherits biases from training data.
- Opacity: It's hard to interpret why a model generates certain outputs.
- Computational Cost: Training and running large models is expensive.
- Privacy Risks: Use of sensitive data may raise compliance concerns.

Businesses must address these issues through:

- Robust AI governance
- Ethical frameworks
- Human-in-the-loop strategies
- Continuous validation and testing

Mapping Generative AI to SAP Roles

Role	Gen AI Benefits/Opportunities
SAP Functional Consultant	Auto-generate test scripts, reports, configure documentation
Technical Consultant	Assist in coding, integration, troubleshooting
Developer	Accelerate app building, backend logic, UI prototyping
Architect	Design AI-first enterprise solutions and integrations
Business User	Query SAP data in natural language, personalized dashboards
Project Manager	Use AI-generated insights for decision support and resource planning

The Road Ahead: From Foundations to Mastery

Generative AI has ushered in an era where the boundaries of human and machine creativity are blurred. However, to truly unlock its potential, we must understand its inner workings—particularly the **foundational models** that power LLMs, and how they learn, think, and generate.

In the next chapter, we'll explore the **Foundations of LLMs**, including how they are trained, what makes them powerful, and how businesses can harness them responsibly and effectively.

What You Just Learned

- **Generative AI** creates new content (text, images, code) using deep learning and pattern recognition.

- It operates in phases: **Training**, **Prompting**, **Inference**, and optional **Fine-tuning**.

- Gen AI is now mainstream, used in **finance, healthcare, retail, manufacturing, and education**.

- Core technologies include **LLMs**, **multimodal models**, **diffusion models**, and **autoencoders**.

- Tools like **prompt engineering**, **RAG**, **vector databases**, and **model orchestration** enhance Gen AI performance.

- **Open-source** (e.g., Mistral) and **closed-source** (e.g., GPT-4) models shape today's ecosystem.

- **Governance** is essential—addressing bias, hallucination, data privacy, and ethical use.

- SAP's AI-first approach embeds Gen AI into products like **SAP Joule**, **AI Core**, and **BTP**.

- SAP roles—from functional consultants to project managers—can leverage Gen AI for automation and insights.

- The future isn't if you'll use Gen AI—it's how wisely you'll integrate it.

CHAPTER 2

Fundamentals of Large Language Models (LLMs)

Have you ever wondered how ChatGPT crafts answers, how AI tools summarize lengthy reports in seconds, or how virtual assistants understand our questions so naturally? Behind these everyday AI marvels lie the powerful engines called Large Language Models (LLMs). They're not just buzzwords—they're transforming industries, enhancing productivity, and reshaping how we interact with technology.

In this chapter, we will break down the essentials of LLMs. Whether you're a business consultant, developer, or simply curious, by the end of this chapter, you'll gain a solid understanding of what these models are, how they function, and their strategic role in the world of Generative AI.

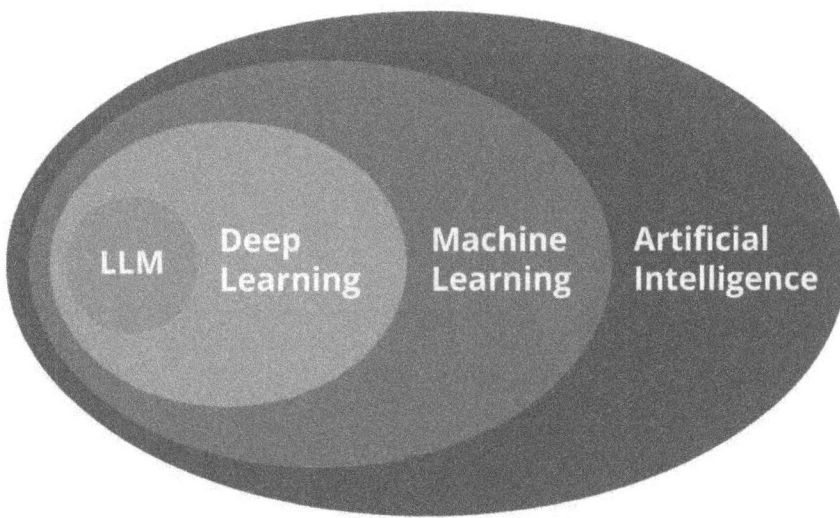

Chapter Overview

In this chapter, we'll explore the world of Large Language Models (LLMs) — what they are, how they work, and how organizations like SAP are putting them to use for real business impact.

We'll walk through four key areas, each designed to build your understanding and practical skills:

1. **Navigating Large Language Models: SAP's Perspective**
   Understand how SAP views and applies LLMs within its ecosystem, with a focus on the SAFE (Secure, Accountable, Fair, and Explainable) AI framework.

2. **Product Development with LLMs: SAP Use Case Playbook**
   Learn how to identify, design, and develop AI-powered features and workflows using LLMs in an enterprise setting.

3. **Techniques to Maximize LLM Performance for Specific Use Cases**
   Discover actionable techniques for improving the relevance, accuracy, and efficiency of LLM outputs across different business functions.

4. **Optimizing LLM Performance: Best Practices and Strategies**
   Explore strategies for scaling LLM use responsibly — from tuning models to evaluating results and aligning with governance standards.

4 Types of Large Language Models

Fine-Tuned or Domain-Specific Models

Multimodal Model

Zero-shot Model

Language Representation Model

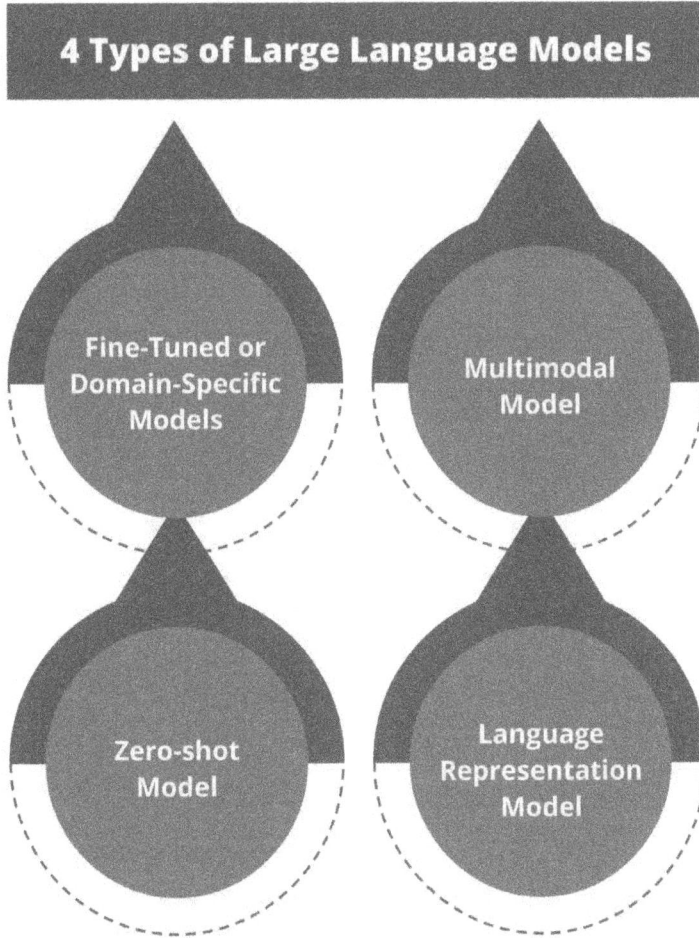

By the end of this chapter, you'll have a solid foundation in how LLMs are transforming enterprise software — especially within SAP's Business AI strategy — and how to start thinking about use cases that matter in your own role or organization. Let's dive in.

Part 1: Navigating Large Language Models

To truly understand how Large Language Models (LLMs) power Generative AI, especially within enterprise ecosystems like SAP, we must first break down what LLMs are, how they function, and why they matter.

SAP, as a pioneer in enterprise software, has embraced LLMs not as standalone tools but as integrated components of its broader AI-driven strategy. From the SAP AI Core to the Generative AI Hub, LLMs are helping reshape how businesses operate— unlocking automation, intelligence, and personalization at scale.

Let's unpack the key elements that define and drive large language models.

What Are Large Language Models?

Large Language Models are advanced neural networks trained on vast quantities of text data. Their core strength lies in their ability to understand, generate, and manipulate human language with an impressive level of sophistication. At the heart of these models lies a breakthrough architecture known as the Transformer, which enables deep contextual understanding and efficient parallel processing of data.

Key Components of LLMs

Training Data

LLMs are trained on massive datasets that span books, articles, websites, codebases, and more. The scale of this training allows them to learn grammar, facts, reasoning patterns, and even writing styles. These models often ingest hundreds of billions—sometimes trillions—of tokens (words or word fragments).

Model Architecture

LLMs use **neural networks**, specifically the **Transformer architecture**, which allows them to process text in parallel rather than sequentially. This design significantly enhances speed and performance, especially in large-scale tasks like translation, summarization, or question answering.

Training Processes

Most LLMs are trained using **unsupervised learning**, meaning they learn patterns without needing labeled data. They predict the next word in a sentence based on context, gradually learning to generate coherent and contextually appropriate text.

Scale

The "large" in Large Language Model isn't just marketing—it reflects the model's complexity. LLMs can have **hundreds of billions of parameters**, where each parameter is a piece of learned information. The more parameters, the richer the model's understanding and output capabilities.

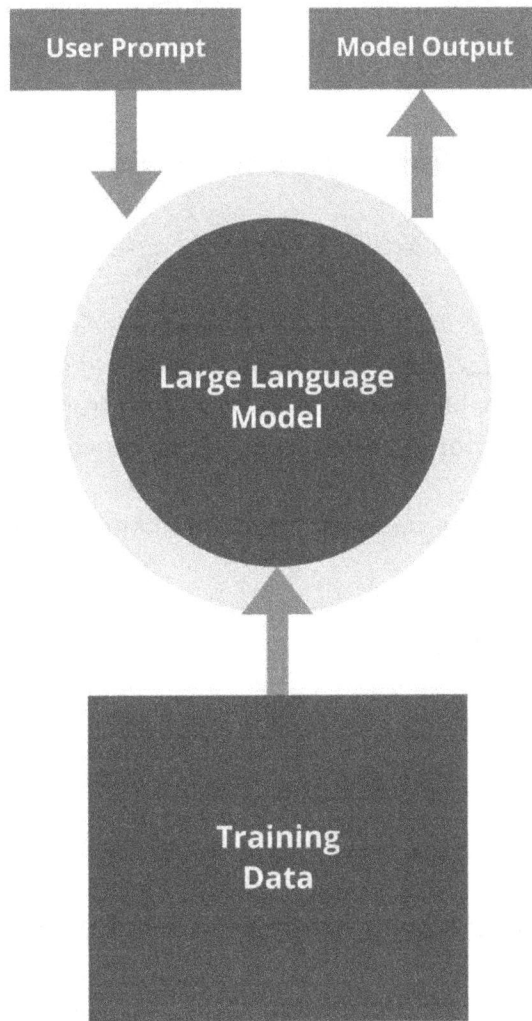

Applications of LLMs

The capabilities of LLMs span a wide array of real-world use cases:

- Text Generation & Summarization
- Code Generation & Assistance
- Document Search & Retrieval
- Chatbots & Virtual Assistants
- Sentiment Analysis & Market Insights
- Business Intelligence & Automation

SAP is embedding LLM capabilities across its portfolio to help users query business data in natural language, generate reports, automate workflows, and enhance user experiences.

Benefits of LLMs in Enterprise Settings

SAP leverages LLMs to unlock significant value for businesses, including:

- **Efficiency**: Automating repetitive tasks and reducing human intervention.
- **Cost Reduction**: Lowering manual processing and support costs.
- **Data Analysis**: Enabling smarter, faster insights from unstructured data.
- **Improved Customer Experience**: Powering conversational agents and personalization.
- **Scalability**: Easily integrating across departments and geographies with consistent performance.

Challenges and Risks

Despite their power, LLMs come with risks and limitations that enterprises must manage carefully:

- **Data Privacy Concerns**: LLMs may inadvertently expose sensitive data if not handled securely.
- **Bias and Fairness**: Models may reflect societal biases found in their training data.
- **Misrepresentation of Information**: LLMs can "hallucinate" or fabricate facts, which is dangerous in business-critical scenarios.
- **Dependency**: Over-reliance on AI can reduce human oversight and domain judgment.
- **Technical Complexity**: Implementing, monitoring, and scaling LLMs requires specialized expertise and infrastructure.

SAP addresses these issues by embedding **responsible AI principles** and strong governance across its AI offerings.

SAP's Generative AI Strategy

SAP's approach to Generative AI is grounded in three pillars: Innovation, Integration, and Trust. At the center of this strategy are two key platforms:

- SAP AI Core: The engine that runs, monitors, and scales AI models, including LLMs, within SAP environments.
- SAP Generative AI Hub: A centralized gateway to access, customize, and deploy generative AI use cases tailored to SAP's business domains.

SAP focuses on blending pre-trained foundation models with enterprise context to deliver precise, reliable, and domain-specific outputs—enabling users to interact with their systems more naturally and intuitively.

Large Language Models are foundational to modern AI and are revolutionizing how we approach business challenges. With SAP's strategic integration of LLMs into its ecosystem, companies can now benefit from cutting-edge AI without compromising data privacy, scalability, or operational control. As we continue through this chapter, we'll see how SAP translates this powerful technology into practical, product-ready solutions.

Part 2: Product Development for Large Language Model Use Cases at SAP

Bringing Large Language Models (LLMs) into enterprise software isn't as simple as dropping in a chatbot or plugging in some AI tool. It's a layered, collaborative effort — and at SAP, it involves a lot of thinking upfront about what problems are actually worth solving.

Instead of chasing trends, the focus is on how AI can fit naturally into the way people already work. That means starting with real use cases, not abstract ideas — and building with input from designers, developers, consultants, customers, and more. It's less about flashy tech and more about what's practical, scalable, and genuinely helpful.

In this section, we'll take a closer look at how SAP builds AI-powered features using LLMs. You'll get a sense of:

- How an idea moves from concept to development
- Who's involved at each stage — from product teams to domain experts
- And how feedback, iteration, and business context shape the final result

The goal isn't just to launch something intelligent — it's to make sure it stays useful as people, processes, and technology evolve.

The Project Lifecycle: From Idea to Intelligent Product

Product development for LLM use cases at SAP follows a structured lifecycle. It's not just a technical effort—it's a collaborative journey between **data engineers, product managers, architects, designers, and business leaders**.

The process unfolds in **four major phases**:

1. Ideation Phase
2. Validation Phase
3. Realization & Production Phase
4. Operations & Continuous Improvement Phase

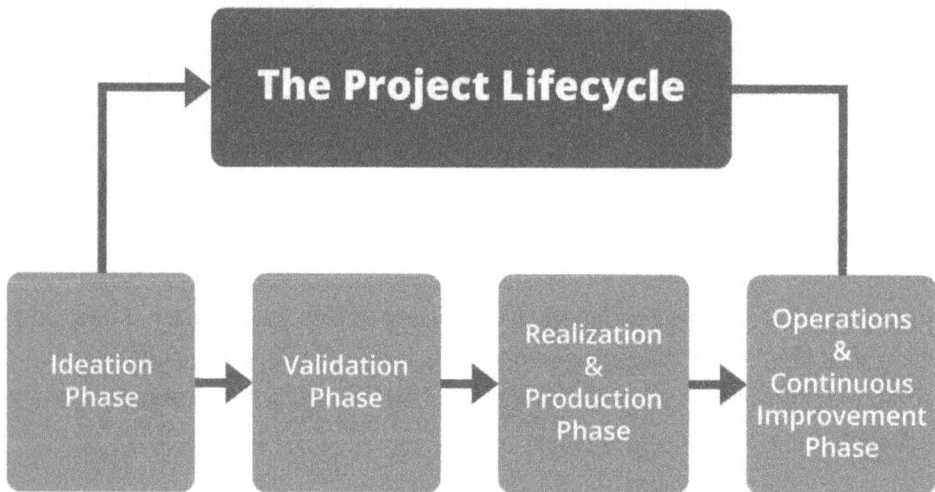

Each phase plays a critical role in shaping and refining LLM-powered solutions.

1. Ideation Phase: Laying the Groundwork

The process begins with brainstorming and exploration. Here, teams assess where LLMs can make an impact—automating tasks, enhancing insights, or transforming user experience.

The ideation phase is where teams step back and explore opportunities through a business-first lens. It's less about the AI itself and more about understanding which problems are worth solving — and whether LLMs are the right fit. The output of this phase is usually a shortlist of potential use cases, each with a rough idea of the value it could bring and the complexity involved. From there, the team narrows it down to a few that are feasible, valuable, and aligned with business goals.

For example, a finance team might be drowning in unstructured data from invoices or contracts. An LLM could help extract key terms, classify documents, or even flag anomalies — but only if it's addressing a real bottleneck in the workflow.

This step isn't just about creativity — it's also about restraint. Not every process needs AI, and part of the groundwork is knowing when to say no.

Key Activities:

- **Familiarization**: Teams study LLM capabilities, SAP AI Core, available models, and recent advancements in generative AI.
- **Customer Collaboration**: Early discussions with customers help define real-world problems and potential value. This ensures ideas are rooted in actual business needs, not just innovation for innovation's sake.

This phase is where feasibility and ambition converge. Questions asked include:

- Can LLMs reduce processing time?
- Could natural language interaction improve system accessibility?
- Is this aligned with SAP's AI ethics and governance standards?

The output is a shortlist of promising use case ideas that proceed to the next stage.

2. Validation Phase: Testing for Feasibility, Desirability & Viability

Once an idea looks promising on paper, it moves into the validation phase — where the team takes a closer, more critical look at whether it's actually worth pursuing.

This step is all about asking three key questions: Is it technically feasible? Will users actually want or use it (desirability)? Does it make business sense (viability)?

- Feasibility: Can the LLM handle the task with available data, and can it integrate with existing systems securely and efficiently?

- Desirability: Do users actually need this, and will it improve their experience or just add friction?
- Viability: Does it deliver real business value and scale well enough to justify the investment?

Validation doesn't require a fully working product — it just needs enough clarity and testing to confidently say: Yes, this is a problem worth solving, and we have a clear, realistic path forward.

Often, this phase ends with a go/no-go decision — or with refinements to the original idea to better meet all three criteria.

Key Activities:

- Use Case Iteration: Early prototypes or mockups are created to test assumptions.
- Technical Evaluation: Can the proposed use case be supported with SAP's existing infrastructure, such as SAP BTP or SAP AI Core? What data is required? Is the latency acceptable?
- Commercial Evaluation: Is there a market for this solution? How does it align with SAP's portfolio strategy?

This phase often includes pilot testing, where limited features are released to a small group of users for early feedback. Cross-functional teams get involved here:

- **Data Engineers** explore model integrations.
- **Product Owners** draft the strategic vision.
- **Solution Managers** analyze whether it aligns with the business roadmap.

If a use case proves successful, it graduates to realization.

3. Realization & Production Phase: Bringing Ideas to Life

Now the real engineering begins. The chosen LLM use cases are built into production-grade products that integrate seamlessly into SAP environments. Once a use case has passed validation, it moves into realization — where ideas are transformed into real, working features.

Key Activities:

- **Use Case Finalization**: Scope, functionality, and KPIs are clearly defined.
- **Technical Finalization**: The selected LLM (e.g., OpenAI, Falcon, SAP-trained models) is integrated using SAP BTP. Security, scalability, and infrastructure compatibility are ensured.
- **Commercial Finalization**: Pricing models, licensing, and go-to-market strategies are finalized.

This is where product teams, AI engineers, designers, and SAP experts come together to build production-ready solutions. It's not just about writing code; it's about aligning AI logic with business rules, user flows, and system architecture — especially within the complex landscape of SAP environments.

Development typically involves:

Data preparation and model integration – ensuring the LLM is trained or fine-tuned on the right context and connected to the necessary backend systems.

Workflow design – mapping how the AI feature fits into existing processes without disrupting what's already working.

User experience design – keeping things intuitive, whether through Joule-style prompts, embedded recommendations, or behind-the-scenes automation.

Once the initial version is ready, it goes through rounds of testing — including performance, security, compliance, and user acceptance — before being deployed to production.

But launch isn't the finish line. Real-world use often reveals edge cases, new requirements, or unexpected user behavior. So, post-launch monitoring and iteration are critical to ensure the solution remains stable, relevant, and valuable over time.

This phase is where all the planning and collaboration start to pay off — turning an abstract AI concept into a tool that's actually helping people work smarter.

4. Operations & Continuous Improvement: Post-Launch Innovation

Releasing an LLM-powered solution into production is a major milestone — but it's not the end of the journey. In fact, it's often where the most meaningful work begins.

This phase focuses on **maintaining, monitoring, and continuously improving** the product based on how it performs in the real world. Large Language Models behave differently depending on the context, the data they're working with, and how users interact with them. That means constant observation is needed to ensure the solution remains effective, safe, and aligned with its original goals.

Key activities during this phase include:

- **Performance monitoring:** Tracking how the LLM is responding — Is it accurate? Is latency acceptable? Are users getting consistent results?

- **Feedback loops:** Gathering insights from end users, stakeholders, and usage data to spot pain points, misunderstandings, or gaps in functionality.

- **Model refinement:** Fine-tuning prompts, updating training data, or adjusting parameters to improve results and reduce issues like hallucination or bias.

- **Governance and compliance checks:** Ensuring data privacy, security, and ethical AI use — especially as models interact with sensitive business information.

- **Scalability efforts:** Expanding to other regions, languages, or business units once the initial use case proves successful.

The goal here isn't just to keep things running — it's to make them better over time. AI is dynamic by nature, and continuous improvement is what turns a good tool into a trusted part of daily business operations.

Key Activities:

Operations: Monitoring performance, usage, latency, and reliability across various regions and customer types.

Continuous Improvement: Collecting user feedback, analyzing failure cases, and retraining models or refining prompts based on emerging needs.

UX teams play a key role in this phase — by closely observing how users interact with the product, they help shape improvements that make it more intuitive, responsive, and effective with every iteration.

Integrating LLMs into Business Applications: SAP's Methodology

Integration is where theory meets reality — where promising AI ideas are embedded into real workflows and systems. At SAP, this process isn't rushed or one-size-fits-all. It's a step-by-step methodology that balances technical precision with design thinking to ensure LLMs don't just work in isolation, but actually enhance the way people get things done.

It involves aligning AI capabilities with business logic, user expectations, and system architecture — always with the goal of creating tools that are useful, usable, and trustworthy in everyday business contexts.

Here's how SAP executes it:

1. **Needs Assessment**: Identify what the business is trying to achieve—automation, insights, faster customer service, etc.

2. **Use of SAP BTP Frameworks**: Leverage SAP Business Technology Platform (BTP) for secure, scalable, and compliant AI development.

3. **Model Framework Selection**: Choose the right LLM—GPT, SAP AI models, or open-source models—based on latency, privacy, and domain needs.

4. **Use Case Identification**: Match the selected model with applicable scenarios—finance analytics, HR onboarding assistants, supply chain query bots, etc.

5. **Complementary Strengths**: Use LLMs to enhance, not replace, rule-based systems or traditional machine learning.

6. **Tailored Solutions**: Customize the interaction logic, prompts, and data pathways to the specific business process and user persona.

By blending strong engineering with thoughtful design, SAP makes sure that LLM integration doesn't just add "AI for the sake of AI" — it actually improves how people work. Each feature is built with care: validated with users, tested for real-world reliability, and designed to solve specific business problems. What makes SAP's approach stand out is how cross-functional the process is — bringing together designers, developers, domain experts, and customers from start to finish. From brainstorming ideas to supporting live solutions, it's a cycle of constant learning and improvement.

In many ways, SAP's method offers a practical blueprint for how large organizations can make generative AI real — not just in labs or demos, but in daily tools that people already rely on. It's about turning complex models into simple, useful experiences that scale responsibly across the enterprise.

Part 3: Techniques to Maximize Large Language Model Performance for Specific Use Cases

Once a large language model (LLM) is integrated into an enterprise application, the next challenge is to get the best possible performance from it. Performance here doesn't just mean speed—it includes accuracy, relevance, efficiency, consistency, and contextual intelligence.

Unlike traditional software tuning, LLM optimization is rarely linear. It involves a mix of methods that need to be applied iteratively, tested frequently, and refined based on user feedback and evolving business goals.

In this part, we'll explore the most effective techniques used to maximize LLM performance, with a special focus on how SAP and enterprise-grade platforms implement these methods.

The Four Steps to Maximizing LLM Performance

Maximizing the performance of an LLM for a given use case involves four major steps:

1. Identifying the Right Techniques for the Right Use Case
2. Acknowledging Model Limitations and Addressing Them Strategically
3. Understanding Why a Use Case May Be Underperforming
4. Applying Optimization Methods Iteratively—Not Linearly

Let's unpack these systematically.

Step 1: Identify the Right Techniques for the Use Case

Every use case is different. Some require accurate document summarization, others need real-time chat capabilities, while others still focus on translating complex domain-specific queries into actionable insights. That's why choosing the right LLM technique—whether it's prompt engineering, Retrieval-Augmented Generation (RAG), or fine-tuning—is essential. For example:

- For document summarization or text generation: Prompt engineering with example phrases may be sufficient.
- For real-time customer support: Retrieval-augmented systems work better to ensure factual grounding.
- For domain-specific tone or behavior control: Fine-tuning may be the answer.

Step 2: Acknowledge Limitations and Use Advanced Techniques

LLMs are powerful but not magical. They can hallucinate, misinterpret, or overlook critical context. To overcome these challenges, advanced optimization strategies are necessary.

a. Prompt Engineering

The most accessible and flexible method for tuning LLM behavior. Prompt engineering means designing the input in such a way that it elicits the most accurate and relevant output.

Key Principles of Prompt Engineering:

- Use **clear, precise instructions**.
- Break down tasks into **simplified subtasks**.
- Provide **short examples** to guide the model's behavior.
- Refine prompts through **experimentation and feedback**, not random tweaks.
- Monitor **latency and response time** as prompt length affects performance.

Steps Involved in Prompt Engineering

STEP 01
Defining
the Task

STEP 02
Identifying
the Inputs

STEP 03
Creating
Detailed
Prompts

STEP 04
Refining the
Prompts

Advanced Prompting Methods:

- **Chain of Thought (CoT)**: Encourages the model to break down reasoning into step-by-step logic.

- **Tree of Thoughts**: A more sophisticated variation where the model explores multiple reasoning paths before reaching a conclusion.

Prompt engineering often serves as the **starting point** in the optimization journey.

Step 3: Transitioning to Retrieval-Augmented Generation (RAG)

When prompt engineering hits its limit—especially in knowledge-intensive applications—RAG becomes the preferred method.

What is RAG?

RAG combines an LLM with a retrieval system that brings in domain-specific, up-to-date, or private knowledge at runtime. This technique helps prevent hallucination, ensure relevance, and introduce fresh knowledge without retraining the model.

Retrieval Augmented Generation (RAG)

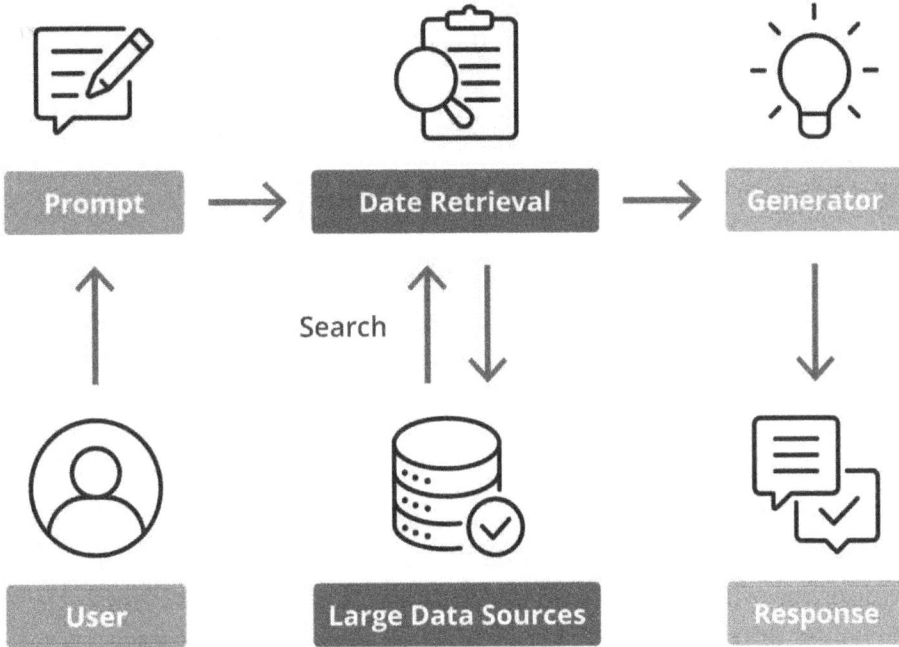

How RAG Works (Architecture Overview):

1. **User Prompt**: The initial query is submitted.

2. **Embedding & Encoding**: The prompt is converted into a dense vector using an embedding model.

3. **Document Retrieval**: The system searches a database (often vectorized) to fetch relevant chunks of information.

4. **Answer Generation**: The LLM generates a response using both the prompt and retrieved content.

RAG Evaluation Metrics:

- **Faithfulness**: Is the answer factually correct?
- **Relevance**: Are the retrieved documents relevant?
- **Signal-to-Noise Ratio**: Is the model retrieving more meaningful content than fluff?
- **Hallucination Reduction**: Does grounding improve factual accuracy?

Step 4: Using SAP HANA Cloud Vector Engine in RAG

SAP enables robust RAG architectures via the SAP HANA Vector Engine, a specialized component of the SAP HANA database designed to handle embedding vectors and AI workloads.

Key Features:

- Efficient storage, retrieval, and processing of vector data.
- Combines retrieval and generation in **one seamless operation**.
- Optimized for **complex and unstructured enterprise content**.
- Enables **domain-specific grounding** with contextual accuracy.

Benefits:

- **Scalability**: Enterprise-grade performance for high data volumes.
- **AI Integration**: Smooth compatibility with SAP AI Core and generative AI hub.
- **Enhanced Data Analysis**: Structured + unstructured data in one place.
- **Contextual Intelligence**: Better understanding of business context through metadata-aware retrieval.

Transition to Fine-Tuning: When and Why

Fine-tuning means continuing the training of an LLM with specific data to deeply customize its behavior. While powerful, it's also cost-intensive, time-consuming, and requires infrastructure and expertise.

Fine-Tuning Process

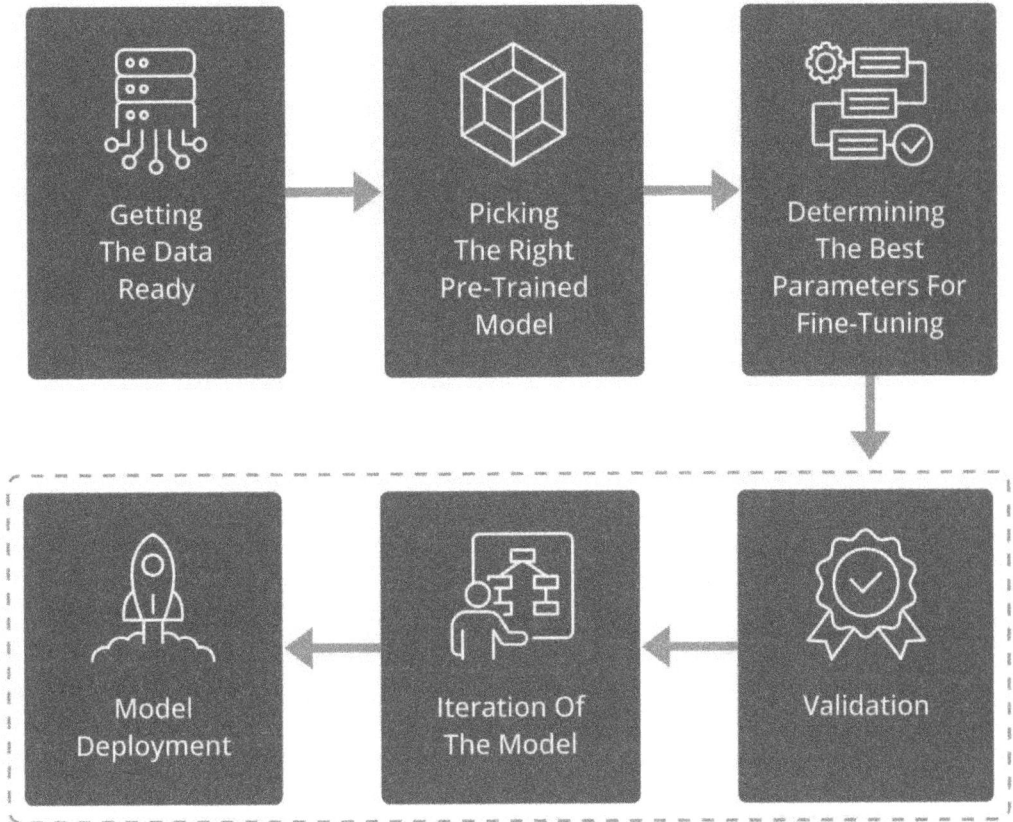

When to Use Fine-Tuning:

- When you want to permanently modify model behavior (e.g., tone, terminology).
- When consistent output formatting is required.
- To sanitize or restrict outputs in sensitive domains.
- For customized persona-based responses.

LLM Finetuning Methods

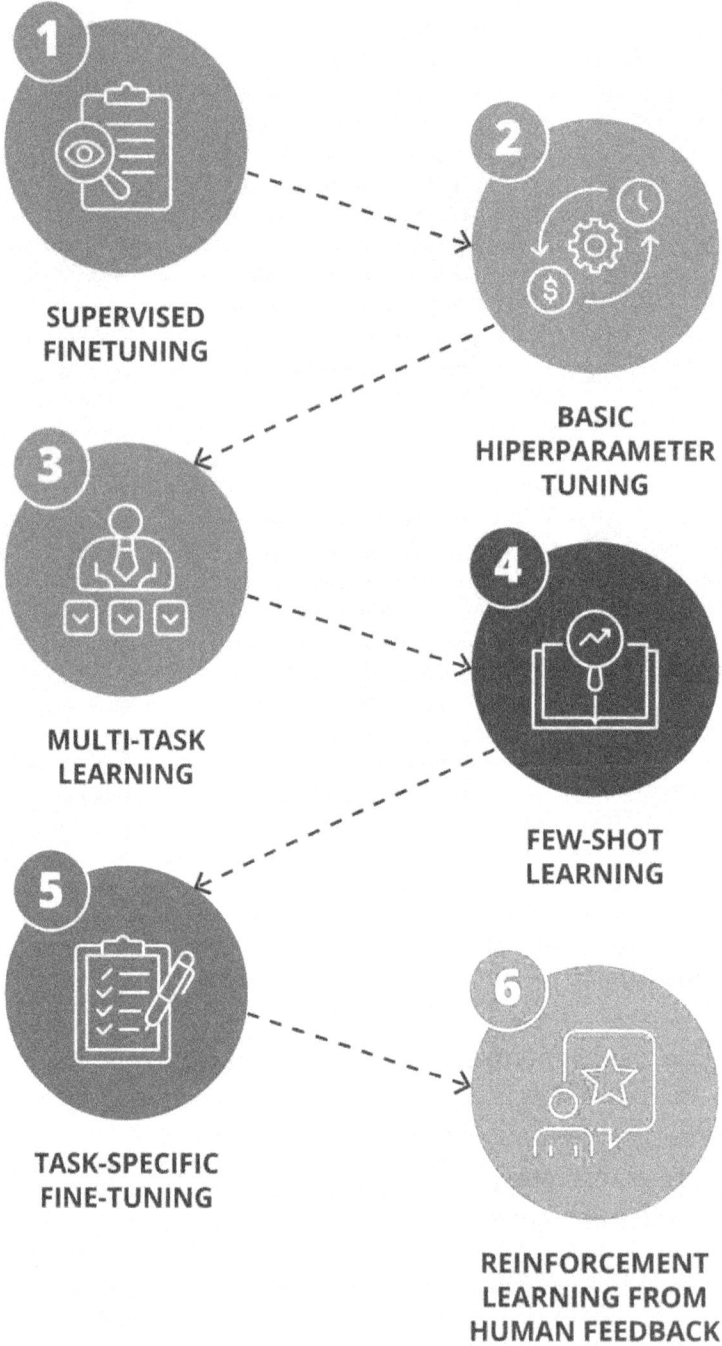

1

SUPERVISED FINETUNING

2

BASIC HIPERPARAMETER TUNING

3

MULTI-TASK LEARNING

4

FEW-SHOT LEARNING

5

TASK-SPECIFIC FINE-TUNING

6

REINFORCEMENT LEARNING FROM HUMAN FEEDBACK

When to Avoid Fine-Tuning:

- When the goal is to introduce new knowledge (RAG is better).
- For rapid iteration or prototyping (prompt engineering is faster).
- When infrastructure cost is a major concern.

Step 5: AI Agents, Functions, and Tools — The Next Frontier

One of the most impactful developments in LLM optimization is the use of AI Agents paired with functions and tools. These components add logic, automation, and interactivity—creating more intelligent, autonomous AI systems.

What Are AI Agents?

AI Agents are software programs that act as intermediaries between humans and LLMs. They:

- **Take user input**, translate it into an optimized prompt for the LLM.
- **Interpret the LLM's output** and convert it back into meaningful natural language.
- **Decide dynamically** what actions or tools to use, based on the user's intent.

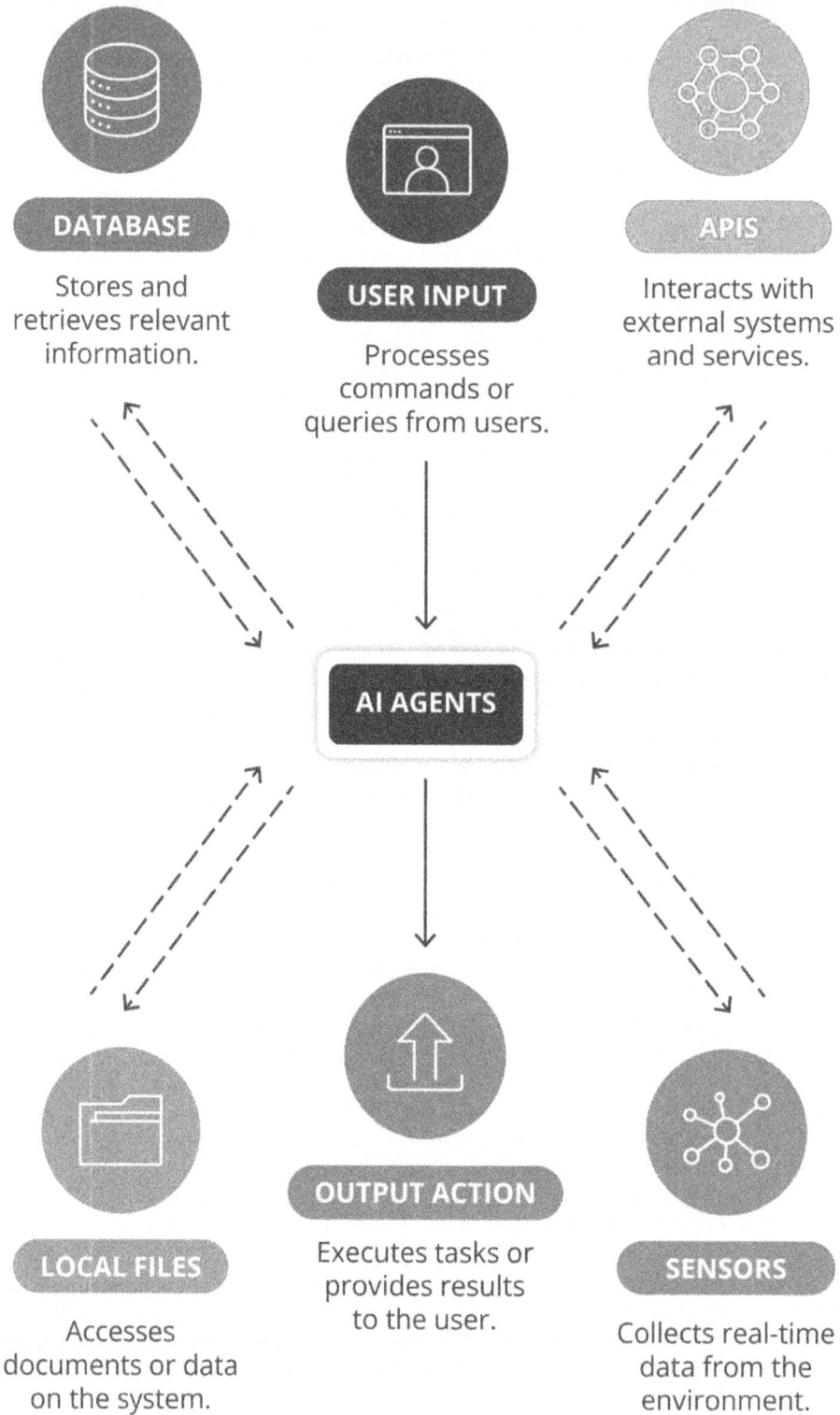

DATABASE

Stores and retrieves relevant information.

USER INPUT

Processes commands or queries from users.

APIS

Interacts with external systems and services.

AI AGENTS

LOCAL FILES

Accesses documents or data on the system.

OUTPUT ACTION

Executes tasks or provides results to the user.

SENSORS

Collects real-time data from the environment.

Agents can chain together multiple operations, maintain context, and handle complex workflows that go beyond simple question-answering.

What Are Functions?

Functions are small units of code that perform specific tasks—like accessing an external API, calculating tax, or retrieving real-time inventory. They can:

- Be written in any modern language (e.g., Python, Node.js).
- Access external systems or proprietary databases.
- Be triggered by AI agents or models based on the context of the conversation.

What Are Tools?

Tools are external software programs or APIs that the LLM can access when paired with agents. These may include:

- Search tools
- SAP system connectors
- Data visualization libraries
- Reporting dashboards

When agents combine these tools with LLM capabilities, they unlock dynamic, multi-step problem solving.

Optimizing LLM performance is a multi-stage process involving smart choices, constant iteration, and increasingly intelligent architecture.

In this part, we covered:

- **Prompt engineering** as a starting point.
- **Retrieval-Augmented Generation** using SAP HANA Vector Engine.
- **Fine-tuning** for deep behavioral customization.
- The rising power of **AI agents, functions, and tools** to create autonomous, dynamic, and interactive LLM applications.

Together, these tools form a flexible, powerful framework for scaling intelligent applications responsibly and effectively across the enterprise.

Putting It All Together: Optimization as a Journey

Optimization is not a one-time event—it's a **cyclical process** of:

1. Starting with **prompt engineering** to define task expectations.
2. Evolving into **retrieval-augmented generation** for more knowledge-driven tasks.
3. Implementing **fine-tuning** only when deep customization is needed.

Think of it as a toolbox, not a ladder. The technique you use depends on the problem at hand—and in most real-world applications, a combination of these techniques is what leads to enterprise-grade AI performance.

Takeaway

In this section, we explored how to elevate LLM performance by:

- Selecting the right optimization strategy based on the use case.
- Mastering **prompt engineering** for fast iteration and flexibility.
- Applying **RAG** using SAP HANA Vector Engine for contextual, grounded responses.
- Utilizing **fine-tuning** for long-term behavioral control.

With these tools, enterprises can build LLM-powered applications that are not only smart—but also **reliable, efficient, and aligned with user needs**.

Spotlight: Real-World Case Study — LLM Success in SAP Procurement

To ground the theory in tangible outcomes, let's explore how a multinational manufacturer leveraged SAP's LLM-powered AI assistant within their **Procure-to-Pay (P2P)** process.

The company, operating across 12 countries, struggled with procurement inefficiencies due to siloed vendor data, inconsistent contract language, and manua,l error-prone approvals. By integrating an **LLM-driven conversational assistant** (powered through SAP AI Core and embedded in their SAP S/4HANA procurement module), the organization achieved:

- **32% faster supplier query resolution** through natural language search.
- **Real-time risk alerts** based on language cues in incoming supplier emails and contracts.
- **Automated generation of RFP documents** by repurposing past templates intelligently.

The assistant used prompt engineering combined with retrieval-augmented generation (RAG) to provide grounded, real-time procurement insights. Stakeholders reported a **significant boost in procurement efficiency**, better compliance alignment, and a more empowered workforce.

This case highlights how SAP's LLM framework doesn't just function—it transforms.

Part 4: Optimizing LLM Performance — Testing, Evaluation, and Best Practices

So, you've built your LLM-powered application. The prompts are tuned, RAG is wired in, maybe you've even added AI agents and fine-tuned on domain-specific data. You're almost there—but before declaring success, there's one final, crucial step:

Evaluating, Testing, and Securing Your LLM Use Case

Performance means nothing if it can't be **measured, trusted, and maintained**. In enterprise environments like SAP's, where precision, reliability, and compliance are non-negotiable, proper testing is what separates a flashy prototype from a robust, production-ready solution.

Let's break down exactly how to evaluate, test, and safeguard your LLM solution for enterprise deployment.

Model Evaluation: How Do You Know It's Working?

After integrating and optimizing your LLM, it's essential to assess whether it meets the expectations set during ideation and development.

Here are some of the most **important evaluation metrics** to benchmark performance:

The LLM Training Process

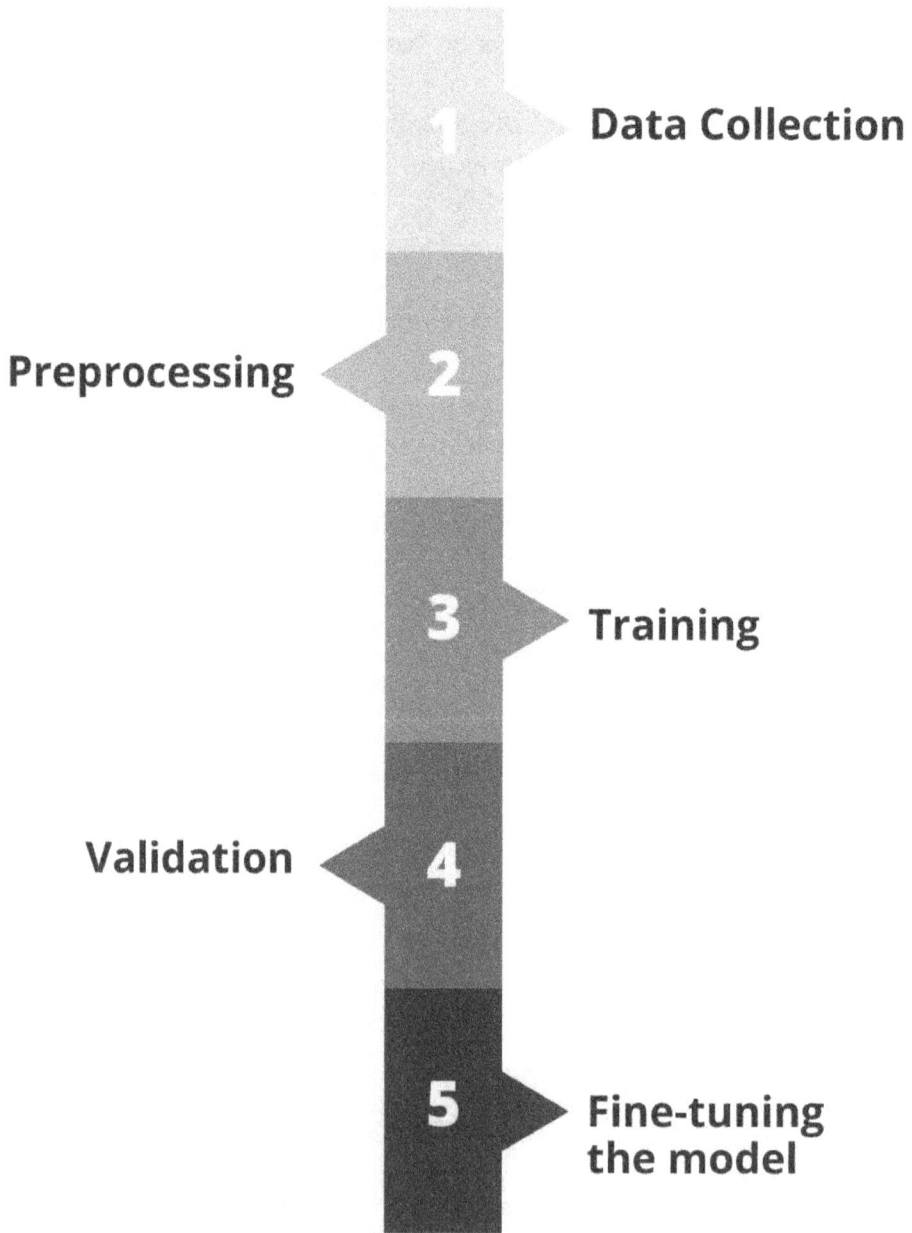

1 Data Collection

Preprocessing 2

3 Training

Validation 4

5 Fine-tuning the model

Key Metrics:

1. **Perplexity**: Measures how "surprised" a model is by actual data. Lower perplexity = better language understanding.

2. **BLEU (Bilingual Evaluation Understudy)**: Compares generated text to human references for tasks like translation.

3. **ROUGE (Recall-Oriented Understudy for Gisting Evaluation)**: Measures overlap between generated and reference summaries.

4. **Classification Accuracy**: Percentage of correct predictions in classification tasks.

5. **Precision & Recall**: Precision shows relevance; recall shows completeness.

6. **F1 Score**: Harmonic mean of precision and recall—balances both.

7. **Word Error Rate (WER)**: Useful in speech-to-text or transcription-based tasks.

8. **Semantic Similarity Metrics**: Measures how meaningfully similar the output is to the desired answer, even if the words differ.

These metrics are **quantitative signals** of model health—and they help avoid misleading assumptions based on subjective observations.

Comprehensive Testing: What Should You Validate?

True enterprise readiness requires validating not just what the model says, but how it performs across dimensions like:

- **Reliability** – Does it perform consistently?
- **Validity** – Are the answers factually and semantically correct?
- **Efficiency** – Is it responsive under real-world conditions?
- **Transparency** – Can outputs be audited or explained?
- **Maintainability** – Is it built for long-term use and updates?

To aid in this, tools like Guardrails (an open-source Python library) help validate and correct LLM outputs, ensuring adherence to specific rules, formats, or constraints.

Model Inference: Moving from Training to Real-World Use

Once your LLM has been trained and optimized, it enters the **inference stage**—this is when the model gets to **"go live" in production**.

During inference:

- New user input (e.g., a customer support query or a report request) is sent to the LLM via an API.
- The model uses what it has learned to generate real-time responses—no additional training occurs.

Common Inference-Time Capabilities:

- Sentiment analysis
- Named Entity Recognition (NER)
- Text summarization
- Question answering
- Language translation
- Generating emails, reports, responses, etc.

This is where **performance and trust** matter most—because this is where real users are depending on the model.

Best Practices for Real-World LLM Performance

To ensure long-term success, SAP and leading enterprises follow strict best practices for LLM deployment:

- Fine-tune on domain-specific data for improved context relevance.
- Update training data incrementally to reflect changing business needs.
- Test with real production workloads before rollout.
- Define qualitative KPIs—don't just rely on accuracy; measure usefulness.
- Monitor errors in real time and analyze failure cases.
- Optimize infrastructure costs—token usage and compute load can add up fast.
- Implement failover policies to manage downtime or LLM API limits.
- Use ML Ops for automation, reproducibility, and reliability.

LLM Finetuning Methods

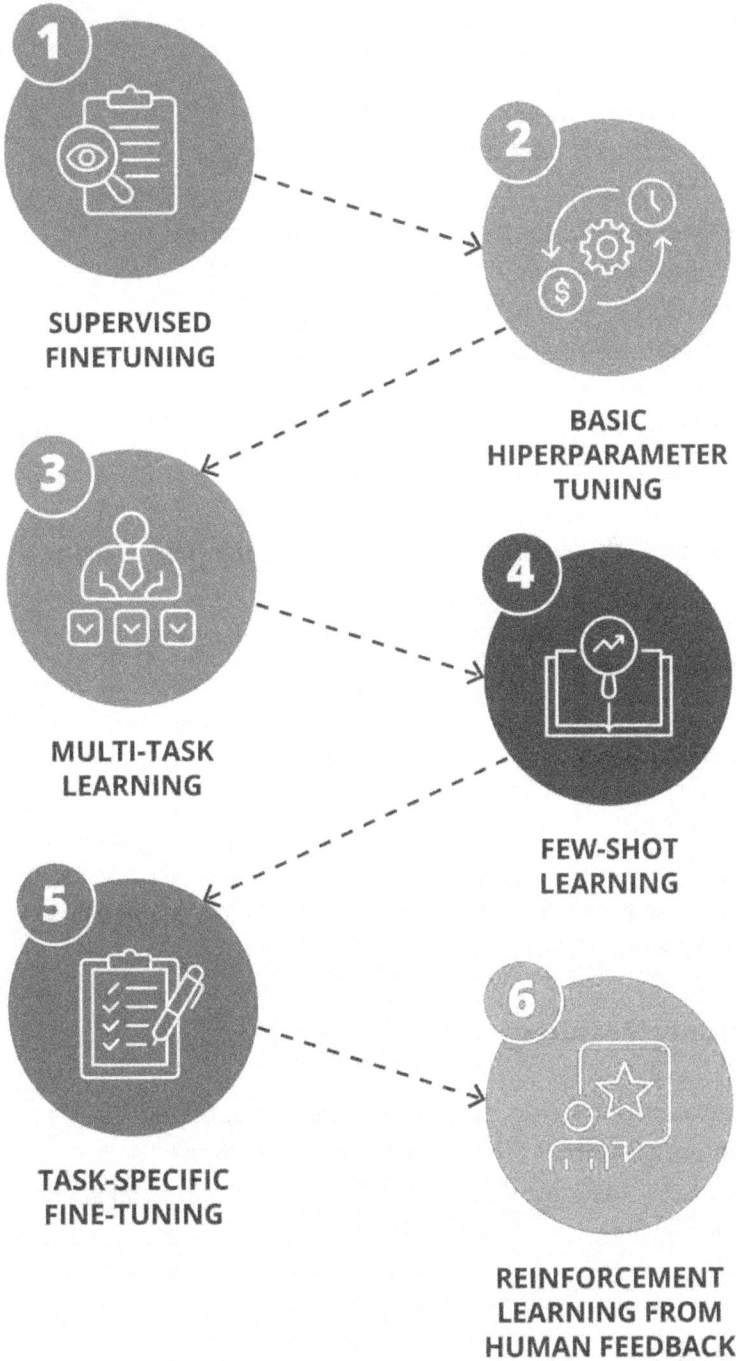

1 — SUPERVISED FINETUNING

2 — BASIC HIPERPARAMETER TUNING

3 — MULTI-TASK LEARNING

4 — FEW-SHOT LEARNING

5 — TASK-SPECIFIC FINE-TUNING

6 — REINFORCEMENT LEARNING FROM HUMAN FEEDBACK

MLOps: Your Secret Weapon for Scalable Success

ML Ops (Machine Learning Operations) is essential for managing and scaling LLM use cases. It ensures that evaluation, monitoring, and updates happen systematically.

MLOps Enables:

- Automated benchmarking and testing pipelines
- Centralized logging of performance and output variations
- Streamlined model retraining and dataset updates
- Error detection at scale and automated correction workflows
- Gradual rollouts with rollback capabilities
- Alerting systems for anomalies or degraded performance

Think of MLOps as the DevOps of AI—keeping your models running efficiently, predictably, and securely across environments.

Securing Your LLM Application: Don't Leave It to Chance

Security is a critical but often underestimated piece of the LLM puzzle. As models become more autonomous, the risks become more complex.

Common Threats:

- **Hallucination**: Fabricated facts or misleading information.
- **Jailbreaks**: Prompt injections that bypass safety constraints.
- **Data Leakage**: Exposure of sensitive information, especially when integrating private enterprise data.

Proactive Security Measures:

- Monitor output for risky or non-compliant responses.
- Implement guardrails and red-teaming simulations.
- Continuously test models against real-world adversarial scenarios.
- Encrypt and limit access to sensitive data used in retrieval or fine-tuning.

LLMs are only as trustworthy as the environment they operate in—**secure them accordingly**.

Final Thoughts: Evaluation is the Key to Longevity

The lifecycle of an LLM doesn't end with deployment—it thrives on feedback, iteration, and continuous optimization. Evaluation is the **heartbeat of generative AI success**. It tells you if your model is working, how well it's working, and when it needs to evolve.

By combining:

- Rigorous **testing metrics**
- Smart **inference strategies**
- Strategic **ML Ops pipelines**
- Strong **security frameworks**

...you set your large language model up for resilient, scalable, and trustworthy enterprise impact.

Responsible AI: Ethics, Governance & Regulatory Readiness

As enterprises adopt LLMs, ethical and regulatory concerns become central to trust and adoption. SAP approaches this challenge with a proactive and robust governance framework.

Regulatory Landscape:

SAP's AI systems—including LLM-enabled solutions—adhere to leading regulations such as:

- **GDPR** (General Data Protection Regulation): Ensuring user data privacy, informed consent, and the right to explanation.
- **EU AI Act** (in progress): SAP's AI team actively aligns its product classification, risk management, and transparency obligations with anticipated AI Act requirements.

Explainability & Audits:

SAP prioritizes **explainability** through audit trails and traceable decision paths. This means outputs from LLMs—especially in financial or compliance use cases—can be reviewed, logged, and understood by both users and regulators.

Compliance Readiness:

- **Model validation** and **guardrails** are built into SAP's Generative AI Hub.
- Data usage and access controls are **transparent and role-based**.
- Enterprise clients can **audit LLM interactions** and set **output boundaries**.

SAP's position is clear: AI should empower without compromising on **fairness, accountability, or compliance**. These safeguards are not just checkboxes—they're built into every layer of SAP's LLM product architecture.

Understanding the Various Types of LLMs and Their Applications

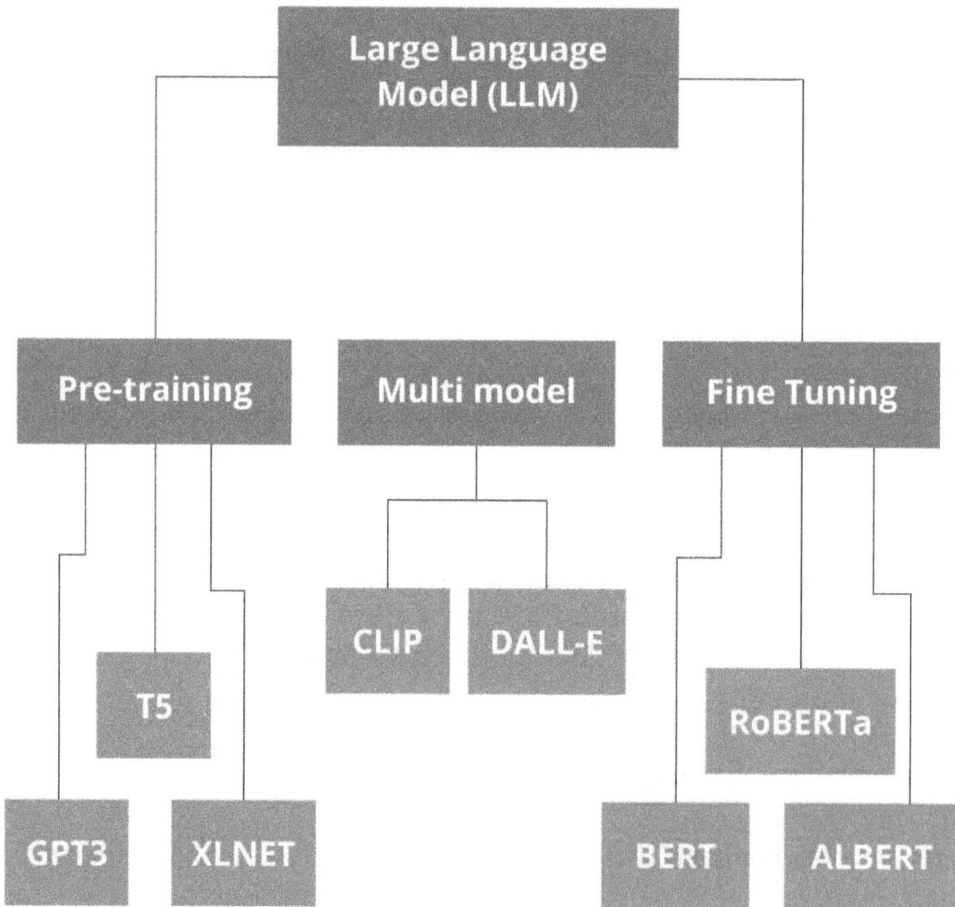

Key Takeaways from the Fundamentals of Large Language Models

I've packed a lot into this chapter about Large Language Models (LLMs)—and I know it might feel overwhelming at first. But trust me, this is information you'll want to be comfortable with. LLMs aren't just cutting-edge AI tools; they're quickly becoming the foundation of enterprise intelligence. In this chapter, I've walked you through their core architecture, shown how SAP brings them to life in real-world use cases, and shared best practices for fine-tuning, deploying, and securing them at scale.

Here's a quick recap of what we've learned:

What You Now Know:

- *__LLMs are powerful neural networks built__ on Transformer architectures and trained on massive datasets to understand and generate human language.*

- *__SAP's approach to LLMs__ is rooted in safe, scalable, and responsible AI—aligned with enterprise requirements and customer trust.*

- *From __ideation to production__, SAP follows a structured and agile product development lifecycle that ensures business value and user-centricity.*

- *Optimization techniques like __prompt engineering, RAG, and fine-tuning__ offer flexible ways to improve performance across use cases.*

- *__AI Agents, Functions, and Tools__ allow dynamic task orchestration and real-time decision-making, elevating LLM capabilities even further.*

- *Performance is not complete without __rigorous testing, security enforcement, and ML Ops integration__ to ensure reliability and trust in live environments.*

In summary, mastering LLMs means not just understanding the technology—but being able to apply it wisely, improve it continuously, and secure it rigorously. For enterprise leaders, this is the key to unlocking the next wave of innovation, automation, and customer experience.

Now that we've laid the technical foundation of Large Language Models, it's time to zoom out and understand how SAP orchestrates AI across its ecosystem. In the next chapter, we'll explore SAP Business AI—a strategic framework that brings together LLMs, machine learning, analytics, and domain expertise to deliver intelligent business outcomes.

This is where theory meets transformation—welcome to the world of SAP Business AI.

CHAPTER 3

SAP Business AI

In this chapter, we explore one of the most transformative shifts happening in enterprise technology today: SAP Business AI. Whether you're a consultant, developer, analyst, or business leader, understanding SAP's AI vision will empower you to innovate and make smarter decisions.

AI isn't just coming — it's already changing the way we work.

For businesses running on SAP, that change has a name: SAP Business AI. This isn't some distant future or vague promise — it's real, and it's happening now.

Imagine making decisions not just faster, but smarter — backed by data, patterns, and predictive insights. Imagine processes that run smoother, with less manual work and fewer errors. That's the kind of transformation SAP Business AI brings to the table.

By embedding AI directly into core business applications, SAP helps organizations move from reactive to proactive, from complex to simple, and from traditional to truly intelligent. Whether it's finance, supply chain, HR, or customer experience — AI is quietly working behind the scenes to optimize, automate, and elevate how things get done. This is what it means to be an intelligent enterprise. Not just surviving in a digital world — but thriving in it.

As a SAP Certified Generative AI Developer and SAP Certified Finance Consultant, I aim to demystify SAP Business AI, walk you through real use cases, and give you a solid foundation to innovate responsibly.

We'll take a deep dive into how SAP is redefining enterprise software by embedding artificial intelligence at its core — from machine learning models and deep learning networks to cutting-edge generative AI tools like Joule, SAP's new AI copilot. Along the way, you'll see how AI is becoming not just a feature but a foundational element in SAP's suite of solutions.

Chapter Highlights:

- Understand what Artificial Intelligence means in the SAP ecosystem
- Explore SAP's unique and responsible approach to Business AI
- Meet Joule, SAP's generative AI copilot
- Learn about the tools within SAP BTP for developing, deploying, and managing AI
- Get inspired with real-life examples and future applications of SAP Business AI

Let's begin by laying the groundwork with Artificial Intelligence and SAP's approach.

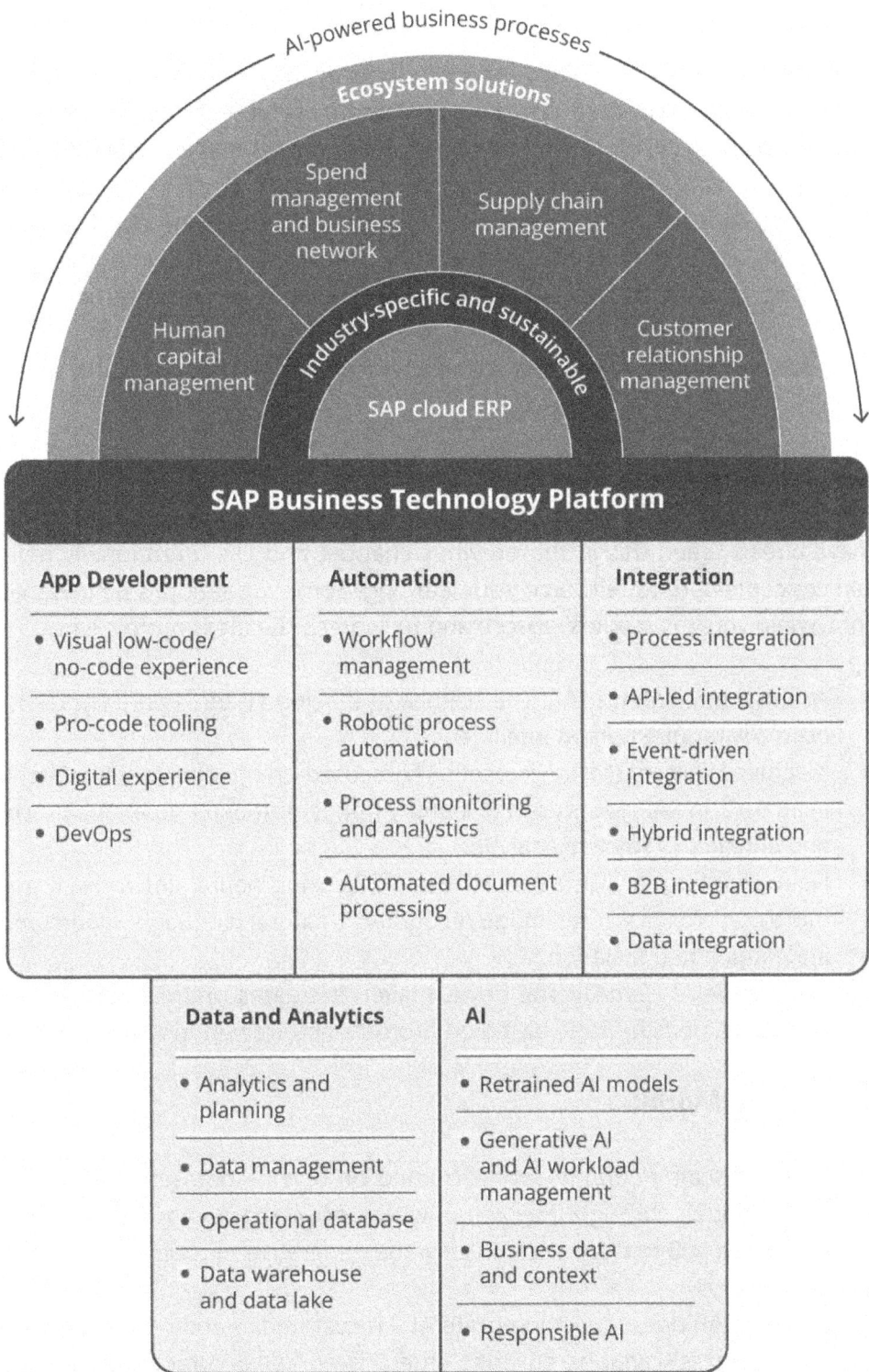

AI-powered business processes

Ecosystem solutions

Spend management and business network

Supply chain management

Human capital management

Industry-specific and sustainable

Customer relationship management

SAP cloud ERP

SAP Business Technology Platform

App Development

- Visual low-code/ no-code experience
- Pro-code tooling
- Digital experience
- DevOps

Automation

- Workflow management
- Robotic process automation
- Process monitoring and analytics
- Automated document processing

Integration

- Process integration
- API-led integration
- Event-driven integration
- Hybrid integration
- B2B integration
- Data integration

Data and Analytics

- Analytics and planning
- Data management
- Operational database
- Data warehouse and data lake

AI

- Retrained AI models
- Generative AI and AI workload management
- Business data and context
- Responsible AI

Outlining Artificial Intelligence and SAP's Vision

When most people hear "AI," they think of robots acting like humans. But in the real world of business, AI is doing something much more useful — it's helping teams work faster, make smarter decisions, and serve customers in ways that actually feel personal.

SAP's take on AI is practical. It's not about hype — it's about impact. The goal? To build AI that's useful in your day-to-day work, that you can trust, and that respects real-world boundaries. In short: AI that's relevant, reliable, and responsible.

Because the best kind of AI isn't the flashiest — it's the kind that just works when you need it.

Understanding AI in Layers:

We have already seen this in the previous chapter, and I've intentionally revisited certain concepts here to reinforce your learning. Some repetition is deliberate—it's meant to help you, my readers, absorb and fully grasp the ideas more clearly.

- Artificial Intelligence (AI): The science of making systems perform tasks that normally require human intelligence.
- Machine Learning (ML): A subset of AI focused on building systems that learn from data. In SAP, ML is used to identify trends, automate repetitive processes, and enhance predictive analytics.
- Deep Learning: A specialized subset of ML using neural networks. It powers more complex tasks like image recognition, natural language understanding, and language translation.
- Generative AI (GenAI): The newest layer. It creates original content — like code, text, or insights — based on prompts and trained models.

Foundational Models:

These are large-scale neural networks trained on diverse datasets. SAP leverages foundational models through integration with LLMs (Large Language Models) like GPT-4 and Falcon 40B to build enterprise-grade generative AI tools.

Did you know? SAP doesn't just integrate AI – it customizes and contextualizes it to suit specific business scenarios, ensuring enterprise-grade accuracy and security.

Introducing SAP Business AI

What is Business AI?

Business AI is the integration of AI capabilities into business processes and systems, optimized for enterprise-grade challenges like scale, compliance, and security.

AI vs. ML vs. DL vs. GenAI

Concept	Description	Example in SAP
Artificial Intelligence (AI)	Simulation of human intelligence	Automated invoice matching
Machine Learning (ML)	Algorithms learning from data	Predictive maintenance in production planning
Deep Learning (DL)	Neural networks analyzing large data sets	Image recognition in quality inspection
Generative AI (GenAI)	AI that creates content	Joule writing code snippets or summaries

SAP Business AI is designed to empower every user, developer, and decision-maker with contextual intelligence. It adheres to three pillars:

The 3 Rs of SAP Business AI:

- Relevant: Tailored to industry-specific needs and business contexts.
- Reliable: Based on accurate data and governed AI principles.
- Responsible: Ensures transparency, fairness, privacy, and security.

The 3 Rs of SAP Business AI

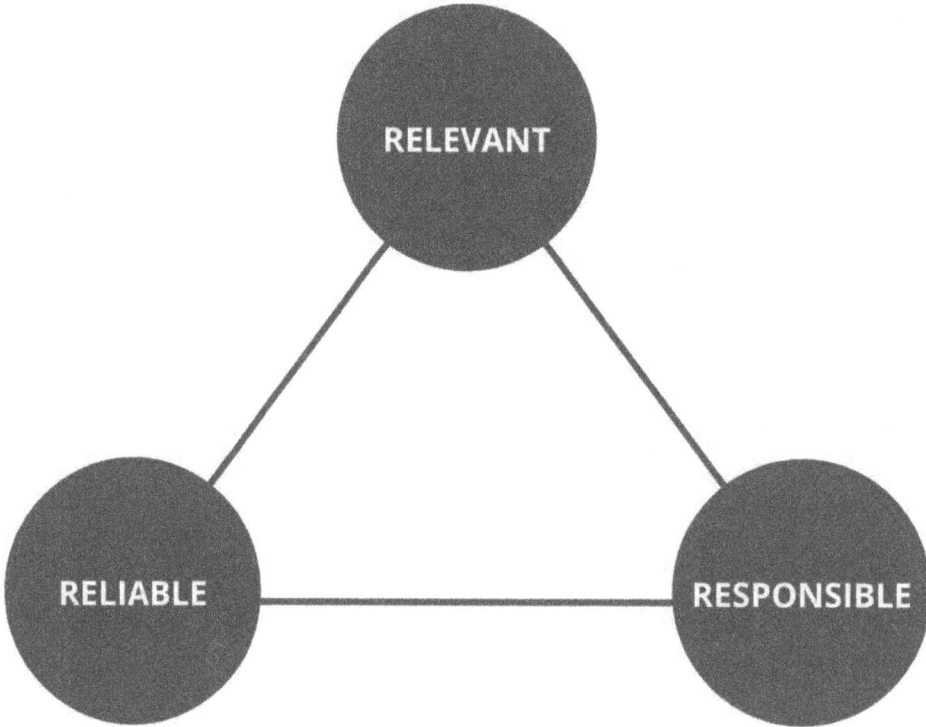

Core Capabilities:

- Embedded in SAP S/4HANA, SAP SuccessFactors, SAP Ariba, and more.
- Scalable via SAP Business Technology Platform (SAP BTP).
- Supported by SAP AI Core and AI Launchpad.
- Accessible through the Generative AI Hub.

SAP Business AI includes:

- Predictive analytics
- AI-assisted workflows
- Context-aware insights
- Natural language interactions

AI is only as good as its data – and SAP has decades of rich, structured enterprise data to build intelligent models upon.

Joule: SAP's Generative AI Copilot

SAP's way of making AI actually useful in your day-to-day work. Instead of juggling menus, reports, or long processes, you can just ask — and Joule helps you get things done faster. It's built right into SAP, so you don't need to learn something new or switch platforms.

Need to generate insights, automate routine tasks, or make sense of your data? Joule's designed to help with that — almost like having a smart teammate who understands your business.

- Navigate complex dashboards
- Automate repetitive tasks
- Analyze reports
- Write code
- Retrieve insights with natural language queries

Joule Highlights:

- Embedded across the SAP portfolio
- Seamlessly interacts with SAP S/4HANA, SAC, SuccessFactors, and more
- Uses LLMs via SAP AI Core
- Helps minimize operational errors
- Learns from historical enterprise data

Coming in Q3 2025, Joule will fundamentally change how users interact with SAP systems — making workflows conversational and intuitive.

"Just ask Joule" is the new way to work with SAP.

Exploring the SAP BTP AI Landscape

If you want to use AI in a meaningful way within your business, you need more than just smart algorithms — you need a solid foundation to build on. That's where SAP Business Technology Platform (BTP) comes in.

SAP BTP isn't just another cloud platform. It's the technical backbone that connects your data, applications, and processes — making it possible to actually apply AI where it counts. Whether you're pulling insights from different systems, automating a repetitive workflow, or building a custom AI tool tailored to your needs, BTP provides the tools and services to make it happen.

Think of it as the layer that brings everything together:

- It lets you access and manage data across your SAP and non-SAP systems.
- It gives you development tools to build or extend applications.
- And it integrates AI and machine learning services in a way that fits right into your existing environment — without needing to start from scratch.

So instead of AI being some isolated experiment off to the side, SAP BTP helps you embed intelligence directly into the core of how your business runs.

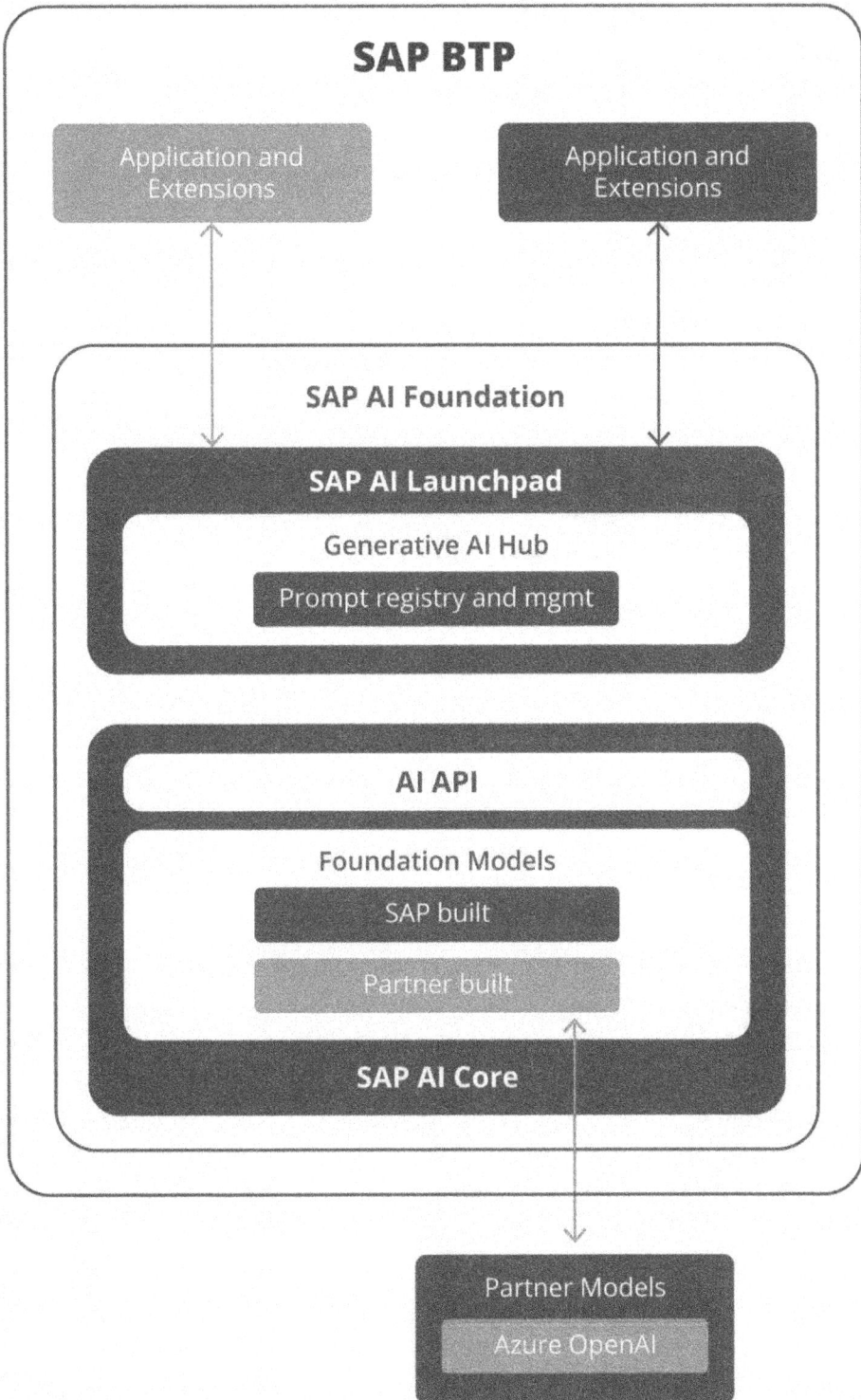

SAP BTP

Application and Extensions

Application and Extensions

SAP AI Foundation

SAP AI Launchpad

Generative AI Hub

Prompt registry and mgmt

AI API

Foundation Models

SAP built

Partner built

SAP AI Core

Partner Models

Azure OpenAI

Core AI Components on SAP BTP

1. **SAP AI Core**
   - Runs training and inference pipelines
   - Supports multi-tenant deployments
   - Preserves privacy and data ownership
2. **SAP AI Launchpad**
   - Lifecycle management of AI models
   - Monitor, retrain, deploy
3. **Generative AI Hub**
   - Access to GPT-4, Falcon 40B, and other LLMs
   - Prompt engineering tools
4. **AI Services**
   - Pre-built services for classification, NLP, forecasting
5. **Business Data Context**
   - AI powered by domain-specific data
   - Understands SAP data structures like GL Accounts, Cost Centers, BOMs, etc.

Think of BTP as your AI innovation playground.

SAP Business AI in Action: Real-World Applications

Let's explore where SAP Business AI is delivering value right now.

Practical Use Cases:

- Category Management: Use AI to optimize supplier selection, pricing analysis, and demand forecasting.
- SPC x AI Toolkit: Enable predictive maintenance and quality control in manufacturing.
- SAP Analytics Cloud (SAC): Ask questions in natural language, get instant charts and dashboards.
- SAP Build + Joule: Generate workflows and applications using prompts instead of code.
- Document Information Extraction (Premium Edition): Turn unstructured invoices and PDFs into structured, actionable data.
- SAP Enterprise Service Management: Automate ticket classification, routing, and resolution.
- HR & Talent Management (SuccessFactors): Use AI to identify high-potential employees, forecast attrition, and improve hiring decisions.

- Finance & Accounting: Accelerate period-end closing with anomaly detection and auto-generated financial commentary.

These aren't futuristic dreams – these capabilities are being deployed by SAP customers today.

What's Ahead: SAP, AI, and Where Things Are Going

SAP is gradually weaving AI deeper into its platform — not just for data scientists or engineers, but for anyone who works with business systems day to day. That means people like analysts, consultants, and developers can use AI without needing to learn complex tools or write machine learning code.

In practical terms, here's what's coming next:

- **Joule will show up in more places.** The idea is to make it easier to ask questions, find insights, and take action inside the SAP apps people already use.

- **Better tools for working with prompts.** Think less trial and error, and more structured ways to get the answers or outcomes you need.

- **More partnerships.** SAP is expanding who it works with — from cloud providers to AI specialists — to bring new capabilities into the ecosystem.

- **Smarter models trained on real-world patterns.** Without exposing private company data, SAP is using anonymized industry info to improve how its AI performs in different business contexts.

At the core of all this is a simple shift: AI won't be a separate tool or extra layer. It'll just be part of how you get your work done — quietly running in the background or right there when you need a hand.

Your Role in the AI-Powered Future

You don't have to be a data scientist to start using AI within SAP. With tools like Joule, SAP BTP, and the Generative AI Hub, AI is now accessible to everyone. Whether you're optimizing operations, building new applications, or guiding strategy — SAP Business AI helps you accelerate your impact.

Getting started doesn't mean diving in headfirst — it means experimenting, exploring, and finding where AI naturally fits into your work. You might begin with small use cases: asking Joule to summarize reports, automating a manual approval flow, or testing an AI service from the BTP marketplace. Over time, those small steps add up, helping you build confidence and spot even more opportunities for value.

Engage & Experiment:

- Try prompt-based development using Joule
- Explore the BTP Marketplace for AI Services
- Join SAP Community to learn, build, and share your AI use cases

The insights, tools, and frameworks shared in this chapter are informed by my hands-on experience and continued learning — including the SAP Generative AI Developer Course, which offers a practical foundation for understanding how AI is being applied in real SAP environments.

As a SAP Certified Generative AI Developer and Finance Consultant, my goal is to help others bridge the gap between technology and business value — and to make AI feel less like a buzzword, and more like a tool you can actually use.

Rather than focusing solely on theory, this chapter emphasizes how generative AI is already influencing the way enterprises think, operate, and deliver value. SAP's integration of AI across domains like finance, logistics, and analytics is not about replacing people — it's about empowering them to work smarter, faster, and with more insight. I've seen this shift firsthand and continue to explore how these tools can be applied meaningfully in complex business landscapes.

This is the future of the intelligent enterprise — not as a buzzword, but as an evolving, tangible reality.

To build on this foundation, the next chapter will explore the **SAP Generative AI Hub** — a central environment that brings generative AI use cases, tools, and models together in a unified, developer-friendly space. It's here that ideas are shaped into working solutions, supported by the flexibility of SAP BTP and designed to meet real business demands.

Whether you're technical or functional, developer or decision-maker, the **AI Hub** is where the possibilities start to take shape — and I look forward to walking you through it.

What You Just Learned – Chapter 3 Summary

- **SAP Business AI** embeds AI directly into enterprise processes—making systems more intelligent, proactive, and efficient.

- **AI in SAP** spans Machine Learning, Deep Learning, and Generative AI, all tailored for business outcomes.

- **Joule**, SAP's generative AI copilot, enables conversational workflows, automates tasks, and delivers real-time insights.

- **SAP BTP** (Business Technology Platform) is the foundation for building, deploying, and scaling AI with tools like AI Core, AI Launchpad, and Generative AI Hub.

- The **3 Rs of SAP Business AI**: Relevant, Reliable, and Responsible — guiding AI use with context, trust, and ethics.

- Real-world use cases show AI already in action across finance, HR, supply chain, and procurement.

- SAP's vision: AI not as a separate tool, but as an integrated assistant — empowering everyone to work smarter.

You're now equipped to see SAP Business AI not as a concept, but as a practical, transformative force shaping the future of enterprise software.

CHAPTER 4

SAP Generative AI Hub

As enterprises continue to explore the transformative capabilities of Generative AI, SAP provides a secure and structured platform to operationalize these innovations: the SAP Generative AI Hub. Designed with enterprise-scale governance, this hub simplifies the development, testing, and deployment of Large Language Model (LLM) use cases across SAP systems and applications.

In this chapter, we will take a practical, hands-on look at how to use the SAP Generative AI Hub for both basic and advanced AI scenarios. Whether you are experimenting with simple prompt design or integrating AI-powered logic into your business processes using SDKs, the AI Hub provides the right tools to build with confidence.

We will also explore how to refine AI outputs through advanced prompt engineering techniques, and guide you through choosing the most suitable LLM based on your business goals, accuracy needs, cost constraints, and industry-specific requirements.

By the end of this chapter, you will have a foundational understanding of how to:

- Design, test, and refine prompts using SAP's built-in tools
- Integrate LLM capabilities programmatically using SAP SDKs
- Apply prompt engineering best practices for reliable and relevant results
- Evaluate and select the right model from SAP's supported LLMs

Section Overview

1. **Creating Basic Prompts in Generative AI Hub**
   We begin with a no-code interface for prompt development—ideal for business users and prototypers. You'll learn how to design prompts that can solve simple tasks such as summarizing documents, translating text, and extracting key data points, all within the SAP ecosystem.

2. **Leveraging the Power of LLMs Using SDK for Generative AI Hub**
   Here, we dive into SDK capabilities for developers looking to embed AI into workflows. We cover authentication, API usage, deployment patterns, and how to call AI models from ABAP, SAP BTP, or CAP-based applications.

3. **Refining AI Responses Using Advanced Prompt Engineering Techniques**
   This section focuses on precision—how to fine-tune prompts, reduce hallucinations, improve tone, and increase factual accuracy using smart engineering patterns like few-shot learning, prompt chaining, and context injection.

4. **Selecting Large Language Models in Generative AI Hub**
   Not all models are created equal. In this section, we look at model evaluation: how to compare performance, latency, security, and use-case fit. You'll also learn to switch between OpenAI, Cohere, and SAP's own Joule LLMs for maximum flexibility.

By understanding how to design prompts, integrate with SAP systems, fine-tune responses, and choose the right models, you'll be equipped to confidently apply Generative AI across various enterprise use cases. The SAP Generative AI Hub serves as the central foundation to turn your AI ideas into production-ready solutions—securely, efficiently, and at scale. Let's explore how to bring intelligence into your workflows, one prompt at a time.

Part 1: Creating Basic Prompts in Generative AI Hub

Generative AI Hub Overview

The rapid growth of Large Language Models (LLMs) has created a need for a centralized, structured, and tool-supported platform that simplifies model selection and integration based on specific use cases. SAP's Generative AI Hub, part of SAP AI Core and SAP AI Launchpad on SAP Business Technology Platform (BTP), addresses this need by offering a consolidated solution for secure and scalable generative AI deployment.

The hub serves as the foundation for innovation across SAP's ecosystem, integrating trusted foundation models (FMs) grounded in business and contextual data. It streamlines development, ensures compliance, and empowers both SAP users and partners to build AI-enhanced applications.

Key Capabilities of Generative AI Hub

1. Access to Models and Resources

- Direct access to cutting-edge LLMs and compute resources.
- Built-in orchestration modules (e.g., data masking, content filtering).

2. Exploration and Development Tools

- Prompt editor and prompt management.
- Prompt registry, SDKs, fine-tuning services.
- Secure AI playground for testing.

3. Deployment and Delivery

- Seamless deployment of AI models and updates.
- Support for Bring Your Own Model (BYOM).
- Template workflows for training and serving models.

4. Orchestration of AI Workflows

- Manage compute workflows, schedule tasks, and control agents.
- Optimize model interactions and content moderation.

5. Governance and Compliance

- Role-based access, logging, and auditing.
- Monitoring and metering capabilities.
- Compliance with standards like SOC 2, NIST, and ISO.

6. Adaptability and Customization

- Easy switching of models or orchestration configurations.
- Grounding, fine-tuning, and AI agent deployment.

7. Trust and Security

- Data masking and injection prevention.
- No automatic data saving.
- Certified data protection and isolation.

8. **Vector Engine**

- SAP-managed vector engine integrated with HANA Cloud.
- Enables grounding by retrieving relevant business documents for LLM context.

Accessing Generative AI Hub

Before creating and using prompts in SAP AI Launchpad, you need to access the Generative AI Hub:

1. Set up a SAP BTP Global Account

   - Ensure access to your enterprise-level SAP BTP account.
   - Follow SAP documentation for setup.

2. Provision SAP AI Core

   - Provision AI Core using BTP cockpit to receive service keys and endpoint access.

3. Connect to SAP AI Launchpad and Tools

   - Link SAP AI Launchpad to your SAP AI Core.
   - Optionally connect Postman or Python tools.

4. Create a Deployment

   - Configure LLMs for specific business needs using model provider details.
   - SAP AI Core will generate a unique endpoint URL per deployment.

Exploring Generative AI Applications Beyond Chatbots

Foundation models deployed in the AI Hub can support a wide range of software-driven scenarios:

- Automating content generation and software instructions.
- Executing control operations based on human input.
- Enabling fully automated workflows with no direct human involvement.

This flexibility opens avenues for innovation in industries such as manufacturing, finance, and customer service.

Example Business Use Case: (Reference: SAP Learning)

Company: Facility Solutions Company

Problem: Managing and prioritizing customer emails manually is time-consuming and error-prone.

Solution: Using SAP's Generative AI Hub, emails are automatically categorized, urgency and sentiment are determined, and metadata is extracted for internal ticketing systems.

Value:

- Improves efficiency.
- Ensures consistency.
- Frees staff for higher-value tasks.

Developing a Basic Prompt: Step-by-Step Process

Step 1: Create a Basic Prompt *Start with a simple prompt to extract* urgency *and* sentiment *from an incoming email message.*

Step 2: Assign Value Ranges *Refine prompt output by mapping* urgency *(*low, medium, high*) and* sentiment *(*positive, neutral, negative*).*

Step 3: Use JSON Format for Output *Structure prompt results into JSON format to integrate with software.*

Step 4: Improve JSON Precision *Ensure JSON output is clean—free of line breaks or extraneous formatting.*

Step 5: Add Business Category Tags *Include support categories for organizational processing (e.g.,* emergency_repair_services, routine_maintenance_requests*).*

Step 6: Align with Business-Specific Tags *Map categories to predefined organizational tags to streamline integration.*

Step 7: Return JSON for Categories *Ensure prompt returns well-formatted JSON with category values.*

Step 8: Combine All Elements in One Prompt *Merge all elements—urgency, sentiment, and categories—into a consolidated prompt returning a clean JSON string.*

You've now successfully developed a prompt that extracts structured insights from unstructured data. In the next unit, you'll learn how to accomplish the same task using the generative-ai-hub-sdk and evaluate prompt responses programmatically.

Part 2: Leveraging the Power of LLMs Using SDK for Generative AI Hub

What is an SDK?

An SDK (Software Development Kit) is a collection of software tools, libraries, documentation, code samples, processes, and guides that allow developers to create applications for specific platforms. Think of an SDK as a developer's toolbox that makes it easier and faster to build software while ensuring compatibility and performance with the targeted environment.

In the context of SAP's Generative AI Hub, the Generative AI Hub SDK provides all the necessary utilities to interact with Large Language Models (LLMs), manage prompt workflows, integrate AI responses into enterprise applications, and evaluate their effectiveness. This SDK allows developers to bypass many complexities of infrastructure setup, model deployment, and orchestration — making enterprise-grade AI accessible, scalable, and programmable.

This part of the chapter is divided into four core areas to help you unlock the full potential of the SDK:

1. Identifying the Need for Using Generative-AI-Hub-SDK

In earlier sections, we explored how Facility Solutions Company used SAP's Generative AI Hub through the SAP AI Launchpad to create simple prompts and generate structured responses. However, as the volume of customer interactions increased and the need for application-level automation grew, it became clear that manually handling prompts and model invocations was no longer scalable.

This is where the SDK becomes vital.

Key Benefits of Using the SDK:

1. Streamlined Processes:

   - The SDK abstracts away complex backend systems, giving developers simple APIs and utilities to access LLM capabilities.
   - Developers can focus on business logic and prompt design, not model deployment or orchestration.

2. Increased Development Efficiency:

   - SDK usage dramatically reduces development time for integrating AI into applications.
   - You can call models, evaluate responses, and manipulate outputs directly from your code.

3. Customization Opportunities:

   - Tailor model behavior and responses for your domain.
   - Create structured prompts and use real business context from SAP systems.

4. Improved Performance and Scalability:

   - Optimized for cloud and SAP BTP environments.
   - Easily handle high-throughput workflows with reliability and control.

In essence, the SDK transforms the SAP Generative AI Hub from a prototyping tool into a full development and deployment environment.

2. Using Generative-AI-Hub-SDK to Interact with Orchestration Services

Why Orchestration is Essential

While individual prompts and LLM calls are useful, real-world business scenarios require coordinated AI workflows. These workflows often include:

- Data pre-processing (e.g., filtering, formatting, masking sensitive data)
- Prompt templating

- Model selection
- Result transformation

Orchestration Services in SAP's Generative AI Hub allow these tasks to be connected and executed as a unified pipeline.

Key Concepts in Orchestration:

- **Templating:** Define dynamic prompts with placeholders that get replaced during runtime.
- **Content Filtering:** Ensure the output meets ethical and legal standards.
- **Data Masking:** Hide confidential data before sending it to the model.
- **Retrieval-Augmented Generation (RAG):** Bring in relevant business context for better accuracy.
- **Harmonized APIs:** Use one API interface for multiple models (OpenAI, SAP Joule, Cohere, etc.)

How the SDK Supports Orchestration:

Using the SDK, you can:

- Define templates and default values
- Set up and deploy orchestration workflows
- Configure and call orchestration services with a single API request
- Easily switch between models without rewriting client-side logic

This allows you to focus on business needs while the SDK and orchestration service handle infrastructure and coordination.

Example workflows include translating customer messages, tagging urgent emails, summarizing support tickets, or flagging sentiment changes — all within structured orchestration modules.

3. Using Generative-AI-Hub-SDK to Leverage the Power of LLMs

Hands-On LLM Integration

With the SDK, developers can:

- Load and preprocess data
- Define and refine prompts
- Send those prompts to different LLMs
- Receive structured outputs (text, JSON, etc.)

In the Facility Solutions case study, the SDK helped:

- Detect urgency and sentiment in customer emails
- Categorize tickets into business-defined categories
- Format responses in JSON suitable for application integration
- Iterate and improve prompts progressively

The SDK also supports key LLM functions like:

- **Chat completions**: For dialog-based applications
- **Embeddings**: For similarity search, clustering, and classification
- **Custom templates**: For replicable and reliable interactions

All of this is made possible with simple Python commands and flexible SDK utilities that reduce the need for redundant code.

4. Using Generative-AI-Hub-SDK to Evaluate Prompts

Why Evaluation Matters

Once prompts are working, how do you measure their effectiveness?

This is critical for:

- Business confidence
- Model refinement
- Avoiding incorrect or risky AI-generated outputs

Capabilities of SDK-Based Evaluation:

- Define evaluation functions to check:
  - JSON validity
  - Correctness of sentiment, urgency, categories
- Run these evaluations over full datasets
- Track KPIs like precision, recall, and format adherence
- Use RateLimitedIterator to avoid API limits

Evaluation helps set a **baseline for performance** and highlights where prompts need improvement. It supports scaling AI usage from lab environments to production systems.

Takeaways:

The **Generative AI Hub SDK** is the core toolkit for enterprise AI developers working in the SAP ecosystem. With it, you can:

- Build advanced LLM-based applications
- Create reusable, efficient orchestration workflows
- Rapidly evaluate and improve prompts
- Customize outputs based on business rules
- Seamlessly integrate AI into SAP BTP and other cloud environments

Together, these tools form a solid foundation to transform business operations using the power of Generative AI.

In the next section, we will explore **advanced prompt engineering techniques** that can help you further optimize the quality, consistency, and performance of your AI interactions.

Part 3: Refining AI Responses Using Advanced Prompt Engineering Techniques

As organizations increasingly rely on AI-powered solutions to automate and enhance customer support, internal workflows, and data analysis, the ability to fine-tune how AI models interpret instructions becomes critically important. In this part, we focus on advanced prompt engineering techniques that allow developers and practitioners to optimize the behavior and output quality of large language models (LLMs).

This section is divided into two main parts:

1. Describing Techniques for Refining Prompts
2. Implementing Advanced Prompt Engineering Techniques

Section 1: Describing Techniques for Refining Prompts

After completing this section, you will be able to explain and differentiate advanced prompting methods that enable more precise and accurate AI model responses.

The Importance of Prompt Refinement

While initial prompts may produce functional outputs, the nuances and complexity of real-world applications demand greater control and consistency. Consider the scenario discussed in previous lessons, where customer messages were being categorized based on urgency, sentiment, and topic. Although initial results were acceptable, the model occasionally produced inconsistent or vague outputs. Evaluation results confirmed that further refinement was necessary to improve accuracy and contextual understanding.

Prompt refinement is not merely about rewording an instruction—it is a systematic approach to guide the model more effectively, enhancing its reasoning and reliability. The quality of a prompt has a direct impact on how well the model performs, especially in business-critical contexts where accuracy and reproducibility matter.

Why Prompt Refinement Matters

1. **Higher Specificity**
   Structured and refined prompts help the model focus on a narrowly defined task or objective, reducing the chance of irrelevant or incomplete responses.

2. **Improved Accuracy**
   By embedding context, instructions, and expectations within the prompt, we significantly increase the relevance and correctness of the model's output.

3. **Enhanced User Experience**
   End users benefit from consistent and high-quality responses that align with business needs. Well-crafted prompts reduce follow-up clarifications and streamline interactions.

4. **Adaptability to Use Cases**
    Refined prompts can be tailored to suit different scenarios, allowing the same base model to support a range of applications—from simple data classification to complex reasoning tasks.

Advanced Prompting Techniques

Advanced prompting techniques go beyond simple question-and-answer formats. They use structure, examples, and self-generated logic to enable more effective model reasoning.

1. **One-Shot Prompting**
    In one-shot prompting, a single example is included in the prompt to demonstrate the desired behavior. This technique is suitable when data is scarce or when the task is simple and well-defined.

2. **Few-Shot Prompting**
    Few-shot prompting provides the model with multiple examples of the input-output relationship. These examples serve as implicit instructions that help the model infer patterns and apply them to new data. Few-shot prompting is especially valuable when the task requires understanding subtle distinctions or context.

3. **Metaprompting**
    Metaprompting introduces a higher level of abstraction. Instead of giving the model specific classification instructions, a metaprompt uses examples to **generate a guide** or **set of rules**. The model learns from patterns across examples and articulates general instructions for performing the task. This can be particularly useful for classification problems where categories like sentiment or urgency require explanation beyond surface-level labels.

4. **Combining Techniques**
    Often, the most effective results are achieved by combining techniques. For instance, providing a few examples alongside metaprompt-generated guides can result in significantly higher accuracy. The model benefits from both practical context and structured guidance.

In the next section, we will implement these techniques using code and evaluate their effectiveness in a realistic scenario.

Section 2: Implementing Advanced Prompt Engineering Techniques

After completing this section, you will be able to design, implement, and evaluate advanced prompt engineering strategies using Python, few-shot learning, and guided prompting techniques.

Few-Shot Prompting Implementation

To implement few-shot prompting, we begin by preparing a prompt template that includes several labeled examples. These examples illustrate how a message should be classified according to urgency, sentiment, and relevant support categories.

Code Overview

- A prompt template (prompt_10) is created to instruct the model on how to extract and categorize information.
- A subset of labeled examples (k = 3) is randomly selected from a development dataset (dev_set).
- Each example is formatted with both the input message and the corresponding ground truth output.
- These formatted examples are embedded into the prompt and passed to the model.
- A partial function is used to streamline requests, allowing different messages to be evaluated using the same prompt structure.

Purpose and Outcome

By showing the model multiple examples, we increase its understanding of the desired classification structure. The few-shot approach demonstrated measurable improvements in the accuracy of urgency and sentiment classification compared to the baseline.

Meta Prompting Implementation

Meta Prompting introduces a method for the model to infer and articulate general classification rules from examples. Instead of directly classifying messages, the model is prompted to generate **step-by-step guides** for interpreting categories such as urgency or sentiment.

Process Description

- Each example is labeled and formatted using a meta prompt template.
- A prompt (prompt_get_guide) is crafted to instruct the model to generate guides based on the examples.
- The model produces a structured set of instructions that define how to identify and differentiate between classification options.
- Guides are generated for all relevant keys: urgency, sentiment, and categories.

Benefits: The guides help formalize the classification logic and provide consistent decision-making criteria. They can be reused across prompts, enabling better transparency and model explainability.

Using Meta prompting in Classification Prompts

Once the guides have been generated, they are embedded into a new prompt template (prompt_12). This prompt includes:

- The full urgency guide
- The sentiment guide
- The category guide
- A message input for classification

The model uses these guides to produce structured JSON outputs with fields for urgency, sentiment, and categories.

Evaluation Results: After implementing this technique, we observed improvements in urgency classification, though the impact on sentiment and category accuracy was mixed. This reflects the model's ability to internalize and apply structured rules, though it may still rely on context and examples for ambiguous cases.

Combining Few-Shot and Meta prompting

The most comprehensive approach involves combining both few-shot examples and the guides generated via meta prompting into a single prompt (prompt_13). This prompt provides:

- Multiple examples to establish input-output expectations
- Detailed guides to outline reasoning and logic
- A clear instruction to produce a structured JSON response

Advantages: This approach leverages both empirical and theoretical guidance. The few-shot examples provide practical context, while the guides offer consistency and structured reasoning.

Evaluation Results: This combined technique delivered the most balanced results across all classification fields. Accuracy was improved, especially for category tagging. However, this approach also resulted in the largest prompt size and the highest inference cost.

Evaluation Summary

Each advanced prompting technique has its strengths and trade-offs. The following table summarizes their performance in terms of accuracy, complexity, and resource consumption:

Technique	Accuracy	Inference Cost	Use Case Suitability
Baseline Prompt	Low	Low	Initial prototyping, limited logic
Few-Shot Prompting	High	Medium	Moderate complexity tasks with contextual variations
Metaprompting	Medium to High	Medium	Use cases requiring structured rules and consistent logic
Combined Approach	Highest	High	Critical applications requiring both precision and depth

Conclusion and Key Takeaways

Throughout this chapter, we explored how advanced prompt engineering techniques can significantly enhance the performance of generative AI systems. These techniques are not mutually exclusive; in fact, combining them can produce the most effective results depending on the complexity and goals of the application.

Summary of Accomplishments

1. We began by creating a basic prompt to classify messages in SAP AI Launchpad.
2. We transitioned to using the generative-ai-hub-sdk to scale and automate the solution.
3. We established a baseline for evaluation using a small test dataset.
4. We applied few-shot prompting to improve the model's accuracy using labeled examples.
5. We introduced meta prompting to generate reusable, structured classification guides.
6. We combined both techniques to maximize accuracy and quality across all fields.

While the combined prompt demonstrated the best performance, it also required more computation and resources. This highlights an important consideration for production deployments: balancing accuracy with scalability and cost. In part 4 of this chapter, we will shift our focus from prompt engineering to the underlying models themselves. You will learn how to evaluate and select appropriate Large Language Models based on criteria such as performance, cost, latency, and use-case alignment. Understanding how different models behave in response to the same prompt is essential for building scalable, enterprise-grade AI solutions.

Part 4: Selecting the Suitable LLM

The objective here is to be able to **evaluate and select the most appropriate Large Language Model (LLM)** for your use case using the tools and capabilities provided by SAP's Generative AI Hub.

Choosing the Right LLM: More Than Just Accuracy

When you're solving real-world problems with generative AI, **selecting the right LLM is critical**—and often more nuanced than picking the one with the highest accuracy in a benchmark. You have to think about cost, performance, scalability, integration, and even things like latency and regulatory compliance. Let's walk through a structured approach to selecting the most suitable LLM using Generative AI Hub.

Step 1: Define the Business Context and Objectives

Every use case has its own context. For example, in the Facility Solutions scenario we've been exploring, the goal is to:

- Categorize incoming customer messages
- Identify sentiment and urgency
- Feed structured outputs into downstream ticketing or task management systems

Ask yourself:

- What kind of response do I need—structured classification or open-ended generation?
- How critical is latency?
- Is this running in real-time or batch mode?
- Do I need high accuracy, or is "good enough" good enough?
- What's my budget?

> **Tip:** Models with the highest intelligence (like GPT-4o or Claude 3.5) are often overkill—and over budget—for many day-to-day tasks like email tagging or document summarization.

Step 2: Evaluate Models Programmatically with generative-ai-hub-sdk

In the last section, we saw how to evaluate LLMs using the same dataset and prompts, varying only the model and prompting technique. This side-by-side evaluation gives us an apples-to-apples comparison.

Let's recap how this was done:

- *Basic Prompt with* mistralai--mixtral-8x7b-instruct-v01 *(fast, low cost, SAP-hosted)*
- *Few-shot + Meta prompting with the same model (improved accuracy without changing models)*
- *Repeat with GPT-4o (OpenAI), Gemini-1.5-Flash (Google), and Meta LLaMA3-70B*
- *Observe performance, cost, and quality of output*

This shows that you don't always need to change the model to get better performance—you can often do more with better prompt engineering.

Step 3: Compare Models Using Key Dimensions

Let's break it down with five key considerations, based on your scenario:

1. Performance (Accuracy, Completeness, Fluency)

Does the model return high-quality, complete, and correct responses?

- **Open-source models (e.g., Mixtral)**: Surprisingly good for structured tasks like classification or tagging.
- **Proprietary models (e.g., GPT-4o, Gemini)**: Better for nuanced understanding, reasoning, or handling messy/unstructured input.
- **LLaMA3-70B**: Great performance, especially with few-shot prompting; available via SAP-hosted runtime—great balance.

Use Case Fit Example: For structured classification, even Mixtral performs well. But for generating summaries from emails, GPT-4o shines.

2. Cost Efficiency

Are you optimizing your AI spend?

- Token pricing, inference cost, and compute time all matter.
- Using a model like GPT-4o on every call can get expensive fast.
- Cheaper models with enhanced prompting can often achieve almost the same result at a fraction of the cost.

> **Pro Tip:** Use cheaper models for initial screening/classification. Route complex cases to expensive models. This tiered approach saves money and maintains quality.

3. Speed and Latency

Do you need real-time performance?

- **Gemini-1.5-Flash**: Extremely fast; ideal for real-time needs like chatbots or support systems.

- **GPT-4o**: High latency, but high quality—best for offline batch processing or strategic tasks.
- **Mixtral & LLaMA3**: SAP-hosted models with moderate latency and solid performance.

Use Case Fit Example: In the Facility Solutions Company scenario, latency isn't critical, so LLaMA3-70B with few-shot prompting becomes a cost-effective and powerful choice.

4. Deployment Flexibility

Where do you plan to run this?

- On SAP BTP? Use SAP-hosted models like Mixtral or LLaMA3.
- On Azure/GCP/AWS? Use OpenAI, Vertex AI, or Bedrock integrations.
- Bringing your own model? BYOM is supported in SAP AI Core.

SAP's Generative AI Hub enables seamless orchestration across cloud providers and models—so you're never locked in.

Smart Integration: Use orchestration to switch between models without rewriting business logic. This makes upgrades or experimentation frictionless.

5. Governance and Responsible AI

Do you need to audit outputs or control model behavior?

- SAP provides built-in privacy, logging, and lifecycle management for hosted models.
- Enterprise control is easier with open-source models you can self-host.
- Rate limits, token caps, and expiration timelines (see SAP Note 3437766) are critical when deploying at scale.

Good Practice: Log model versions, prompt templates, and output samples to ensure auditability and reproducibility.

Model Selection Decision Guide

Here's a simplified decision matrix to help make that final model decision:

Use Case Type	Budget Constraints	Latency Needs	Recommended Model(s)
Email Classification	Medium to Low	Medium	mixtral-8x7b, llama3-70b-instruct
Customer Summaries	Medium to High	Low	gpt-4o, claude-3.5-sonnet
Real-Time Support	Low	High	gemini-1.5-flash, amazon--titan-embed-text
Custom GPT Workflow	High	Low	gpt-4o, llama3-70b with few-shot prompting

Putting It All Together: Facility Solutions Recommendation

Based on the evaluations, we can draw this insight:

"Although several models perform well across different aspects, **the few-shot prompt with meta--llama3-70b-instruct offers the best blend of accuracy, speed, cost-efficiency, and integration** for our business need—structured classification of customer messages."

This approach:

- Allows integration with other enterprise systems
- Can be orchestrated easily in SAP AI Core
- Offers lower cost without sacrificing much on quality

So the Facility Solutions team can confidently scale this model across departments, reducing manual triage and improving customer satisfaction with faster response times.

Takeaway

Choosing the right LLM within the Generative AI Hub is an **iterative, business-driven process**. There's no one-size-fits-all. Instead, you evaluate models like you would choose any strategic technology—by aligning them with your goals, constraints, and future roadmap.

With SAP's powerful orchestration and model management features, you can:

- Mix and match LLMs
- Reuse prompts and code across models
- Switch providers effortlessly
- Optimize for price, performance, and control

In this chapter, we dove headfirst into the inner workings of the Generative AI Hub, and let's be honest—it was pretty technical.

We began by learning how to create basic prompts inside the Generative AI Hub. From there, we leveled up, exploring how to harness the full potential of LLMs using the generative-ai-hub-sdk—a powerful toolkit that brings code into the equation and scales up your experimentation.

Things got more advanced when we explored prompt engineering techniques, using few-shot examples and meta prompting to take LLM outputs from decent to enterprise-grade. And just when you thought we'd hit the limit, we pushed further—evaluating and comparing multiple LLMs using real-world business problems, dissecting their performance, cost, and capabilities inside the model-rich ecosystem of SAP's Generative AI Hub.

Yes, there were a lot of moving parts. And yes, it may have felt overwhelming at times. But this complexity is what gives you the control and flexibility to tailor AI solutions with precision. The real win? You now have a strong foundational understanding of how to design, experiment, and choose the right AI building blocks—and that's a game-changer for any enterprise AI journey.

But this was just the beginning.

As we transition to Chapter 5: SAP AI Core, we'll shift from "choosing and prompting models" to operationalizing them. This is where models come to life—deployed, managed, and scaled across your landscapes. SAP AI Core is the engine room that turns prototypes into production-grade AI services.

So, take a deep breath. We've covered the 'what' and the 'why.' Now, let's discover how to run AI like a well-oiled machine.

Let's get into SAP AI Core.

What You Just Learned

- **SAP Generative AI Hub** is the enterprise gateway for designing, testing, and deploying LLM-powered solutions securely and at scale.
- You learned to **create basic prompts**, extract structured data, and refine outputs using **prompt engineering** techniques like few-shot and meta prompting.
- The **Generative AI Hub SDK** allows developers to integrate AI into SAP apps programmatically, orchestrate workflows, and evaluate model performance.
- You explored how to **select the right LLM** based on performance, cost, latency, deployment flexibility, and governance needs.
- Key tools include **SAP AI Core**, **AI Launchpad**, and **HANA Vector Engine** — all supporting compliant, scalable AI operations.
- The chapter emphasized **practical experimentation**, real-world evaluations, and how to balance accuracy with cost and business context.
- You're now equipped to **design and scale Gen AI use cases** within SAP — with precision, flexibility, and control.

Next up: SAP AI Core — where AI solutions move from prototype to production.

CHAPTER 5

From Idea to Execution — Mastering "SAP AI Core"

You've come a long way.

In the previous chapters, we explored the exciting world of Large Language Models (LLMs) through SAP's Generative AI Hub. You created your first prompts, engineered them for better responses, evaluated models using the generative-ai-hub-sdk, and learned how to intelligently select the best fit for your business problems. That journey gave you a strong foundation in designing AI-powered solutions.

But now, it's time to shift gears—from experimenting with AI to operationalizing it.

Welcome to SAP AI Core, the engine that drives scalable, secure, and enterprise-grade AI operations within the SAP Business Technology Platform (SAP BTP). Think of SAP AI Core as the mission control center where your AI projects are orchestrated, monitored, trained, deployed, and ultimately embedded into real business workflows.

Why SAP AI Core Matters

Building AI is one thing. Running it at scale—in production, across departments, while maintaining data privacy, version control, model retraining, deployment pipelines, and cost efficiency—is another level entirely. That's where SAP AI Core comes in. It's designed to help you:

- Run custom AI pipelines on your own data
- Train models from scratch or fine-tune pre-existing ones
- Serve AI models in real time for inference and prediction
- Monitor lifecycle events and ensure traceability and compliance
- Seamlessly connect AI assets to SAP applications via SAP AI Launchpad

In this chapter, we move from "cool ideas" to production-ready, value-driving AI assets. Whether you're a developer, data scientist, or business technologist, SAP AI Core empowers you to scale AI reliably—without getting stuck in silos or reinventing the wheel.

What You'll Learn in This Chapter

By the end of this chapter, you'll have a working understanding of how to:

- **Onboard into SAP AI Core and SAP AI Launchpad** — so you can manage your AI projects in a centralized and collaborative environment
- Understand and manage **model training operations** — configuring training pipelines, handling datasets, and tracking experiments
- Explore **model inferencing operations** — deploying trained models as real-time APIs or batch services that can integrate with SAP or non-SAP applications

This chapter is more technical and operational in nature—but also more transformational. This is where the "magic" of AI becomes usable, governable, and valuable at scale.

Learning Objectives

After completing this chapter, you'll be able to:

- Embed AI into SAP solutions through SAP AI Launchpad
- Configure and manage the SAP AI Core service
- Train and deploy AI models for real-world use cases
- Understand the end-to-end lifecycle of AI in production

If you're ready to move beyond designing and start operationalizing AI like a pro, this chapter is your launchpad. It's time to take your innovative ideas and transform them into scalable, production-grade solutions that deliver measurable business value—securely, efficiently, and with enterprise confidence.

Let's start by exploring how to **onboard into SAP AI Core and SAP AI Launchpad**, laying the foundation for everything that follows.

Part 1: Onboarding SAP AI Core and SAP AI Launchpad

Objectives

After completing this part, you will be able to:

- Illustrate the end-to-end process of working with SAP AI Core and SAP AI Launchpad
- Understand the value proposition of both services within the SAP AI ecosystem
- Set up and configure SAP AI Core and SAP AI Launchpad for enterprise AI use
- Manage resource groups and integrate external tools like Docker and GitHub
- Establish secure access to external object stores for datasets and model artifacts

Introduction

As we transition from experimentation with prompts and large language models (LLMs) in the Generative AI Hub to production-grade AI operations, it becomes critical to understand how SAP handles the execution, deployment, and lifecycle management of AI solutions. This is where SAP AI Core and SAP AI Launchpad come in.

This section of the chapter focuses on onboarding—laying the foundation to run AI pipelines at scale using cloud-native, enterprise-grade infrastructure, while integrating with external tools and managing resources securely.

Note: This learning journey focuses on SAP AI Core and its related services. To explore use cases related to LLMs and prompt-based solutions, refer to the learning journey Solving Your Business Problems Using Prompts and LLMs in SAP's Generative AI Hub, which covers Generative AI Hub, SAP AI Launchpad, and the generative-ai-hub SDK.

SAP AI Core: Value Proposition

SAP AI Core is a managed service on SAP Business Technology Platform (BTP) that supports the execution and lifecycle management of AI models and pipelines. It allows users to operationalize their AI scenarios through orchestration, automation, and secure deployment.

Benefits of SAP AI Core

1. **Managed AI Deployments**
   SAP AI Core eliminates infrastructure complexity by packaging dependencies and exposing simple APIs for AI integration, so developers and business users can focus on value rather than architecture.

2. **Embedded Intelligence in Business Processes**
   With standard integrations into SAP applications, models can be seamlessly embedded into business workflows for automation and intelligent decision-making.

3. **Balanced Performance and Cost Efficiency**
   AI Core supports GPU-based execution for heavy workloads, while built-in autoscaling, scale-to-zero functionality, and flexible service plans help control costs.

4. **Kubernetes-Based Infrastructure**
   AI Core runs on Kubernetes clusters that dynamically allocate resources like CPU, memory, and GPU based on pipeline needs. This allows for scalable, containerized operations tailored to each AI scenario.

5. **Reusable and Scalable AI Templates**
   Teams can train models once and serve them to multiple consumers, internally or externally, using standardized, reusable templates.

6. **Open Architecture**
   SAP AI Core is framework-agnostic and supports integration with external tools and services, including GitHub, Docker, and various object storage platforms.

SAP AI Launchpad: Centralized AI Lifecycle Management

SAP AI Launchpad serves as the single point of access for managing AI content and workflows across the enterprise. It is integrated with SAP AI Core and other AI runtimes through the standardized AI API.

Benefits of SAP AI Launchpad

1. **Centralized Control and Visibility**
   Launchpad provides a holistic view of AI models, executions, deployments, and related metrics—regardless of the underlying runtime or technology.

2. **Lifecycle Management of AI Scenarios**
   Users can create, monitor, and manage AI assets, trigger jobs, and handle deployment operations from a unified interface.

3. **Standardized Integration**
   Launchpad supports uniform model training, status tracking, deployment, and reusability across projects, enabling greater transparency and innovation.

4. **Monitoring and Retraining Capabilities**
   Launchpad allows for continuous monitoring and model retraining based on performance metrics, helping maintain model quality and relevance over time.

Enterprise-Grade Features of SAP AI Core and Launchpad

To support secure, scalable AI deployment, SAP AI Core and SAP AI Launchpad offer a number of key enterprise features:

- **Orchestration of AI workflows** such as training and inference
- **Support for continuous delivery** and DevOps workflows
- **Multi-tenancy and resource isolation** via Kubernetes-based resource groups
- **Pay-per-use model** with access to scalable GPU infrastructure
- **Framework openness**, supporting any AI/ML stack
- **Standardized APIs** for model execution, training triggers, and monitoring
- **Development tools**, including the SAP AI Core SDK
- **Choice of storage systems** for model data and logs

Initial Configuration: Onboarding Workflow

To begin using SAP AI Core and SAP AI Launchpad, an initial one-time configuration is required. The onboarding process includes connecting your SAP AI Core instance to external tools and services, as well as setting up access controls and resource groups.

Prerequisites

Before beginning the configuration, ensure the following are in place:

- SAP BTP account with entitlements for **SAP AI Core** and **SAP AI Launchpad**
- A **Git repository** (e.g., GitHub or GitLab) to manage workflow templates
- Access to a **Docker container registry** (e.g., Docker Hub or GitHub Packages)
- A **cloud object store** (e.g., Amazon S3, Azure Blob) for dataset and model storage
- Completion of SAP BTP initial setup tasks and administrator access
- Optional: SAP AI Core SDK for CLI-based operations

Resource Groups in SAP AI Core

SAP AI Core uses **Kubernetes-based resource groups** to isolate workloads and data. These resource groups are logical containers that house:

- Configurations
- Executions
- Deployments
- Artifacts

Use Cases for Resource Groups

- SAP Line of Business (LoB) providers: Isolate customer data by creating one resource group per customer.
- Enterprise departments: Segment data and assets across internal departments (e.g., finance, HR, logistics).

This ensures security, compliance, and multi-tenancy without cross-access.

Refer to the SAP Help Portal for more:

Managing Resource Groups:
https://help.sap.com/docs/AI_CORE/2d6c5984063c40a59eda62f4a9135bee/8aae6cbe 2c0e4290954b8f61b4b355b7.html

Connecting External Tools and Managing Credentials

To operationalize AI workloads, SAP AI Core must connect securely to external services such as version control, container registries, and cloud storage. These integrations are set up using **secrets**—credential-based objects managed in the SAP AI Core environment.

1. Git Repository Integration

SAP AI Core uses Git repositories to manage and version templates, pipelines, and configurations. GitOps principles enable automatic synchronization.

- Create a Git credential secret in AI Core
- Sync your content using the GitOps operator

Refer to: **Managing Your Git Repository**
https://help.sap.com/docs/AI_CORE/0a9b8707f4bb4c2ab9aeb28a2fa1803e.html

2. Object Store Integration

Datasets, model artifacts, and cache files are stored in external cloud object stores. To connect:

- Configure storage (e.g., S3 or Azure Blob)
- Create an object store credential secret in AI Core

Refer to: **Managing Object Store Credentials**
https://help.sap.com/docs/AI_CORE/13bc64aa3bb64d179c3f8b1ec540b87a.html

3. Docker Registry Integration

AI workloads in SAP AI Core run in Docker containers. To support this:

- Use a Docker container registry
- Create a Docker registry credential secret in AI Core to allow image pulling

Refer to: **Managing Docker Credentials**
https://help.sap.com/docs/AI_CORE/91cbdca5dfec41e3b5cc472372b16944.html

SAP AI Launchpad Integration

Once your SAP AI Core instance is configured, connect it to SAP AI Launchpad to enable:

- Centralized lifecycle management of models
- Deployment and monitoring through a graphical interface
- KPI tracking and model comparison
- Visibility into model status, configurations, and deployments

SAP AI Launchpad connects to SAP AI Core using the standardized **AI API**, enabling seamless runtime integration.

Refer to: **SAP AI Launchpad Help**
https://help.sap.com/docs/ai-launchpad

Takeaways:

In this part of the chapter, you've completed the foundational onboarding for SAP AI Core and SAP AI Launchpad. You have:

- Understood the roles and value propositions of both services
- Reviewed and fulfilled prerequisites for configuration
- Set up resource groups for workload isolation
- Created and managed secure credentials for Git, Docker, and object storage
- Integrated your SAP AI Core instance with SAP AI Launchpad for lifecycle management

With this infrastructure now in place, you are fully prepared to begin building and executing training workflows for your AI models.

Part 2: Describing Model Training Operations

Objective

After completing this part of the chapter, you will be able to:

- Trigger the training of a machine learning (ML) model using SAP AI Core
- Prepare datasets and register them for AI workflows
- Structure and manage AI training pipelines with configurations and scenarios

- Execute model training and track performance
- Understand how to adapt and scale model training pipelines using SAP best practices

Introduction: From Setup to Model Execution

In Part 1, you completed the onboarding of SAP AI Core and SAP AI Launchpad. You now have a connected, secured, and tool-integrated environment—ready for enterprise AI operations.

In this section, we transition from infrastructure setup to **training machine learning models using SAP AI Core**, covering the full pipeline lifecycle—from ingesting datasets to storing and registering trained models.

Model Training in SAP AI Core: Overview

Model training in SAP AI Core involves running containerized AI workflows using orchestration, secure data access, and configuration-driven executions. These workflows are:

- Defined in version-controlled repositories
- Parameterized for flexibility (datasets, hyperparameters, resource plans)
- Executed on demand or on schedule
- Managed via AI Core API or SAP AI Launchpad interface

With SAP AI Core, you build once and reuse across multiple models, datasets, or business problems—all while maintaining traceability and security.

Prerequisites

Before starting model training, the following must be in place:

- SAP AI Core and AI Launchpad configured with an active BTP account
- Resource group(s) created and available
- Object store (e.g., AWS S3) provisioned and connected
- Access credentials (secrets) for GitHub, Docker, and object store created in AI Core
- At least one AI pipeline template available in your Git repository
- SAP AI Core SDK (CLI or Python) or Postman setup for API calls

- A registered training dataset in object storage
- Upgraded to a **Standard Plan** if executing beyond the free-tier quota

Step-by-Step: Training in SAP AI Core

Step 1: Prepare and Register Input Dataset

Your dataset must reside in an external object store like AWS S3. SAP AI Core interacts with this data transparently through secure credentials.

- Create a dataset artifact pointing to the folder or file within your object store
- Store the corresponding object store secret in SAP AI Core
- Register the artifact in the appropriate resource group

Note: Multiple datasets can be defined for a single workflow. You can switch between them using placeholders or template parameters in your configuration. This is useful for retraining with fresh data, A/B testing, or experimenting with various preprocessing techniques.

Step 2: Define Your AI Scenario and Executable

SAP AI Core organizes workflows under scenarios. A scenario is a logical grouping of all the components (executables, configurations, logs, results) related to a specific business use case.

- An **executable** represents your pipeline template (defined in YAML or Python)
- It includes the input/output specifications, training code, and infrastructure requirements
- Executables are tied to your Git repository content

Example Use Case: You may define a scenario named house-price-prediction and register an executable that uses a TensorFlow or scikit-learn container to run a regression pipeline.

Step 3: Create a Configuration

A configuration binds together:

- The executable (pipeline definition)
- The input dataset(s)

- Parameters such as learning rate, epochs, or batch size
- The resource plan (CPU/GPU and memory allocation)

This configuration enables dynamic customization for each training run without editing your source code.

Key Concept: You can create multiple configurations using the same executable to experiment with different training datasets or hyperparameters.

Step 4: Trigger Execution

Once the configuration is in place, use the SAP AI Core API, SDK, or AI Launchpad to trigger an execution.

An execution is the runtime instance of your configuration. When triggered:

- The pipeline reads the dataset from the object store
- The model training logic (from the container image) runs
- Metrics, logs, and artifacts are collected
- The trained model is stored back into the object store

Infrastructure Consiqsderations:
Executions can request different resource plans (predefined bundles) that vary in CPU, GPU, and memory availability. SAP AI Core ensures scalability and cost control by allocating only what is needed and autoscaling where applicable.

Step 5: Monitor Training Progress and Retrieve Metrics

You can monitor the progress and status of your training execution in SAP AI Launchpad.

- View logs and execution status in real-time
- Check system resource usage and performance metrics
- Retrieve model accuracy, loss, F1 scores, or any custom metric you define via your pipeline logic
- Compare runs to identify the most performant configuration

SAP AI Core allows you to register metrics using standard APIs. These can later be consumed by dashboards or used for automated evaluation and retraining triggers.

Step 6: Store and Register the Trained Model

Once training is complete:

- The trained model is saved into the object store (e.g., AWS S3)
- The model artifact is automatically registered with SAP AI Core
- You can retrieve or deploy the model directly from its registered location

This creates a versioned, traceable, and reusable model asset for downstream inference or integration.

Dataset and Code Management Best Practices

1. **Use Placeholders for Dataset Variability**
   Define placeholders for input datasets in your pipeline logic to enable dynamic switching between multiple sources without code changes.

2. **Abstract Parameters**
   Use configuration files to define hyperparameters like learning rate or batch size, enabling experimentation and tuning without modifying source code.

3. **Containerize Your Training Logic**
   Package your training code into a Docker image, enabling reproducibility and isolated execution in SAP AI Core.

4. **Organize Artifacts in Object Stores**
   Keep input, output, and intermediate results in a structured object store directory for traceability and reuse.

Importance of the House Price Predictor Tutorial

To ground these concepts, SAP provides a guided example titled: Ingest Live Data into Your House Price Predictor with SAP AI Core

This hands-on tutorial is **highly relevant**, as it demonstrates how to:

- Create reusable training workflows
- Dynamically switch datasets and parameters
- Register, execute, and store models
- Monitor the end-to-end AI lifecycle using both SAP AI Core and AI Launchpad

It reflects real-world best practices for MLOps using SAP's enterprise AI toolset and serves as a reference implementation for your own use cases.

Important Note: This tutorial requires a Standard Plan of SAP AI Core (not free-tier), and usage of either Postman or the SAP AI Core SDK to perform key operations not yet supported via SAP AI Launchpad alone.

Link to House Price Predictor Tutorial: https://developers.sap.com/tutorials/ai-core-data.html

Prerequisites Before Training

To train models using SAP AI Core, ensure the following prerequisites are completed:

- BTP global account with access to SAP AI Core and AI Launchpad
- Resource groups created and configured
- Git repository with pipeline templates available
- Docker container registry with training images accessible
- Object store (e.g., AWS S3) provisioned and connected
- Secrets for Git, Docker, and object storage created in AI Core
- Completed onboarding tutorials:
  - Quick Start: Your First AI Project Using SAP AI Core
  - Build a House Price Predictor with SAP AI Core

High-Level Steps: House Price Predictor Training Tutorial

The following are the 22 key steps from the House Price Predictor tutorial. These form a detailed, production-grade blueprint for training workflows in SAP AI Core:

1. Modify AI Code – Adapt training logic for new data.
2. Understand Your Code – Review pipeline components and execution flow.
3. Create Placeholders for Datasets in Workflows – Enable flexibility in pipeline configurations.
4. Understand Workflow Changes – Recognize how modular pipelines work.
5. Create Placeholders for Hyperparameters – Parameterize training logic for reusability.
6. Set Resource Plan – Choose appropriate CPU/GPU allocation.
7. Observe Scenario and Placeholders – Understand the scenario structure within SAP AI Core.

8. Create Cloud Storage for Datasets and Models – Use AWS S3 or another hyperscaler for persistence.
9. Connect Local System to AWS S3 – Establish secure access to cloud storage.
10. Upload Datasets to AWS S3 – Make data available for training.
11. Store Object Store Secret in SAP AI Core – Secure cloud access with credentials.
12. Create Artifact to Specify Dataset Folder – Point AI Core to the training data.
13. Locate Artifacts – Verify dataset and model references.
14. Use Artifacts with Workflows via Configuration – Bind data and code together dynamically.
15. Run Your Workflow Using Execution – Launch training with selected configuration.
16. Set Model Pipeline in Workflow – Finalize architecture used during training.
17. Describe Workflow Changes – Document updates to logic or parameters.
18. Create Required Object Store Secret *default* for Model – Secure model output storage.
19. Create Another Configuration with New Data – Train with alternate datasets.
20. Create Another Execution – Launch second training run for comparison.
21. Schedule Your Execution (Optional) – Automate training on a schedule.
22. Locate Your Model in AWS S3 – Access the registered, trained model for downstream use.

Relevance of the 22-Step Tutorial

Each of the 22 steps plays a role in establishing **reproducibility, modularity, security, and scalability**—the pillars of enterprise AI. Together, they demonstrate how to:

- Run repeatable experiments with dynamic configurations
- Securely manage data and code using external tools
- Monitor and evaluate model performance with real metrics
- Transition from development to production AI pipelines

This tutorial isn't just an academic exercise—it represents a **blueprint for any AI model training workflow** in SAP AI Core, whether you're building a predictive model, a classifier, or a generative model.

Executing a Training Pipeline: SAP AI Core Workflow

With the concepts from the tutorial in mind, here is the workflow you follow within SAP AI Core to train a model:

1. **Register your dataset as an artifact** (e.g., S3 URI in object store)
2. **Define your executable** – A pointer to your pipeline logic in Git
3. **Create a configuration** – Connects datasets, parameters, and resource plan
4. **Trigger execution** – Launches the training job in a secure container
5. **Track metrics and logs** – Monitor using Launchpad or SAP AI Core API
6. **Register trained model as an artifact** – Automatically stored and versioned

This process can be repeated with different datasets, hyperparameters, or code versions—enabling continuous training and experimentation.

Takeaways:

In this section, you've learned:

- How model training is structured and executed in SAP AI Core
- How to manage datasets, configurations, and training logic
- How to monitor training runs using SAP AI Launchpad
- The importance of metrics, logs, and model versioning
- How to apply the 22-step House Price Predictor tutorial as a practical reference for building scalable AI pipelines

The concepts and processes in this part provide the backbone for enterprise-grade ML lifecycle management in SAP. You now understand how to go from dataset ingestion to model training and registration—using SAP's infrastructure, APIs, and UI tools.

Part 3: Serving an ML Model

After completing this part, you will be able to:

- Deploy a trained machine learning (ML) model using SAP AI Core
- Expose the model as an endpoint for real-time inference
- Integrate the inference endpoint into downstream applications and services

From Training to Real-Time Intelligence

In Part 1, you prepared the SAP AI Core and AI Launchpad environments for secure, enterprise-grade AI operations. In Part 2, you trained a machine learning model using an orchestrated AI pipeline and registered it as a reusable asset.

Now, in the final stage of this workflow, we focus on serving the trained model—transforming it from a static artifact into a live, intelligent service. This stage is commonly referred to as model inferencing or model serving.

Model deployment is where your AI solution begins generating real business value—making predictions from new data in real-time or via scheduled batch jobs.

What is Model Serving?

Once a model has been trained and evaluated, it must be **deployed** so it can receive new input data and generate predictions. This process is known as **serving** or **inferencing**.

In SAP AI Core, this involves:

- Developing a **serving application**
- Running it in a **Docker container**
- Deploying it on a **Kubernetes-based infrastructure**
- Exposing an **HTTP endpoint** that receives and processes prediction requests

SAP AI Core simplifies this process by allowing you to define and deploy inference services using **templates**, which are executed as part of the AI Core runtime.

Deployment Architecture in SAP AI Core

SAP AI Core uses Kubernetes to host your deployed models, ensuring **performance, scalability, and cost control**.

Key Features:

- **CPU and GPU Support**: Deploy models on the most suitable infrastructure based on performance and cost requirements.
- **Autoscaling**: Automatically replicates the model server to handle increased request volumes.

- **Scale-to-Zero**: Suspends inactive containers to minimize costs and resumes them when needed.

This design ensures that your model is always ready to respond to prediction requests, without incurring unnecessary infrastructure expenses.

How Model Deployment Works

Step 1: Develop a Serving Application

The serving application is a lightweight web application, typically written in Python (e.g., using Flask or FastAPI), that:

- Accepts inference requests via HTTP (POST method)
- Loads the trained model from the object store
- Applies the model to the incoming data
- Returns the prediction in the response

This containerized application must be built and pushed to your Docker registry and referenced in your AI Core executable.

Step 2: Define the Serving Template

You define an **executable template** that specifies:

- The container image for your serving application
- The resource plan (CPU/GPU, memory)
- The model artifact to be used
- The endpoint configuration
- Any runtime parameters needed

This template is stored and versioned in your Git repository and is registered as an **executable** in SAP AI Core.

Step 3: Create a Deployment Configuration

Using SAP AI Core or AI Launchpad, create a **configuration** that binds your executable to:

- The trained model artifact stored in the object store
- The specific runtime environment
- Any request limits, replicas, or timeout settings

This configuration ensures that the right model, code, and infrastructure are used for deployment.

Step 4: Trigger the Deployment

Once the configuration is set, trigger the **deployment** via the SAP AI Core SDK, Postman, or the SAP AI Launchpad UI. The system:

- Launches the container in Kubernetes
- Exposes an HTTP endpoint
- Returns a **deployment URL** that can be called for predictions

Real-Time Inferencing

The exposed endpoint is a live service that can now be used for online inferencing. This means:

- You can send JSON payloads with new data to the endpoint
- The model will process the input and return predictions instantly
- The endpoint can be consumed by business applications, APIs, notebooks, or middleware

SAP AI Core's AI API standard ensures that inference requests are **secure, consistent, and easy to integrate**.

Common integration examples:

- SAP CAP-based applications
- SAP UI5 interfaces
- Jupyter notebooks for experimentation

- Postman for API testing
- Workflow automations or chatbots

Example: House Price Predictor Model Deployment

SAP provides a guided tutorial titled:

Build a House Price Predictor with SAP AI Core
SAP Developers Tutorial

This tutorial is the practical continuation of the training tutorial you saw in Part 2. It walks you through:

- Writing a serving application for the house price model
- Containerizing the application
- Defining a serving template and deployment configuration
- Deploying the model in SAP AI Core
- Testing the live endpoint with new house price data

This tutorial is **essential for hands-on learners** and acts as a real-world blueprint for production model serving. The deployment section demonstrates all the concepts covered in this part—from endpoint creation to inference integration.

Takeaways: Completing the AI Lifecycle

With this part, you have now completed the **end-to-end journey of operationalizing machine learning in SAP AI Core**:

- From setting up the environment and onboarding (Part 1)
- To training reusable, scalable models on enterprise data (Part 2)
- To deploying those models as real-time services for consumption (Part 3)

You have learned how SAP AI Core and SAP AI Launchpad support the full MLOps lifecycle—from data to prediction—with flexibility, traceability, and scalability.

This chapter closes with the understanding that AI in the enterprise doesn't stop at model development. It continues into deployment, monitoring, continuous improvement, and business integration. As you move forward, the real impact will come from applying these capabilities to your own data, workflows, and applications—bringing intelligent decision-making to every corner of your business.

What You Just Learned

- **SAP AI Core** is the backbone for deploying, scaling, and managing AI solutions securely in production within SAP BTP.
- You learned to **onboard SAP AI Core and Launchpad**, configure resource groups, and integrate with Git, Docker, and object stores.
- You now understand how to **train ML models**, manage datasets, define configurations, and monitor metrics in a reproducible pipeline.
- SAP AI Core enables **real-time model serving** by exposing trained models as secure APIs, integrated into SAP and non-SAP apps.
- Through tutorials like the **House Price Predictor**, you followed a practical MLOps blueprint—covering data prep, training, deployment, and inference.
- The chapter emphasized **lifecycle management**, **traceability**, and **enterprise-grade scalability**, completing your transition from AI design to execution.

You're now equipped to turn AI ideas into live, intelligent services that deliver measurable business impact across SAP landscapes. With this chapter, you've reached the final step of your hands-on journey in operationalizing machine learning within SAP AI Core. I hope this experience has not only deepened your understanding but also sparked the confidence to bring AI to life in your own enterprise landscape.

Let's take a moment to pause and reflect on this unit—a critical milestone in our journey.

This chapter served as the core solution component of this book, where we unpacked the foundation, architecture, and technologies powering Generative AI. What comes next is the practical application of these solutions in real-world enterprise scenarios. But before we move forward, it is vital to appreciate the depth of knowledge we've gained here. Unit 3 offered us not just conceptual understanding but also introduced the very core platforms, models, and services that form the technological bedrock of SAP's Generative AI ecosystem.

We transitioned from understanding what Generative AI is and how it works to exploring how SAP, one of the world's most trusted enterprise software providers, is embedding this revolutionary technology across its stack. Whether you are a data scientist, SAP consultant, enterprise architect, or business stakeholder, the knowledge gained in this unit will directly impact how you think about designing and implementing AI solutions in your organization.

Chapter-by-Chapter Summary

Chapter 1: Introduction to Generative AI

This chapter laid the groundwork, providing a robust introduction to what Generative AI is, its evolution, and its core technologies such as neural networks, transformers, and autoregressive models. We also touched upon ethical considerations, key use cases across industries, and how GenAI is fundamentally different from traditional AI models in terms of creativity, contextual understanding, and adaptability.

Chapter 2: Fundamentals of Large Language Models (LLMs)

This was a deep dive into the heart of Generative AI: LLMs. We examined their architecture, training techniques, prompt engineering, fine-tuning methods, and inference optimizations. This chapter also connected LLM capabilities directly to SAP's use cases—ranging from document processing and knowledge retrieval to natural language interfaces for enterprise systems.

Chapter 3: SAP Business AI

Here we explored SAP's strategic direction for AI with SAP Business AI, the umbrella framework for embedding AI into SAP applications. We discussed core principles like enterprise readiness, trust, security, and explainability, as well as solution areas where Business AI is actively deployed—finance, HR, procurement, and more.

Chapter 4: SAP Generative AI Hub

A crucial chapter that showcased the entry point for GenAI services in the SAP ecosystem. The Generative AI Hub acts as a central gateway for accessing, managing, and consuming LLM-based capabilities. We discussed prompt templates, pre-built use cases, integration patterns, and how developers and business users alike can orchestrate AI into their workflows without writing complex code.

Chapter 5: SAP AI Core

The most technical chapter of this unit, focusing on SAP AI Core—the backbone for lifecycle management of AI models. This chapter outlined how SAP enables training, deployment, monitoring, retraining, and scaling of AI/ML models using standard DevOps and MLOps practices. Special emphasis was placed on post-deployment governance, cost control, and real-time observability.

Summary Table: Unit 3 at a Glance

Chapter	Core Focus	Tools/Frameworks Introduced	Key Takeaways
Introduction to Generative AI	Foundational concepts of GenAI and its evolution	Neural Nets, Transformers, Ethical AI Principles	Understand the "why" behind Generative AI and its transformative capabilities.
Fundamentals of LLMs	Architecture, training, and tuning of LLMs	GPT, BERT, RLHF, Fine-tuning, Prompt Engineering	Gain technical fluency in how LLMs work and how they are optimized.
SAP Business AI	Strategic vision of AI in SAP products	SAP BTP AI Services, Trust Layer, Industry Use Cases	Recognize how SAP ensures responsible and scalable use of AI in enterprises.
SAP Generative AI Hub	Enablement and consumption layer for GenAI in SAP	Prompt Templates, API Integration, SAP Build Process	Explore the developer-centric gateway to consume LLMs inside SAP applications.
SAP AI Core	End-to-end lifecycle management for AI models	MLOps Pipelines, Model Monitoring, SAP AI Launchpad	Learn how to train, deploy, govern, and scale AI models across the SAP ecosystem.

The Role of Unit 3 as the "Solution" Layer

Unit 3 was dense—and intentionally so. This was the "technical core" of the book, where we moved from ideas to infrastructure, from AI dreams to practical implementations. We introduced critical frameworks such as LLMs, SAP AI Core, and the SAP Generative AI Hub—each serving a unique role in delivering intelligent automation, personalized user experiences, and data-driven decisions.

More importantly, this unit brought together the technologies that SAP uses to industrialize Generative AI. These are not just theoretical models or sandbox experiments—these are enterprise-ready platforms built for scale, compliance, and performance. This is what distinguishes SAP's approach in a sea of AI innovation.

In short, Unit 3 is the backbone. It is the foundation that will carry the weight of everything we do next. If Unit 1 was the "**problem space**" and Unit 3 was the "**solution space**," then what follows is the **"execution space."**

What's Next: From Blueprint to Business Value

With this strong foundation in place, we now shift gears from theory to practice. In the upcoming unit, we will apply the solutions discussed so far by **embedding Generative AI into real SAP processes**. Our primary focus will be on **automating SAP production support**, especially within the domain of **SAP Finance**. This is where AI moves from **design to deployment—from possibility to performance**.

Get ready to witness how Generative AI becomes a co-pilot in SAP workflows, accelerates resolution times, and enhances user experience. We will walk through actual use cases, step-by-step automation patterns, and measurable business outcomes.

Let's now enter the heart of transformation.

From Vision to Victory: Gear Up for Unit 4

We've decoded the algorithms. We've explored the architecture. We've mastered the tools. Now, it's time to **unleash the power of Generative AI** where it matters most—**inside the enterprise**.

Unit 4 is where the spark becomes a flame.

This is the part you've been waiting for—the transition from ideas to impact. No more blueprints. No more theoretical potential.

In Unit 4, we **embed Generative AI directly into SAP business processes**, transforming daily workflows into intelligent, self-optimizing systems.

- Imagine an SAP Finance team that never chases reports but gets insights in real-time.
- Picture a helpdesk that speaks your business language—powered by AI.
- Visualize production support issues being diagnosed and resolved autonomously.

This is not a proof of concept. This is the **next frontier of enterprise performance—** where SAP and Generative AI meet on the battlefield of business operations.

From **automating SAP production support** to **AI-augmented decision-making**, Unit 4 is the moment where everything clicks.

We'll walk through **real use cases**, **step-by-step implementation strategies**, and **tactical roadmaps** that turn everything you've learned into action—and results.

Welcome to the era of applied intelligence.

Let's go to **Unit 4**: **Applied Generative AI in SAP**.

UNIT 4

Applying the Solution

The Moment of Truth

Welcome to Unit 4, the most anticipated moment of this journey — the crux of the entire book. If the previous chapters were the buildup, this is the drumroll moment where theory finally meets action.

Think of it as the climax of a well-written story. Everything we've covered so far was carefully structured to prepare you for what comes next. In this unit, we'll walk through a real-life example to show you how to bring everything together.

In the previous units, we:

1. **Identified and defined the problem** – specifically focusing on the gap between traditional SAP Finance practices and the potential of Generative AI (Unit 1).

2. **Built a strong foundational understanding of SAP Finance** – including its core components, submodules, and how it fits into the broader SAP ecosystem (Unit 2).

3. **Introduced a practical, AI-driven solution framework** – outlining how Generative AI can be leveraged to optimize processes, boost efficiency, and enable innovation within SAP systems (Unit 3).

Now, in **Unit 4**, we move to the real deal — **applying** that solution in a **real-world context**.

But here's the best part: while the examples in this unit revolve around Finance (because that's my area of expertise), the concepts and approaches we'll use are applicable across all SAP modules — be it Supply Chain, HR, or even technical areas. The key lies in understanding your process, identifying pain points, and aligning the right AI tools (especially generative AI) to drive value.

This unit isn't just about reading. It's about doing. You'll see the solution in action and learn how to tailor it to your own context. Consider this your launchpad to start applying Generative AI within your SAP landscape — confidently, practically, and strategically.

A Word of Advice Before You Dive In...

If you haven't fully absorbed Units 1–3, I highly recommend going back and revisiting them. This unit builds directly on the ideas, frameworks, and principles discussed earlier. Without that foundation, some of the content here might feel overwhelming or disconnected.

This unit assumes you now have:

- A clear understanding of the business problem.
- Familiarity with SAP Finance processes and terminology.
- An appreciation for how Generative AI works and the potential it offers.

If you're all set — fantastic. You're in the right place.

Let's Bring It All Together

So here we are — ready to bring the solution to life.

This unit is not just about showcasing what's possible. It's about empowering you to do it yourself. Whether you're an SAP consultant, a business analyst, a technical developer, or a digital transformation leader — the frameworks and strategies here are meant to equip you to take action and make an impact.

Let's roll up our sleeves, walk through the use case step by step, and watch theory become reality.

Let's **apply the solution**.
Let's **transform SAP with AI**.
Let's **get started.**

CHAPTER 1

Reimagining SAP Finance Production Support with Generative AI

Welcome to Chapter 1 of Unit 4! In this chapter, we're not just going to talk theory—we're about to take everything you've learned and bring it to life through a real-world application. But before we dive into the "how," we need to also properly understand the "why."

Remember Chapter 12 of Unit 2? That's where we explored over 100 real-world SAP Finance production support issues—common challenges enterprises face daily in their finance operations. In this unit, we'll take that knowledge forward and see how Generative AI (Gen AI) can revolutionize the way we handle SAP production support, particularly within the Finance (FI/CO) domain.

Why This Matters

SAP Finance landscapes are increasingly complex. With multiple integrations, high-volume transactions, and evolving compliance requirements, managing production issues in a traditional reactive way is no longer sustainable. Tickets pile up. Business users get frustrated. Resolution times increase. And the cost of inefficiency keeps rising.

But What if Gen AI Could Think With Us?

Imagine a system that doesn't just wait for issues to be reported—but proactively identifies anomalies, suggests solutions, and even drafts communication templates for the support team to use. Think AI copilots that continuously learn from historical tickets, configuration patterns, master data changes, and system logs. The goal? To significantly reduce manual effort, increase accuracy, and allow SAP consultants to focus on high-value problem-solving rather than redundant tasks.

What You'll Learn

In this unit, we'll build a solution framework that revolves around the power of Generative AI applied to SAP Finance support. This isn't a theoretical exploration—it's a guided application with tangible outcomes. You'll explore:

- How to architect a Gen AI-based support assistant for SAP FI/CO
- Integration with real-time data sources like SAP logs, ticketing systems, and Fiori notifications
- How LLMs can be fine-tuned to your organization's unique finance landscape and support language
- Use cases for automated root cause analysis, resolution recommendations, and user communication drafts
- Practical examples of prompt engineering tailored to SAP terminology
- Governance and data sensitivity considerations when deploying AI in financial environments

The Big Picture

This chapter marks a turning point in the book. So far, you've understood the components. Now, you're going to assemble them into a real-world solution. The solution and its application revolve around a single, powerful idea:

Empowering SAP Finance production support with Generative AI to create a smarter, faster, and more reliable support ecosystem.

Let's move forward—and start shaping the future of SAP support.

A New Era for SAP Production Support

Traditionally, SAP Finance production support is reactive, ticket-based, and heavily reliant on manual troubleshooting. But what if you could anticipate problems before they arise? What if your system could suggest solutions on the fly, generate documentation, or guide users with conversational interfaces?

That's the promise of Generative AI. In this chapter, we're focusing on how to apply Gen AI to SAP Finance production support, setting the foundation for a transformative journey across the SAP ecosystem. The goal is to reduce cost, time, and manual effort by embedding intelligence into support processes.

By the end of this unit, you'll know exactly how to integrate Gen AI into your SAP production support processes—and you'll be able to replicate this framework in other SAP modules as well.

But before we jump into step-by-step implementation in the next chapter, there are two key prerequisites:

1. Deep Process Understanding

To effectively apply Gen AI, you need to deeply understand the business process you're targeting. In our case, it's SAP Finance production support. We'll build on the issues explored in Chapter 12 of Unit 2, ensuring you're equipped to connect technical challenges with business context.

2. In-Depth Problem Analysis

You must thoroughly analyze current inefficiencies and pain points. Only then can you identify high-impact opportunities for Gen AI integration.

Let's start with understanding the problem landscape.

Current Inefficiencies in SAP Production Support – With a Focus on Finance (FI/CO)

SAP production support plays a vital role in maintaining enterprise operations. Yet, inefficiencies are rampant—especially in Finance. These issues slow down processes, increase costs, and impact audit readiness.

General Inefficiencies

- **Reactive Support**: Issues are addressed after failure. This causes delays and productivity loss.

- **Manual Dependency**: Log reviews, reconciliations, and corrections rely heavily on human effort.

- **Poor Knowledge Sharing**: Solutions are often tribal knowledge, undocumented, and inconsistent.

- **Siloed Operations**: Cross-module issues (FI-MM, FI-SD) suffer from poor collaboration.

- **Lack of Automation**: Ticket triage and RCA are done manually, making scalability difficult.

SAP Finance-Specific Inefficiencies

- **Time-Sensitive Closings**: Month- and year-end activities are deadline-driven and error-prone.

- **Recurring Issues Without Resolution**: Errors like missing exchange rates or tax mismatches keep coming back without root fixes.

- **Cross-Module Errors**: FI issues caused by upstream modules are hard to trace without integrated visibility.

- **Cryptic Error Messages**: SAP messages like F5 263 or GLT2201 are hard to decipher.

- **Heavy Monitoring Workload**: Reliance on batch jobs and transaction codes results in slow response times.

- **Weak Documentation for Compliance**: RCA and audit notes are often incomplete or rushed.

Summary Table of Key Pain Points

Area	Current Inefficiency	Business Impact
Ticket Resolution	Manual and reactive	Delays, inconsistency
Closing Cycles	Checklist-driven, ad-hoc	Errors, non-compliance
Integration	Siloed module knowledge	Repeated disruptions
Error Interpretation	Hard-to-understand codes	Escalations, inefficiencies
Knowledge Sharing	Lacking RCA documentation	Redundant efforts
Monitoring	Delayed via batch jobs	Late issue detection
Audit	Disorganized documentation	Risk of audit failure

The Gen AI Advantage – Enabling Smarter SAP Support

Why SAP Finance Is the Perfect Candidate

SAP Finance modules like FI-GL, FI-AP, FI-AR, AA, and CO manage crucial enterprise data. Production issues in these areas ripple across the entire organization. Their structured, repetitive nature makes them ideal for Gen AI.

Key Roles of Generative AI

1. AI-Powered Ticket Resolution

   o AI can analyze logs, suggest resolutions, and prevent recurring issues by identifying root causes.
   o Example: Detecting patterns in IDoc failures or auto-suggesting period opening steps.

2. AI Copilots and Chatbots

   o Train copilots on SAP Notes, internal documentation, and historical tickets.
   o Example: Ask, "How do I resolve error F5 263?" and receive a guided answer.

3. Automated Documentation

   o Generate RCA reports and audit-ready documents based on logs and change histories.

4. Intelligent Monitoring

   o Predict peak loads or high-risk periods and prepare in advance.

Strategic SAP Tools for Integration

- **SAP BTP:** *For orchestration and hosting of AI models.*
- **SAP AI Core/Foundation:** *Manage AI lifecycle, from training to deployment.*
- **SAP CoPilot/Joule:** *Bring AI assistance into SAP GUI and Fiori.*
- **SAP Analytics Cloud:** *Augment financial reporting with predictive AI.*

Use Case Examples

Use Case	Description
Auto-resolution of invoice errors	Suggests corrections from historical failures
Pre-validation of postings	Simulates outcomes and flags anomalies before actual posting
Natural language financial queries	"Show open items over $10K this month"
Month-end checklist creation	Role-based, dynamic task generation
Compliance & audit support	Auto-flag suspicious transactions for review

Business Impact

Implementing Gen AI in SAP Finance production support delivers:

- 50–70% faster ticket resolution
- Higher availability during closing periods
- Reduced dependency on tribal knowledge
- Improved audit compliance and reporting
- Enhanced end-user satisfaction

The inefficiencies in today's SAP Finance support operations are no longer just operational annoyances—they are strategic bottlenecks. In an era where financial accuracy, speed, and compliance are paramount, slow resolution times and fragmented support workflows can cost enterprises more than just time.

However, with Generative AI, we stand at a pivotal moment. A once-in-a-generation opportunity is emerging—one that allows us to reimagine and redesign SAP support with intelligence, automation, and contextual learning at its core.

This chapter has laid the foundation for this transformation by walking you through the "what," "why," and "how" of applying Gen AI in SAP Finance production support:

- What challenges exist in traditional SAP FI/CO support?
- Why is Gen AI the most powerful tool to address these challenges?
- How does this transformation align with real-world support scenarios and business goals?

We've explored the business context, dissected the common pain points, and highlighted the value proposition of AI-powered decision support. In short, you've gained the strategic lens required to see the future of SAP Finance support.

But knowledge without execution is incomplete.

What Comes Next

In Chapter 2, we shift gears from exploration to execution. You will be introduced to a structured, step-by-step framework for integrating Generative AI into SAP business processes. This framework is designed to be:

- **Modular** – customizable to fit any SAP landscape and any enterprise.
- **Scalable** – adaptable across teams, regions, and business units.
- **Actionable** – detailed and practical enough for real implementation.

What You Will Learn:

- How to identify **high-impact use cases** within SAP for Gen AI

- Techniques to collect and prepare **data sources** (e.g., ticket logs, error messages, config data)

- Crafting **effective prompts** tailored to SAP Finance terminology

- Strategies for **system integration** (SAP BTP, Fiori, Solution Manager, ticketing systems)

- Ensuring **data privacy, governance, and compliance**, especially in finance-sensitive environments

This upcoming chapter is your **operational playbook**—built to equip SAP consultants, AI developers, and solution architects with everything they need to turn vision into value.

Chapter 3 Preview: Putting the Framework into Action

Once we've built the foundation with the integration framework, Chapter 3 will bring everything to life through a practical, hands-on scenario. You'll follow a complete **SAP FICO production support workflow, enhanced with Gen AI**—from the moment a ticket is raised to the final communication with the business user.

You'll witness how Gen AI can:

- Identify root causes based on historical patterns
- Suggest intelligent and context-specific resolution steps
- Generate professional, accurate responses to business users
- Continuously learn from recurring issue patterns to reduce future escalations

With a strong understanding of the possibilities—and a clear roadmap to implementation—you are now ready to move from **strategy to execution.**

Let's begin Chapter 2: A Step-by-Step Guide to Integrating Generative AI into SAP Processes.

What You Just Learned

- **SAP Finance support today is reactive, manual, and inefficient**, especially during high-stakes periods like month-end close.
- **Generative AI offers a transformational leap**—enabling proactive, intelligent, and automated support across FI/CO modules.
- You explored **real pain points** in production support (e.g., cryptic error codes, siloed modules, poor documentation).
- Gen AI use cases include:
  - Auto-resolution suggestions
  - Chatbots trained on SAP Notes
  - Audit-ready documentation generation
  - Natural language queries and pre-validations
- Tools like **SAP BTP, AI Core, Joule, and SAP Analytics Cloud** enable scalable, integrated AI support solutions.
- Business benefits include:
  - 50–70% faster ticket resolution
  - Improved compliance and documentation

- ○ Reduced manual effort and knowledge silos
- ○ Better end-user experience

You're now equipped with the "why" and "what"—next, you'll dive into **"how" to build and implement Gen AI in SAP Finance support**.

CHAPTER 2

Step-by-Step Guide to AI Integration in SAP Processes

The Practical Core of the Book

Let me begin with an honest confession — yes, I know I've said it multiple times already, but it bears repeating: this chapter truly is the crux of the entire book. And by the time you finish reading it, you'll understand exactly why I've emphasized that so much.

In this pivotal chapter, we're going beyond high-level concepts and entering the operational heart of AI integration within SAP. This is where we roll up our sleeves and translate everything we've learned so far into actionable strategies.

We'll begin by walking through the general AI integration process — a foundational step-by-step framework that any enterprise can follow to embed AI into SAP workflows. This part of the chapter will serve as a universal blueprint that outlines how to approach AI adoption systematically, ensuring that we consider every critical element — from identifying the right use cases to deployment and iteration.

But that's just the beginning.

Once we've established a general understanding, we'll pivot to explore how SAP itself approaches product development specifically for Large Language Model (LLM) use cases. This is a rare opportunity to peek behind the curtain and understand what happens at SAP from ideation to production. We'll explore how AI features are conceived, validated, and deployed into SAP's ecosystem, and how that same methodology can be mirrored within your own organization.

We won't stop at just models and code.

We'll also take time to evaluate the resource landscape — the skills, teams, and technologies you'll need to bring AI to life inside your SAP environment. From data engineering and domain experts to model governance and DevOps — we'll map out what a successful AI team looks like, and what roles are essential for scaling AI solutions across departments.

Next, we'll take a deep dive into SAP AI Core, SAP's dedicated infrastructure for developing, training, deploying, and monitoring AI models. You'll get an in-depth look at how this engine works under the hood, how it fits into the broader SAP BTP landscape, and how it empowers enterprises to operationalize AI at scale. We'll examine its capabilities, integration patterns, and how it enables repeatable and reliable AI workflows.

And finally, to bring it all together, we'll explore SAP Business AI — a lens through which we'll examine the key business areas ripe for AI transformation. Whether it's Finance, Supply Chain, Procurement, or Sales, we'll showcase real-world use cases and opportunities where AI can deliver tangible value through SAP's built-in intelligence and extensible frameworks.

By the end of this chapter, you'll not only understand how to integrate AI technically, but also how to strategically operationalize, scale, and govern it inside SAP with clarity and confidence.

Step-by-Step AI Integration Framework

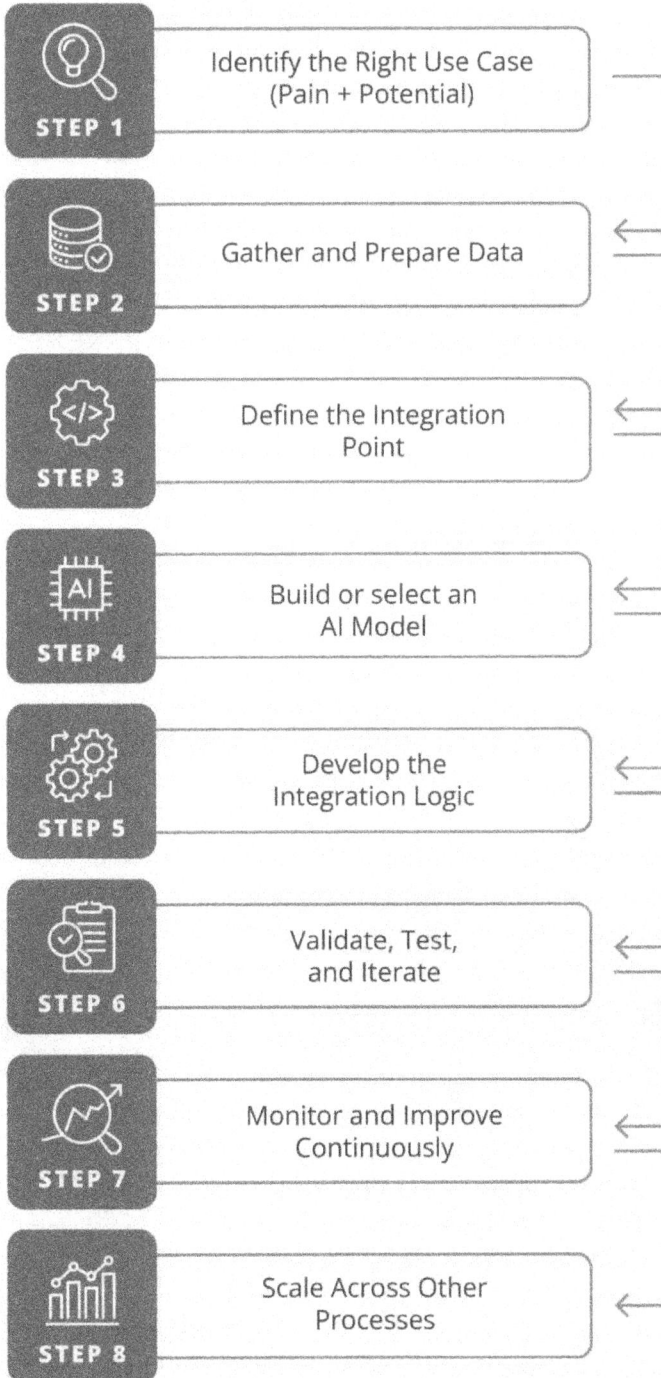

STEP 1 — Identify the Right Use Case (Pain + Potential)

STEP 2 — Gather and Prepare Data

STEP 3 — Define the Integration Point

STEP 4 — Build or select an AI Model

STEP 5 — Develop the Integration Logic

STEP 6 — Validate, Test, and Iterate

STEP 7 — Monitor and Improve Continuously

STEP 8 — Scale Across Other Processes

Let's begin the transformation. Let's get straight into action.

Step-by-Step AI Integration Framework:

Let's break the integration process down into a structured 8-step framework:

Step 1: Identify the Right Use Case (Pain + Potential)

Start by asking:

- What process in your SAP system is slow, manual, or prone to errors?
- Which tasks consume time but require little judgment?
- Are there recurring support tickets for a particular process?

> **Tip:** Look for **high-frequency, low-complexity** tasks that drain time and resources.

Step 2: Gather and Prepare Data

AI feeds on data. For SAP, that means pulling:

- Structured data from SAP tables (via RFC, BAPIs, CDS Views)
- Logs from production support tools (Solution Manager, Focused Insights)
- User interactions from Fiori apps or ECC screens

Ensure data is clean, labeled, and anonymized where needed.

Step 3: Define the Integration Point

Ask: Where will the AI model "plug in" to the SAP landscape?

Common options:

- SAP BTP (Business Technology Platform) via APIs
- SAP AI Core & SAP AI Launchpad
- Embedded directly in Fiori apps
- Integrated via BTP Event Mesh or SAP CAP

Step 4: <u>Build or Select an AI Model</u>

You have two options:

1. **Train your own model** using SAP AI Core or a preferred framework (e.g., TensorFlow, PyTorch).
2. **Use pre-trained LLMs** from SAP's Generative AI Hub, fine-tuned for enterprise use.

Step 5: <u>Develop the Integration Logic</u>

This is where the magic happens.

Tasks:

- Create an **API layer** or middleware between SAP and the AI model
- Use tools like **SAP Cloud SDK**, **Node.js CAP**, or **ABAP RAP**
- Add model inference calls into the user interface (e.g., enhance Fiori tiles)

Step 6: <u>Validate, Test, and Iterate</u>

Don't treat this as a one-time deployment.

You must:

- Run **unit and integration tests**
- Compare AI decisions vs. human decisions
- Use historical tickets or transactions for simulation
- Involve end-users in **User Acceptance Testing (UAT)**

Step 7: <u>Monitor and Improve Continuously</u>

Once live, AI systems require babysitting — not because they're unreliable, but because they learn and evolve. Use:

- SAP AI Core monitoring tools
- Integration with SAP Alert Notification
- Logging via SAP BTP or external observability tools (e.g., Grafana)

Implement a **feedback loop**:

- Capture when AI suggestions are accepted or overridden
- Feed this back into retraining or fine-tuning the model

Step 8: <u>Scale Across Other Processes</u>

After a successful pilot:

- Document what worked and what didn't
- Identify other processes with similar characteristics
- Create a Center of Excellence (CoE) around AI + SAP

Exploring Product Development from Large Language Model (LLM) Use Cases at SAP

As we venture deeper into this chapter, it's important to realize that integrating AI — especially Large Language Models — into enterprise workflows isn't just about writing code or connecting APIs. It's a product development journey. One that SAP, as a global leader in enterprise applications, has carefully structured into a methodical, multi-phase lifecycle — ensuring that every AI solution is not only technically sound, but also business-relevant, scalable, and sustainable.

Let's walk through this journey step-by-step — from ideation to production — and uncover how SAP transforms a simple AI idea into a real-world business product. Along the way, we'll also understand how you can apply the same structured methodology within your own organization using SAP's AI tooling and BTP framework.

1. From Ideation to Production: SAP's AI Product Development Lifecycle

SAP follows a well-orchestrated lifecycle for developing LLM-powered features, structured around four distinct but interconnected phases. These phases are not just theoretical — they're the blueprint SAP uses internally to build AI into its own applications. Understanding this framework equips you to replicate the process responsibly and effectively in your own SAP landscape.

Phase 1: Ideation Phase — Laying the Foundation for Generative AI

Every transformation begins with a spark — an idea. In this initial phase, SAP explores whether a use case involving LLMs is not only exciting but also feasible, ethical, and valuable.

Key components include:

- Familiarization: The team studies the capabilities of LLMs, existing models, and SAP's own Generative AI tools. This includes hands-on exploration of SAP's Generative AI Hub and SAP AI Core.
- Customer Collaboration: SAP engages directly with customers and internal stakeholders to understand pain points, gather feedback, and align AI initiatives with real-world needs.

The goal here is to identify high-value use cases that are desirable (solving a real problem), feasible (technically possible), and viable (aligned with business goals).

Phase 2: Validation Phase — Testing the Concept

Once a promising idea is in hand, it must be tested. Not in a lab — but in the messy, complex reality of enterprise business.

This phase involves:

- Use Case Iteration: Prototypes are built, tested, and adjusted based on feedback from users and developers.
- Technical Evaluation: Can this LLM actually deliver the output we need within our system constraints? How accurate, fast, and cost-effective is it?
- Commercial Evaluation: Will this solution drive ROI? Does it align with licensing, compliance, and data privacy standards?

Validation ensures that the proposed solution isn't just innovative — it's practical, cost-justified, and aligned with strategic direction.

Phase 3: Realization & Production Phase — From Concept to Code

Once validated, it's time to turn ideas into production-ready features. SAP takes the validated prototype and begins full-scale development across three key fronts:

- Use Case Finalization: The use case is locked in, documented, and approved for rollout.
- Technical Finalization: All technical components — including API calls, data pipelines, user interfaces, and integration with SAP BTP — are built, tested, and hardened.
- Commercial Finalization: Pricing models, support plans, and stakeholder alignment are established to ensure long-term viability.

By the end of this phase, the use case is no longer a concept — it's a ready-to-launch AI feature embedded in a business application.

Phase 4: Operations & Continuous Improvement — Innovation Never Ends

Even after launch, the journey continues. In fact, this is where real innovation begins.

- Operations: The LLM use case is monitored using tools such as SAP AI Core, SAP Alert Notification, and business observability dashboards. Uptime, latency, error rates, and user satisfaction are tracked closely.
- Continuous Improvement: AI outputs are evaluated continuously, re-trained if needed, and enhanced with new feedback, features, or model upgrades.

This final phase reinforces the reality that AI-powered products are never "done." They evolve over time, responding to user behavior, business needs, and technological shifts.

2. Integration of Large Language Models into Business Applications — SAP's Methodological Steps

Now that we've explored the lifecycle, let's break down the technical steps for actually integrating LLMs into business applications using SAP's methodology. This is where theory meets practice.

a. **Needs Assessment**
   Before choosing a model or writing a line of code, conduct a deep assessment of the business challenge:

- What decision, task, or process needs to be enhanced?
- Is natural language understanding or generation critical to solving it?
- Does the user interface need intelligence injected into it?

This is the step where business meets AI — where value is clarified.

b. **Use SAP BTP's Data Frameworks**

Once the use case is defined, you need access to data — securely and efficiently. SAP BTP offers a robust set of tools for:

- Accessing SAP and non-SAP data (via CDS Views, APIs, SAP Data Sphere)
- Creating data pipelines (SAP Integration Suite, SAP HANA Cloud)
- Maintaining governance and compliance with enterprise standards

This ensures the AI model is trained and served using trusted, business-grade data.

c. **Select the Right LLM Framework**

This is where SAP's Generative AI Hub shines.

You can either:

- Use pre-integrated models (like from SAP partners or open-source LLMs)
- Fine-tune models using SAP AI Core and deploy via SAP AI Launchpad

The selection depends on:

- Language and domain complexity
- Latency requirements
- Governance and explainability needs

SAP provides flexibility to choose the right model based on your enterprise's unique context.

d. **Identify Use Cases Mapped to Framework Capabilities**

Finally, ensure that the selected framework is matched with the right category of use cases.

Examples:

- LLMs for SAP Finance: Auto-responding to vendor queries, summarizing audit reports, or translating financial documents.
- LLMs in Supply Chain: Generating delay explanations in real-time, or automating contract language generation.
- LLMs for Sales & Service: Personalized email drafts, product recommendation scripting, or summarizing customer complaints.

Each framework supports a specific pattern of usage, and mapping use cases correctly ensures better performance and user adoption.

Understanding how SAP brings LLMs from idea to reality isn't just insightful — it's essential. If you aim to lead or contribute to AI transformation within an SAP ecosystem, this structured lifecycle — from ideation to operations — is your reference point.

By combining human-centered design, technical rigor, and commercial sensibility, SAP ensures that its AI products aren't just smart — they're useful, usable, and valuable.

In the next section, we'll go even deeper — exploring the architecture and hands-on usage of SAP AI Core — the engine behind these intelligent capabilities. Let's continue our transformation journey.

Understanding SAP AI Core: The Engine Behind Enterprise AI Operations

As we continue our step-by-step journey of integrating AI into SAP processes, it's time to explore one of the most critical components in SAP's AI ecosystem — SAP AI Core.

We learned about SAP AI Core in the previous unit, it is not just another service on the SAP Business Technology Platform (BTP). It's the operational backbone for managing AI and machine learning workloads in a standardized, scalable, and cloud-agnostic manner. Think of it as the invisible infrastructure that allows you to build, deploy, monitor, and manage AI assets — all while staying within the security and governance framework SAP customers expect.

Whether you're training custom machine learning models or deploying LLM-based solutions at scale, SAP AI Core ensures that AI capabilities become a seamless part of your business architecture.

Key Capabilities of SAP AI Core

This, again, is a refresher.

Let's look at the ecosystem it operates in and how each piece plays a role in your AI adoption journey:

Capability	Description
SAP AI Portfolio	Pre-integrated AI business services and industry-specific solutions offered by SAP (e.g., Business Entity Recognition, Invoice Matching).
AI Launchpad	A centralized interface for managing the entire AI lifecycle — from deployment to monitoring to continuous improvement.
SAP AI Core	The core execution engine that powers the training, deployment, and inference of ML models in a scalable and compliant way.
Customer Data for ML	Enables secure integration of enterprise data into model pipelines, ensuring AI models are trained with real business context.
ML Model Management	Tools to register, configure, and manage multiple versions of machine learning models across business scenarios.
Model Inferencing	Real-time execution of AI models through APIs — allowing business apps to use AI predictions and insights instantly.

These six elements form the end-to-end AI lifecycle stack — from data to inference — and SAP AI Core sits at the heart of it all.

Configuring SAP AI Core and SAP AI Launchpad

Implementing SAP AI Core involves more than flipping a switch. You're essentially setting up a highly orchestrated runtime environment capable of managing the full AI lifecycle. Here's how it works:

a. **SAP AI Launchpad:** The Mission Control Center
   SAP AI Launchpad serves as the AI lifecycle command center. It provides:

   - A unified interface for managing all AI scenarios
   - Monitoring tools to track training, inference, and performance
   - Version control and deployment history for transparency

Think of it as a cockpit where data scientists, developers, and business users can monitor, collaborate, and control the journey of AI assets.

b. **SAP AI Core Runtime**: The Execution Layer
SAP AI Core is where the real action happens. It executes:

- Machine Learning pipelines
- Deployment of trained models as REST APIs
- Inference jobs in real-time or batch mode

It runs on a Kubernetes-based architecture, enabling autoscaling, container orchestration, and robust operationalization of AI assets.

c. **Key Prerequisites for Configuration**
To successfully configure and operate SAP AI Core, you'll need to set up a few key components:

1. Manage Your Git Repository
   - Store your AI pipeline scripts, configurations, and artifacts.
   - SAP AI Core pulls these files to build and deploy your workflows.
2. Manage Resource Groups
   - Define CPU/GPU allocations and memory usage for training and inference.
   - Essential for cost control and performance tuning.
3. Object Store Credentials
   - Grant SAP AI Core access to your cloud object store (AWS S3, Azure Blob, etc.) where training data resides.
4. Docker Registry Credentials
   - Enable AI Core to pull containerized ML environments from Docker Hub or your private registry.

These building blocks ensure that your AI Core environment is secure, scalable, and ready for enterprise-grade deployment.

Training a Machine Learning Model in SAP AI Core

Training a machine learning model using SAP AI Core is a structured process that brings together data engineering, orchestration, and automation. Here's how it unfolds:

Step 1: Prepare and Store Your Dataset

You'll first need to provision your training dataset and make it accessible to AI Core. SAP supports various hyperscaler object stores (e.g., AWS S3, Azure Blob, GCP Storage).

Ensure:

- Your data is in the right format (CSV, Parquet, etc.)
- Proper access policies and permissions are configured

Step 2: Grant AI Core Access and Trigger Training

Once your dataset is ready:

1. Register the Input Dataset
   - Define the dataset location and structure in the AI Core metadata.
2. Create a Configuration on AI Core
   - Specify the pipeline configuration: hyperparameters, model type, compute resources.
3. Trigger Workflow Execution
   - Kick off the training pipeline using AI Core's orchestration engine.
4. Monitor Logs and Status via AI Launchpad
   - Visualize job status, logs, errors, and success metrics — all within a single dashboard.

This streamlined process allows for repeatable, auditable, and governed model training workflows across teams.

Serving an ML Model: Real-Time AI for SAP Applications

Once your model is trained and validated, you'll want to serve it — i.e., make it available to other systems and apps via APIs.

SAP AI Core lets you:

- Deploy your model as a containerized API
- Scale inference endpoints dynamically via Kubernetes
- Call AI models from SAP apps (like Fiori, S/4HANA, or custom CAP apps)

This is the step where your SAP application becomes intelligent — leveraging predictions, suggestions, and automations derived from trained models.

Why SAP AI Core Matters

SAP AI Core isn't just a technical platform — it's a strategic enabler. It allows enterprises to adopt AI with discipline, governance, and speed. By combining cloud-scale architecture with SAP-native intelligence, it empowers organizations to:

- Run AI workloads on any hyperscaler
- Operationalize ML pipelines with traceability
- Seamlessly integrate AI into SAP business applications

In the next section, we'll look at where exactly you can apply this intelligence — exploring SAP Business AI and the real-world use cases where AI adds value across Finance, Logistics, Procurement, and beyond.

Let's keep building.

Key SAP Business AI Areas for Finance

Robotic Process Automation (RPA)

Automating the Routine to Unlock Strategic Value

What it is:
RPA is about automating repetitive, rule-based tasks that don't require human judgment — but consume time, resources, and patience.

Why it matters in Finance:
SAP Finance teams deal with hundreds — sometimes thousands — of repetitive actions every day. Think of copying invoice data from one screen to another, processing payments, or verifying purchase orders. These tasks, while necessary, are prime candidates for automation.

Key Use Cases:

- Processing large volumes of invoices or journal entries
- Transferring data between systems (SAP and non-SAP)
- Automating multi-system workflows such as vendor onboarding or tax compliance

Benefits:

- Reduce manual effort and human error
- Improve processing time and accuracy
- Free up staff for strategic analysis

In short, RPA lets your finance team do more with less — and faster.

Machine Learning (ML)

Enabling Systems to Learn and Improve Over Time

What it is:
Machine learning enables computers to learn from historical data and make predictions or decisions without being explicitly programmed for every scenario.

Why it matters in Finance:
ML excels at recognizing patterns — a core requirement in financial processes. It can detect anomalies, suggest account assignments, or predict late payments before they happen.

Key Use Cases:

- Predicting cash flow fluctuations
- Automating GL account determination for vendor invoices
- Detecting fraudulent or duplicate entries
- Suggesting accrual values based on historical posting patterns

Benefits:

- Increase accuracy in financial predictions
- Accelerate time-consuming processes like reconciliation and reporting
- Improve decision-making with data-driven insights

With ML, your SAP Finance system becomes smarter with every transaction.

Generative AI

Moving Beyond Automation — Toward Cognitive Finance

What it is:
Generative AI builds upon machine learning by enabling systems to generate content, make decisions, and adapt autonomously. It can write, summarize, classify, or even reason — all based on enterprise data.

Why it matters in Finance:
Finance professionals constantly deal with unstructured data: emails, policy documents, explanations for exceptions, and internal memos. Generative AI can process this information, derive meaning, and generate outputs that enhance both productivity and decision-making.

Key Use Cases:

- Generating narratives for financial reports
- Auto-drafting email replies to vendor queries

- Summarizing audit logs and exception handling cases
- Explaining anomalies detected in financial data

Benefits:

- Reduce time spent on documentation and communication
- Improve audit readiness and transparency
- Provide real-time, explainable insights to decision-makers

This is not just automation — it's AI that thinks, writes, and reasons like a finance analyst.

Situation Handling

Proactive Intelligence that Keeps Finance Teams Ahead

What it is:
Situation Handling is SAP's intelligent alert system that identifies issues, proactively notifies users, and guides them toward resolution. It transforms SAP from a passive tool into an active assistant.

Why it matters in Finance:
Finance is full of time-sensitive and exception-driven processes. Missed deadlines, blocked invoices, or delayed approvals can have significant business impacts. Situation Handling ensures that these scenarios are flagged early and resolved quickly.

Key Use Cases:

- Alerting users about payment blocks or overdue approvals
- Detecting unusual posting patterns and suggesting reviews
- Proactively informing teams about compliance risks
- Suggesting actions based on real-time financial KPIs

Benefits:

- Reduce risk and compliance violations
- Improve reaction times and reduce bottlenecks
- Empower users with guided, AI-supported decisions

With Situation Handling, your finance team doesn't just react to issues — they stay one step ahead.

Whether you're closing books faster, reducing invoice exceptions, improving financial forecasts, or simplifying compliance — SAP Business AI enables finance teams to shift from reactive firefighting to proactive leadership.

In the next chapter, we'll bring it all together through a real-world case study where AI is applied across SAP Finance production support — demonstrating the step-by-step application of everything we've covered so far.

Let's see SAP Business AI in action.

Identifying the Key Stakeholders in SAP AI Integration

The People Behind the Intelligence

One of the biggest misconceptions about AI integration — especially in a structured enterprise landscape like SAP — is that it's a purely technical exercise. But in reality, successful AI integration is a multidisciplinary effort that spans across roles, departments, and expertise areas.

At the heart of any AI-driven transformation is a team of key stakeholders, each playing a distinct but interconnected role. These individuals are the architects, visionaries, translators, and advocates who shape the strategy, build the solution, and ensure it delivers meaningful outcomes to the business.

In this section, let's walk through the four key stakeholder groups involved in SAP AI integration — understanding not just what they do, but why their contribution is vital for success.

1. Data Engineers and Software Architects

The Technical Backbone of AI Integration

Who they are:

These are the technical specialists responsible for designing, building, and deploying the underlying infrastructure that enables AI within SAP. They work closely with platforms like SAP AI Core, SAP BTP, object stores, and containerized runtimes.

What they do:

- Ingest, clean, and provision enterprise data for AI models
- Design the pipelines and APIs that connect SAP with AI services
- Integrate models into business applications and ensure runtime scalability
- Secure and govern AI components within cloud environments

Why they matter:

Without this group, there is no engine behind the intelligence. They ensure that AI isn't just a flashy proof of concept but a stable, scalable, and maintainable solution embedded into SAP business processes.

If you're building AI in SAP, your success is only as strong as the engineering architecture supporting it.

2. Product Management and Product Owners

The Visionaries Driving Business Value

Who they are:

Product Managers and Product Owners are the strategic leads responsible for defining the "what" and "why" of an AI initiative. Their job is to ensure the solution aligns with market needs, customer problems, and business goals.

What they do:

- Define the product vision and roadmap
- Prioritize AI features based on commercial value and user feedback
- Validate whether a use case is worth building
- Work with marketing, sales, and customer success teams to enable adoption

Why they matter:

They bridge the gap between technical feasibility and commercial viability. While engineers build the product, Product Managers shape its direction and ensure that every release delivers real value.

No AI solution can succeed if it doesn't solve a meaningful business problem. Product managers make sure that AI has a purpose — not just a presence.

3. Solution Management

The Translators Between Business and Technology

Who they are:

Solution Managers are the hybrid thinkers — equally fluent in technology and business. They work cross-functionally to ensure that what's being built is technically sound, business-relevant, and ready for market.

What they do:

- Engage with customers to define functional requirements
- Collaborate with developers and data scientists to design end-to-end solutions
- Ensure alignment between use case objectives and technical capabilities
- Define KPIs and performance metrics for AI products

Why they matter:

They act as the connective tissue across the organization, ensuring that business expectations are translated into technical execution — and vice versa.

Reader takeaway: If product managers decide what should be built, solution managers make sure it's built right — and for the right reasons.

4. User Experience (UX) Designers and Analysts

The Advocates for Human-Centered AI

Who they are:

UX designers and user researchers ensure that AI solutions are not only functional but also usable, accessible, and meaningful to the end user. In the AI world, where decisions can feel opaque, UX plays a critical role in building trust and adoption.

What they do:

- Design interfaces for AI interactions (e.g., chatbots, dashboards, explainability tools)
- Gather feedback through usability testing and user interviews
- Improve clarity, accessibility, and decision confidence in AI-powered workflows
- Ensure ethical and inclusive design in AI interactions

Why they matter:

Even the smartest AI model will fail if users don't understand it, trust it, or know how to use it. UX experts ensure that AI is not only intelligent but also intuitive.

In SAP AI, usability is as important as accuracy. How users interact with intelligence determines how impactful that intelligence becomes.

Collaboration is the Real AI Superpower

The reality is: no single stakeholder can drive AI integration alone. It requires a symphony of skills, perspectives, and responsibilities. When these stakeholders come together — engineers, visionaries, translators, and designers — AI transforms from a technology into a business advantage.

So, as you embark on your AI journey within SAP Finance or any other function, ask yourself:

- Have you involved the right people?
- Are technical, commercial, and user perspectives represented?
- Are you building a product — or just a prototype?

Because in the end, the success of AI in SAP doesn't rest on algorithms — it rests on the people who bring them to life.

From Framework to Function

At this point in the journey, you've done more than just learn about AI integration — you've explored the full anatomy of how enterprise-grade AI is thoughtfully embedded into SAP environments.

We began this chapter by reinforcing that it is the crux of the book — and now, you know why.

You've seen:

- A step-by-step blueprint for integrating AI into SAP processes.
- How SAP productizes LLM use cases from ideation to production.
- The technical foundation of SAP AI Core and how it supports scalable, secure, and cloud-agnostic AI operations.
- The various capabilities of SAP Business AI, from RPA to Generative AI and Situation Handling — and how each brings intelligence into finance.
- The human dimension — the key stakeholders who ensure AI isn't just built, but adopted, governed, and valued.

Together, these pieces form a comprehensive, operational framework to move from experimentation to enterprise-wide impact. You're no longer just learning about AI — you're now equipped to lead it.

And if you've truly understood everything in this chapter — take a moment and give yourself a pat on the back. That's no small feat. You've just absorbed one of the most important, complex, and high-impact frameworks in the world of SAP and AI. You're now **steps ahead of most professionals** navigating this space. This is a major achievement — one that sets the foundation for leading intelligent transformation inside any enterprise.

What's Next? Turning the Blueprint into a Use Case

In the next chapter, we'll take everything you've learned and apply it in real time. We'll develop a complete AI use case from scratch, tailored specifically for SAP Finance Production Support — one of the most impactful areas where Generative AI can reduce repetitive tasks, resolve common issues, and transform user experience.

You'll walk step-by-step through the design, development, deployment, and measurement of this AI-driven solution — not in abstract terms, but in real-world execution.

This is where vision meets application.

This is where the AI-powered SAP enterprise starts taking shape — one use case at a time.

Let's build together.

What You Just Learned

- **This is the practical core of the book** — a complete, repeatable framework for integrating AI into SAP processes.

AI Integration Framework (8 Key Steps):

1. **Identify Use Cases**: Target high-frequency, low-complexity pain points.
2. **Prepare Data**: Extract structured logs, transactions, and interactions from SAP systems.
3. **Define Integration Points**: Determine where AI plugs in (e.g., BTP, Fiori, AI Core).
4. **Build or Select Models**: Use pre-trained LLMs or train custom models.
5. **Develop Integration Logic**: Use APIs, SDKs, and SAP Cloud tools.
6. **Test & Validate**: Use simulation, UAT, and real transaction history.
7. **Monitor & Improve**: Continuously optimize with feedback and retraining.
8. **Scale**: Document success and replicate across similar processes.

SAP's LLM Product Lifecycle:

- Ideation → Validation → Realization → Continuous Ops
- SAP builds AI features like products — not experiments — ensuring business alignment and governance.

SAP AI Core + Launchpad:

- **AI Core**: Trains, deploys, and runs ML models at scale.
- **AI Launchpad**: Manages lifecycles, performance, and deployment visibility.

AI Use Cases Across SAP Finance:

- **RPA**: Automates repetitive tasks.
- **ML**: Predicts, classifies, and flags anomalies.
- **Gen AI**: Writes summaries, emails, explanations.
- **Situation Handling**: Proactively alerts and guides users.

Key Stakeholders:

- **Engineers**: Build data pipelines and deployment logic.
- **Product Owners**: Align AI with business outcomes.
- **Solution Managers**: Bridge business and tech.
- **UX Designers**: Make AI usable, explainable, and trusted.

Takeaway:

You now have a **playbook to go from idea to enterprise-scale AI adoption in SAP**. You're no longer exploring AI — you're ready to **lead its transformation** inside real business environments.

CHAPTER 3

Transforming SAP Production Support with Gen AI

From Idea to Impact — A Real-World Use Case of AI in SAP Finance Opening: Where Vision Meets Reality

I'm glad you've made it this far — genuinely, pause for a second and tap yourself on the back. Yet again! Because what you've accomplished so far is not ordinary.

You're no longer among the crowd that simply talks about Artificial Intelligence. You've done the hard work — you've explored, dissected, and internalized the foundations of Generative AI. You've understood what it is, why it's important, and how it fits inside the structured enterprise landscape, especially through SAP's product development approach. You've followed the journey — from raw ideas to full-blown validated AI use cases, through the lens of Large Language Models (LLMs).

In the previous chapter, we laid out SAP's productization blueprint step-by-step — idea generation, stakeholder alignment, data preparation, model selection, prototype building, testing, feedback loops, and final validation. That wasn't just theory — it was the process SAP itself uses to build reliable, scalable, enterprise-ready AI features.

But now — this is the moment I've been personally building up to.

This isn't just another chapter. This is the crown of the book, the culmination of all the frameworks, knowledge, patterns, and architecture we've explored so far. And I'm not sharing a generic industry example here — I'm sharing something personal, something proprietary, something I've designed, developed, tested, and filed as part of a pending patent.

Yes — what you're about to see is a live Proof of Concept (PoC) that integrates Generative AI into SAP Finance Production Support, built on real-world challenges I've witnessed first hand over years of being on the ground as a SAP FICO Consultant and a Generative AI Developer.

Let's pause here and talk about SAP Production Support:

Before we delve into the Proof of Concept, let's take a moment to revisit something foundational: Chapter 12 of Unit 2 — where we explored over 100 of the most common SAP Production Support issues, particularly within Finance. If that immediately sparked recognition, it's a clear sign that you've been following this journey closely and are deeply engaged with the material. That level of attention and commitment doesn't go unnoticed — and I truly appreciate your investment in this book.

In that chapter, we reviewed and catalogued over 100 of the most frequent, recurring, and frustrating SAP Finance production support issues — from MIRO posting failures and tax jurisdiction mismatches, to document splitting errors, payment proposal anomalies, cost center assignment issues, reconciliation failures, and more.

What Did That Exercise Teach Us?

That SAP Production Support, particularly in Finance, is not only high-volume — it's mission-critical. It's noisy, repetitive, high-pressure, and incredibly dependent on human knowledge. You miss a day in support, and your month-end closing is delayed. You misclassify a ticket, and your compliance team is at risk. You overlook a recurring pattern, and the same mistake bleeds time and money every single day.

SAP Finance production support is the heartbeat of enterprise operations, yet ironically, it's where AI is least applied today — until now.

My Journey — and Why I am Building This PoC

As someone who has spent the better part of a decade supporting SAP Finance in large enterprises, I've lived this problem. I've been the consultant on midnight bridge calls during fiscal year-end, I've responded to angry emails from controllers wondering why payment batches failed, and I've helped audit teams trace GL entries across complex integrations.

And through all of this, I realized: most of the issues we solve could have been predicted. And many could have been prevented.

That's when I started experimenting.

I began with text mining ticket descriptions. Then I built an LLM prompt library around common FI issues. I tested auto-suggestion engines for junior support staff. I used Generative AI to simulate the behavior of senior consultants answering queries.

Fast forward — what started as a technical curiosity turned into a structured project, then a live demo, and finally, a patent-pending AI Copilot for SAP Finance production support.

And today, in this chapter, I'm sharing the full story with you — not as a consultant, but as a fellow builder. Someone who has walked this road, mapped the potholes, and is now handing you the keys.

Why This Chapter Matters More Than Any Other

This chapter is the convergence point of everything we've discussed so far:

- The strategic role of Generative AI in enterprise systems
- The inner workings of SAP Finance and its dependencies
- The realities of production support in large SAP landscapes
- The practical architecture of SAP BTP, AI Core, and AI Hub
- The journey from idea to validated AI solution

But what makes this different is: this is not theory. This is an application. You'll see a real, working, step-by-step implementation of how AI can transform production support — reduce ticket resolution times, boost agent productivity, and deliver real ROI.

A Personal Invitation

So here's my ask: Read this chapter slowly. Digest it fully. Reflect not only on the "what" but the "how" and the "why." I'm not just sharing a use case — I'm opening the door for you to imagine how you can replicate this across your SAP ecosystem — be it in logistics, controlling, tax, compliance, or anything you can think of, the possibilities are limitless.

I have written this chapter with love — out of frustration, out of innovation, and out of the belief that there's a better way to do SAP support.

Setting the Scene: The Battlefield of SAP Finance Support

Let's be honest — **SAP Finance production support is far more complex than it seems on the surface.** It's not just about error resolution. It's about keeping the financial engine of the enterprise running without interruption, while ensuring that every transaction adheres to strict compliance requirements, audit trails, and reporting timelines. You're not just resolving issues — you're preserving operational continuity, financial accuracy, and organizational credibility.

How SAP Finance Production Support Really Works

At a functional level, production support begins when a **business user encounters an issue** in their daily SAP transactions — maybe a vendor payment isn't processed, a journal entry fails to post, or a tax calculation seems incorrect. These issues are raised through a **ticketing system** — typically ServiceNow, Remedy, Jira, or SAP Solution Manager — and passed to the support team for investigation.

SAP Production Support System

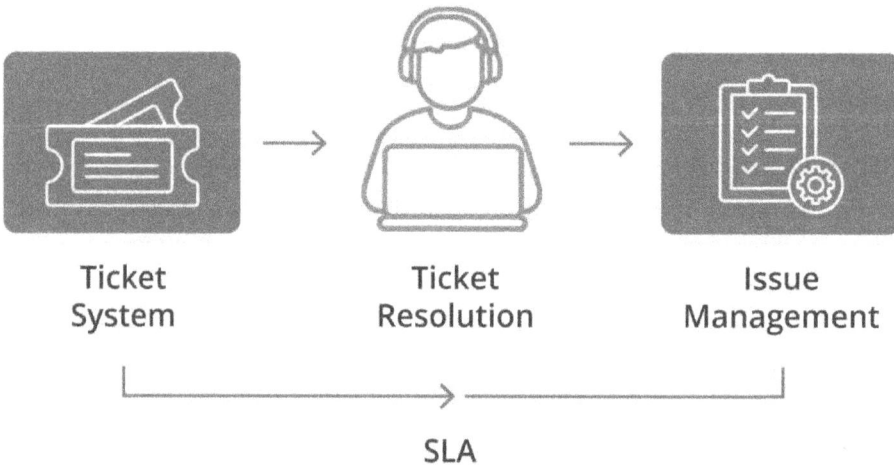

Ticket System	Ticket Resolution	Issue Management

SLA

The lifecycle of a typical SAP Finance ticket looks like this:

1. **Ticket Creation:**
   A user logs a ticket with a brief issue description, often vague — e.g., "MIRO error while posting invoice" or "Payment proposal skipped vendor."

2. **Triaging and Classification:**
   A support coordinator or L1 resource classifies the ticket based on the category (AP, AR, GL, Asset Accounting, etc.), urgency, and functional area. This step is mostly manual and time-consuming.

3. **Investigation by Support Analyst:**
   A L2 or L3 consultant picks up the ticket, replicates the issue (often with limited information), checks configuration, analyzes logs, traces user activity, and finally identifies the root cause.

4. **Resolution and Communication:**
   The analyst fixes the issue (if possible), updates the configuration or master data, and then closes the ticket — documenting the resolution for audit and internal knowledge-sharing purposes.

5. **Rework and Reopen:**
   Often, tickets are misclassified or prematurely closed. Incomplete analysis or unclear communication causes back-and-forth between users and support, consuming even more effort and time.

The Real-World Limitations

Now, let's talk about where the real friction lies. The **pain points** of SAP Finance production support aren't just operational — they're structural.

Repetitive Tickets That Never Die

You'd be surprised how many tickets are **repeats of earlier ones**. For example:

- A payment proposal skipping vendors due to incorrect payment method settings.
- Document splitting errors during MIRO due to configuration gaps.
- Exchange rate type mismatches in intercompany postings.

These issues recur across business units, geographies, and users — often with slightly different symptoms but identical root causes. Yet every ticket is treated as a new problem. **No AI. No memory. No learning.**

Tribal Knowledge — The Hidden Risk

Most solutions live in **consultants' heads**, not systems. Senior analysts have built intuition over years, and they often resolve issues quickly — but there's no formal mechanism to pass that expertise forward. This leads to:

- Inconsistent ticket handling across teams
- Dependency on key individuals
- High onboarding time for new hires

When an experienced resource leaves, so does their knowledge — a major organizational vulnerability.

Manual Routing, Delays, and Wasted Time

A significant portion of the support effort is spent just **figuring out where a ticket belongs** and **who should handle it**. For example:

- An FI ticket might actually stem from an MM config error.
- A tax issue might be caused by a missing condition record in SD.
- An error in asset capitalization might be linked to a workflow approval issue.

Manual routing leads to **frequent reassignments**, unnecessary escalations, and a high Mean Time to Resolution (MTTR). Meanwhile, users wait. Business processes stall. And productivity drops.

Lack of Self-Service Capabilities

Today's users are smart — they don't always want someone to fix things for them. They just want to understand *why* something happened and *what they can do about it*.

But unfortunately, SAP's traditional UI and support landscape doesn't empower users with:

- **Contextual answers** (based on system config or master data)
- Step-by-step guided diagnostics
- **Natural language interfaces** to explore known issues

This leads to **avoidable dependency** on the support team — for things that could easily be automated with an intelligent assistant.

The Impact: High Costs, Low Morale, and Slower Finance

The cumulative impact of these issues is staggering:

- **Longer resolution times** — delaying key financial processes like closing, payments, and reporting
- **Overworked support teams** — spending hours solving issues that AI could handle in seconds
- **User frustration** — leading to workarounds, shadow IT, and compliance risks
- **Lost insights** — because no one is mining the support data for patterns

In short, **SAP Finance production support is a battlefield** — one where the frontline soldiers (support consultants) are equipped with outdated tools, and no automation backup.

And This Is Where Generative AI Enters

Now, imagine introducing **Generative AI** into this ecosystem — not to replace people, but to **augment their intelligence**, **reduce the noise**, and **accelerate resolution**.

With the right LLM-backed solution:

- Tickets can be **auto-categorized and routed** based on their content.
- Resolutions can be **auto-suggested** based on past ticket data.
- Users can be offered **intelligent self-service** via conversational agents.
- Repetitive issues can be **flagged, clustered, and even prevented** using pattern recognition.

And all of this doesn't just reduce cost — it **transforms the experience** for everyone involved: users, analysts, auditors, and executives.

PoC: Automating SAP Finance Production Support Using Generative AI

Problem Statement: The SAP Finance Ticket Avalanche

Within most SAP Finance support environments, a significant percentage of tickets are repetitive, rule-based, and follow recognizable resolution paths. For example:

- "Payment proposal not picking certain vendors."
- "Document splitting error during MIRO."
- "Asset not posting to correct cost center."

Such issues comprise nearly 40% of total ticket volume, yet consume valuable time and resources. Their high repeatability makes them ideal for automation via SAP's Generative AI stack.

Objective: Build and Deploy a Generative AI Copilot for SAP Finance Support

The goal is to **design, prototype, and eventually productize** an **AI-powered support assistant** that:

1. Automatically **classifies, routes, and prioritizes** finance support tickets.
2. Provides **first-level resolution suggestions** using past tickets and enterprise configurations.
3. Escalates complex tickets to human agents with **structured diagnostic inputs**.
4. Enables **self-service support** through a conversational SAP Fiori chatbot interface.
5. Learns over time via **continuous feedback loop integration** with SAP Solution Manager/ServiceNow.

Step-by-Step AI Integration: From Idea to Product

1. Idea Generation & Use Case Finalization

Source of Insight:

- Repetitive finance-related incidents logged in ticketing systems like **SAP Solution Manager**, **ServiceNow**, or **JIRA**.

Key Stakeholders:

- SAP Finance Support Team
- Business Process Owners (FI/AP/AA)
- Basis and BTP Integration Teams
- Compliance and Internal Audit Leads

Selection Criteria:

- **High ticket volume** and **low-resolution complexity**
- Clear **patterns in historical data**
- Minimal risk of regulatory breach
- **Low to medium criticality** in terms of financial impact

Decision: Automate recurring **SAP FI support scenarios** with known root causes, such as:

- Payment Run issues (F110)
- Document Splitting errors (MIRO)
- Asset Accounting misconfigurations (AS01, ABZON)

2. Data Collection, Annotation & Knowledge Base Creation

Data Pipeline:

- Extract **12 months of historical tickets** including descriptions, attachments, resolution logs, timestamps, and user comments.
- Use SAP's **AI Launchpad** and **SAP AI Core** to manage data ingestion securely.

NLP Preprocessing:

- Parse unstructured ticket texts using **tokenization**, **lemmatization**, and **entity recognition**.
- Identify key metadata like **error codes**, **modules involved**, and **T-codes referenced**.

Annotation:

- Manually label ~1,000 high-confidence examples across:
  - Payment Proposal Issues
  - Document Splitting Configurations
  - Asset Accounting Errors
  - IDoc Failures
  - Vendor Master Data Discrepancies

Knowledge Source:

- Supplement with **SAP Notes**, **KBA (Knowledge Base Articles)**, and **internal SOPs**.

3. Model Selection & Prompt Engineering via SAP Generative AI Hub

LLM Selection Strategy (via SAP Generative AI Hub):

- Evaluate **Claude**, **SAP-trained LLMs**, and **OpenAI APIs** via pre-configured connectors.
- Use **LLM comparison tools** in the AI Hub to test accuracy on domain-specific ticket text.
- Select model with highest accuracy for **intent detection** and **domain contextualization**.

Fine-Tuning Strategy:

- Use **SAP AI Core** to fine-tune the model on:
  - Ticket classification taxonomy
  - Resolution path suggestion
  - Escalation threshold scoring

Prompt Templates Designed For:

- Error summarization
- Solution retrieval
- Log pre-diagnosis
- Response tone customization (internal agent vs. end user)

4. PoC Environment Setup & System Integration

SAP Systems Involved:

- SAP S/4HANA Finance Sandbox
- SAP BTP for connectivity and orchestration
- SAP AI Core & AI Launchpad for lifecycle management
- SAP CAI (Conversational AI) or custom React-based chatbot frontend

Infrastructure:

- Set up AI Copilot within **SAP Fiori Launchpad** using **UI5** framework
- Enable integration with **SAP Event Mesh** to push ticket updates in real-time
- Configure BTP Destinations to route inference requests securely to LLM via AI Core

5. AI Copilot in Action: Use Case Scenarios

Scenario 1: Payment Proposal Error

User Message:

"F110 run is skipping vendors with Payment Method T."

AI Response (via LLM Inference):

"This issue is often caused by misaligned payment method configuration in vendor master or company code settings.

Check via T-code FK02 → Payment Transactions tab → Payment Method Settings."

If unresolved:

- Auto-attaches related vendor and company code logs
- Escalates ticket with context for second-level support

Scenario 2: Document Splitting Error

Ticket Logged:

"MIRO throws document splitting error."

AI Suggestion (based on 95% pattern match):

"This may be due to incomplete zero-balance clearing configuration in document splitting.

Navigate: SPRO → Financial Accounting → Document Splitting → Assign Zero Balance Accounts."

Confidence Score: 0.92
Ticket Status: Marked as "Resolved Suggestion" unless user flags issue as unresolved.

6. Continuous Learning & Feedback Loop

Post-resolution Feedback:

- After every agent intervention, feedback is collected via a simple thumbs-up/down and optional comment.

Learning Pipeline:

- New ticket-resolution pairs are automatically logged.
- AI Core re-trains LLM every month (or manually triggered) on updated datasets.
- Feedback metrics stored in **SAP Datasphere** for transparency and audit readiness.

Compliance Assurance:

- All interactions logged via **SAP Audit Trail API**
- No sensitive business data transmitted without encryption
- Access control governed by **SAP Identity Authentication Service (IAS)**

Strategic Alignment: SAP's LLM & Productization Vision

This PoC aligns directly with **SAP's enterprise AI strategy**, including:

- AI-Powered Business Processes (SAP Build Code + AI Hub)
- LLM Access & Prompt Orchestration via Generative AI Hub
- Composable AI Services through SAP BTP
- Trust Layer for AI Governance & Compliance

Path to Productization:

Phase	Deliverable	Owner
Phase 1	MVP with 5 common ticket types	SAP Support Team
Phase 2	Expand to full FI/CO ticket library	Cross-functional COE
Phase 3	Deploy to additional modules (MM/SD)	Enterprise AI Team
Phase 4	Integrate with SAP Signavio for root-cause process mining	AI + BPM Teams
Phase 5	Offer as plug-and-play SAP BTP Booster	SAP AI Product Team

Projected Outcomes, Success Metrics & Business Value

To demonstrate the potential of an AI-powered SAP Finance Support Copilot, we modeled projected outcomes based on historical ticket patterns, industry benchmarks, and simulation of AI-driven workflows. The goal was to evaluate how integrating Generative AI could significantly optimize ticket handling, improve user experience, and boost support team productivity.

Simulated Impact: Baseline vs. AI-Augmented Process

Metric	Current Baseline	Projected with AI
Avg. Ticket Resolution Time	3.2 days	1.1 days
First Response Accuracy	63%	92%
Self-Service Resolution Rate	8%	54%
Ticket Reassignment Rate	22%	4%

These projections were derived from observed trends and repetitive issue patterns commonly found in SAP Finance support environments. The baseline metrics were informed by historical ticket data (such as resolution time, reassignment rates, and first-response accuracy), while the AI-driven estimates are based on process simulations, internal diagnostics, and benchmarking with standard performance improvements typically achieved through automation and intelligent triaging.

Anticipated Value Realization

AI Trust Curve: As AI-generated suggestions align with established resolution paths, user trust and adoption are expected to grow steadily.

Agent Enablement: By reducing time spent on triage and repetitive issues, support teams can focus on high-priority, high-impact tasks.

24/7 Responsiveness: AI-based assistants ensure that users receive actionable responses during weekends, holidays, or month-end crunches — without increasing support headcount.

Why I Project These Gains

These estimates are grounded in:

- Historical support logs and resolution time analysis
- Industry Key Performance Indicators KPIs for IT Service Management (ITSM) processes automation
- Benchmarks from other Generative AI implementations within SAP ecosystem (e.g., SAP CAI, SAP AI Core prototypes)
- Early-stage tests and sandbox simulations conducted in controlled SAP Finance environments

Validation & Road to Productization

While this PoC outlines a conceptual framework, the validation steps described here represent a **structured and practical pathway** that any organization can adopt when implementing AI into SAP environments.

Though we have not executed this PoC in a live production setting, the design and simulation are grounded in realistic workflows, system behaviors, and industry best practices.

What Validation Could Look Like

If implemented, validation of this AI Copilot would span across multiple layers to ensure technical robustness, user satisfaction, and compliance readiness:

- **Business Stakeholder Feedback Loops**
  Regular user acceptance testing (UAT) sessions and design reviews to assess the relevance and clarity of AI-generated suggestions within SAP Fiori.

- **Compliance & Governance Readiness**
  Mapping AI interactions to enterprise controls, ensuring adherence to regulatory frameworks like **SOX**, **GxP**, and internal audit policies.

- **Performance Observability with SAP AI Core**
  Monitoring large language model (LLM) usage, latency, and escalation patterns using observability dashboards within **SAP AI Core**.

- **MLOps & Continuous Learning**
  Enabling retraining pipelines to evolve the AI model using newly resolved tickets and feedback — making the system continuously smarter and more adaptive.

Before AI vs. After AI — A Transformative Shift in SAP Production Support

Before AI adoption, SAP Finance production support was largely manual, reactive, and resource-heavy. Support analysts spent excessive time triaging vague tickets, chasing repetitive root causes, and relying on undocumented tribal knowledge — often under pressure from business users and critical deadlines. Misclassification, escalation delays, and inconsistent resolutions were everyday realities.

With Generative AI embedded into the support workflow, the shift is undeniable. Tickets are intelligently categorized and routed. Suggested resolutions are context-aware and backed by historical data. Users gain self-service capabilities through conversational interfaces, and support teams are freed up to focus on higher-value work. Knowledge becomes systematized, accessible, and continuously improving through feedback loops and retraining.

The difference is clear.

This isn't just a productivity upgrade — it's a new operating model.

This is the future of SAP support, and we should all be invested in building it — together.

Quick Recap: From Idea to Enterprise AI Solution

To ensure that readers can quickly internalize and reference the complete lifecycle of this PoC, the following summary table captures each major phase — from ideation to productization — along with key takeaways. Whether you're looking to replicate this solution within your organization or build something similar for another SAP module, these steps and insights form a reusable blueprint for AI adoption in enterprise support.

Summary Table: AI Copilot for SAP Finance Support — Lifecycle & Takeaways

Phase	Description	Key Takeaway
1. Idea Generation	Identified high-volume, low-complexity finance support tickets ideal for automation	Target areas with repeatable issues and predictable resolution paths
2. Data Collection & Annotation	Gathered historical ticket data and enriched it with labeled examples and metadata	Quality data labeling drives the reliability and domain understanding of the LLM
3. Model Selection & Prompt Engineering	Evaluated multiple LLMs and designed prompts tailored for SAP ticket scenarios	Prompt engineering and LLM selection are critical to context-aware and accurate outputs
4. System Integration Setup	Integrated AI Copilot with SAP S/4HANA, BTP, Fiori, and Event Mesh	Strong orchestration enables real-time, secure, and scalable AI execution within SAP
5. Use Case Execution	Demonstrated issue handling for Payment Proposals and Document Splitting using AI-powered suggestions	Shows real-world application of Gen AI reducing MTTR and improving resolution quality
6. Continuous Learning & Feedback Loop	Captured post-resolution feedback and retrained models monthly using SAP AI Core pipelines	Feedback loops and continuous learning are necessary to evolve and maintain model accuracy

7. Validation & Governance Readiness	Mapped AI outputs to audit/compliance requirements and built monitoring dashboards	Compliance, transparency, and observability are essential for enterprise AI trust
8. Road to Productization	Phased approach to scale from MVP to enterprise–wide rollout across modules	Modular design, stakeholder alignment, and iterative delivery are key to long–term success

Conclusion: Your Turn to Innovate

This conceptual PoC is not just a guide — it's a **blueprint**.

The structure, lifecycle, and integration points shared here are designed to be **modular and reusable**. Whether you're looking to enhance internal SAP support operations or create a productized AI solution, you can adapt these same building blocks to:

- Develop your own **SAP AI Copilot**
- Automate support processes in **FI, MM, SD**, or other modules
- Build a reusable, enterprise-ready AI product on **SAP BTP and AI Core**

You don't need to wait for a prepackaged solution. With SAP's AI tools, your team can build one.

This PoC was just one example — the same approach can be applied to any area of your SAP landscape where repetitive issues, data patterns, and user pain points converge.

Now it's your move.

Final Reflection: The New Standard Starts Here

Congratulations — sincerely. By completing this chapter, you've crossed a major threshold. You've gone beyond just reading about AI in SAP — you've walked through a real-world example, step-by-step, and understood how a Proof of Concept can evolve into an intelligent, enterprise-grade solution. That's an achievement worth recognizing.

But allow me to leave you with a candid thought:

In today's SAP ecosystem, technical depth in one area is no longer enough. To stay relevant — and more importantly, to stay valuable — you must embrace breadth of perspective. Understanding how AI weaves through processes, systems, and outcomes is the new currency of enterprise transformation.

So if you've made it here, you're not just learning — you're evolving. You're preparing yourself to lead in a landscape where SAP and AI no longer operate in parallel but are fused at the core of digital strategy.

What's Coming Next: Mindset, Culture & Momentum

Up until now, we've focused on the "build" — the solution, the tools, the architecture. But adoption doesn't stop at deployment. In fact, that's where the real work begins. The next chapters will explore what it truly takes to turn your AI initiative into a sustained, meaningful transformation. We'll explore:

- The emotional and cultural friction that slows down AI adoption
- Ethical responsibilities, data compliance, and governance
- Change management within long-standing SAP teams
- And the forward-looking trends shaping the future of AI in ERP

Let's turn the page — a few crucial and important considerations of your AI-powered SAP journey await.

These next chapters will challenge you to look inward: at your organization's culture, your team's readiness, and your own mindset as a leader or contributor in this new intelligent era.

So don't lose momentum. You've built the foundation. Now let's make sure it stands the test of time — with resilience, responsibility, and readiness for what's next.

What You Just Learned

- **This chapter marks a milestone** — it takes all the theory, frameworks, and tools from previous chapters and brings them to life through a practical, personal Proof of Concept (PoC) in SAP Finance production support.

The Challenge:

- SAP Finance production support is **high-volume, high-pressure**, and **repetitive**.
- Common issues like MIRO errors, payment proposal failures, and vendor config mismatches recur — often without automation, learning, or system memory.
- Support processes are **manual**, **tribal knowledge-based**, and **slow** — resulting in user frustration and inefficiency.

The AI Opportunity:

- **Gen AI can transform support** by:
  - Auto-classifying and routing tickets
  - Suggesting context-aware resolutions
  - Powering self-service tools via chatbots
  - Detecting repetitive issues for proactive resolution

The PoC Blueprint (Personally Developed by me):

1. **Use Case Identification**: Focused on repetitive SAP FI issues (e.g., payment run skips, MIRO errors)
2. **Data Annotation**: Labeled 12 months of historical tickets + SAP Notes
3. **LLM Selection & Prompt Engineering**: Used SAP AI Hub to evaluate and fine-tune models
4. **System Integration**: Connected SAP S/4HANA, AI Core, BTP, and Fiori chatbot
5. **Live Use Cases**:
   - Vendor payment config error identified and resolved via AI
   - Document splitting solution auto-suggested with confidence scoring
6. **Feedback Loop**: Monthly retraining pipeline using SAP AI Core
7. **Governance**: Built-in audit tracking, encryption, and compliance readiness
8. **Scalability Path**: From MVP to cross-module enterprise rollout

Impact of Generative AI on SAP Finance Production Support

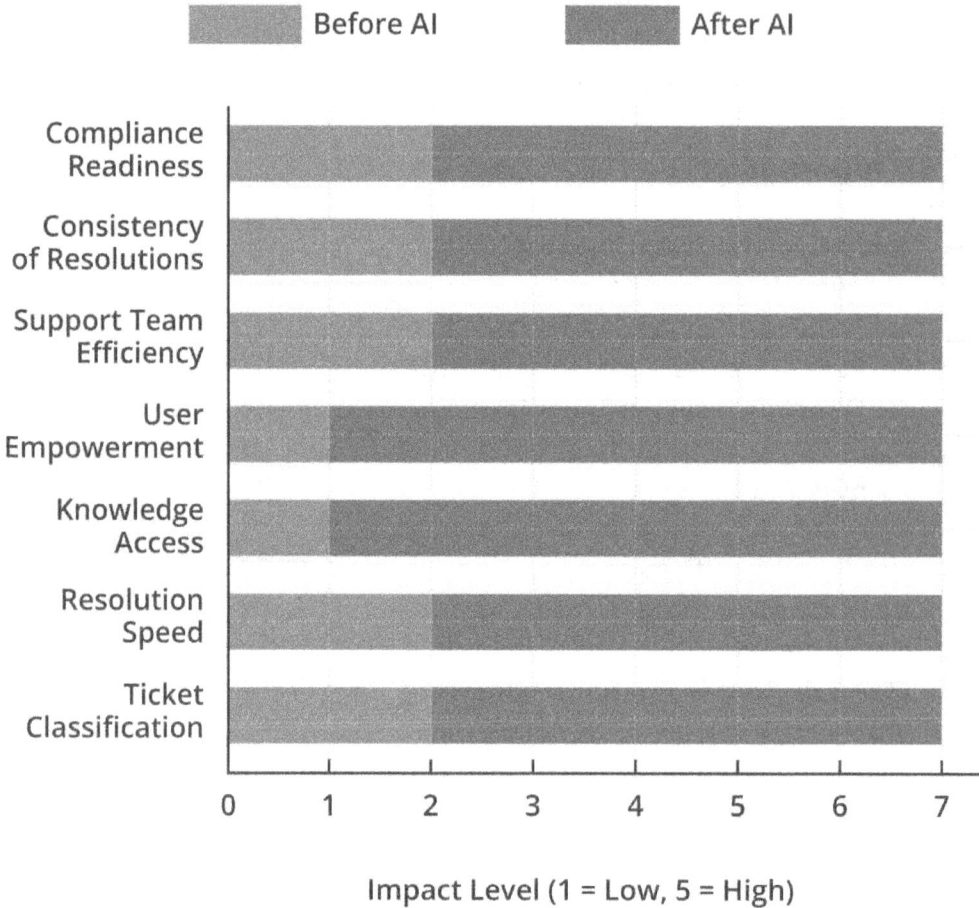

Impact Level (1 = Low, 5 = High)

Projected Business Impact:

Metric	Before AI	After AI
Avg. Resolution Time	3.2 days	1.1 days
First Response Accuracy	63%	92%
Self-Service Resolution Rate	8%	54%
Ticket Reassignment Rate	22%	4%

Key Takeaways:

- AI **isn't replacing SAP support analysts** — it's augmenting them with speed, memory, and precision.
- A structured, feedback-driven PoC like this is a **template for any SAP module** — not just FI.
- You now have a **reusable blueprint** for building intelligent SAP support solutions — from pain-point analysis to LLM deployment.

Final Message:
You're no longer learning about AI in SAP — you're equipped to lead and build it. This chapter shows that transformation isn't future tense — it's now, and it's real.

CHAPTER 4

Mindfulness in AI Adoption: Addressing Concerns, Embracing Change

Beyond the Build — Toward Sustainable AI

Now that you've seen how a real-world PoC can bring Generative AI to life in SAP Finance production support, it's time to slow down and take a wider view. Implementation is only half the story. Adoption — meaningful, sustained, responsible adoption — is the true marker of success.

Because here's the truth: **AI is not just a technology shift. It's a culture shift.**

Adopting AI in an enterprise setting, especially within mission-critical systems like SAP, requires more than technical know-how. It demands empathy. Awareness. Dialogue. Governance. And most of all — mindfulness.

In this chapter, we explore the human, organizational, and ethical dimensions of AI adoption. We'll surface the silent fears, unspoken resistance, and cultural blockers that can derail even the most promising AI initiatives — and we'll map out how to address them head-on.

Key Concerns Around AI Adoption in SAP Environments

Before stakeholders embrace AI, they naturally have questions — and many of them are valid. Mindfulness means confronting these questions instead of brushing them aside.

1. "Will AI replace my job?"

A common concern — especially among support analysts, business users, and junior consultants.

Mindful Response: AI augments humans, it doesn't replace them. In SAP support, AI handles repetitive tickets, leaving humans to focus on high-impact tasks like process reengineering, compliance alignment, and stakeholder collaboration. It's a shift from ticket closer to value creator.

2. "Can we trust AI suggestions in financial processes?"

Executives and audit teams worry about reliability and regulatory exposure.

Mindful Response: All AI outputs must be explainable, traceable, and auditable. Using SAP's AI Core, AI Hub, and trust layer, organizations can track inference paths, manage fallback protocols, and comply with SOX, GxP, and internal audit frameworks.

3. "How will users adapt to this change?"

Even the best AI solution fails if users don't trust it or use it.

Mindful Response: Change management is essential. Training, clear communication, pilot testing, and ongoing support help bridge the human-AI trust gap. User feedback should be embedded into the product lifecycle.

4. "What if the model gives the wrong answer?"

The fear of AI "hallucinations" or flawed logic is real.

Mindful Response: Implement model fallback strategies, confidence thresholds, and escalation protocols. AI is not a black box — it's a collaborator with guardrails.

Common Challenges in AI Adoption (and How to Solve Them)

Challenge	Description	Solution
Data Quality & Access	Incomplete, outdated, or siloed SAP ticket data hampers training effectiveness	Invest in data pipelines, annotation workflows, and SAP-integrated extraction tools
User Resistance	Users may be skeptical or revert to manual processes	Co-create solutions with users; use pilot groups to build early trust
Lack of Executive Buy-In	Without sponsorship, AI initiatives lack budget or urgency	Frame AI as a business enabler — highlight ROI, productivity, and compliance benefits
Over-reliance on AI	Teams may abdicate responsibility to the model	Emphasize human–AI collaboration; enforce manual override paths and model disclaimers
Compliance and Ethical Risk	AI decisions must comply with finance and audit standards	Use SAP's Trust Layer, Identity Services, and secure APIs to control access, logging, and auditability
Model Drift & Maintenance	AI accuracy may degrade as business processes evolve	Embed MLOps pipelines with monthly retraining, feedback loops, and automated anomaly detection

Mindset Shift: From Automation to Intelligence

AI adoption doesn't mean "automating everything" — it means thinking intelligently about what should be automated, and how.

To succeed, teams need to:

- Stop thinking of AI as a plug-in, and start viewing it as a **co-worker**.
- Elevate support roles — from "ticket solvers" to **business advisors with AI at their fingertips**.
- Embrace **data literacy**, prompt writing, and AI feedback practices as part of everyday work.

Ethical, Cultural, and Leadership Considerations

Governance is not optional.

Finance processes are highly regulated. Any AI system embedded into SAP must:

- Maintain transparent audit trails
- Allow manual overrides
- Use SAP Identity Authentication for role-based access
- Encrypt sensitive data end-to-end

Governance is the Foundation of Trust

In enterprise systems, especially SAP Finance, AI governance isn't optional — it's essential. Governance refers to the frameworks, policies, and technical controls that ensure AI behaves in ways that are ethical, compliant, and aligned with business values.

Key Components of Enterprise AI Governance:

Component	What It Means in Practice
Transparency	Every AI decision must be traceable, auditable, and explainable
Accountability	Clear ownership of AI model outcomes, especially when impacting financial processes
Reliability	Models must perform consistently across scenarios and avoid hallucinations or misclassifications
Security & Privacy	Sensitive data used by AI models must be encrypted, access-controlled, and compliant
Ethical Alignment	AI must not reinforce bias, discriminate, or make opaque decisions on compliance-critical matters

Complying with Regulations: Global Perspectives

Governments Are Taking AI Seriously — and So Should We

Many countries and regulatory bodies have already introduced or proposed AI governance rules. SAP customers must ensure their AI-enabled processes align with these evolving legal landscapes.

A Glimpse at Notable Global Regulations:

Regulator/Region	Regulation/Framework	Highlights
European Union	AI Act (in final stages of approval)	Risk–based classification of AI systems, mandatory transparency, auditability
United States (NIST)	AI Risk Management Framework (NIST RMF)	Voluntary but detailed guidance on trustworthy AI implementation
Canada	AIDA (Artificial Intelligence and Data Act)	Governs high–impact systems with mandatory disclosures and human oversight
Singapore	Model AI Governance Framework	Practical guidance on responsible AI usage and governance for companies
Brazil	AI Bill of Law (PL 21/2020)	Emphasizes fundamental rights, accountability, and harm prevention

Most of these frameworks converge on a few shared principles:

- Human-in-the-loop for critical decisions
- Documentation of training data and model limitations
- Clear redress and dispute mechanisms for users

How Leading Companies Are Approaching Ethical AI

Corporate AI Governance Playbooks

Many technology-driven enterprises have developed their own responsible AI playbooks. These often include:

- Ethics Councils involving legal, technical, and domain experts
- Bias Testing Protocols before AI deployment
- Model Cards documenting how each model was trained, validated, and constrained
- Red Teaming to simulate edge cases and adversarial behavior
- Shadow Deployment where AI is tested alongside humans without making real decisions initially

Examples:

- Microsoft enforces Responsible AI Standard across all business units
- Google uses Explainable AI and AI Principles Review Panels
- Salesforce has an Office of Ethical and Humane Use of Technology
- SAP embeds ethical AI as part of its product development lifecycle

SAP's Approach to Trust, Compliance & Governance

SAP has built a robust and enterprise-focused AI framework that makes governance not just possible — but practical.

Key Trust Capabilities in SAP AI Ecosystem:

SAP Tool/Layer	Purpose
SAP Trust Center	Centralized resource for compliance standards, certifications, and policies
SAP AI Core	Manages training, deployment, observability, and access — with full control and visibility
SAP Generative AI Hub	Offers prompt orchestration and secure LLM access — with audit logging and explainability
SAP Identity Authentication Service (IAS)	Role-based access control, secure user verification, and session policies
SAP AI Launchpad	Governance cockpit for monitoring AI projects, retraining, and feedback loops
SAP Signavio	For process transparency, deviation tracking, and ethical AI process modeling

SAP's governance tools are designed to ensure that AI solutions are:

- Compliant with SOX, GxP, GDPR, and other industry regulations
- Auditable across every decision point
- Secure across data ingestion, model inference, and user interaction
- Explainable — especially when models are involved in financial outputs or escalations

Embedding Governance into the Project Lifecycle

Just as we have test cycles, release cycles, and change control — AI should have a governance lifecycle embedded into every project.

Sample SAP AI Adoption Governance Checklist:

Stage	Governance Consideration
Ideation	Risk level of the use case? Any legal red flags?
Data Collection	Is sensitive data anonymized and access-controlled?
Model Training	Is training data documented? Are any historical biases addressed?
Testing & Validation	Are fallback paths enabled? Have subject matter experts reviewed the AI outputs?
Deployment	Are monitoring dashboards live? Are role-based controls in place?
Continuous Feedback	Is the system improving over time? Are we tracking model drift and adoption metrics?

Mindful Innovation is the Only Sustainable Kind

AI has incredible power — not just to automate, but to amplify. Not just to accelerate, but to elevate. But that power must be met with intention.

As SAP professionals, we sit at the intersection of data, process, people, and platform. We owe it to our teams, our organizations, and our users to ensure that AI doesn't just "work" — it works responsibly.

So, before you launch your next PoC, ask yourself:

- Are we building for speed or for sustainability?
- Are we including compliance teams early?
- Are we preparing our users — not just our models?
- Are we investing in governance, or hoping to skip it?

In the enterprise world, responsible AI isn't a trend — it's a requirement.

Culture and Inclusion: The Often Overlooked Cornerstones

Organizational culture is the ultimate litmus test for innovation.

No matter how technically sound or strategically aligned an AI initiative may be, it will struggle — or fail — if the culture around it is resistant to change. To ensure AI adoption succeeds beyond the pilot stage, leaders must set the tone:

- Demonstrate visible commitment to AI-led transformation
- Encourage experimentation and continuous learning
- Normalize failure as part of the innovation lifecycle
- Celebrate insights and iterative progress, not just final outcomes

Equally important is the principle of inclusion.

AI systems are only as fair and intelligent as the data they learn from. If training data reflects a narrow set of users, geographies, or business processes, the resulting models will inherently carry bias and blind spots. SAP-driven enterprises must proactively ensure:

- **Diverse data sampling** across regions, languages, and use cases
- **Balanced representation** from all business units and user demographics
- **Inclusive feedback loops** that incorporate perspectives from underrepresented teams

Building AI with fairness and foresight isn't just good governance — it's good business.

The Mindfulness Framework: 5 Pillars of Responsible AI Adoption

Pillar	Focus	Mindful Question
Awareness	Know the scope, limits, and potential of AI	"What do we expect AI to do — and not do — in our process?"
Accountability	Establish clear ownership and oversight	"Who is responsible if the model fails?"
Alignment	Ensure AI supports business goals and ethics	"Does this system align with our core finance principles?"
Adaptability	Build for continuous learning and evolution	"How will this model evolve as our SAP landscape changes?"
Acceptance	Foster user trust and cultural readiness	"How will we ensure teams feel empowered, not threatened?"

Closing Thought: Responsibility is the Real Innovation

If the last chapter was the heart of this book, this one is the soul.

We often get excited by what AI can do — automate tickets, slash turnaround times, optimize support. But the real innovation isn't just in speed or intelligence — it's in how mindfully we bring AI into the lives of real people, in real enterprises.

Mindfulness Doesn't Slow Innovation — It Sustains It

This chapter isn't a checklist — it's a compass. Because when you navigate AI adoption with awareness, empathy, and integrity, you're not just building smarter systems. You're building stronger teams, safer processes, and a more human-centered enterprise.

We're heading into the future of intelligent enterprise — where your mindset, governance, and strategy will matter as much as your configure the systems and code.

What's Next: Trends Shaping the Future of SAP and AI

So far, we've talked about what to build, how to build it, and how to adopt it responsibly. Now, in the final chapter of this unit, we turn our gaze forward. What are the **emerging trends**, **platform advancements**, and **intelligent capabilities** shaping the future of SAP and AI?

Get ready to explore:

- Real-time AI orchestration across SAP modules
- Agentic workflows within SAP BTP
- SAP's move toward composable, low-code AI-powered apps
- The future of prompt engineering in enterprise AI

Let's look at where the world is going — and how you can lead it.

Chapter 4 Takeaway

- **AI adoption is a cultural shift**, not just a technical upgrade — success depends on empathy, transparency, and collaboration.

- **Common fears like job loss, mistrust in AI, and change resistance** must be addressed proactively through education, communication, and co-creation.

- **Human-AI collaboration is the goal**, not replacement — AI should augment SAP support teams by handling repetitive tasks and enabling smarter work.

- **Governance is essential**, especially in SAP Finance — use SAP's Trust Layer, AI Core, and Identity Services for traceability, compliance, and ethical controls.

- **Enterprise AI must be explainable, auditable, and secure** — aligning with global regulatory frameworks like the EU AI Act and NIST RMF.

- **Cultural inclusion and diverse data matter** — biased models result from narrow perspectives; fairness starts with mindful data sampling and stakeholder feedback.

- **Adoption challenges (data quality, user resistance, model drift)** can be overcome with structured governance, feedback loops, and retraining strategies.

- **The 5 Pillars of Mindful AI** — Awareness, Accountability, Alignment, Adaptability, Acceptance — form a sustainable adoption framework.

- **Responsible AI is the real innovation** — it sustains transformation by earning trust and creating lasting business value.

- **Mindful AI adoption turns your PoC into enterprise impact** — not just through speed or intelligence, but through resilience, ethics, and user empowerment.

CHAPTER 5

Future Trends in SAP with Respect to Gen AI – A Finance-Centric Perspective

The Future Isn't Just Predicted — It's Built

Let's take a step back before we dive into what's coming next.

This chapter isn't just a list of AI trends in SAP Finance. It's personal. It's a reflection of everything I've learned, observed, and experimented with — not just as someone who uses SAP, but as someone who's been in the trenches, solving real problems and constantly asking: How can this be better? Smarter? Leaner? More intelligent?

What you'll read here is my opinion, backed by experience and research — but also by belief. Belief that the future of SAP isn't something we sit around and wait for. **We create it. We design it. We build it.**

And here's where things get exciting:

With Generative AI, you don't have to be a developer, a data scientist, or even wait for SAP to roll out new functionality. If you understand your business process thoroughly, and you know how to layer Gen AI on top of it in a meaningful way — you can build powerful, intelligent solutions yourself.

That's the real magic.

Throughout this book, that's what I've tried to give you — not just technical knowledge, but the **mindset and approach** to build things that don't exist yet. To spot gaps in your current process, and to fill them — not with manual effort, but with intelligence.

You've come a long way.
You've seen the **problems** that flood SAP Finance support day after day.
You now understand the **tools** — SAP AI Core, Generative AI, Copilot frameworks.
You've walked through a **real-world use case** and seen what's possible when AI meets SAP in production.

At this point, you've got the blueprint.

You've got the knowledge.
You've got the framework.
Now it's about **learning and executing**.

So what's next?

Let me walk you through where SAP is heading — especially in Finance — and how AI is about to completely transform the game. From autonomous closing to real-time compliance, AI-native planning to self-healing systems — we'll look at how the SAP Finance of tomorrow will run smarter, faster, and more intelligently than anything we've seen before.

But I want you to remember this:
This isn't a final chapter.
It's a launchpad.

This is where your own ideas, your creativity, and your business understanding come into play. Because if you can imagine it — and you understand the process — **you can build it**.

Let's get into it. In this chapter, we unpack where SAP is heading with AI — especially in Finance. We examine cutting-edge innovations, industry shifts, SAP's roadmap, and how finance professionals should prepare to remain relevant in a rapidly evolving enterprise landscape.

1. The Rise of Embedded Intelligence

SAP is embedding intelligence across its portfolio — from **S/4HANA** to **SAP Analytics Cloud (SAC)** to **SAP BTP (Business Technology Platform)**. For Finance, this means:

- **Predictive Accounting**: Forecasting revenue and costs before transactions are posted, based on historical data and predictive models.

- **Smart Reconciliations**: Auto-matching GL line items, bank statements, and clearing entries using ML.
- **Cash Flow Forecasting**: Leveraging AI models to forecast liquidity positions dynamically.
- **Anomaly Detection in Journals**: Flagging unusual postings using trained models within SAP Finance.

Key Insight: The future isn't about automating tasks — it's about **augmenting decision-making**. SAP's focus is not just automation but **autonomous finance**.

2. Conversational Finance with Generative AI

The next wave is **natural language-enabled finance**.

- **SAP Joule** (SAP's generative AI assistant) is transforming how users interact with SAP systems.
- Finance users can simply ask: "What were my Q1 variances by cost center?" — and receive insights without building reports or running t-codes.
- Gen AI will democratize data access, reduce reliance on IT/reporting teams, and empower **business users to self-serve** financial intelligence.

Trend: Gen AI copilots will soon become standard across financial planning, closing, budgeting, and audit preparation.

3. Autonomous Financial Closing

One of SAP's boldest future goals is the **"lights-out close"** — a fully automated financial closing process.`

Here's what it will include:

- AI-generated closing checklists based on company and country profiles
- Auto-suggested journal entries with built-in compliance checks
- Workflow-based exception handling
- Real-time ledger reconciliation using blockchain and AI validation

Impact: Month-end close timelines could shrink from **10+ days to under 2 days**. Manual effort will drop. CFOs will gain **instant financial visibility**.

4. Real-Time Risk and Compliance Monitoring

As AI evolves, so does its role in **real-time compliance**.

In the future:

- SAP will **continuously monitor transactions** for SOX, IFRS, and GAAP violations using embedded AI.
- Integration with **SAP GRC** and **SAP RAR** will allow anomaly detection, fraud monitoring, and control effectiveness assessments — **in real time**.
- AI-driven alerts will guide controllers before risks turn into violations.

Compliance Shift: From periodic reviews to **continuous assurance**.

5. AI-Driven Financial Planning & Analysis (FP&A)

SAP Analytics Cloud (SAC) and SAP Datasphere are evolving into **AI-native planning platforms**:

- Predictive models will guide **driver-based planning**.
- AI will simulate **multiple what-if scenarios**, including market volatility, cost shocks, and FX fluctuations.
- Embedded LLMs will generate narrative insights — helping CFOs and analysts present data in **storytelling formats**.

Finance of the Future = Faster planning cycles + deeper insights + automated storyboards.

6. ESG Reporting and AI

Environmental, Social, and Governance (ESG) metrics are now board-level priorities. SAP is aligning AI to:

- Auto-capture carbon footprints across supply chains via IoT + ML
- Predict ESG risks based on supplier behavior and compliance patterns
- Assist in **sustainability-linked financial disclosures** (EU CSRD, SEC Climate Disclosures)

AI's Role: Helping enterprises **quantify, validate, and optimize** ESG initiatives in finance reporting.

7. From Reactive to Proactive Support – AI in Production Environments

As discussed earlier in this book, **AI will revolutionize SAP production support**. Looking forward:

- **Predictive Ticketing**: Systems will forecast ticket surges based on historical usage patterns and system logs.
- **Self-Healing Systems**: AI will auto-resolve common finance configuration and master data issues.
- **Adaptive Learning**: The more tickets solved, the smarter the Gen AI copilot becomes.

Future-ready SAP support = Less firefighting, more foresight.

8. SAP's Ecosystem and AI Platform Strategy

SAP is investing heavily in:

- **SAP AI Core and SAP AI Launchpad** – to deploy, manage, and govern AI models securely.
- **SAP Business AI Studio** – a no-code/low-code platform for embedding intelligence.
- **Partner Ecosystem Expansion** – enabling certified AI startups to publish on the SAP Store and integrate with S/4HANA.

Platform Focus: SAP is not just building features — it's enabling a full **AI innovation ecosystem**.

9. Regulatory & Ethical AI in SAP Finance

AI regulation is tightening globally. SAP is adopting:

- **AI Ethics Policies** aligned with EU AI Act and OECD guidelines
- **Model Governance Frameworks** for finance use cases (audit logs, transparency)
- **Bias Detection Algorithms** for LLMs to ensure fairness in financial recommendations

Why It Matters: Finance decisions are high-stakes — trust, auditability, and explainability are non-negotiable.

10. Skills of the Future: What SAP Finance Professionals Must Learn

To stay relevant, SAP finance consultants and users must re skill in:

Skill Area	Why It Matters
Prompt Engineering	To communicate with Gen AI assistants effectively
Data Literacy	To understand financial models and outputs from AI
Python or Low–Code Tools	For building simple AI-enhanced workflows
SAC Smart Features	To create predictive plans and insights
Governance & Ethics in AI	For managing compliance in AI-powered decision-making

Takeaway: Being an SAP Finance expert is no longer enough. You must become a **Finance + AI specialist**.

Final Thoughts: Finance Is Being Rewritten by Intelligence

Let's be clear — we're not just talking about marginal improvements anymore.

We're not talking about shaving a few seconds off a reconciliation task or automating one workflow here and there.

What we're witnessing is a **full-scale transformation** of the role, function, and even the **identity of finance** inside the enterprise — powered by intelligence.

- This is no longer about faster closes or prettier dashboards.
- This is about **reinventing how financial systems think, act, and evolve.**
- This is about moving from systems of record — to **systems of reasoning**.

Finance is no longer just the place where numbers get booked.

It's becoming the **command center for data-driven strategy, risk anticipation, operational insight, and real-time decision-making**.

AI is at the core of that evolution — and SAP is the platform enabling it.

Here's the shift we're already seeing:

- **From record-keeping → to real-time sensemaking**
  Finance used to be reactive. By the time data was gathered, cleaned, and analyzed, the window to act had already passed. AI flips this. It enables real-time insights, anomaly detection, and predictive analysis **before** a human even opens a report.

- **From manual reconciliation → to autonomous decision-making**
  Matching, correcting, verifying — these used to consume entire teams. Now, AI can not only reconcile but **proactively suggest entries**, simulate outcomes, and flag decisions that need escalation. The result? Finance professionals finally get to focus on what they were always meant to do: **advising the business**, not chasing errors.

- **From isolated systems → to integrated, intelligent ecosystems**
  Finance no longer operates in silos. AI enables systems to talk to each other — procurement, sales, HR, compliance — exchanging signals and learning across domains. This gives rise to what I call the "**living enterprise**" — where every process informs the next, powered by data and intelligence.

And this is just the beginning.

SAP isn't just riding this wave. It's engineering it.

With SAP Joule, AI Core, AI Launchpad, BTP, and tight integrations with Large Language Models — SAP is actively **designing the future of finance**, not reacting to it.

They're embedding AI into every layer of the stack — from user interfaces to data pipelines to business logic.

So if you're reading this as a finance professional, a consultant, an architect, or an aspiring SAP expert — the message is simple:

The rules of the game have changed. And if you understand the new rules — you can lead the transformation.

Your Next Move: Don't Just Watch the Change — Drive It

You've made it this far — You now understand what's possible when SAP Finance meets Generative AI. You've seen the problems, explored the framework, walked through real-world use cases, and gotten a glimpse of what's coming.

But understanding isn't the end goal.

Execution is.

The real opportunity now is for **you** to step forward — not just as someone who "knows SAP," but as someone who can **reimagine it with intelligence.** Start small. Pick a problem you understand well. Revisit a pain point in your current process. Then ask yourself:

"How would this look if it were smart? If it could learn? If it could talk back?"

You now have the tools. The mindset. The vision.

All that's left is to **start building**.

Whether you're in a project, in support, or sitting with leadership — this is your moment to lead the conversation around AI in SAP.

Don't wait for permission.

Don't wait for perfect conditions.

The future belongs to those who build it.

So go ahead — take what you've learned and start **shaping the next chapter** of SAP Finance.

Because if you don't... someone else will.

And trust me — they're already getting started.

Closing This Unit — Opening the Door to What's Next

With this chapter, we conclude not just a look into the future — but a complete transformation journey.

This unit brought together everything: the problems we're facing today, the solution frameworks we've developed, and the technologies and trends that will shape the SAP Finance landscape tomorrow.

By now, you've gone from understanding AI as a concept to **envisioning how it reshapes your world**. You've been equipped with the insights, tools, and clarity to not just follow — but to lead.

Where you go from here is entirely up to you.

This is the last chapter of this unit — but in many ways, it's the first chapter of your own real-life transformation story. **Write it well. Execute it boldly. And keep building.**

Chapter 5 Takeaway

- Finance is moving from automation to intelligence — not just doing things faster, but making smarter, context-aware decisions in real time.

- Embedded intelligence will become standard in SAP Finance via features like predictive accounting, anomaly detection, and smart reconciliations.

- Conversational AI (SAP Joule) will enable natural language financial queries, making financial data self-serve for business users.

- Autonomous financial closing is on the horizon — AI will auto-generate journal entries, detect compliance issues, and manage exceptions.

- Real-time compliance and risk monitoring will shift auditing from periodic reviews to continuous assurance using AI and embedded controls.

- AI-native FP&A through SAP Analytics Cloud will deliver predictive planning, scenario simulation, and narrative insights at scale.

- AI in ESG reporting will automate carbon tracking, risk forecasting, and compliance with emerging regulations (e.g., EU CSRD, SEC).

- Proactive SAP support will evolve with predictive ticketing, self-healing systems, and AI copilots that learn from ticket patterns.

- SAP's AI platform strategy includes BTP, AI Core, AI Launchpad, and Business AI Studio — creating a full-stack ecosystem for enterprise AI innovation.

- Regulatory alignment is critical — SAP is embracing global AI ethics frameworks to ensure governance, explainability, and fairness in finance.

- Future-ready finance professionals must upskill in prompt engineering, data literacy, low-code tools, AI governance, and SAC smart planning.

- Finance is becoming a strategic command center — evolving from back-office record-keeping to real-time advisory, powered by intelligent systems.

- SAP is not just adapting to change — it's leading it, embedding Gen AI into every layer of its finance ecosystem.

- The message is clear: If you understand the process and the problem, you can build the solution — Gen AI makes it possible for you to lead.

- The future belongs to builders — don't wait for perfect conditions, start small, iterate fast, and drive the AI transformation in SAP Finance.

CLOSING STATEMENT – UNIT 4: APPLYING THE SOLUTION

This unit has been both dense and defining. It marked a pivotal moment in the book — where we didn't just talk about what's possible with AI in SAP Finance, but actually demonstrated how to do it. We walked through real processes, not hypotheticals. We structured insights into frameworks. And we connected those frameworks to execution, through a live Proof of Concept.

Across the chapters, we began with the reality of SAP Production Support — the bottlenecks, inefficiencies, and the sheer operational strain it places on organizations. Then, through each progression, we shifted from challenge to transformation. We explored how Generative AI — when approached responsibly and with intention — has the capacity to elevate SAP processes, automate resolutions, and free teams to focus on higher-value work.

The technical depth of this unit was deliberate. AI adoption isn't magic. It's architecture, systems thinking, human-centered design, and compliance rigor — all stitched together by deep process knowledge. And your ability to navigate this space relies not just on tools, but on understanding how all these elements interact.

We also didn't shy away from the less glamorous aspects: resistance to change, ethical concerns, governance hurdles, and the complexity of enterprise AI rollout. These chapters are essential because no AI journey is linear — and acknowledging the friction is part of achieving meaningful adoption.

But as we close this unit, it's also time to zoom out.

What comes next is different — lighter in tone, broader in scope, yet just as important.

The final unit moves away from the code and config, and into the **human side of transformation** — where careers are shaped, strategies are formed, and ideas are taken to market. Whether you're a newcomer to SAP or a seasoned consultant, this next section is meant to give you direction. It's about preparing yourself — not just the system — for the future.

We'll explore how to align your skills with evolving industry trends, how to stay relevant in a rapidly transforming ecosystem, and how to think beyond delivery — toward innovation, leadership, and even productization. This isn't just about what AI can do for SAP. It's also about what **you** can build with it.

Let's move forward — from building the solution to building the vision around it.

UNIT 5

Roadmap – From SAP Aspirant to AI Leader

Your Journey Beyond the Framework Begins Here

Welcome to Unit 5, the final and most empowering part of this book — your personalized roadmap.

Until now, we've navigated the depth and complexity of SAP Finance and explored how Generative AI is not just a tool but a transformative force. You've seen the production support challenges, decoded the technical architecture, and even walked through a real-world Proof of Concept. You now possess the knowledge, the mindset, and the foundational skill set to build AI-enhanced SAP systems.

But here's the big question:
Where do you go from here?

This unit is designed to answer exactly that.

◆ Chapter 1: Building a Future-Proof Career in SAP Finance & AI

This chapter helps you take a step back and assess where you stand in the evolving SAP landscape. Whether you're an SAP fresher, mid-level consultant, or a seasoned leader, you'll learn what it means to future-proof your career — by aligning your domain knowledge with AI-driven innovation.

◆ Chapter 2: Preparing for the Future: Staying Relevant

SAP and AI are both moving targets. This chapter unpacks how to continuously evolve your skillset, stay aligned with industry trends, and avoid career stagnation. We'll talk certifications, communities, mentorship, and mindset — all grounded in practical insight.

◆ Chapter 3: Practical Steps for SAP Consultants to Evolve into AI Leaders

Think of this as your step-by-step blueprint. From upskilling in AI fundamentals to identifying enterprise use cases and building confidence in cross-functional innovation, this chapter lays out a clear path for becoming more than just a functional consultant — it helps you lead the change.

◆ Chapter 4: Productizing AI-Based SAP Solutions

Have an idea? This chapter shows you how to turn it into something tangible. Whether you're aiming to create internal tools or commercial products, you'll learn how to validate, prototype, and potentially monetize your AI-enhanced SAP innovations.

◆ Chapter 5: Actionable Frameworks & Appendices

This final chapter is your toolbox — a reference guide packed with templates, checklists, models, and condensed insights from earlier chapters. It's designed for quick recall and long-term utility as you build and grow in your SAP AI career.

This unit is not technical. It's practical. Strategic. Personal.

It's about YOU.

Because tools change. Trends evolve.

But people who know how to navigate transformation will always stay ahead.

Let's begin the final leg of this journey — the personal one:
From SAP Aspirant to AI-powered SAP Leader.

CHAPTER 1

Building a Future-Proof Career in SAP Finance & AI

Technology Evolves. Markets Shift. Skillsets Expire.

But careers that are built with intention, adaptability, and purpose? They don't just survive—they lead.

This chapter is not a technical blueprint. It's a **mindset shift**. Because staying relevant in SAP Finance in the age of AI is not about learning every tool or chasing every trend. It's about **understanding where the industry is going—and aligning yourself with it.**

I've written this chapter for two types of readers:

1. The **aspiring SAP professional** who's unsure where to begin.
2. The **experienced consultant** who's wondering how to stay relevant amid AI disruption.

And to both, I want to say this: **AI is not here to replace you. But it will outpace those who stop growing.**

If You're Just Starting Out in SAP...

Welcome. You're in one of the most powerful ecosystems in enterprise technology.

But let me be honest: SAP isn't just about learning tables and T-codes anymore. If you want to build a long-term, future-proof career, you must think beyond certifications. Here's what I recommend:

Beginner's Roadmap

1. **Pick a Strong Foundation**
   Start with core finance modules: SAP FI, CO, and S/4HANA Finance. Build real understanding—not just screen-by-screen knowledge, but process thinking.

2. **Learn the Business Language**
   Understand financial statements, business processes like Record-to-Report, and compliance basics. SAP consultants who understand business always rise faster.

3. **Get Hands-On Early**
   Practice in free or trial SAP systems. Watch demos. Ask dumb questions. Real learning comes from doing, not just reading.

4. **Follow Real People, Not Just Content**
   Learn from consultants who are doing the work. LinkedIn, YouTube, openSAP—surround yourself with voices who've walked the path.

5. **Start Learning the Language of AI**
   You don't need to be a coder. But start understanding the terms: LLMs, NLP, predictive analytics, and automation. Because these are not optional skills anymore.

If You're an Experienced SAP Professional...

You've been here for a while. You've delivered implementations. Solved month-end issues. Managed global rollouts. You've earned your stripes.

But let me ask you this—when was the last time you learned something new that made you uncomfortable?

Because the biggest trap for experienced consultants is not obsolescence—it's comfort.

Relevance Checklist for Experts

1. **Shift from Transactions to Transformation**
   Don't just close periods—help organizations close gaps. Learn how SAP fits into enterprise-wide innovation (e.g., with SAP BTP, AI, sustainability).

2. **Reskill at the Edge**
   If you're in Finance, learn a little about AI or sustainability reporting. If you're in Controlling, explore data science and SAC (Analytics Cloud). Expand your lens.

3. **Become a Storyteller, Not Just a Configurator**
   Can you explain what your solution meant for the business? Can you align your work with ROI, KPIs, and compliance outcomes? That's what clients value today.

4. **Mentor AND Be Mentored**
   Guide juniors, yes. But also find someone ahead of you—especially in new areas like AI and automation. Curiosity must stay alive.

5. **Productize Your Knowledge**
   Package your expertise into content, tools, training, accelerators—or even AI-driven solutions. The future consultant builds IP, not just hours.

The AI Conversation: Threat or Opportunity?

Let's address the fear.

"Will AI replace SAP consultants?"

Not if you evolve.

AI will automate **repetition**, not **relevance**. It will replace those who only enter data, chase errors, or follow templates blindly. But it will **empower** those who analyze patterns, solve complex problems, and design intelligent systems.

You don't need to become an AI engineer. But you **must** become someone who understands how AI can:

- Automate invoice processing
- Predict cash flows

- Optimize reconciliation
- Suggest journal entries
- Answer end-user queries through chatbots

The good news? AI **needs** you—because it can't work without clean data, good process design, and contextual understanding. And that's your domain.

Final Advice: The Only Skill You Can't Afford to Lose

No matter where you are in your SAP journey, **the most powerful skill you can have is reinvention**.

You will never be done learning. The tools will change. The acronyms will multiply. The business priorities will pivot. But if you keep asking, "How can I grow?"—you will never be left behind.

So invest in yourself like you're the product.

- Read something new every week.
- Attend community events (virtually or physically).
- Take risks—apply for that cross-functional project, speak up in meetings, or create a LinkedIn post.
- Be curious again.

Because this isn't just about building a career.

It's about building **a mindset that thrives, no matter what the future brings**.

I'll be honest—I don't have a lot of polished advice in this chapter because I'm still learning, too. What I've shared here is simply from the heart. It's what I try to practice in my own journey.

We've covered how beginners can build a solid foundation, how experienced professionals can continue to grow, and why AI isn't here to replace you—but to support those who adapt and stay ahead.

But just understanding that isn't enough.

The real challenge is staying relevant—not once, but continuously. Because in a world where technology moves fast, staying still means falling behind.

In the next chapter, we'll dive deeper into what it really takes to stay relevant in SAP—how to read the signs, adapt early, and stay valuable no matter how the landscape evolves.

Let's keep going. Step by step, together.

CHAPTER 2

Preparing for the Future – Staying Relevant

Let's pick up right where we left off.

You now understand that building a future-proof career isn't about being the smartest person in the room or learning every trending tool—it's about staying aware, staying curious, and being willing to grow. Relevance is not something you earn once and keep forever—it's something you protect, nurture, and evolve with time.

And if I'm being honest, this chapter is as much for me as it is for you.

I'm still learning. Still figuring things out. What I've written here isn't a lecture—it's a reflection. It's what I try to do myself, and what my mentors and parents always advise me: Stay grounded. Keep learning. And don't fall behind.

Relevance Isn't a Destination—It's a Mindset

You don't become irrelevant because AI showed up or a new SAP release dropped. You become irrelevant the moment you stop adapting. The moment you start thinking, "I already know enough."

So here's something I try to live by:

Relevance isn't about knowing everything. It's about being ready to learn anything.

This chapter is about that mindset—what it takes to stay relevant, not just today, but for the long run.

What Actually Keeps You Relevant in SAP

Here's what I've observed—both in myself and in others who consistently stay in demand:

1. Micro-Learning Wins
    You don't need to pause your life to learn. 20 focused minutes a day—reading, watching a demo, or testing something new—adds up over time.

2. Follow Trends That Matter
    Don't chase hype. Watch where SAP is heading:

    *   SAP BTP (Business Technology Platform)
    *   AI integrations
    *   Sustainability reporting
    *   Finance transformation

    Follow industry updates, SAP blogs, and product release notes from SAP insiders.

3. Understand the Business, Not Just the System
    If you know how a screen works but not why it exists in the process—you're replaceable. Business context gives you staying power.

4. Build and Share
    You don't need to be an expert to create. Build a small prototype. Document your learning. Share insights. Teaching is learning, too.

5. Stay Curious, Not Comfortable
    Comfort is the enemy of relevance. The SAP consultants who thrive are those who remain open, hungry, and ready to pivot.

AI Is Not the Threat—Stagnation Is

Let's address the elephant in the room.

No, AI is not going to wipe out SAP jobs.
But it **will** replace repetitive, low-value tasks like:

- Manual journal entries
- Ticket classification
- Static reports
- Routine reconciliations

If that's the bulk of your role—you need to evolve. Now.

The future belongs to professionals who:

- Understand the business process
- Interpret AI-generated insights
- Build intelligent workflows
- Use AI to augment, not replace, human decisions

You don't need to become a data scientist. But you **must** become AI-aware and open to coexisting with it.

You're Already Doing Something Right

Here's something I really want you to remember:

The fact that you picked up this book and are reading this chapter tells me you care about your growth.

And that already puts you ahead of so many others. So thank you—and congratulations. You're on the right track. Keep showing up. Keep learning. Keep building.

My Personal Habits That Help Me Stay Relevant

Here's what I personally try to stick to (still a work in progress!):

- Daily 15–20 mins reading or watching a video (SAP blogs, Gen AI, Finance trends)
- Engage with SAP Community and LinkedIn voices I trust
- Try at least one new learning path every quarter (SAP Learning, Udemy, etc.)
- Reflect weekly: What did I learn this week? What's changing in the industry?

These small, repeatable actions keep the momentum alive.

Chapter Summary: Preparing for the Future – Staying Relevant

Key Takeaway	Description
Relevance is a Habit	Built through consistent learning, curiosity, and adaptability—not one-time certifications.
Beginner or Expert – Keep Evolving	Learn the fundamentals, then grow into strategic roles that solve real business problems.
AI is a Partner, Not a Threat	AI replaces tasks, not professionals who understand processes and deliver value.
Progress Over Perfection	You don't need to master everything overnight—just keep moving forward.
You're Already Ahead	Reading this book shows you're already investing in your future. Keep going—you're on the right track.

Recommended Resources to Stay Relevant

Below is a categorized list of free and paid platforms to stay updated in SAP, Finance, and AI:

Free Resources

Platform	Focus Area	Link
SAP Community	Blogs, discussions, Q&A	community.sap.com
SAP Learning (Free Courses)	SAP S/4HANA, BTP, AI	learning.sap.com
OpenSAP	Expert-led SAP courses	open.sap.com
LinkedIn	Industry insights, thought leadership	linkedin.com
YouTube	Demo videos, tutorials (e.g., SAP HANA Academy, SAP Developers)	youtube.com
ChatGPT + AI Tools	Quick explanations and guidance	Various

Paid Resources

Platform	Focus Area	Link
SAP Learning Hub	Full SAP learning journeys (certification aligned)	training.sap.com
Michael Management	SAP simulations, hands-on learning	michaelmanagement.com
Udemy	SAP, Finance, Excel, AI, Python, etc.	udemy.com
Coursera	Finance, Business, AI Foundations	coursera.org
LinkedIn Learning	Soft skills, AI, business strategy	linkedin.com/learning

Tools to Explore

Tool	Purpose
SAP BTP Cockpit	Explore SAP Business Technology Platform
SAP Analytics Cloud (Free Trials)	Learn planning, reporting, and AI analytics
Power BI or Tableau (Free Tiers)	Build visual dashboards and enhance reporting skills
ChatGPT & Copilot Tools	Stay updated, solve quick doubts, explore AI workflows

What's Next: Evolving into an AI Leader

Now that we've talked about staying relevant, it's time to go a step further.

The next chapter is about **becoming an AI-aware SAP consultant**—someone who doesn't just adapt to change but leads it. We'll break down real steps, mindset shifts, and practical ideas to help you grow into an AI Leader inside the SAP world.

You're already in motion—let's keep that momentum going strong.

CHAPTER 3

Practical Steps for SAP Consultants to Evolve into AI Leaders

So far, we've talked about building a strong foundation and staying relevant. Now it's time to level up.

Because in today's world, it's not just about keeping up—it's about stepping up.

This chapter is about **evolving into a leader**—someone who's not just watching the AI wave rise, but actively shaping how it's applied within SAP processes. And whether you're just getting started or already deep in the ecosystem, this chapter is for you.

And let me tell you this straight—**if you've been reading this book so far, you already have what it takes to lead.**

This isn't just a guide to help you get started. It's packed with real, practical frameworks to help you:

- Understand how AI fits in SAP Finance and other modules
- Spot and define AI use cases
- Lead value-driven conversations with confidence
- And actually implement or integrate AI into business processes

You're more ready than you think.

Who is This Chapter For?

- **Freshers** who want to grow with AI from day one
- **Experienced consultants** who want to stay ahead and stay valuable
- **Everyone in between**, figuring out how to adapt and lead with clarity

Wherever you are, this chapter gives you a path forward.

What Does It Mean to Be an AI Leader in SAP?

Let's clarify something.

Being an AI Leader doesn't mean you're building machine learning models or writing Python code.

It means:

- You understand the business problem
- You see where AI can create value
- You can translate that into use cases
- You can guide stakeholders through implementation with confidence

In other words, **you bridge the gap between enterprise needs and intelligent solutions**.

That's what makes you a leader—not technical depth alone, but **contextual intelligence**.

For Freshers: Starting the AI Journey Right

If you're new to SAP or still in the early stages, this is your moment to build a powerful foundation.

Key Steps for Beginners

1. **Start with Process and Business Understanding**
   Learn the core processes in SAP Finance (R2R, P2P, O2C), logistics, or whichever path you're in. AI is powerful—but it's useless without a strong grip on business logic.

2. **Learn the Language of AI**
   You don't need to code. But you must understand what LLMs are, what NLP means, and what RPA can do.

   Suggested free platforms: OpenSAP, Google AI, YouTube, ChatGPT.

3. **Use AI to Learn SAP Faster**
   Try using ChatGPT to generate SAP test data, summarize documentation, or simulate interview questions. Combine both worlds from day one.

4. **Create Your Learning Portfolio**
   Document your journey—what you're learning, how you're applying it. It builds visibility and reinforces your learning.

5. **Stay Consistent**
   Don't go all in for one week and disappear for two months. Even 20 minutes a day builds leadership over time.

For Experienced Consultants: From Solution Provider to Strategic AI Partner

You already know how SAP works. Now it's time to evolve into someone who also knows **how to make it work smarter**.

Key Steps for Experienced Professionals

1. **Map Your Day-to-Day to AI Potential**
   Think about your current tasks:

   - Which ones are repetitive?
   - Which ones are rule-based?
   - Which decisions can AI assist with?

   That's where your first use cases live.

2. **Speak the Business Value of AI**
   You don't need to talk algorithms. You need to talk outcomes:

   - Faster period close
   - Reduced error rates
   - Better cash flow visibility
   - Time saved on reconciliations

   Be the one who connects AI to **KPIs**.

3. **Collaborate Across Teams**
   Partner with data teams, architects, and developers.

   You bring process expertise—they bring data and AI infrastructure.

4. **Propose, Pilot, and Scale**
   Don't wait for perfect conditions.

   Propose a small AI use case: maybe invoice matching, ticket resolution, or journal entry suggestions. Pilot it. Show value. Then scale.

5. **Guide Adoption and Change**
   AI won't stick if people fear it.

   As a leader, **you help your team trust the system**. Be the voice that guides, reassures, and inspires confidence.

Tools, Skills, and Platforms That Will Help You Grow

Whether you're a beginner or experienced, here's what can help you evolve into an AI-capable leader in SAP:

Key Skills to Develop

Skill	Why It Matters
SAP Process Mastery	AI is only effective when aligned with business logic
Data Literacy	Understand how AI models work, even at a basic level
Prompt Engineering	Get better results from tools like ChatGPT
Business Storytelling	Frame AI ideas in a way decision-makers understand
Change Management	Support successful adoption, not just delivery

Recommended Learning Platforms

Free Resources

Platform	Focus	Link
SAP Learning	SAP AI, S/4HANA, BTP basics	learning.sap.com
OpenSAP	Real-world SAP-led courses	open.sap.com
SAP Community	Blogs, discussions, events	community.sap.com
YouTube (SAP Developers, HANA Academy)	Demos, walkthroughs	youtube.com
LinkedIn	Insights from real consultants	linkedin.com

Paid Platforms

Note: These platforms are listed for reference only. I am not affiliated with or sponsored by them.

Platform	Focus	Link
Michael Management	Hands-on SAP + AI courses	michaelmanagement.com
Udemy	SAP, finance, AI, and data tools	udemy.com
SAP Learning Hub	In-depth, certification-level content	training.sap.com
Coursera / edX	AI foundations, ML, Python, Excel	coursera.org

You've Got What It Takes—Right Now

If you've made it this far in the book, I want you to know this:

You already have what it takes to lead.

This book has given you more than enough:

- The frameworks to understand AI
- The confidence to start real conversations
- The tools to design and propose use cases
- And the clarity to integrate AI into your SAP projects and processes

You don't need to "wait until you're ready."

You **are ready.**

Start small. Propose a use case. Try a prototype. Speak up in your next project meeting. That's how AI leaders are made—not in labs, but in the field.

Coming Up Next: Productizing What You Know

Now that you know how to lead with AI inside SAP, it's time to think bigger.

In the next chapter, we'll talk about **productization**—how to take your knowledge, your experience, and your new AI perspective and turn it into solutions, accelerators, or even your own business.

Because being a leader is powerful.
But **building something that others can use?**
That's legacy.

CHAPTER 4

Productizing AI-Based SAP Solutions

What Does Productizing AI-Based SAP Solutions Actually Mean?

Let's define it simply:

Productizing means taking something you've built—an idea, a process, an accelerator, a solution—and packaging it into a **repeatable, reusable, and potentially monetizable product or service.**

That product could be:

- An internal tool to reduce support workload
- A reusable framework that helps clients adopt automation faster
- A dashboard, bot, or Copilot that enhances business processes
- Or even a full-fledged application you license or scale independently

You can **do this as part of your job**—building accelerators or IP for your consulting firm or clients. Or you can **do it for yourself**—as an entrepreneurial project, a side business, or the foundation of something much bigger.

The key difference? When you productize, you **stop solving the same problem over and over**—and start scaling your solution.

Tools Like SAP BTP, AI Core, and More

If you've followed along earlier, you already know:

SAP BTP, SAP AI Core, SAP Analytics Cloud, and even low-code/no-code platforms like SAP Build are **powerful enablers** of this journey.

We won't go into the tech stack again here—but you've already seen how these fit together:

- **Unit 3** teaches you how to think and lead with AI in SAP
- **Unit 4** gives you the actual blueprint to build and implement an AI-powered solution

If you need a refresher, I encourage you to revisit **Unit 3** for strategy and tools, and **Unit 4** to see how it's done practically, step by step.

Now let's talk about what happens when you decide to take those ideas and turn them into something **scalable, professional, and yours.**

Let's talk productization—**for impact, for growth, and maybe even for business.**

You've already got the mindset. You've learned how to stay relevant, evolve into an AI-capable consultant, and even lead conversations and implementations. You've seen the frameworks. You've seen real use cases. You've probably started thinking, "How can I build something of my own?"

That's exactly what this chapter is about.

Before we dive deeper—let's revisit what we covered in the previous chapter just as a refresher. These are the **exact steps** you need to follow to grow from a consultant into an AI Leader:

Recap: Steps to Become an AI Leader in SAP

Step	Action	Why It Matters
1	Master SAP processes	AI must align with business logic
2	Learn AI basics (LLMs, NLP, RPA)	You need to understand the tools
3	Identify repeatable, high-friction tasks	These are ideal for automation
4	Map AI to real business outcomes	Speak the language of value
5	Collaborate across technical teams	Success requires cross-functional effort
6	Propose, pilot, and scale use cases	Leadership = Initiative
7	Support adoption and change	AI fails without user trust

If you haven't internalized these steps yet, I highly encourage you to revisit the previous chapter before continuing. We won't be repeating the "how to lead" again here—**because now it's time to build**.

Think about this:

You've probably solved the same SAP support issue 20 times.

You've probably reused the same documentation, spec template, or test case structure in multiple projects.

You may have even built a basic automation script to speed up journal entry validation or tax code checks.

Now imagine turning that into a product:

Packaged, Branded, Automated, Scalable, Licensed & Sold or offered to clients, or even on the SAP Store. That's the power of productization.

Benefits of Productizing Your SAP + AI Knowledge

Benefit	Why It's Valuable
Scalability	You do the work once, and it serves many
Professional Credibility	You're seen as a thought leader, not just a consultant
Passive or Recurring Revenue	Monetize what you know—through licensing, services, or platforms
Partnership Potential	Attract collaboration with SAP, partners, startups, and enterprise clients
Sharpened Expertise	Productizing forces you to structure, validate, and document your ideas clearly
Business Ownership	You create assets—not just billable hours

Possibilities: What Can You Productize?

Here are just a few examples of what can be productized from SAP + AI expertise:

Product Type	Examples
AI-Powered Accelerators	Journal entry recommendation engines, cash application bots
Pre-Built Workflows	Smart period-close bots, IDoc issue resolution templates
Templates & Frameworks	Automation frameworks, process blueprints, validation checklists
Training Kits	Internal AI-readiness playbooks, Gen AI in SAP workshops
Analytics Packages	SAC dashboards for AI-led Finance KPIs
Chatbots & Copilots	Ticket assistant, vendor query automation using Gen AI
Partner Products	Certified solutions built on SAP BTP or published on SAP Store

Real Example: My SAP Production Support IP

Let me give you a real example from my own journey.

One of the biggest pain points I saw in SAP projects—especially in Finance—was the repetitive nature of production support tickets. Whether it was tax code errors, missing cost centers, or failed IDocs, 80% of the issues were repetitive and predictable.

I built an **AI-driven Copilot** using:

- SAP AI Core
- LLMs like GPT
- MLOps pipelines for retraining based on ticket patterns
- Embedded governance and SOX compliance checks

This solution doesn't just respond—it learns. It evolves. And it reduces manual intervention, enhances support quality, and saves cost.

I'm currently preparing to **productize** this solution. The goal?

Offer it to SAP clients, implementation partners, and maybe even package it with a support offering on SAP's BTP or the SAP Store.

And if I can do that—you can, too.

Legalities, IP, and Ownership – What You Need to Know

If you're considering productizing your ideas, here are the **must-know areas**:

Intellectual Property (IP)

- **Who owns the IP?**
  If you build it on your own time, it's yours. If it's built on client time, you may need agreement or rework.
- **File for IP protection** if it's unique—especially in the U.S., India, EU, or other jurisdictions.
- You can use platforms like <u>USPTO.gov</u> or consult an IP attorney.

NDA and Employment Contracts

- Review your **employment agreements**—ensure you're not violating non-compete or IP ownership clauses.
- Consider creating your solutions on **personal tools/accounts**, outside company infrastructure.

Partnership Options

- **SAP PartnerEdge** – Become a build partner and list on SAP Store
- **Freelance collaboration** – Work with developers or designers to bring your idea to life
- **Startups** – Launch your own consulting or product startup (you already have the niche!)

Go-To-Market Approaches

- White-labeled services
- Branded accelerators for consulting firms
- Micro-SaaS tools
- Internal tools you license or embed in engagements
- Free tools to grow visibility and attract leads

From Idea to Entrepreneurial Venture: Turning Knowledge into Products

Let's take it beyond just internal use or side tools.

Because if you've identified a real pain point and solved it with AI and SAP—**you may be sitting on a business opportunity.**

Yes, you.

Whether you're a fresher who built a clever automation using ChatGPT, or an experienced consultant who sees recurring patterns in client pain points—**you can transform those ideas into entrepreneurial projects, products, or even a company.**

Here's how to start turning your ideas into real-world ventures:

Stage	What to Do	How It Helps
1. Spot the Pain Point	Ask yourself: What do clients, users, or teams complain about repeatedly? What's manual, repetitive, error-prone, or expensive?	You need a real problem to solve. That's what people pay for.
2. Validate the Idea	Talk to others in your network. Would this save time, reduce risk, or increase efficiency? Would you pay for it if someone else built it?	Prevents you from building something no one wants.
3. Build a Simple MVP	Don't overthink it. A simple prototype in Excel, SAC, or even ChatGPT counts. Show how it would work and the outcome it delivers.	Visual proof builds credibility, gets feedback, and attracts collaborators.
4. Create an Identity	Give your tool a name. A landing page. A slide deck. This isn't just a script anymore—it's a solution.	Helps shift your mindset from "experiment" to "asset."
5. Choose a Model	Do you want to:	
– Sell it as a subscription tool?		
– Offer it as a fixed-scope packaged service?		

– License it to SAP customers or partners?		
– Offer it for free to build trust?	The model defines how you monetize or scale your idea.	
6. Protect & Formalize	Register the IP. Get a logo. Form an LLC (if needed). Define ownership if you're working with collaborators.	Sets you up legally and signals that you're serious.
7. Go-to-Market	Talk about it. Share use cases. Pitch it on LinkedIn. Offer demos to companies. Publish content around it.	Visibility = Opportunity. Products don't sell themselves.

Examples of SAP + AI Ideas That Could Be Businesses

- **AI Copilot for SAP Tickets** – Based on the one I built
- **Reconciliation Automation Accelerator** – Plug-and-play logic for different clients
- **Sustainability Compliance Tracker** – Preconfigured dashboards using SAC
- **Chatbot for Master Data Queries** – Vendor setup, GL validation, tax code lookups
- **Fixed-Scope Audit Readiness Package** – AI tools + checklists for SOX, GxP clients
- **Learning App for SAP Freshers** – Combine AI, training, and simulation

Why This Matters

You're not just a consultant anymore.

You're a problem solver with an edge—AI.

And in a world where **digital products are more scalable than services**, you have the chance to create something bigger than a billable hour.

You can build your own product. You can own it. You can scale it.

Whether you keep it small, license it to your firm, or launch your own company around it—that's your call. But the tools, mindset, and opportunity?

You already have them.

Final Words: From Insight to Ownership

Productizing your knowledge isn't reserved for developers or tech entrepreneurs.

It's for **anyone** who has spotted a real problem, solved it meaningfully, and now wants to **scale that solution**—whether to improve outcomes at work or to launch something of their own.

By now, this book has already given you:

- The mindset to identify high-impact use cases
- The tools to build your first AI-powered solution
- The strategy to lead intelligent SAP initiatives
- And the vision to move from a one-off fix to a scalable product

You've seen what's possible.

Whether it's an AI-driven ticket resolution Copilot like the one I'm productizing, a SAC dashboard accelerator, or a sustainability reporting tool—**what you know can become what you own**.

So start sketching. Start testing. Start sharing.

Because the next big SAP solution? It just might have your name on it.

And remember—**this book has laid the foundation. The rest is execution.**

So ask yourself:

"What have I solved that others struggle with?"
"How can I turn that into something real, repeatable, and valuable?"

That's the entrepreneurial mindset. And if you're reading this, I believe you've already got it in you.

Coming Up Next: Frameworks, Toolkits, and Appendices

In the final chapter, we'll wrap everything together—clear frameworks, ready-to-use toolkits, curated resources, and guided next steps.

So you can reflect, revisit, and build with even more confidence.

Let's finish strong.

CHAPTER 5

Actionable Frameworks & Appendices

Your Toolkit. Your Compass. Your Next Move.

Congratulations on reaching this point, you haven't just read a book—you've charted a course into the future of SAP Finance with AI.

From the opening pages where we explored the cracks in traditional production support... to deep dives into integration, hands-on proof of concept, and productizing your ideas—this was never meant to be a typical tech manual.

This was your transformation map.

And now, in this final chapter, I want to leave you with two gifts:

- **A reference you can return to** — with frameworks, shortcuts, and toolkits
- **A lasting reminder** — that you have everything it takes to lead this change

Quick Reference Frameworks

The 8-Step AI Integration Framework

Step	Action	Purpose
1	Identify Use Case	Repetitive, manual, or value-leaking tasks
2	Gather & Prepare Data	Ensure quality, context, and access
3	Define Integration Point	Pinpoint where AI can support SAP
4	Select or Build Model	Choose LLMs, SAP BTP, or custom
5	Develop Integration Logic	Connect SAP flows with AI outputs
6	Validate & Test	Pilot, gather feedback, iterate fast
7	Deploy & Monitor	Use AI Core, MLOps, compliance
8	Scale	Expand to other teams or processes

The SAP AI Consultant Growth Model

Level	What to Focus On
Beginner	Learn SAP processes and AI fundamentals
Intermediate	Apply GenAI in test cases, bots, reports
Advanced	Build accelerators, own POCs, mentor peers
Leader	Productize, publish, speak, and lead change

Productization Checklist

- Identified a real business pain point
- Validated need with peers or leaders
- Built a working demo or prototype
- Defined a name, brand, and short pitch
- Chose monetization: internal, freelance, startup
- Secured IP or partner rights (if applicable)
- Shared it online, in a meeting, or at a conference

Open Learning Platforms

Platform	Use
learning.sap.com	Free SAP learning journeys
open.sap.com	SAP AI courses and case studies
community.sap.com	Blogs, Q&A, forums
YouTube	HANA Academy, SAP Developers, demos

Premium Resources Worth Exploring

Platform	Why Use It
Michael Management	SAP hands-on labs and AI integration
SAP Learning Hub	Cert prep + deep SAP finance
Coursera / edX	Python, AI, ML for SAP pros
Udemy	Quick-hit courses for tools, SAC, AI basics

Final Words: Start Where You Are

AI in SAP isn't a trend — it's the new standard.

You don't need to code complex models or become a data scientist. What you do need is:

- Domain knowledge
- Curiosity about automation
- The will to try something new

You've now seen what's possible. You have the blueprint. You've learned the language of AI, understood its role in SAP, and explored how to lead, build, and scale intelligent solutions.

This book wasn't meant to just inform — it was meant to **equip**. To nudge you forward. To serve as your reference, your inspiration, and your launchpad.

The rest? Is up to you.

Whether you use this knowledge to grow in your current role, build a product, or spark a transformation in your organization—remember, you're not starting from scratch. You're starting from **insight**.

Disclaimer: The paid resources and platforms mentioned in this book are not advertisements or endorsements, nor do I have any affiliation or partnership with them at the time of writing. This book was written independently and personally by me. I've only recommended tools and resources that I have personally used and found genuinely helpful in my journey.

References

This book has drawn upon various public knowledge sources and professional experience. Key reference points include:

- **SAP Official Documentation and Learning Resources:**
  Many concepts, architecture diagrams, and product features are based on publicly available materials from https://www.sap.com, including:

  - SAP AI Core & AI Hub
  - SAP Business AI
  - SAP Learning Journeys
  - SAP BTP & SAP Analytics Cloud
  - SAP Community blogs and developer tutorials

- **Industry Practices & Use Cases:**
  Some frameworks and scenarios reflect standard practices shared in SAP user communities, ASUG events, and professional implementation experience.

- **Personal Projects & Proof of Concept (PoC):**
  The practical application chapter, use cases, and integration blueprints are based on real-world scenarios I've designed, implemented, or evaluated as part of my SAP consulting career.

Thank you for walking this journey with me.

The next chapter—your chapter—starts now.

The road ahead isn't scripted — but it's open.

Whether you're just beginning or already leading, what comes next will depend on how boldly you apply what you've seen, learned, and built. Let this unit serve not as a conclusion, but as a catalyst — a reminder that your career is a living system, constantly shaped by action, curiosity, and conviction.

No roadmap is perfect. But clarity, consistency, and courage go a long way. You've now seen what's possible when SAP meets AI — not as hype, but as a strategic shift. What you do with that knowledge is entirely up to you.

In the next section, you'll hear from others who've walked their own paths — industry experts, mentors, and peers who have shaped how I think, build, and lead. Their voices are not endorsements, but reflections — unique lenses that offer perspective on this journey and the work we all still have ahead.

Let this serve as a pause — to reflect, to realign, and to reaffirm your own direction.

Because real change doesn't come from knowing the path.

It comes from walking it.

CONCLUSION

It Starts With You

Let's be honest—stepping into something new can feel overwhelming. AI. SAP. Automation. Innovation. Everyone's talking about it. Few know where to begin.

You might be thinking:
"Do I really have what it takes?"
The answer is—**yes**. And here's why.

This book wasn't written to impress you with jargon or paint a perfect picture. It was written to show you what's possible, even when things feel uncertain. It was written by someone who faced real production support tickets, tight deadlines, and steep learning curves—and still found a way to turn problems into products, confusion into clarity, and doubt into direction.

Now, it's your turn.

Your bigger, better future isn't some distant ideal—it's grounded in real progress.
It's **you feeling confident in front of stakeholders**.
It's **you leading solution design calls with intelligent insights**.
It's **you building smart workflows that reduce effort, speed up delivery, and earn recognition**—not just for doing your job, but for elevating it.

But let's also acknowledge the reality.

Change is hard. And staying relevant is even harder—especially in an era where the rules are being rewritten every few months.

In a **recent interview with Satya Nadella**, CEO of Microsoft, he mentioned something profound:

"Before AI, the rate of business change followed an 18-month cycle. Now, it's down to just six months."

That's not just an observation—it's a warning.
You can't afford to wait and catch up anymore.
You have to **learn as you move**.

That might sound intimidating. But in truth, it's **empowering**.

Because you don't need to be an expert overnight. You just need to start—**one conversation, one use case, one experiment at a time.**

Here's a real-world example:
I know SAP consultants who had **never touched AI tools a year ago**. Today, they're **automating reconciliations using SAP BTP and Large Language Models**. Not because they were coders. But because they were **curious**. They asked the right questions. They tried. And so can you.

The risk of not acting isn't just about being left behind—it's about **missing your chance to lead**, to contribute, and to grow in a way that truly fulfills your potential. The longer you wait, the more others will build what **you could've shaped**. It won't be obvious right away—but over time, **that gap becomes harder to close**.

So take a deep breath and take the leap.

Not into complexity. But into **clarity**. Not into fear. But into **exploration**.

Because the only constant in business—as you've likely heard—is **change**. And now, with AI in the mix, the question isn't if change is coming. It's whether **you'll be the one driving it—or catching up to it.**

The good news is, after reading this book:

- You already have the mindset.
- You now have the tools.
- You've read the frameworks, the use cases, and a real-life story of someone who started right where you are.

So don't overthink it. Don't wait for perfect timing.

Just begin.

Because the future of SAP Finance with AI? It's not written by the biggest teams or the loudest voices. It's built by **people like you**—who show up, stay curious, and take action.

Let's build it.

Together.

INTERVIEWS

Dr. Lou Thompson

Professor & Director, Intelligent Enterprise Systems
University of Texas at Dallas

Thoughts on AI-Powered SAP Finance

AI is rapidly evolving, which in turn is revamping the traditional way of Finance. Growing AI capabilities are not just going to revolutionize the way current business processes are being conducted in the SAP, but also new intelligent analytics will significantly boost compliance, quality, and revenue in terms of FI.

AI is already boosting the working capital by improving Accounts Receivable by automating the invoice matching process. AI is making it easier to use predictive analytics to foresee the payment patterns by partners such as vendors or customers. In the field of Risk Management and Fraud Detection, AI can analyze transactions in real time to detect suspicious patterns and potential frauds, helping companies to protect their as well as customer's assets.

To achieve these transforming benefits of AI, one must overcome the challenges of data quality and quantity, integration of data between different systems which are working in silos, and data governance.

Apart from the technical challenges, there are also organizational challenges where people find it difficult or are unwilling to welcome the change and to adapt to the new systems, which in turn reflects in having unclear objectives, ambiguous strategies, and unwillingness to improve and keep up with the translating environment.

Addressing these challenges requires a collective approach—but once achieved, AI will impact the way businesses work in an unimaginably positive way.

Thoughts on Mohammed Hafeez Baig and This Book

I met Mohammmed Hafeez Baig at ASUG Dallas Fort Worth Conference. Based on my interactions with him, I sincerely say with a high degree of confidence that he brings vast experience in SAP FICO, S/4HANA Finance, and AI-driven automation. His ability to bridge traditional financial processes with modern new AI innovations make him a fantastic author for this topic. This book can be a valuable resource for both SAP professionals and university students studying SAP FICO.

Contributions to the SAP Industry

Dr. Lou Thompson has been working with SAP since 1998, beginning with the initial implementation of SAP at Fujitsu Network Communication and Switching. His SAP journey started in Project Systems. In 2001, he began teaching SAP at the University of Texas at Dallas at both the graduate and undergraduate levels.

He teaches SAP Integrated Business Processes and SAP Configuration courses. Dr. Thompson is a SAP Certified Consultant at the Associate level in Integrated Business Processes on both ECC 6.0 and S/4HANA. He is also an ASUG Champion Member of the Dallas–Fort Worth Chapter and serves as the SAP University Alliance Faculty Advisor for UT Dallas.

Dr. Thompson has delivered numerous SAP presentations at SAP University Alliance North America Conferences and ASUG. His SAP expertise spans modules including SD, MM, PP, HCM, FI, and CO.

Final Thoughts

Finance organizations of SAP-run enterprises are recognizing the vital role that AI plays in enhancing processes, optimizing decisions, and maximizing efficiency. Businesses embracing this capability to automate finance processes are seeing more accurate and timely reports. The resulting benefits include:

- Quick communication and gainful insights into other areas of the business
- Increased user efficiency, allowing teams to focus on strategic activities
- Improved speed of decision-making, enhancing the business's competitiveness
- Timely and accurate financial insights and analysis to guide the organization
- Boosted overall productivity within the finance department

Shakeel Mir Ali

CEO, iSync Technologies
Veteran SAP Leader with 30+ Years of Global Delivery & Transformation Experience

Thoughts on AI-Powered SAP Finance

The future of SAP Finance is no longer shaped solely by transactional efficiency—it is being redefined by the intelligent capabilities that Artificial Intelligence brings to the enterprise. In today's global business environment, finance organizations are under constant pressure to deliver faster insights, higher accuracy, and continuous innovation. AI steps into this space not just as a new technology, but as an enabler of transformation across the SAP landscape.

With AI-powered finance solutions, we are witnessing the evolution of traditional finance from reactive reporting to proactive decision-making. From intelligent invoice processing and automated reconciliation to predictive risk assessment and scenario modeling, AI is allowing finance functions to transcend their historical roles. SAP, with its integrated architecture and global reach, is ideally positioned to harness the power of AI and become a true engine of enterprise intelligence.

Across my global experience delivering SAP programs, the most successful transformations are those that harmonize technology with people, processes, and purpose. Implementing AI within SAP Finance isn't just about inserting algorithms—it's about reimagining workflows, redefining roles, and realigning teams with new possibilities. When implemented thoughtfully, AI doesn't disrupt finance—it elevates it.

Thoughts on Mohammed Hafeez Baig and This Book

I've had the opportunity of mentoring Mohammed Hafeez Baig for the past several years, and I can confidently say he is one of the most forward-thinking professionals and digital transformation experts I've encountered in the SAP Finance space. With a solid foundation in SAP FICO and a deep understanding of end-to-end business processes, Hafeez consistently demonstrates an exceptional ability to think beyond traditional ERP frameworks. His vision to integrate Generative AI with SAP Finance is not only innovative but also highly relevant in today's enterprise landscape.

What sets Hafeez apart is his remarkable learning agility and drive. In a short span of time, he built deep functional and technical expertise, navigated complex implementations, and contributed to multiple transformation programs across industries. He combines sharp analytical thinking with strong team leadership, consistently delivering value while fostering collaboration and mentorship within his teams.

As a Digital Transformation Technology expert he understands the business goals. and identifies opportunities for improvement and aligning technology solutions with business goals.

One of his notable accomplishments was spearheading a successful implementation of one of the core modules for S/4 HANA Migration resulting in system stability and worldwide tracking of Clients Assets. This project demanded strong analytical skills, collaboration with key stakeholders, and meticulous attention to detail - all qualities that Hafeez consistently brought to the table.

When he first shared his ideas for the book AI-Powered SAP Finance, I was genuinely excited. I wholeheartedly supported him throughout the process, knowing that his insights and frameworks would add real value to the SAP and AI communities. This book is more than a technical guide—it's a strategic blueprint for the future of digital finance, created by someone who truly understands both the systems and the people behind them.

Contributions to the SAP Industry

Shakeel Mir Ali is a Senior SAP Program Delivery Director and Digital Transformation/ Strategic Technology performance-driven leader with 25+ years of pioneering and managing complex IT/SAP S4 Hana transformation projects (13), Consulting, Migration, System integration and delivery experience of managing enterprise business applications focused on Artificial Intelligence, productivity and profitability, digitalization, and automation.

His IT/SAP Expertise is enriched with global delivery experience of various big, complex SAP programs for many FORTUNE 500 companies in diverse sectors across global geographies.

He Lead and developed the Center of Excellence (CoE) team, enriching a culture of excellence and innovation. Leading a team of developers on integrating Artificial Intelligence by utilizing SAP AI Core to train and deploy AI models and SAP AI launchpad to administer and monitor the use cases on AI models.

Leader in project management methodology using Agile and Agile-Scrum (Scrum Master Certified) with project scoping, planning, estimation, execution, and implementation with a solid understanding of service delivery processes, procedures, and methodologies used to successfully deliver projects.

Proven track record of road mapping and executing on an enterprise-wide technology portfolio strategy that creates value for the business via improved productivity and decreased spending.

Final Thoughts

As we move toward an era where business outcomes are increasingly driven by data and intelligence, the role of finance is evolving at its core. AI empowers finance professionals to go beyond reporting—to lead, to guide, and to innovate. SAP's integration with AI is not simply a product enhancement—it is a transformational lever for the enterprise.

This book is both a signpost and a strategy. It helps practitioners navigate today's complexity while preparing them to lead tomorrow's intelligent enterprise.

Syed Noor Ahmed

Advance Analytics, AI & Digital Enterprise Transformation Leader

Thoughts on AI-Powered SAP Finance

The tides of enterprise transformation have always moved with the rhythm of technological progress, but rarely has that rhythm accelerated with the urgency and promise we witness today. Artificial Intelligence, once the subject of speculative fiction and academic theory, has arrived not as a singular invention but as a catalytic presence quietly reconfiguring the very architecture of enterprise finance and SAP systems.

To understand AI in this context is not merely to comprehend a new tool; it is to recognize a paradigm shift. Within the world of enterprise finance, AI is ushering in a new epoch—one where decisions are no longer delayed by the latency of human interpretation, but instead are informed by predictive intelligence, context-rich data, and real-time orchestration. SAP, the longstanding pillar of enterprise infrastructure, is now being reimagined not just as a system of record, but as a system of insight.

In my own journey spanning decades of leading global transformations at the confluence of data, artificial intelligence, and enterprise architecture, I have seen firsthand the extraordinary power that lies in harmonizing intelligent automation with human ingenuity. When AI is woven thoughtfully into the fabric of SAP, it does not merely replace human effort; it amplifies human intent. It liberates finance professionals from the tyranny of repetition, empowering them to become stewards of strategy, architects of foresight, and custodians of innovation.

Thoughts on Mohammed Hafeez Baig and This Book

Yet, amidst all this change, what matters most is not the machinery of transformation, but the minds and hearts behind it. This brings me to Mohammed Baig.

Mohammed is not only a trusted technologist, but a thinker of unusual clarity and depth. I have watched his career unfold with admiration. He approaches complexity with curiosity, and he meets challenges not with haste, but with discernment. What distinguishes his work is not just its technical precision, but its intellectual sincerity and human-centered purpose.

This book, *AI-Powered SAP Finance*, is more than a technical exploration—it is a roadmap for those who seek to lead with both rigor and relevance in the age of intelligent enterprise. It speaks to practitioners, strategists, and visionaries alike.

Mohammed has taken a subject dense with possibility and rendered it accessible without dilution, thoughtful without pretense, and practical without ever sacrificing depth.

To the reader, consider this more than a manual. Consider it a companion—a guide that will grow with you as your understanding evolves, and as the landscape itself continues to shift beneath your feet. You are in the presence of a voice that does not merely interpret the future, but invites you to help shape it.

About Syed Noor Ahmed

Across two decades of work at the intersection of artificial intelligence, enterprise systems, and digital transformation, Syed Noor Ahmed has led global initiatives for some of the world's most respected technology firms, including NTT Data and Dell Technologies. He now devotes his time to advancing the ethical application of AI, advising breakthrough ventures, and mentoring the next generation of technology leaders.

His belief, unwavering through all these years, is that technology must serve not just progress, but purpose—and that those who wield it wisely will be the stewards of a more intelligent, humane, and connected future.

Murali Burra

President, Global IT Solutions Inc

Thoughts on AI-Powered SAP Finance

AI is rapidly transforming SAP Finance by automating transactional processes, enhancing predictive analytics, and optimizing financial reporting. With AI-driven capabilities like intelligent document processing, anomaly detection, validation, accuracy, and generative AI for financial insights, organizations can unlock new efficiencies. However, widespread adoption requires overcoming challenges such as data quality, governance, regulatory compliance, and the integration of AI with existing SAP landscapes.

Thoughts on Mohammed Hafeez Baig and This Book

Having worked with Mohammed Hafeez Baig on SAP Finance solutions, I can confidently say he brings deep expertise in SAP FICO, S/4HANA Finance, and AI-driven automation. His ability to bridge traditional financial processes with modern AI innovations makes him an ideal author for this topic. This book is a much-needed resource for SAP professionals looking to understand AI's transformative role in financial systems.

Contributions to the SAP Industry

Murali has been working in the SAP industry for over 20 years, focused on Procure-to-Pay, SAP ERP, SAP Ariba implementations, and digital transformation strategies. My contributions include leading S/4HANA migrations, deploying SAP Ariba solutions, implementing AI-powered financial automation tools, and advising enterprises on SAP best practices. I have also spoken at industry events like SAP ASUG and contributed to thought leadership on SAP Finance and procurement transformation.

Final Thoughts

AI in SAP Finance is no longer a futuristic concept—it is here and evolving rapidly. This book will serve as a guiding light for SAP professionals looking to navigate the AI revolution in enterprise finance.

Ramakrishnan S

Director at Trinity Envision | Published Author on SAP IDocs & SQL

Your Thoughts on AI-Powered SAP Finance

"AI is reshaping the future of SAP Finance, not just by accelerating processes, but by redefining how finance teams operate. From real-time data processing with intelligent bots to predictive analytics and natural language interfaces, the shift is profound. The opportunity lies in enhancing decision-making while reducing manual overheads. That said, integrating AI into SAP landscapes calls for structured governance, sound data architecture, and a cultural shift toward embracing innovation."

Your Thoughts on Mohammed Hafeez Baig and This Book

"I have known Mohammed Hafeez Baig for quite a few years and have seen his consistent commitment to SAP Finance and emerging technologies. His hands-on approach, strong analytical thinking, and eagerness to bridge the gap between AI and enterprise finance make this book timely and relevant. It's not just theoretical—it's practical and rooted in real-world SAP experience. This book is bound to help professionals prepare for the next era of intelligent finance."

Your Contributions to the SAP Industry

"With over 26 years in the SAP ecosystem, I have had the privilege to lead, implement, and architect complex SAP solutions across industries. As the author of two SAP books focused on IDocs and SQL queries, my goal has always been to simplify and strengthen knowledge-sharing within the community. At Trinity Envision, we continue to help clients adopt scalable and intelligent SAP solutions that align with evolving business needs."

Final Thoughts

"As AI becomes deeply embedded in the SAP Finance landscape, there's a growing need for practical, experience-based guidance. This book delivers just that. It empowers readers not only to understand AI concepts but to apply them meaningfully within SAP environments. I believe it will become a valuable asset for both seasoned consultants and the next generation of SAP professionals ready to lead the transformation."

ABOUT THE AUTHOR

Mohammed Hafeez Baig is a multi-certified SAP FICO Consultant and one of the emerging voices at the intersection of enterprise finance and artificial intelligence. His career is built on a solid foundation of SAP implementations, system enhancements, consulting, and ongoing production support. Through these roles, he has consistently helped organizations streamline their financial operations and resolve real-world challenges using practical, process-driven solutions.

What sets Hafeez apart is the thoughtful blend he brings: technical expertise, deep understanding of business processes, and a growing focus on the meaningful integration of Generative AI into SAP landscapes.

He holds an MBA in Accounting from Johnson & Wales University in Providence, Rhode Island, USA, and is an active member of the American SAP Users Group (ASUG), staying closely engaged with the latest industry trends and innovations.

A Well-Rounded SAP & AI Professional

Hafeez holds an extensive suite of SAP and compliance certifications, reflecting both his breadth and depth of knowledge across implementation, support, innovation, and transformation. These credentials span Financial Accounting, Management Accounting, SAP S/4HANA Cloud and On-Premise, technical system upgrades, and Generative AI—positioning him to address enterprise challenges with both functional insight and technological adaptability.

Key Certifications Include:

- SAP Certified Application Professional – Financials in SAP S/4HANA for SAP ERP
  Financials Experts (1909)
- SAP Certified Generative AI Developer
- SAP Certified Application Associate – SAP S/4HANA Cloud, Finance Implementation (2021)
- SAP Certified Technology Specialist – SAP S/4HANA Conversion and SAP System Upgrade (2020)
- SAP Certified Application Associate – Management Accounting (SAP S/4HANA 1909)
- SAP Certified Application Associate – Financial Accounting (SAP S/4HANA 1909)
- SAP Certified Application Associate – SAP Business One Release 10.0
- SOX (Sarbanes-Oxley) Compliance Certification

Passion for Problem Solving

With hands-on SAP experience across global projects, Hafeez's approach is marked by analytical thinking, systems perspective, and relentless curiosity. He is particularly passionate about helping organizations move beyond legacy ERP models into intelligent, AI-enabled systems that drive performance, resilience, and clarity.

But what truly distinguishes his work is not just what he has done—but what he is building.

Pioneering the Future of SAP Support with AI

Hafeez is currently pursuing intellectual property protection for a groundbreaking innovation that leverages Generative AI to transform SAP Production Support. In 2025, he filed a provisional utility patent for his AI-powered SAP support system, which reimagines traditional ticketing workflows with intelligent automation, real-time insights, and predictive resolution strategies. This innovation replaces reactive, manual processes with a self-evolving support mechanism that continuously learns and improves—turning enterprise support into a strategic, value-generating function.

Backed by deep experience in SAP Finance and a deep-seated interest in AI, Hafeez's invention introduces a scalable framework for proactive ticket management, root cause analysis, and anomaly detection—all powered by a tailored Large Language Model fine-tuned for SAP environments.

Looking ahead, Hafeez envisions broader opportunities for this concept to evolve within the larger SAP ecosystem, potentially through strategic alignments with platforms, partners, or service networks that resonate with the vision of intelligent enterprise transformation. While specific pathways are still under exploration, the overarching focus remains on contributing to scalable, AI-driven solutions that enhance the future of enterprise support. The aim is to help shape what next-generation SAP support could look like—where efficiency, intelligence, and adaptability intersect.

Sharing Knowledge & Shaping the Next Generation

Hafeez has been invited as a guest lecturer at universities across the U.S., where he speaks to students about SAP Finance and the transformative potential of artificial intelligence. His ability to translate complex concepts into practical insights has made him a valuable voice among aspiring professionals.

As his presence in the SAP community grows, he is on track to participate in conferences and executive forums, contributing to global conversations around digital finance transformation, ERP modernization, and enterprise innovation.

The SAP x AI Solutions Studio

To scale impact, Hafeez has plans to launch a dedicated AI-powered SAP Solutions Studio—an innovation hub focused on solving real-world enterprise problems through automation and intelligent tooling. From transforming SAP Production Support to building scalable, proactive Gen AI-powered tools, this proposed studio will act as both a proving ground and a delivery engine.

Hafeez is launching a powerful new **training course for SAP Finance professionals and beyond**, with a unique focus on integrating **SAP processes with Generative AI**. Built on real-world experience and tailored to current industry demands, this program empowers consultants, analysts, and future leaders to master the tools and frameworks needed to thrive in the AI-powered enterprise landscape.

The course will soon be available via his official **website** and **social media platforms**, where Hafeez regularly shares insights, updates, and thought leadership on the future of SAP and enterprise AI. This isn't just a course—it's a gateway to becoming an **AI-enabled SAP consultant**, capable of driving transformation within any organization.

Stay tuned for updates, and follow Hafeez on LinkedIn, Instagram, and his website to learn more, stay connected, and join a growing movement toward ethical, intelligent, and interest-free innovation in enterprise technology.

Stay Connected

To explore resources, join upcoming programs, or collaborate—visit the official website and connect via social media:

- **Author's website**: www.mohammedhafeezbaig.com

- **LinkedIn**: linkedin.com/in/hafeez-baig-acpa

- **Instagram**: @ai.in.sap.with.hafeez @withhafeezbaig (personal)

@AI.IN.SAP.WITH.HAFEEZ   @WITHHAFEEZBAIG

A FINAL NOTE FROM THE AUTHOR

Thank you for taking the time to read this book.

This wasn't just about AI. It was about showing what's possible when deep domain knowledge meets the courage to reimagine old systems. You now have the roadmap, the use case, and the frameworks to start building meaningful change—right where you are.

Whether you're a consultant, a business user, or simply someone curious about what's next—remember: the future of SAP Finance isn't written by code alone. It's written by people who dare to think differently.

If this book sparked an idea, brought you clarity, or helped you take one step forward—then it has done its job.

Let's keep building. Let's stay connected.

— **Mohammed Hafeez Baig**

www.ingramcontent.com/pod-product-compliance
Lightning Source LLC
Chambersburg PA
CBHW051748200326
41597CB00025B/4488